Y0-BRB-805

The extent to which a knowledge of sixteenth-century theological doctrines can help readers interpret the works of Edmund Spenser has long been a matter of controversy. In *Interpretation and theology in Spenser* Darryl J. Gless offers a new approach: drawing on recent literary theories, he focuses less on what Spenser intended than on the ways readers might construe both the poet's works and the theological doctrines which those works invoke. Professor Gless demonstrates the seldom-admitted fact that theological texts, like literary ones, are subject to the interpretive activity of readers. Informed by this approach to Elizabethan theology, he provides a useful survey of major doctrinal concepts, and develops a thorough analysis of the first, most widely studied, book of Spenser's Elizabethan epic *The Faerie Queene*. He concludes with series of concise illustrations of ways in which theological perspectives can enrich significant moments in later, less overtly theological, passages of Spenser's great poem.

Interpretation and theology in Spenser

INTERPRETATION AND THEOLOGY IN SPENSER

DARRYL J. GLESS

Department of English
University of North Carolina, Chapel Hill

Published by the Press Syndicate of the University of Cambridge
The Pitt Building, Trumpington Street, Cambridge CB2 1RP
40 West 20th Street, New York, NY 10011-4211, USA
10 Stamford Road, Oakleigh, Victoria 3166, Australia

First published 1994

Printed in Great Britain at the University Press, Cambridge

A catalogue record for this book is available from the British Library

Library of Congress cataloguing in publication data

Gless, Darryl J., 1945–
Interpretation and theology in Spenser / Darryl J. Gless.
        275 p. cm. –
Includes bibliographical references and index.
ISBN 0 521 43474 2 (hardback)
1. Spenser, Edmund, 1552?–1599. Faerie queene. 2. Christian poetry, English – History and criticism. 3. Spenser, Edmund, 1552?–1599 – Religion.
4. Theology, Doctrinal, in literature. 5. Christianity and literature. I. Title.
PR2358.G57 1994
821' .3 – dc20   93-43766   CIP

ISBN 0 521 43474 2   hardback

KB

For Victoria

CONTENTS

ACKNOWLEDGMENTS

Despite its modest scope, this book has been in process so long that I may be unable properly to remember all my patrons and advisors. First, then, my gratitude to all colleagues, friends, students, and others whose good offices may go unrecorded here. My students, first at the University of Virginia, subsequently at the University of North Carolina at Chapel Hill, have supplied continuing, indispensable energy, and constant provocation to think and to know at the highest levels my abilities can reach. They have ensured that I continue to seek to meet the level of intellectual testing that scholarly publications alone impose.

For material support, my thanks to the National Endowment for the Humanities, which provided me time in an especially stressful year to undertake a large portion of the research in primary sources that grounds this book's theological explorations. The University of North Carolina at Chapel Hill provided research time through a younger faculty summer development grant, at a time when I could still be counted among the young. The College of Arts and Sciences, especially Dean Gillian Cell, also contributed importantly, through arrangements for two semesters of "earned leave," in 1987 and 1990. Throughout my years in Chapel Hill, the geniality and intellectual example and engagement of colleagues in the English Department has made productive scholarly labor both possible and enjoyable. Among the many who have contributed to this sustaining environment, I owe special thanks to Laurence Avery, Reid Barbour, Doris Betts, Alan Dessen, Lee Greene, Ritchie Kendall, Jerry Mills, Mark Reed, and James Thompson. A remarkable extramural extension of this stimulating collegiality occurred at the NEH Institute on Spenser's *Faerie Queene,* held at Princeton University in summer 1988. I learned constantly there, from the Institute's originator and impresario, Tom Roche, from our learned fellow professor, Annabel Patterson, and from the energetic college teachers who were our "students." The contributions of all the colleagues so far mentioned have built upon foundations firmly set down by the love of learning evident in my grandparents and parents, especially by my mother Vivian I. Gless; by the example of my accomplished brothers and sister, Francis, Alan, and Valerie; and by the unmerited interventions of my earlier teachers, Paul A. Olson, Ted Beck, Alastair Fowler, and the late D. W. Robertson, Jr.

Most recently, I have benefited from the exceptionally high standard of manuscript evaluation performed by the readers at Cambridge University Press. For their exemplary combination of receptiveness, accurate description, acute analysis, wise advice on rhetorical strategy, and helpful proposals for specific improvement and correction, my warm thanks to Dr. Colin Burrow (Gonville and Caius College, Cambridge), Professor Patrick Collinson (Trinity College, Cambridge), and Dr. Dennis Kay (Lincoln College, Oxford). Thanks, too, to Kevin Taylor, my patient and highly professional editor at the Press, for selecting readers whose scholarly publications are themselves superlative. For the book's remaining lapses, these helpful scholars should be held blameless.

For assiduous aid with the chore of checking citations and quotations, and correcting errors of logic and style, I owe gratitude to two young scholars: Scott Heulin, who worked on an earlier version of the manuscript, and Amy Strong, who much improved the final version.

For permitting me to reproduce photographs of Albrecht Altdorfer's "Maria mit dem Kind in der Glorie," my thanks to Alte Pinakothek München. For providing Spenserians with an excellent, richly annotated edition of *The Faerie Queene*, my thanks to A. C. Hamilton, whose Longman edition (London, 1977) is cited throughout my text.

Finally, for her constant wise counsel and intellectual engagement, and for restoring the author's confidence in his ability not only to complete this book but also to confront life's more significant human challenges, my deepest thanks to this book's dedicatee, Victoria Fisher Reed Gless.

ABBREVIATIONS

ABR	*American Benedictine Review*
CritI	*Critical Inquiry*
ELH	*English Literary History*
ELR	*English Literary Renaissance*
Hamilton, *FQ*	Spenser, *The Faerie Queene*, ed. A. C. Hamilton, London: Longman, 1977
HLQ	*Huntington Library Quarterly*
JWCI	*Journal of the Warburg and Courtauld Institutes*
MLR	*Modern Language Review*
MP	*Modern Philology*
PMLA	*Publications of the Modern Language Association of America*
RES	*Review of English Studies*
SEL	*Studies in English Literature*
SP	*Studies in Philology*
SSt	*Spenser Studies*
TSLL	*Texas Studies in Language and Literature*

INTRODUCTION

READING THEOLOGY / READING
THE FAERIE QUEENE

Those of us who have the good fortune to teach Spenser have all witnessed our students' insistent, sometimes desperate yearnings for the
comfort provided by a nurturing footnote. Most students and many of
their teachers will on occasion grasp at any prop that might lighten the
pleasurable but sometimes scarcely tolerable burdens imposed by this
poet's unique combination of eclectic learning, conspicuous archaism,
and prodigal inventiveness. It is no surprise that many such students,
at length turned professors, have frequently set out to manufacture aids
for readers, earnestly seeking to help others control the poem, as we
sometimes think we have come to control it, by establishing beachheads
in its "backgrounds." Nor is it surprising that religious doctrines have
long been welcomed as reliable sources of stabilizing contexts.

What could be more definite, after all, than religious doctrine? The
Bible, biblical commentaries, doctrinal treatises, sermons, and articles
of religious belief all continue to be treated, by Spenser specialists and
Renaissance scholars generally, as if their meanings were easily available,
unambiguous, and therefore unproblematically applicable to literary interpretation. Our widely shared inclination to treat these materials so
simply and confidently stems in part from the aggressive assertiveness
of doctrine itself. The varied genres which belong to theological discourse have frank and comprehensive designs upon readers. Yet the habit
of treating doctrine as if it were both simple in itself and a ready mechanism for interpreting literature also manifests an oversimplification we
often impose more broadly on the idea of "history." Because humanistic studies lack absolute standards with which to adjudicate interpretive
conflicts, literary scholars frequently turn to history, on the wishful assumption that it provides a place to stand "effectively free of the kind of
epistemological and methodological disputes that agitate their own area
of inquiry." Late-twentieth-century historiography has cast doubt on
that assumption.[1]

One aim of this book is to cast doubt on that assumption as it is applied to the content and the history of theology. But I want to perform this task of unsettling easy assumptions without resorting, by way of the always tempting binary impulse, to the opposite conviction – that religious contexts and content, once shown to be problematic, have also been exposed as useless. I proceed instead in the conviction that scholarly interest in Spenser's doctrinal contexts and commitments can illuminate us, not only as readers of his works, but as readers of many other Elizabethan and Jacobean texts that draw on theology, and as students more generally of Renaissance culture. Many colleagues share this opinion, of course, and scholarly engagement with the religious contexts of Spenser's works has remained strong in recent years. Much of the scholarship this interest has yielded proceeds, however, without paying sufficient heed to the topics that organize the bulk of this Introduction: (1) the variability that characterizes processes of perception in general and of reading in particular, (2) the roles which generic categories can play in the process of reading Spenser, (3) the uneven reception of Protestant orthodoxies in sixteenth-century England, and (4) the pervasive complexity, occasional indeterminacy, and not infrequent self-contradiction of theological doctrines themselves – even those that fall within the restricted range of "Reformed Protestant orthodoxy."

We will take up these topics now, in the sequence I have just given. The Introduction will then conclude with two sections readers may want to know about here. These include, first, an excursus that begins to suggest how the theological and interpretive sections of this book might guide responses to many significant portions of Spenser's oeuvre; and, second, an overview of chapters 2–6, where our main business is to examine The Legend of Holiness in detail.

THE FLUIDITY OF PERCEPTION

Studies of Spenser's theological contexts incline unselfconsciously to adopt a common strategy: the poet's convictions are inferred from passages in his poems, read in light of what little evidence remains of his political and social affiliations; this inferentially constructed "Spenser" is then considered solid enough to validate further interpretive inferences. Overtly or obliquely, hypothetical reconstructions of the author's political, religious, or literary allegiances provide the ground on which interpretive authority finally rests. This is as true of books by, say, Stephen Greenblatt and John Guillory, who are not primarily concerned with theological matters, as it is of studies that focus on those concerns, by (for instance) Anthea Hume and John King.[2] The unquestioned reliance on authorial intention which these books share does not significantly diminish their differing sorts of value.

Yet much is to be learned by acknowledging and tracking the operations of the circularity that makes guesses about authors' intentions our primary guarantees of the accuracy of meanings discovered in their works.[3] I intend to acknowledge the inescapable intentionalism of my own interpretations, and to recognize this intentionalism as a consequence of the hermeneutic circle that circumscribes acts of reading. According to the accounts that most persuasively describe it for me, reading is a process governed by anticipations, guesses about the meanings and nature of the whole utterance we are encountering. Because these guesses condition and help to constitute the reception of details we encounter in sequence, the texts we read are always somewhat like Narcissus' pool. To a significant degree, they reflect us, what we already are, know, and desire. Reading need not, however, become the self-deluding and potentially self-destructive mirroring which this image implies. While we are reading, most of us persistently imagine an author whose linguistic traces allow us not only to construct ideas that match our own but also to notice other views that extend or conflict with them. This mirroring-with-a-difference helps ensure that the "making" which occurs in acts of reading can "also always [be] a finding."[4] More or less consciously, too, most of us also apply tests of validity to determine which of various possible interpretations of any work or passage seems most plausible. According to Paul Armstrong's helpful formulation, these tests can be labeled "inclusiveness" (the interpretation's capacity to account for what readers judge to be a sufficiently extensive array of the text's details), "intersubjectivity" (the interpretation's power to persuade people that it is reasonable), and "efficacy" (the interpretation's capacity to solve interpretive difficulties without creating new ones).[5] I will persistently if implicitly invoke these tests in the following pages.

This somewhat paradoxical recognition – that readings can be subject to processes of validation and yet that texts, their meanings, and the authors we perceive through them are products in part of our own imaginings – can exert a healthy influence on interpretive practices. The paradox should at least make us less assured about the ideas we take to be a literary author's favorite dogmas. The further recognition that readers can create part of what they find even in doctrinal texts might also induce us to become less dogmatic about dogma. Shifting our attention from authors to readers may be, as Harry Berger has said, a small

leap for an old new critic to make. But despite the forceful start provided by Paul Alpers nearly a quarter century ago, this shift has not often been energetically and persistently achieved in Spenser studies.[6] And
Spenser studies have not yet begun to recognize that the documents
which propagate religious doctrine – in spite of their authors' efforts to
impose more limits on interpretation than literary texts normally do –
remain subject nonetheless to the constructive activities of readers. In
the following chapters, I seek always to be attentive to the ways readers
might construct not only the meanings of Spenser's texts but also the
content of what we believe to be his doctrinal contexts. Sustained study
of primary theological sources provides ample evidence that the
"textuality" which characterizes history, as new historicism and compatible theories understand "history," also characterizes what it is possible
for us to know of the history and content of religious doctrine.[7]

Even those of us who become convinced that readers themselves supply much of what they believe they find in texts often unconsciously
revert, while practicing literary interpretation, to two articles of implicit
faith: that meaning is contained in the text, and that the author's deliberate intentions led him or her to put it there.[8] The kind of evidence
that most effectively helps me resist such relapses, and helps my students begin to see how they construct as well as discover meaning in
texts, is (literally) graphic evidence. E. H. Gombrich's studies of "the
beholder's share" in perception and interpretation provide especially
effective assistance in this.[9] The profusion of vivid examples Gombrich
adduces from the visual arts helps to explain why the Shakespearian or
Spenserian texts I teach semester after semester invariably look somewhat different, excite classroom discussions that have differing content
and emphases, and yet (at least in the heat of discovery and presentation) possess me and some of my students with the illusion that our
current construction of the work is, quite simply, true and for all time.

What Gombrich illustrates convincingly is the usefulness of the idea
that perception is controlled by "schemata" or "frames."[10] As cognitive
psychology describes them, these mental structures filter out some features of the object under scrutiny, make other features perceptible, and
supply still other features which are not empirically present in that object. In their filtering and accessing functions, the schemata operate like
"formats" of the sort computers employ to "specify that information must
be of a certain sort if it is to be interpreted coherently." Schemata are
less rigid than formats, however, because they also function as "plans
for finding out about objects and events, for obtaining more informa-

tion to fill in the format." The information that fills in the format at one moment in the cyclic process becomes a part of the format in the next, and so helps to determine how further information will be accepted. The schemata do not absolutely determine what can be perceived, for "at any given moment," an individual schema "resembles a *genotype* rather than a *phenotype* . . . It offers a possibility of development along certain lines, but the precise nature of that development is determined only by interaction with an environment."[11]

Because schemata develop over time, divergent perceptions of an object can become available to the same viewer at different moments of perception. This divergence is the more likely to occur because the schemata provide material that supplements what is actually there, in the world, painting, or text. Among numerous wonderful instances of the degree to which viewers co-create works of art by projecting expected specific patterns onto inchoate shapes or blank screens, Gombrich adduces the illustration reproduced here. (See next two pages.) In what is actually a mere "series of luminous dots" that appear in Altdorfer's "The Virgin amidst Angels," we are induced to "see" infinite multitudes of angels. By means of gradual transitions, "[t]he artist leads the willing beholder from the charming angels in the foreground to more and more indistinct shapes and thus makes him project a vision of infinite multitudes of the heavenly host into the sparkling dots that fade into the distance." We succumb, in short, to a very persuasive illusion, and become convinced that we see more detail and locate more definite meaning than could be found, by empirical means, in the objects themselves.[12]

The guesses that interpret shapes *as* something can also modify our perceptions of their visible form, their very scale and orientation. Particularly striking instances of this control of perception by interpretation appear in unstable figure-ground and counterchange patterns. The checkerboard pattern, so commonplace that we seldom notice its instability, can become the focus of complex visual explorations if placed in a context in which we are stimulated to attend. This is also true of "certain forms of Gothic tracery which are apt to dissolve and reform in front of our eyes."[13] In sequence, the viewer's eye selects some features of the design, draws connections between them, and allows others to recede into the background. Because individual interpreters' particular assemblages of cognitive schemata control perceptions not only of the appearance but of the meaning assigned to things, a common yet puzzling phenomenon need not disturb us: meaning is available first, and the stimulus only later or not at all; meaning can "[come] to consciousness

Plate 1. Albrecht Altdorfer: "The Virgin amidst Angels" (c. 1525)
Alte Pinakothek München

Plate 2. Albrecht Altdorfer: "The Virgin amidst Angels" (c. 1525) – detail
Alte Pinakothek München

before (or without) the physical properties on which it allegedly depends."[14] When this happens, the interpreter has simply resorted to "the etc. principle," the assumption that the utterance or visual object we have just begun to perceive will display other features of the type to which we have unconsciously assigned it.[15]

CONTINGENCIES OF READING

When joined to a theory that takes into account the temporal dimensions of reading and the interpretive functions of genre, these analogies from the visual arts provide a persuasive description of the experience of reading *The Faerie Queene*. In acts of reading, as Wolfgang Iser describes them, the element of Gombrichian illusion arises from projections by which readers fill indeterminate places in texts, anticipate what will follow, and selectively remember what has come before.[16] Automatically assigning passages to familiar types of language, readers perceive detail and grasp implications of the sort those types have previously exhibited. The anticipated becomes part of the observed. Through these processes of selection and extrapolation, readers perform a version of the operations Renaissance schoolmasters promoted as deliberate strategies when they taught students to seek Christian meanings in the pagan classics.[17] Like those students, modern readers are likely (in less explicitly tutored ways) to imagine some overall sense of the work or passage, some "gestalt." When we "find" that ordering idea, the appropriate patterns and affiliated meanings appear.[18] Memory plays a part in this too. As we shall have occasion to note, *The Faerie Queene* provides numerous illustrations of the reconfiguring that occurs as readers move through its text and continuously adjust recollections of material already read in light of ideas and expectations aroused by passages currently under scrutiny. The text provokes "a continual interplay between modified expectations and transformed memories."[19]

A primary agent of this effect is the poem's diversity of generic signals, signals that often rapidly alter our guesses about the family of linguistic kinds to which successive passages can be assigned.[20] Like cognitive schemata, genres can help us reduce to manageable selections the multiplicity of features which complex linguistic phenomena present. And like schemata, genres can provide materials with which to fill out places of indeterminacy. Even where the text fails to provide them, we can be induced to "see" features of what we merely expect to find in the numerous sub-genres *The Faerie Queene* comprises – romance, epic, psychomachia, georgic, idyl, amatory lyric, satire, creed, parable, sermon, and others. Sometimes as we read *The Faerie Queene* a local shift in the text's generic identity[21] evokes startling implications because the characteristic values associated with the juxtaposed genres are incompatible.[22] In subsequent chapters, we will explore occasions when conflicting types of language – narrative romance and the various genres of theological discourse – meet or overlap. In the Legend of Holiness especially, the persistent confrontation of romance by theological statement and of theology by romance yields some of the text's most striking effects. The opposition of those two major kinds, and of numerous less pervasive ones, ensures that even in the most overtly dogmatic passages of *The Faerie Queene*, Book I, readers can find multiple interpretations. Despite the apparent attempts (through allegorical labels, for example) to limit readers' options, the text of the Legend of Holiness can remain remarkably accommodating. One of my aims is to demonstrate that the Legend not only allows, but also invites, a broader spectrum of particular realizations than critics have been prepared to recognize.[23]

Once we acknowledge that doctrinal ideas exist not as stable backgrounds but as constructs readers assemble from various discursive and literary genres, we can recognize that these readers find themselves in an extraordinarily fluid situation. They will not only undertake the search for meaning with different degrees of seriousness and energy; they will also construct different versions of what they take to be applicable contexts.[24] When constructing doctrinal perspectives from the materials Elizabethan Protestantism made available, moreover, readers will be drawing upon a vast array of ideas that are themselves too extensive and complex, often too self-contradictory, and too active as agents and objects of political contention to supply stable "backgrounds" for anything whatever.

HISTORICAL CONTINGENCY AND THE REFORMATIONIN ENGLAND

Evidence for the assertion with which my previous paragraph concludes often slips from consciousness, especially when commentators ask theology to help them control the protean poetry of *The Faerie Queene*. But many recent historical studies can offset the homogenizing amnesia to which the exigencies of interpretation drive us. For instance, a predominant view of the English Reformation, established in the 1960s by A. G.

Dickens, presented that movement as a popular one whose theological ideas gained rapid acceptance as the English people welcomed the passing of a decadent religious establishment.[25] This view has recently been judged a product of "whig" interpretive assumptions, which presuppose that the Reformation was caused by progressive forces. Once that assumption takes hold, the interpreter will inevitably see the mere existence of legislation like that which established the religious settlement of 1559 as "evidence for the strength of that [progressive] force." But recent studies of the local effectiveness of the Reformation imply that, on the popular ideological level, its influence developed very slowly. According to this reconstruction, the ideological victories of the Reformation began only in "the middle of the reign of Elizabeth I" when for the first time "the universities produced a generation of committed Protestant ministers who could take the evangelical faith to the parishes."[26]

Even then, the success of the ideological Reformation apparently varied by geographical areas. It appears to have met with early success "in towns such as Bristol, Colchester, Coventry, Ipswich and London," but "[i]n Cambridgeshire, Cornwall, Gloucestershire, Lancashire, Lincolnshire, Norfolk, Suffolk, Sussex, and Yorkshire, the Protestant Reformation was an Elizabethan (or often mid-Elizabethan) event. For much of the reign of Elizabeth, the Church of England was a prescribed, national Church with more-or-less Protestant liturgy and theology but an essentially non-Protestant (and in some respects anti-Protestant) laity."[27] Ronald Hutton's studies of churchwardens' accounts provide evidence that "parish religion in 1530 was an intensely dynamic and rapidly developing phenomenon," and that in successive phases of the Reformation under Henry, Edward, and Elizabeth, government commissioners displayed surprising and fierce efficiency in seizing "the endowments of chantries, religious guilds, and perpetual obits," removing images and rood screens, and confiscating and liquidating all the accoutrements of late-medieval worship.[28]

Although this meticulousness showed successive governments to be effective at destroying the traditional faith, they proved less competent at establishing a new one. That would have required an extraordinary and well-financed campaign to build up the new religion in people's esteem. Such a campaign never materialized, partly because the rich church properties and materials confiscated in negative phases of the reform were diverted to other uses, and partly because, even when positive success became possible under Elizabeth, her government showed little eagerness to proselytize. The successes that gradually turned England into a Protestant nation appear to have resulted from individual efforts. Among those efforts, some might well count a major work by a major new poet, for Spenser's Legend of Holiness treats features of doctrine and ecclesiology that were just beginning in many areas to receive adequate formulation and dissemination by the authorities.

Awareness that Elizabethan orthodoxy was unevenly received should somewhat inhibit whatever impulse literary interpreters might still feel to assert confidently what "the English reader" thought about religious issues raised in *The Faerie Queene.* Although we literary scholars have often liked to assume, for example, that the official *Homilies* made a Protestant version of Christianity universally available, the situation was not that simple. Despite the government's sponsorship of the *Homilies* in 1547, "only nineteen out of the ninety-one parishes" in Hutton's sample actually purchased a copy during Edward's reign. "The government had more success with the English translation of Erasmus' *Paraphrases*" – a document that might further the ends of Protestantism, but was not at all points doctrinally consistent with those ends. "[O]f the [ninety-one] parishes in the sample, forty-one had bought it before the end of 1548, and another twelve by the end of Edward's reign." That numerical success seems modest enough, but the book's actual impact may have been less impressive still. As Hutton points out,

[h]ow far [Erasmus'] lively but scholarly work was read or understood by parishioners is . . . a different matter, and some of the entries recording the purchase do not encourage optimism. In the accounts of Yatton, Somerset, the book is called "The Paraphrases and Erasmus", in those of St. Dunstan, Canterbury, "Parasimus", and in those of Sheriff Hutton, Yorkshire, "Coloke of Herassimus".[29]

Moreover, there appears to have been widespread, surreptitious perpetuation of traditional Catholic practices. The endowing of "lights," participation in lay fraternities whose chief function was to pray for the dead, and similar activities, which J. J. Scarisbrick documents for earlier Tudor periods, survived throughout Elizabeth's reign. Such was the vitality of these survivals that Archbishop Grindal, Spenser's "Algrind," had to be relentless in investigating "whether ministers used any 'crossing or breathing or elevation of the bread and wine, any oils, chrism, tapers, prayers for the dead . . .'" Despite such vigilance, "recusancy increased in strength and confidence during the 1570s."[30]

DOCTRINAL CONTINGENCY

Still, it can be argued that late in Elizabeth's reign, England became "a Protestant nation" – not the uniformly Protestant one many of us have been imagining in the wake of Dickens' magisterial work, but one "containing deep tension and potential confusion within an outward shell of consensus."[31] Even if we can accept this view of an eventual if partial success in the widespread propagation of Protestant ideology – or if we were to go still further and assume that the religious consensus literary scholars frequently ascribe to late-sixteenth- and early-seventeenth-century England was absolute, consistently held by people in authority, and effectively and systematically preached to the populace – we still could not assume that it was consistently received. The seed of the word fell on varying soil, some of it stony. Even so conscientious a minister as Richard Greenham appears to have failed to win over many of his charges. As Christopher Haigh reconstructs the story, Greenham,

rector of Dry Drayton in Cambridgeshire from 1570 to 1591, was an exemplary Protestant pastor. At Dry Drayton he preached six sermons a week (about 6,000 in all), and catechised twice a week; he composed his own thoughtful and well-organised . . . catechism; and his commonplace book shows him to have been a diligent visitor of the sick and a sympathetic comforter of troubled souls. But after twenty-one years of exhausting effort he stumped off in disgust to London, because of "the intractableness and unteachableness of that people among whom he had taken such exceeding great pains" – and an analysis of Dry Drayton wills suggests that his conclusion that he had, in all but a few families, failed, was just about right.[32]

This kind of evidence may in part represent not the people's reluctance to forgo old beliefs (as Haigh and other "revisionist" historians assume), but a more pervasive, less historically specific factor. More insistently than the doctrines of the old religion, those of the new set themselves in overt opposition to ordinary ways of viewing the world. When Josias Nichols made a practice of asking people from various parishes in Elizabethan Kent to describe their beliefs "he usually found. . . a kind of folk religion, expressing a Pelagian faith in the social virtues but not even an elementary understanding of the Protestant path to salvation."[33] Other evidence appears to confirm Nichols' report that "the common sort of christians" adhered to an "incorrigibly Pelagian philosophy." In a parish of four hundred communicants systematic catechizing before administering the sacrament had revealed that scarcely one in ten was familiar with the elements of protestant doctrine. Asked "whether it were possible for a man to live so uprightlie that by well doeinge he might winne heaven", there was hardly a man who failed to answer in the affirmative: "that a man might be saved by his owne weldoing, and that he trusted he did so live that by God's grace hee shoulde obtaine everlasting life, by serving of God and good prayers, etc."[34]

The idea that the supreme being works thus sensibly by the measure of humankind's notions of just dealing is so congenial to human capacities that fundamental Protestant doctrines – justification *sola gratia, sola fide* – must fight a perpetual uphill battle against common mental reflexes.[35]

Even for people who might escape Pelagianism's inertial pull and reject all Catholic traditions, Protestant orthodoxy itself could still present diverse aspects when observed at different moments and from different locations. Its content displays diverse colorations that reflect the diversity of its origins. A "portmanteau of religious attitudes" was available and even authorized in differing ways during the Elizabethan period because official religion drew its doctrinal substance from many continental authorities. Calvin was extremely influential, of course, but "English theologians were as likely to lean on Bullinger of Zurich, Musculus of Berne, or Peter Martyr as on Calvin or Beza" – not to mention "Junius, Danaeus, the Heidelberg doctors and their influential Catechism, Ursinus, and above all Zanchius" as well as a list of patristic authorities, among whom Augustine enjoyed a conspicuous place.[36] The eclecticism of Elizabethan theology implies that we should resist historical reconstructions which seek to establish an unrivalled theological authority for the Elizabethan period. Although Martyr or Bullinger might be considered representative in certain respects, neither they, nor for that matter Calvin or Hooker or Perkins, can be viewed as normative. Those authors had much in common, but they could also, actually or apparently, contradict each other, and sometimes even contradict themselves, on major points of doctrine.

For example, as careful readers have noticed, the works of major Swiss reformers can appear remarkably self-contradictory. These Reformers' readiness to exhort their readers to persist in good works seems to imply a pervasive moralism and a corresponding readiness to value the believer's striving. This emphasis appears to challenge the same theologians' explicit insistence on the preeminence of grace. In the works of Bucer and Zwingli, the absolute primacy of grace often becomes manifest in a specific emphasis on the Holy Spirit as primary agent in the process of justification. Yet in Bucer's elaboration of Zwingli's moralist tendencies, this emphasis developed into a notion of double justification. The first justification, Bucer maintained, is awarded on the basis of faith alone, but a "secondary justification takes place on the basis of [the believer's] works," which the Spirit's indwelling presence impels.[37] Cursory readings or partial recollections of Bucer or Zwingli could lead interpreters to contradictory conclusions: either that Bucer and Zwingli believed in justification by faith, or that they believed sinners can in some sense be justified by works.

A comparable conundrum appears in Calvin's works. Readers can find it difficult to reconcile his emphasis on gratuitous justification with his emphatic attention to the demands of obedience to divine law.[38] For readers studious enough to discover it, Calvin did provide a reconciliation, which appears in his distinctive concept of incorporation in Christ: this mystical union of the Savior with the individual human soul is what produces justification and sanctification as "distinct and inseparable" features. An Elizabethan reader who managed to grasp and become convinced of Calvin's solution to the problem of allocating definite roles to grace and human will, and who happened next to turn to the works of Henry Bullinger, another Reformed authority valued by the Elizabethan church, would be confronted by a conundrum. For Bullinger sometimes appears confidently to announce "that justification did not mean the imputation of righteousness" at all; it meant instead "the actualisation of righteousness."[39]

Similarly, to those who bring specifically Calvinist expectations to their reading of the evasively politic Elizabethan Article 17, Elizabethan orthodoxy could appear to include the doctrine of double predestination, which (as Calvin explains) views both salvation and damnation as direct functions of divine will: "[w]e call predestination God's eternal decree, by which he compacted with himself what he willed to become of each man . . . Eternal life is foreordained for some, eternal damnation for others."[40] Readers who follow the lead of Peter Martyr, by contrast, could maintain, and could read the Elizabethan article to imply, that "the reprobate are not predestinate." In the 1580s, adherents of Martyr's view would find support in Hooker's *Discourse on Justification*; their opponents could gain ammunition from Hooker's antagonist, Travers.[41] Protestants who resisted the idea of double predestination could locate further support in Erasmus' *Paraphrase* – "required" reading, as we have noted, for clergymen in Elizabeth's reign – of Paul to the Romans, where the apostle is made to remark (incongruously, many readers will feel) that God condemns "no man . . . but for his own offence." Still more incongruously, Erasmus' "Paul" grounds justification not in the actions of irresistible grace but in a faith that can be freely chosen or rejected: the faithful

be accounted righteous, not for keeping of the law, but for their only faith's sake, whereunto no man is compelled, but rather greatly provoked and allured, which God doth to the intent that our faith in Christ should be a thing of us freely wrought, and of no compulsion, and that our deliverance through him . . . should be a thing of God's free gift and mercy, and of no debt. (Rom. 4:5)[42]

Believers inclined to adopt so voluntarist a conception of faith could discover an influential ally operating quietly in every parish church. For the Elizabethan liturgy could itself at least implicitly undermine any believer's consciously held allegiance to fundamental Reformed doctrines: "the English liturgy implied in its undertones and ethos as much as in any explicitly dogmatic statement the universal availability of grace through the sacraments and the use of petitionary prayer."[43] Clearly, even careful readers can find that Elizabethan Reformed Christianity spoke with more than one voice. As my quotations from early texts will repeatedly imply hereafter, the multiple and often competing voices of Elizabethan Reformed theology were widely disseminated in English translations that received an *imprimatur* from the ecclesiastical and political authorities.[44]

The few disagreements I have mentioned here just begin to expose the inaccuracy of an assumption often held by Renaissance literary scholars – that all or most doctrinal disagreement in England was stilled by the appearance of the Thirty-Nine Articles and *Homilies*, and that Elizabethan controversies focused entirely on liturgy and ecclesiastical governance.[45] Liturgical and ecclesiological disputes were conspicuous, of course, but we should also recognize that the latitude built into the authorizing texts of the religious settlement allowed variations in doctrinal interpretation.[46] This became evident, for instance, when an academic skirmish at Cambridge concerning fundamental features of the doctrine of justification grew into a matter of urgency for the national government. H. C. Porter's exposition of these arguments over what doctrines actually were set down "by authority" deserves rereading by anyone inclined to assume that there was a doctrinal consensus which can provide stable interpretive touchstones for Elizabethan literature.[47]

SPENSER AND THEOLOGICAL INTERPRETATION

If sixteenth-century English Protestant doctrines are complex and contradictory, subject to variable readings determined by interpreters' subjective differences as well as their differing stations within political, economic, and social structures, is there any point in trying to read Spenser in the light of sixteenth-century theology? I think there is. What has been said so far appears to me to guarantee that the experience of reading the Legend of Holiness and related portions of Spenser's oeuvre, in the sixteenth century as now, will evoke attitudes and ideas that conflict with whatever dogmatically tidy interpretations scholars might propose. To seek to describe all the possibilities for divergence would be futile. To describe a few, as I attempt to do in the following chapters, might be instructive. And the discovery of a diversity of possible interpretations of doctrinally implicated passages of Spenser makes the enterprise of reading those passages more intellectually engaging than theological interpretations have often proved to be.

Because we cannot have unmediated access to things themselves, we must settle for versions of the world, versions of history (intellectual and other), and versions of texts.[48] Before exploring the kinds of complexity that result from the marriage of various genres of theological discourse to a variety of literary kinds in *The Faerie Queene*'s first book, we need to explore major elements of the amalgam that constituted "Elizabethan Protestant Orthodoxy." My version of those orthodox doctrines appears in chapter 1. What might make this description of a portion of English intellectual history worth attention? Like any other newly stated version, it claims to be "improved." The improvement derives from my effort to prevent unacknowledged presuppositions about Spenser's private convictions from limiting what I can see of the doctrines available to him and to his earliest readers. The resulting reconstruction of Elizabethan doctrinal history cannot elude the unconscious governance of individual predispositions, of course, but I have sought to use my imperfect consciousness of those predispositions to enable me to notice more features of Elizabethan doctrinal topography than previous surveyers have explored.

Another source of this account's value will be its sheer availability. Because the deceptively simple terms of Christian doctrine – holiness, grace, faith, sin, law, good works – appear to be obligingly self-interpreting, we as yet have no readily available statement of what those terms might mean to an attentive reader of Spenser's *Faerie Queene* who might also be an attentive reader of sixteenth-century theology. What chapter 1 and some sections of later chapters supply, therefore, is a description of particular constructions of those otherwise vague terms. Chapter 1 also contains a rather extensive anthology of quotations and citations that ground my interpretations of theological terms in the English versions of numerous sixteenth-century theologians' specific statements. Although the abundance of these quotations risks explaining too much for specialist readers, and of explaining too elaborately for others who possess a limited appetite for theology, I have insisted on a degree of thoroughness. My aim is to reduce the inaccuracies that appear in more hastily generalizing scholarly descriptions. This seems intrinsically worth doing because the history of theology in the period, like its literary, economic, social, and political history, is rich, interesting, and useful for students of sixteenth-century culture to know. Theology appears in this study as a great deal more than a necessary background, to be gotten out of the way before we hurry to develop either of the options most fashionable in the past few decades – another exposition of the ideological functions of Spenser's text, or another close reading of that text itself. Both the text itself and the ideological functions readers feel it serves will be substantially constructed from contexts, theological and other, which those same readers provide.

That such contexts themselves require construction by readers becomes especially clear at those moments when early texts most forthrightly show Elizabethan Protestant doctrine functioning as a "discipline" in Foucault's sense of the term. We will have occasion to notice (ch. 6, p. 143, below), for instance, Richard Greenham's discussion of a kind of anxiety and depression which his parishioners sometimes suffered, and which he termed "blind griefs." An assiduous physician of souls and practitioner of the discipline of Christian casuistry, Greenham diagnoses this common distress as the work of a "secret providence" which is determined to correct God's wayward children. Greenham's discipline next enables him to construct (though he would have said to "find") and then to treat the deeper, more particular symptoms which that providential cause produced: the sufferers must first be brought "to the sight of sin, as to some cause of their trouble. Herein we must labour to put away all confusion and blindness of sorrow, endeavouring," through the application of confessional techniques new and old, "to bring the parties wounded to some certain object and matter of their trouble; and so draw out of them the confession of some several, especial, and secret sin."[49] No doubt such sessions often produced remarkable discoveries – co-constructed, like narratives which emerge in modern psychoanalytic sessions, by the very instruments of the healer's art and by the physician and patient who employ those instruments.[50] Readers who are inclined toward religious belief may tend to view Greenham's pastoral labors as a search for hidden spiritual realities; devotees of skeptical interpretive practices will appraise his work differently, as I do here.

This question of how one evaluates the results of literary or cultural interpretation raises a crucial issue, the question of "the reader." Whereas interpretations of Spenser invariably if implicitly imagine a set of possible readers, reader-oriented interpretations must do so explicitly. The readers my interpretations posit are interested in theology as well as in poetry like *The Faerie Queene,* and although such readers may have been more numerous in the sixteenth and early seventeenth century than they now are, the species remains extant. These readers require no specialist expertise; they simply possess a more energetic interest in theological ideas and a more comprehensive doctrinal knowledge than nineteenth- and twentieth-century literary scholars have characteristically displayed, and they feel less of the religious historian's need to minimize inconsistencies and uncertainties in order to categorize and clarify. They will in general assign special significance to the abundant features of Spenser's poem that coalesce most effectively when constructed in part from materials which Reformed orthodox theology supplies. Such readers can construe *The Faerie Queene* quite differently than established modern interpreters so far have done. And although these readers' responses will be variously inflected by their differing political, economic, and social circumstances, the theological doctrines they share can provide at least a little consistency. The contexts my version of doctrinal history provide can, I believe, help such readers bring many passages "into focus in a remarkable way," enabling "puzzling or unnoticed details [to] emerge into clarity and distinction" [and] "familiar [passages to] take on new clarity of argument."[51]

EXCURSUS: THEOLOGICAL INTERPRETATION AND
THE SPENSERIAN OEUVRE

Although an exploration of *The Faerie Queene*, Book I, will supply most of my evidence for the foregoing assertion, we should pause here to glance at a few instances that occur elsewhere in Spenser's works. Other examples will receive attention during or after our detailed progress through the Legend of Holiness. For readers informed about theology, familiar or unnoticed passages which emerge into new clarity and distinction can crop up almost anywhere. Let us begin, for instance, with a familiar passage written at the beginning of Spenser's career. In the "September" eclogue of *The Shepheardes Calender*, Diggon Davie's vituperative account of pastoral misdoings in "a farre countrye" develops into an invective against wolves at home, then into a story of an especially crafty wolf that preyed on the flock of a shepherd named Roffy.[52] Since Roffy "is wise, and as Argus eyed" (203), the wolf that repeatedly manages to carry off a "Lambe, or a Kidde, or a weanell wast" (198), must possess special skills. Not only can he wear the "clothing of seely sheepe" (188), but he has also become an expert impersonator. Sometimes he imitates one of the sheepdogs, "[f]or he had eft learned a curres call" (191), but he has also "cond the shepherds call" (215) so perfectly that he easily dupes Roffy's most vigilant dog:

> in the night [he] came to the shepecote,
> And called Lowder, with a hollow throte,
> As if it the old man selfe had bene.
> The dog his maisters voice did it weene,
> Yet halfe in doubt, he opened the dore,
> And ranne out, as he was wont of yore.
> No sooner was out, but swifter then thought,
> Fast by the hyde the Wolfe lowder caught:
> And had not Roffy renne to the steven,
> Lowder had be slaine thilke same even.   (216–25)

A glance at most commentaries demonstrates that all this intriguing detail has aroused little scholarly attention. Eagerness to identify specific historical references ("Does this dangerous wolf allude to Father Preston?"), or to adduce broad scriptural analogues,[53] has deflected critics from noticing that Diggon's elaborate description of the wolf's techniques might itself become the focus of a more than usually inclusive and effective interpretation. Readers guided by interest in theology could readily adopt that focus.

Such readers' attention might be arrested here by an interpretive puzzle. If Lowder is the best of sheep dogs – "Never had shepheard so kene a kurre" (182) – why does the wolf's imitation of the shepherd's voice so completely delude him and the ecclesiastical officers he symbolizes? If the good shepherd-bishop's expert officers can be so taken in by an imitation of their master's voice, what powers of perception can enable humankind to distinguish the sound of true doctrine from false? Are the empirically apprehensible voices of shepherd and wolf, their voicing of doctrinal truth and falsehood, nearly identical? If "the central point of Diggon's tale of Roffy" is that "[i]nstinct is not enough; one must know, perceive,"[54] how can one achieve that accuracy of knowing and perceiving in circumstances so befuddling as the ones Diggon's tale recounts?

The tale's elusiveness is part of its fun.[55] But, as our explorations in sixteenth-century doctrine will soon demonstrate, contemporary theology provides a potential reading of Lowder's susceptibility to wolvish ventriloquism. Certain principles of that theology maintain that even the best informed, most well-intentioned, most learned, most practiced of human minds will fail – not only sometimes but always – to recognize truth unless grace at every moment impels that mind's reason to perform its natural functions effectively (p. 32). A modestly detailed awareness of notions of grace as defined by the theologies prevalent in Spenser's England can therefore explain Lowder's sudden incompetence as a temporary loss of a particular function of grace. As we shall see, such doctrinal awareness can also provide intriguing contexts for recurrent lapses in *The Faerie Queene*, like the unexpected but repeated disappearances of Una's powers of spiritual insight, of the defensive powers of Red Cross Knight's armor, and (especially in later books) of Arthur's perplexing capacity to be overtly allied with grace and yet to display remarkable, sometimes comic and sometimes unsettling faults.

The same doctrinal contexts can cast novel light on Diggon's and Hobbinol's ensuing disagreement about what must be done to protect sheep from such dangerous wolves. Diggon recommends that shepherds must "ever liggen in watch and ward" (234); Hobbinol retorts that "thilke same rule were too straight . . . We bene of fleshe, men as other bee" (236–38). Scholars have sometimes argued that Spenser was promoting Diggon's "Puritan" rigorousness; others have maintained that Spenser wanted us to side with Hobbinol's "'large and moving gesture of acceptance of himself and others'."[56] An interpretation informed by contemporary doctrines of grace could sharpen these perceptions. It can help us recognize that any shepherd's efforts to achieve Diggon's recommended degree of rigor would be exceptional, and yet that such efforts constitute strong evidence that the shepherd in question indeed possesses the grace which will save his own soul while making some imperfect successes, like Roffy's, possible in this world. Such a response would at the same time recognize that Hobbinol's point is true: being flesh, no shepherd can remain perpetually vigilant. No matter how large his portion of grace, the divine source of grace has determined that its human recipients are sometimes most effectively aided by being allowed to fail. Roffy's remarkable degree of grace becomes evident in the rare fact that "with his word his work is convenable" (175), yet sometimes even he will "sleepe" and fail adequately to protect his flock (189–98).[57]

This version of the passage casts a gently critical light on Hobbinol's view, construing it not as a "large and moving gesture of acceptance" but as a pair of unreconciled excuses – a rejection of the obligations divine imperatives impose ("We bene of fleshe . . . Why should we be bound to such miseree?," 239), and an assertion based too easily on natural creatures' need to alternate physical exertion and rest (240–41). However true, the second point sounds like evasion when measured against the divine imperatives for which Diggon here speaks. The doctrines of grace we will examine shortly would induce us to highlight this feature of human weakness in Hobbinol's argument while at the same time providing reason to judge the speaker gently, as a representative of most of humankind.

This passage in "September" illustrates the kind of shift in focus – and the consequent transformation of the object perceived as well as its potential meanings – which doctrinal interests can frequently help readers effect during their progress through Spenser's works. Other instances from *The Shepheardes Calender* come readily to mind. The story of the fox and the kid in "Maye" becomes more textured and engaging if the schemata by which we construct it possess more complexity than the usual questions – of ecclesiastical factionalism, or stark moral contrasts, or E. K.'s simplistic personification allegory – tend to allow. If "the Kidde may be understoode [as] the simple sorte of the faythfull and true Christians. . . [and] hys dame Christe," as E. K. asserts,[58] why does the poet, through Piers, so fully exploit the delightful features of beast fable – detailing the goat's revived sense of loss ("A thrilling throbbe from her hart . . . [of] some old sorowe . . . Seemed shee sawe in the younglings face / The old lineaments of his fathers grace," 208–12); the extension of that loss in her emotional attachment to her kid ("florish[ing] in flowres of lusty head. / For even so thy father his head upheld, / And so his hauty hornes did he weld," 204–6); and her warning about the fox which, though elaborate, fails explicitly to note that the fox may not appear to be a fox when he arrives (215–26)? In what sense is the kid, who receives a comparably elaborate beast-fable portrait, a simple, faithful, and true Christian? Although the fox, disguised as ailing pedlar, plays effectively on his sympathies ("The Kidd pittying hys heauinesse," 259), the kid opens the door specifically because he is "so enamored with the newell [glass]" and entertains the fox "[a]ll for the love of the glasse he did see" (276, 283).

Readers who note this little tale's complexities may indeed conclude that they represent generic features of pastoral dialogues, which "explore what may best be said on either part."[59] But other possibilities of complex construction are available. Reformed Protestant doctrines of grace can enable us to agree that the kid is "simple," perhaps also "faithful" and "true," but knowledge of those doctrines would provide each term with subtle but rapid redefinitions as readers progress through rich and potentially diverse interpretive experiences of the passage. Those redefinitions could account both for the kid's apparent selfishness and for his generosity, natural inheritances from a mother whose devotion to him is at once generous and narcissistic – and therefore fundamentally human in the ways sixteenth-century theological discourse depicted humanity. Doctrinal perspectives can also provide a more than usually sharp intellectual account of the sense of loss readers may feel when the goat discovers her new bereavement: we are to undertake some hard mental adjustments in recognizing that simple innocence, as humans define it, may be a primary characteristic of those determined from all eternity to live and die as goats rather than sheep. Our discussion of Una's sojourn among the fauns and satyrs (*Faerie Queene* I.vi; ch. 4, pp. 106-12, below) will throw retrospective light upon this.

A ROAD MAP

Such darting attention as I have here been giving to *The Shepheardes Calender* will also be provided in the following pages for portions of *The Faerie Queene* that lie beyond the ample territories of the Legend of Holiness. This will occur most persistently in chapter 7, where we will glance briefly, for instance, at the usually unacknowledged generic diversity that characterizes the transition from Book I to Book II; the interplay of genres that casts an often underappreciated comic light upon Guyon's and the palmer's rigidly moral perceptions in Book II; the sometimes strange, sometimes Chaucerian comic gracelessness of Arthur's actions, which seem nonetheless to represent the presence of grace, in Books III and IV; the frequently unnoted surprises in later books, like Mercilla's court prosecutor's (Zele's) use of the moral monster Ate as his trump witness against Duessa/Mary; and Colin Clout's downright Gombrichian/Iserian construction of an interpretation for his vision on Mount Acidale. Sometimes this attention to the wider world of faery will appear in parenthetical or footnote references sprinkled about in my treatment of Book I.

Although the episodes explored in chapter 7 reflect the wonderful variety of Spenser's *Faerie Queene,* they also focus on themes we will confront often in chapters 2–6. These include, especially, the interpretive consequences of generic inclusiveness, the question of closure, and the poem's redefinition of heroism through the character of Arthur. This recurrence of (by then) familiar themes reflects the general aim of my final chapter, which is to hint at ways in which the theological interpretations we have developed for Book I can have intriguing applications elsewhere. In offering these hints, I also mean to imply that interpretations produced by the kind of readers I am positing in this book will be able to meet the tests of validity listed earlier. Without pretending to be the only readings permissible, or that those readings coincide in any simple sense with the author's intended meanings, these interpretations can effectively meet the tests of inclusiveness and effectiveness. (Readers of this book will decide whether its interpretations also meet the test of intersubjectivity.)

Here, then, is our itinerary on the road to chapter 7: chapter 1 assembles theological materials that enable us to achieve fresh insights into portions of *The Faerie Queene* that invoke apparently simple but actually quite complex theological doctrines. Subsequent chapters, which are devoted primarily to Book I, elaborate that claim, beginning in chapter 2 with careful scrutiny of the opening passages of the Legend of Holiness. My aim in this chapter is to provide readers with grounds to resist an overly rapid resort to the "etc. principle," which leads many to perceive dogmatic simplicity where Spenser has provided novelty and complexity. Chapter 2 therefore explores how the prefatory matter of the poem's earliest editions and the grammatical ambiguities and allusiveness of the opening stanzas of Book I, canto i, resist the (always seductive) possibility of construing its content as "allegory," simplistically understood. The chapter then focuses on interpretive consequences of the interplay, in I.i, between theological ideas and other major genres, literary and discursive. These genres include chivalric romance, moral philosophy, and georgic. Chapters 3 and 4 persist in this exploration of the consequences of generic alternation, especially on meanings that arise in I.ii-vi, when theological notions are conjoined with or modulated by generic features of antimonastic satire, political satire, allegorical pageant, epic, and pastoral idyl.

Chapter 5 concerns mainly John's Apocalypse (treated as representative of a genre rather than as a source of *The Faerie Queene*) interacting with romance and epic to enable readers to revalue notions both of holiness and of heroism in the poem's central narrative episodes (I.vii–viii). This section reevaluates interpretations that have taken a political or "historical" slant. What readers have perceived chiefly as "historical allegory" becomes the more ideologically powerful because, as I demonstrate, the Legend's climactic events draw meaning from features of biblical prophecy which claim to transcend history, to represent timeless truths that participants in secular history will reiterate only at the cost of extreme peril. The analyses presented here often reverse established interpretations, and find, in parts of the poem thought to be most static and simple, invitations to engage in an active intellectual exercise – and invitations to resist the widespread assumption that the poem's apocalyptic features induce an automatic expectation of "closure."

Incitements to active intellectual engagement remain insistent, I argue in chapter 6, even in Spenser's presentation of the House of Holiness, a place which illustrates as forcefully as anything in Spenser's works that his great poem may participate in a broad humanist project to employ literature less to disseminate received ideas than to elicit and sharpen active thought.[60] That point becomes still more evidently applicable when, as I have mentioned, we explore in chapter 7 Spenser's use of the final canto of Book I as a transition into the broader world of the poem, and, in a dash through that world's ample domains, we briefly scrutinize selected features of *The Faerie Queene*, Books II–VI. This chapter, which concludes my book, proposes a way of approaching theological materials throughout Spenser's poem. My argument is, in brief, that sturdy acts of faith become increasingly necessary if readers are to sustain optimistic providentialist interpretations as they move from Book II through Book VI. Though complex in content and application, such interpretations can solve many hermeneutic difficulties in Books I and II. Without rendering similar interpretations impossible, Spenser recurrently confronts them, in Books III–VI, with challenges that make his readers' participation in the construction of providentialist meanings increasingly strenuous, and for some, perhaps, increasingly precarious.

We will begin our analysis of theological contexts now, and, because the title of *The Faerie Queene*, Book I, proposes it, a primary focus of our attention in chapter 1 will be the doctrine, or rather the doctrines, of holiness. As we shall see, "holiness" gains meaning from its place in a constellation of terms that includes a number of substantial entries – "predestination," "grace," "will," "faith," "law," and "sin." Viewed from my current location in the history of the disciplines of doctrinal and literary history, these terms describe elements and patterns of emphasis that differ somewhat from the ones visible to Spenserians who have so far studied them.

I should conclude here with a note on style. Because my aim, in accord with reader-oriented criticism generally, is to describe not certain meanings authors put into texts, but potential readings different readers might differently construct from those texts, I have often been obliged to violate the standards of prose style my students are often exhorted to meet, a style in which active verbs describe a definite world. A vocabulary suggesting the possible rather than the actual proliferates below – "can," or "could," or "might" must dominate – except, that is, when the illusion that I am perceiving and describing truth overwhelms my interpretive principles.

Readers will want to know also that I have regularized spelling in quotations from early prose works, including the Geneva Bible. But I have allowed the biblical and ecclesiastical authors to retain forms that will not impede modern readers, e.g. the "-eth" verb ending. I have followed modern usage of i/j, u/v, and w. Finally, I have cited A. C. Hamilton's richly annotated Longman edition of *The Faerie Queene* (London, 1977) throughout my text.

1

HOLINESS: CONSENSUS, COMPLEXITY, CONTRADICTION[1]

Spenser scholarship has often treated the word "holiness" as if it were utterly vague, merely describing a special degree of individual piety. Because our aim here is to explore readings that might occur to interpreters of *The Faerie Queene* who have undertaken a modestly conscientious scrutiny of major doctrines of sixteenth-century English orthodoxy, it will be important to consider contemporary ideas of holiness in some detail. This undertaking must include a brief description of the overall theological system that endowed individual doctrinal concepts with some measure of specificity. Given the complexity of the subject, my description of that system cannot be exhaustive, nor can it be pellucid. It will comprise regions both of greater than usual clarity and of deeper or, at least, more elaborate confusion.

In sixteenth-century England, "holiness" could carry many implications. At its least concrete, the idea of the holy could retain, especially for readers of the Bible, something of its original Mosaic and prophetic cast. Its scriptural origins enabled "holiness" to refer to characteristics of the Lord Himself, to His separateness, absolute purity, and awe-inspiring transcendence – the terrifying majesty displayed in the theophanies of the Pentateuch where no one, not Moses himself, can look upon Yahweh and live (e.g., Exod. 33:20). When this fearful attribute of the divine enters the human sphere, it extends to objects, seasons, people, and priests consecrated to the Lord, and it acquires cultic dimensions from its association with ritual cleanliness.[2]

Later the idea was extended, notably in the Holy God of Isaiah, so daunting in His majesty that the seraphs must cover their eyes for fear of seeing Him (Is. 6:2). This God of transcendent otherness and purity demands an answering if necessarily diminished holiness from men, holiness conceived not merely as separation from things ritually unclean, but as purification from sin (see, e.g., Is. 1:26; 5:16; 6:5–7 and the Geneva commentary, 1587).[3] Isaiah's God demands, in short, "righteousness," a kind of justice or judicial equity that reflects His own unmatchable holiness (see esp. Is. 6:4). Having imposed so extreme a demand, the Lord must first provide whatever degree of purity He requires from humankind.[4]

Isaiah's own and later prophets' conceptions of holiness as spiritual and moral purity became dominant in the New Testament,[5] and its preeminence there helped to ensure that "sanctity" defined as moral purity would dominate Protestant treatments of the subject. Yet Yahweh's awesome otherness does not disappear from sixteenth-century discussions of the holy. It remains particularly marked in the works of Calvin, for whom the "image of God" in man is to be interpreted as "true holiness and righteousness." This apparently ethical interpretation both accompanies and is colored by a notion of the deity which, at its most sublime, is communicated through the magnificent imagery of Job and the awe-inspiring circumstances of the Mosaic theophanies. Calvin's deeply scriptural conception of the Lord as creator, providential sustainer, and divine judge of the world not only conveys a vivid idea of His fearful grandeur; it often accompanies an equally powerful conception of His boundless generosity, expressed through Christ.[6]

This double emphasis on fearful grandeur and incomprehensible generosity reappears throughout the works not only of Calvin but also of other major continental Reformers and their English contemporaries and successors. Although "Calvinists" have often been said to promote the idea of a terrifying and vindictive God, a less schematic reading of their works will discover a shifting focus – on God the Judge, and on God the Savior.[7] To propose a single defining epithet for the "Calvinist" deity and to take that to be the norm in sixteenth-century Europe is to employ a very simple schema that fails to acknowledge not only the complexity of dogma but also the multifariousness of its contexts and employments in human experience. To approach holiness through sixteenth-century responses to scriptural texts is to discover its multiple associations – associations sometimes with the transcendent and fearful Other, sometimes with the comforting image of God in Christ, and sometimes with an intricate set of ethical demands.

The scriptural origins of "holiness" suggest that the idea can invoke extensive horizons of implication. Whatever their personal degrees of commitment, neutrality, or opposition, many of Spenser's earliest readers would probably understand "holiness" in ways conditioned not only by the complexities of scripture but by the theological proclivities of the Elizabethan and early Stuart church, which intellectual and literary historians have with increasing unanimity been describing as "Calvin-ist."[8] Because the religion established in 1559 promoted a doctrine of salvation which comprises a conspicuous configuration of Pauline ideas, that religion certainly warrants the label "Reformed," a term somewhat less reductive than "Calvinist." Reformed paradigms of salvation characteristically include and place somewhat differing values and degrees of emphasis upon the doctrines that (1) God predestines individual souls to salvation or to damnation; that (2) the corrupt human will is utterly incompetent to undertake, much less to accomplish, works that can meet the standards God imposes; that (3) only the gift of predestined, un-merited grace makes such works, and salvation, possible; that (4) salvation results from faith alone, itself a gift of grace which imputes Christ's merits to the believer; and that (5) holiness of life follows from and constitutes an outward sign of this divine gift.

GOOD WORKS

Soteriological systems that so prominently feature ideas of grace and pre-destination inevitably raise questions about the role of good works. "How can your actions matter if everything is predestined?" students will ask. Following Paul (especially Rom. 8:29–30), the Elizabethan Thirty-Nine Articles elucidate the matter somewhat by listing, in Ar-ticle 17, the sequence of events that result from predestination. People whom God has predestined to salvation, the Elizabethan article declares, "be called according to [His] purpose by His Spirit working in due sea-son; they through grace obey the calling; they be justified freely; they be made sons of God by adoption; they be made like the image of His only begotten Son Jesus Christ; they walk religiously in good works, and at length by God's mercy, they attain to everlasting felicity."[9] As this quotation shows, major events in each elect Christian's spiritual life in-clude calling, justification, adoption, sanctification, and glorification. The language presents these events as a sheer list, without explicitly commenting on their interrelations or the energies that achieve them. By including all these weighty theological terms in its treatment of pre-destination, however, the Article allows readers to experience the per-ception – which interpreters influenced by Theodore Beza, Peter Mar-tyr, and Martin Bucer (among others) would readily incline toward – that when God predestines the end (salvation), He also predestines the means to that end (calling, justification, sanctification).[10] From the perspective of interpreters harboring Reformed presuppositions, each crucial spiritual event in the life of the faithful as Article 17 describes it occurs as a consequence of eternal predestination.

The Article points out, furthermore, that to be predestined to salvation means to be "chosen in Christ" and "[brought] by Christ to everlasting salvation." The Elizabethan fathers here and elsewhere in the Articles invite readers to view God's predestinating will in the comforting light of the mercy made available by Christ.[11] The Articles could therefore be taken to share Calvin's insistence on "the personal union of Christ and the believer in justification." This emphasis was particularly important to Calvin, who frequently "speaks of the believer being 'grafted into Christ', so that the concept of *incorporation* becomes central to his understanding of justification."[12] In their treatment of justification, therefore, the Thirty-Nine Articles preserve the doubleness of focus we have noted in Reformed conceptions of the deity Himself. Although the idea of predestination in itself can be frightening, it is presented in ways contrived also to comfort.

A comforting Christological emphasis also appears in official pronouncements concerning faith, defined as the "instrument, wherewith we . . . lay hand on Christ" by whom "all thing is prepared, given, and purchased for us before."[13] This faith awakens in the believer when God's grace effects the predestined calling. With faith comes justification, the instantaneous, complete, and free imputation to the believer of Christ's perfect righteousness.[14] At the same time, the process of sanctification begins, and this process of gradual, uneven, and never (in this life) perfected spiritual cleansing brings a measure of desire and power to accomplish good works.

Described thus as an ineluctable sequence, the doctrine of salvation can appear to be a "comfortable" one, as it was advertised to be, and it will be comforting to the same degree that it remains anti-voluntaristic. By attributing nearly everything in the pursuit of good works to grace rather than voluntary human endeavor, this soteriology offers the consolation many people needed – earnest believers, possessed as Red Cross Knight is, with "wonted feare of doing ought amis" (I.i.49.2) and yet guilty about many things they knew to be deeply "amis." As Luther's own spiritual transformation demonstrated, to be freed of responsibility for one's salvation was a sensation sixteenth-century believers could desire intensely. Yet when discussing Reformed doctrines of the age, it can be misleading to assert, as many historians of dogma and of Christian literature do, that "[m]an's role at each and every stage of the *ordo salutis*" remains "purely passive."[15] True, "justification is merely an aspect of the temporal execution of the eternal decree of election,"[16] but it is important to note that major Reformed theologians, including the English authorities, were adamant in affirming that when true faith results in good works, those works are *collaborative in nature*. Human collaboration with grace raises many issues. By elevating human responsibility, for instance, the idea of cooperation can reduce the theological system's comforts and extend its terrors.

Calvin often insists on human responsibility, asserting that believers are obliged constantly to undertake good works, even though works contribute nothing toward salvation: "we dream neither of a faith devoid of good works nor of a justification that stands without them . . . Christ justifies no one whom he does not at the same time sanctify."[17] This formulation appears to suggest that the sanctifying process results entirely from divine initiative. In treating the point further, Calvin asserts on the authority of Philippians 2:13 that "[E]verything good in the will is the work of grace alone." God does not merely assist a weak will or correct a depraved one, He also works in us the very possibility of willing the good: "For it is God which worketh in you, both the will and the deed, even of His good pleasure." Calvin drives the point home by reference to the opening chapters of Ephesians, which Spenser echoes (as he does Philippians) in the Legend of Holiness: "[I]f even the least ability came from ourselves, we would also have some share of the merit. But Paul, to strip us, argues that we deserve nothing because 'we have been created in Christ . . . for good works which God prepared beforehand.'"[18]

After so firmly establishing this idea, Calvin introduces qualifications that appear to undermine the argument. Commenting on Philippians 2:12, which bids the faithful to "work out [their] own salvation in fear and trembling," Calvin persists in finding no hint that humankind can cooperate in a way that merits any trace of reward. He argues instead that the Holy Spirit here "assigns tasks" for believers "so that they may not indulge the sluggishness of the flesh"; they must "act passively," using the power granted to them. However essentially "passive" the action by which believers shake off their sluggishness, they will not feel passive at all. Each good work has two parts, "the first . . . is will; the other, a strong effort to accomplish it," and that involves "choice, zeal, and effort [which] do not falter, but proceed even to accomplishment." It is worth noting that Calvin can even endorse the idea of cooperation with grace, if one means by the term "that after we have by the Lord's power once for all been brought to obey righteousness, we go forward by our own power and are inclined to follow the action of grace."[19] Although the entire process requires human activity of the most strenu-ous sort, God remains the sole author of each good action. And although Calvin's language now becomes markedly voluntaristic, he treats the potential contradiction as merely apparent – God's grace undertakes good works in the believer, but it does so partly *through* the good will it has created and sustains there. Not everyone will agree that the issue has been resolved in passages like this, but Calvin's attempt to do so does repay attention. It ranks as one of several similarly ambiguous explana-tions of the relations and contributions of grace and human will that appear in the works of Lutheran as well as Reformed theologians both on the Continent and in England.[20]

Official pronouncements of the Church of England exhibit a similar ambiguity. As we have seen, for an interpreter applying Reformed per-spectives to its terse phrasing, Article 17 implies that good works will follow necessarily from one's effectual calling, as direct and inevitable consequences of grace. Yet Article 10, "Of Free Will," seems at once to assert and to undermine the notion of necessity: "we have no power to do good works pleasant and acceptable to God, without the grace of God by Christ preventing us, that we may have a good will, and work-ing with us, when we have that good will."[21] The onset of grace must come first, "preventing us." Yet it initiates a second, persistent opera-tion of grace that, according to the Latin articles, "cooperates" with human will; according to the English articles, this grace "work[s] with" human will. Spenser scholars have sometimes assumed that this refer-ence to active cooperation by the human will registers a distinct differ-ence between Elizabethan and Calvinist doctrines.[22] Although the Eliza-bethan article can, like any other text, be subjected to readers' interpretive wills, it does not necessarily diverge from Calvin by inviting allegiance to the Pelagian idea that mankind can cooperate with grace in achiev-ing salvation. Reformed theology never overtly admits the possibility that human cooperation in good works can actually contribute to one's salvation; good works can be no more than outward signs of the justifi-cation that results entirely from faith in Christ's merits.[23] Interpreters who adhered to these presuppositions could conclude that Article 10 accurately reflects their position.

But other views of the relationship of grace and will were available in sixteenth-century England. A version that differs from Calvin's – and shares many ideas which were typical of English conformist thought during the century's later decades – appears in the works of Richard

Hooker. Before discussing differences, however, it is important to mention some of the similarities these theologians display. This can prove useful for interpreters of Renaissance literature, who often suggest that Hooker spoke for English orthodoxy in opposing both Genevan polity and Calvinist theology. He is said to be a defender of natural reason, who taught that the realms of nature and grace exist in harmonious hierarchy and differ but little in essence.[24] It is true that in *The Laws of Ecclesiastical Polity* Hooker's polemical aims required that he focus on reason and other human faculties and institutions which his adversaries had, he believed, too energetically sought to discredit. And as Hooker describes it, God's grace appears to act chiefly through mediating faculties or virtues. Grace therefore seems to operate somewhat less directly through the indwelling Spirit, or through incorporation in Christ, than it does in the treatments of Zwingli and Bucer, or of Calvin.

As a result – depending on the selection of details from which readers construct interpretations of his work – we might understandably infer that Hooker "argued back towards the papist view of human capacity to contribute towards salvation."[25] But other perceptions are possible, even more likely, for Hooker claims to want everything he teaches "concerning the force of man's natural understanding . . . always . . . to be understood" to presuppose "that there is no kind of faculty or power in man or any other creature, which can rightly perform the functions allotted to it, without perpetual aid and concurrence of that Supreme Cause of all things." Whenever our sins cause God to withdraw this perpetual aid of His grace, humankind – despite its native endowment of "the light of reason" – begins to walk, as Paul says, " 'in the vanity of their mind, having their cogitations darkened . . . being strangers from the life of God . . . because of the hardness of their hearts.' "[26] Hooker appears convinced that the human will is so possessed by "a native evil habit that if God's special grace did not aid our imbecility, whatsoever we do or imagine would be only and continually evil."[27]

Like Calvin, Hooker stresses that humankind must attribute all good actions entirely to God, yet must nevertheless labor strenuously in pursuit of good works. To retain the "grace of sanctification," defined as a "baptism with heavenly fire, which both illuminateth and inflameth . . . 'we must desire, procure, and for ever entertain, with belief and observation of God's laws.' For let the Spirit be never so prompt, if labour and exercise slacken, we fail."[28] Preeminent English Calvinists held similar views. William Perkins, for instance, urgently presses believers to contribute to their sanctification: the elect must "press on to the strait

gait with main and might, [and] with all violence lay hold of the kingdom of heaven."[29] Earlier Elizabethan opinions on the issue differed
little from these. On the relationship of grace and human will, in particular, the corporate voice of the Church of England normally spoke in
terms as uncompromising as those adopted by Hooker and Calvin. According to the *Homilies*, if utterly depraved mankind ("of our own nature . . . carnall, corrupt and naught . . . without any spark of goodness") harbors the least "charitable and godly motions . . . they proceed
only of the Holy Ghost, who is the only worker of our sanctification."[30]
Yet the *Homilies* also relentlessly exhort listeners to the energetic pursuit of good works. However absolutely attributable to grace, works of
holiness will entail all the sensations of strenuous voluntary endeavor.[31]

For readers interested in Spenserian interpretation, an especially instructive instance of this emphasis on good works occurs in Calvin's remarks on the heroic conceit of "the whole armor of God," a symbol that
has been taken automatically to embody an anti-Calvinistic, even panegyric attitude toward human capacity.[32] Sometimes the armor is taken,
just as unproblematically, to represent the opposite – that, in the simplest
sense, "all the good is God's." Reformed theologians would contest both
views, as Calvin does when he corrects biblical commentators who interpret the breastplate "of righteousness" as "a freely bestowed righteousness,
or the imputation of righteousness, by which pardon of sin is obtained."
This is wrong, Calvin argues, for the context in which Paul describes the
armor proves that "the subject now under discussion is . . . a devout and
holy life." This life requires relentless combat against the agents of evil, a
combat that grace makes possible, but one that also demands energetic
engagement of the believer's will.[33] Clearly, the idea of cooperation with
grace in the achievement of good works could occupy a conspicuous place
even in the first Calvinist's paradigm of salvation.

VARIETIES OF HOLINESS

The readmission of cooperative endeavor into the *ordo salutis* introduces
new complexity, but it also provides some clarifications. It helps to
explain, for example, why Reformed Protestantism would so often follow Luther in considering every regenerate person "always just, and always sinful." The phrases can (but need not) be taken to refer to the
commonplace distinction between imputed as opposed to actual righteousness.[34] As we have seen, Bucer speaks of *iustificatio pii* or "secondary justification" as the source of moral improvement in people who have

first received the *iustificatio impii*; Calvin, by contrast, "speaks of the believer being 'grafted into Christ' . . . The two consequences of the believer's incorporation into Christ are *iustificatio* and *sanctificatio*, which are distinct and inseparable." Though Bucer's and Calvin's explanations differ, both find the true source of salvation in free imputation of righteousness; for both, the achieved virtues that flow from imputation represent actual holiness of life.[35] Expounding a similar distinction between "a justifying and a sanctifying righteousness," Hooker declares that the righteousness "whereby here we are justified is perfect, but not inherent. That whereby we are sanctified, inherent, but not perfect." This distinction resolves an apparent conflict between scriptural authorities, Hooker argues, for Paul is discussing the righteousness of justification when he writes that " 'To him that worketh not, but believeth, faith is counted for righteousness' " (Rom. 4:5). By contrast, John refers to the righteousness of sanctification when he asserts that "'He is righteous which worketh righteousness'" (I John 3:7).[36]

To this point, Hooker's reconciliation of voluntarist with anti-voluntarist scriptural texts appears compatible with Calvin's and Bucer's. But Hooker subsequently develops the concept of sanctifying righteousness, which he often calls "holiness,"[37] in ways that could induce readers to construe the relations of grace and will rather differently. Having contrasted the "perfect, but not inherent" imputed righteousness of justification with the "inherent but not perfect" righteousness of sanctification, Hooker explains that the latter exists "in us" and

consisteth of faith, hope, charity, and other Christian virtues . . . God giveth us both the one justice and the other: the one by accepting us for righteous in Christ; the other by working Christian righteousness in us. The proper and most immediate efficient cause in us of this latter, is, the spirit of adoption which we have received into our hearts. That whereof it consisteth, whereof it is really and formally made, are those infused virtues proper and particular unto saints.[38]

To speak of "infused virtues" could for some readers suggest a real human possession of virtues, by and in the elect. Since, after their effectual calling, the elect must always retain the efficient cause of these virtues – the indwelling Spirit – there can be no question of their possessing *autonomous* theological virtues. The possibility that autonomous possession of virtue is being implied appears possible, however, when Hooker further subdivides "sanctifying righteousness" into "Habitual and Actual." "Habitual [is] that holiness, wherewith our souls are inwardly endued, the same instant when first we begin to be the temples of the Holy Ghost; Actual, that holiness which afterward beautifieth all the parts and actions of our life, the holiness for which Enoch, Job, Zachary, Elizabeth, and other saints, are in Scriptures so highly commended."[39] According to this formulation, holiness is therefore both a state and a process. By deeds serially enacted, the process testifies to the presence of the state — that the believer possesses God's grace and consequently *is* holy. The virtues this holiness brings, "being derived from both natures of Christ really into us, are made our own." They belong to us, but, paradoxically, while "the participation of Christ importeth . . . a true actual influence of grace" it remains one "whereby the life which we live according to godliness is his."[40]

Despite this final caveat, Hooker's comfortable use of scholastic terms ("habitual," "infusion"), can appear — to readers whose constructions weight the evidence in appropriate ways — greatly to differ from Calvin's concept of "actual holiness of life." It is true that Hooker's overall context appears designed to exclude the Pelagian implications which scholastic terminology will suggest to some readers. Yet virtues *habitually* our own can appear to credit human behavior with some real if tiny contribution toward salvation. However carefully theologians as rhetorically sophisticated as Hooker — and Thomas Aquinas — might seek to forestall misunderstanding on this point, readers need not cooperate. History demonstrates that they have not.[41]

A comparable opportunity for varying constructions can arise from vocabulary employed even by theologians whose Calvinistic credentials are unimpeachable. In *A Golden Chain*, for instance, William Perkins discusses "vivification," the second part of sanctification, as a process "whereby an inherent holiness being begun is still augmented and enlarged."[42] Perkins is also willing to describe this inherent quality as habitual. For the papists, he explains, what

maketh us righteous before God . . . is the habit of inward righteousness; or charity with the fruits thereof. We [Protestants] . . . grant that the habit of righteousness, which we call sanctification, is an excellent gift of God . . . and is the matter of our justification before man; because it serveth to declare us to be reconciled to God, and to be justified; yet we deny it to be the thing, which maketh us of sinners to become righteous or just before God.[43]

However carefully qualified, the idea of an infused, habitual righteousness will often be misconstrued. Unless readers can retain the overall context and local qualifications Perkins provides for such passages, those readers are likely to find Pelagian implications lurking in the notion that any "inherent holiness" and any "righteousness" can become "habitual."

As with habitual righteousness, so with cooperation. The Church of England can agree, Perkins says, with the Roman Catholic notion that even

in the first conversion of a sinner, man's free will concurs with God's grace, as a fellow or co-worker in some sort . . . at the very time when he is converted, by God's grace he wills his conversion . . . For look at what time God gives grace, at the same time he giveth a will to desire and will the same grace.

Such passages as these appear in contexts that grant priority to the Spirit working within to realize the righteousness of sanctification and the virtues it produces. Perkins exhorts his readers always to remember "that howsoever in respect of time the working of grace by God's spirit, and the willing of it in man go together, yet in regard of order, grace is first wrought, and man's will must first of all be acted and moved by grace, and then it also acteth, willeth, and moveth itself."[44] And yet, if free will is "a fellow or co-worker in some sort," some readers can lose sight of the absolute priority of grace. At least a few such readers will easily return to the notion – seductively congenial to human reason – that justification results from a process of cooperation between grace and a renewed human will.[45]

This possibility is diminished, in Perkins' overall treatment of the matter, because humankind can never achieve good works that are pure enough to please God. By natural means alone, the best we can do is to perform the "outward actions of civil virtues," a list familiar to Spenserians: "as namely, justice, temperance, gentleness, and liberality."[46] More strikingly, Perkins explains that man's renewed will, even when acting in cooperation with grace, must contribute to good works *in a way that corrupts them.* By definition, "holiness" becomes visible only in good deeds which, though enacted by Christ's spirit, necessarily receive corruption from the human faculties through which they work. Roman Catholics hold, Perkins explains,

that we are saved by the works of Christ, which he worketh in us, and maketh us to work . . . [Protestants] confess with them that good works in us are the works of Christ; yet are they not Christ's alone, but ours also, in that they proceed from Christ by the mind and will of man, as water from the fountain by the channel.

The corruption of that channel corrupts the works. If this were not the case, works would merit salvation, an idea which, for Protestants, is "flat against the word."[47] This comparison of Christ to the pure fountain and man's faculties to the corrupting conduit had become a topos long before it appeared in Perkins. Here is the version that appeared in Alexander Nowell's widely disseminated Elizabethan *Catechism*:

The dutiful works of godliness, which proceedeth out of faith, working by charity . . . though they be derived from the Spirit of God, as little streams from the spring-head, yet of our flesh, that mingleth itself with them, in the doing by the way, they receive corruption, as it were by infection, like as a river, otherwise pure and clear, is troubled and mudded with mire and slime, wherethrough it runneth.[48]

This is a point of fundamental difference between Protestant and Catholic theologians. According to the Tridentine decrees, "it is plain, that those are opposed to the orthodox doctrine of religion, who assert that the just man sins, venially at least, in every good work; or, which is yet more insupportable, that he merits eternal punishments; as also those who state, that the just sin in all their works."[49] As we saw in the Introduction, some evidence suggests that many Elizabethan Christians gravitated readily toward Pelagian views comparable to these pronouncements of the Tridentine fathers, who insist that human good works must in some way be counted truly "good."

DIVINE LAW AND THE SCOPE OF SIN

The Protestant refusal to concede that men might achieve meritorious works expresses a conviction that true virtue lies beyond the reach of human capacity. For Protestant theology, the standard of virtue could be found only in God's Law, and one of His Law's primary aims is to reveal humankind's utter incompetence to satisfy its demands.[50] This daunting message appears, for instance, when the Sermon on the Mount concludes by requiring believers to be "perfect" because the Lord is perfect (Matt. 5:48). By its very impossibility, the Law drives the believer "to desire of very necessity the promised Messiah" who alone can make salvation available.[51] This resort to the Messiah was made necessary by the persistent claim that not only actions and words but even thoughts and intentions fall within the purview of the Commandments. As the New Law clearly says, men who feel even involuntary lust for a woman commit adultery, and those who feel anger are in truth committing murder.[52]

In asserting that "sin" includes even the first motions of involuntary thoughts and intentions, Reformed theology adopted a position more severe than influential predecessors had maintained. A gentler tradition transmitted by Augustine and Lombard had located the beginnings of sin not in the soul's first motion toward forbidden fruits, but at the moment when the higher reason permitted the mind to dwell on possible sensual indulgence.[53] Calvin, among others, found this unsatisfactory. In contrast to Augustine, who considered inordinate desires "weakness" rather than "sin," Calvin points out that "[w]e, on the other hand, deem it sin when man is tickled by any desire at all against the law of God. Indeed, we label 'sin' that very depravity which begets in us desires of this sort." The scriptural foundation for this severity is Christ's identification of the "great commandment" of the Law:

For we are bidden to "love God with all our heart, with all our soul, and with all our faculties" [Deut. 6:5; Matt. 22:37]. Since all the capacities of our soul ought to be so filled with the love of God, it is certain that this precept is not fulfilled by those who can either retain in the heart a slight inclination or admit to the mind any thought at all that would lead them away from the love of God into vanity.[54]

Similar meditation on the "great commandment" of Matthew 22:37 causes Hooker to match the most thoroughgoing Calvinists in moral rigor. Since God's judgments weigh especially our intentions, not only do our evil "deeds, words, or thoughts" prove us impure – so too do our good deeds. "Cut off" from our list of good works "all those things wherein we have regarded our own glory, those things which we do to please men, or to satisfy our own liking, those things which we do with any by-respect, not sincerely and purely for the love of God; and a small score will serve for the number of our righteous deeds." No man from Adam onwards can be found "that hath done any one action, which hath past from him pure, without any stain or blemish at all . . . The best things we do have somewhat in them to be pardoned."[55] Perkins gives the same idea a somewhat sharper edge: "the best thoughts, the best desires, affections and endeavours, that be in any natural man, even those that come most near to true holiness, are not only contrary to God, but even enmity itself."[56]

Having established that humankind's best works and thoughts bear the taint of sin, the Reformed conception of human depravity might appear to have reached its furthest possible extension. Certainly its comprehensiveness already betrays the inadequacy of the notion, often presupposed in interpretations of *The Faerie Queene,* that "sin is always the false choice of a lesser or apparent good instead of a greater or real good."[57] The Protestant conception of sin invests it with a reserve of evil far deeper than situations of active choice can comprehend. Human sinfulness is so absolute that the sinner himself cannot fathom it; innumerable sins, and the habit of sinfulness itself, remain largely subconscious.

Reformed preachers took special pains to insist on this. Bradford, for instance, attacks auricular confession on the ground that no one can know all his sins; for, "as David saith, none can understand, much less . . . utter all his sins [Ps. 19]."[58] Calvin employs the same prooftexts to mount an identical argument:

[David] understood only too well how deep is the pit of our sins . . . how many heads this hydra bore, and what a long tail it dragged along. Therefore, he did not catalogue them. But from the depths of his evil deeds he cried out to the Lord: I am overwhelmed . . . I am sunk down into the deep pit . . . may thy hand draw me out, weak and dying.[59]

In some of its expressions, the Protestant insistence that human nature includes an unfathomable depth of sinfulness gives rise to an important paradox: the faithful, unable to plumb the depths of their corruption, are nevertheless obliged to enumerate and seek forgiveness for their particular faults. After observing that even David failed to comprehend all his sins, for example, Bradford repeatedly urges his auditors to effect contrition by taking "God's law as a glass to [search] in; for in it and by it cometh the true knowledge of sin without which knowledge there can be no sorrow. For how can a man sorrow for his sins, which knoweth not his sins?"[60] But as Calvin warns, in this process of enumerating his sins, the sinner can lose sight of the essential point of the exercise of repentance, which is to use the consciousness of particular sins as a means to discover and display that "hidden slough of vices, their own secret transgressions and inner filth," which is "the abyss of our evil" so deep as to be altogether "beyond our comprehension."[61]

This conviction of total depravity is what sinners should achieve when they scrutinize their reflections in the mirror of the Law. Nevertheless, to be sincerely persuaded of utter sinfulness, we must be prepared "to recognize with all our thought how great and how varied is the stain of our sin; to acknowledge not only that we are unclean, but of what sort and how great and how manifold our uncleanness is."[62] Actual sins, raised to consciousness, therefore represent by synecdoche humankind's radical sinfulness, a condition that moved even Richard Greenham to extreme language. Our underlying sinfulness, Greenham proclaims, "is almost continually boiling and walloping in us, foaming out such filthy froth . . . into our minds that . . . it would make abashed the very natural man, to look into so loathsome a sty of sin, and sinkhole of iniquity."[63] "Into our minds" is a phrase worth noticing, for most of these authors appear to agree with a notion of sinfulness akin to that which Calvin also treated under the label "concupiscence." As R. S. Wallace well summarizes Calvin's idea, concupiscence "is something deeper than an evil will, something more fugitive and unformed than an evil desire, and though it is as closely related to the activity of the mind as to the will and the emotions, it cannot be defined in terms of the working of the mind either."[64]

We shall see later how such convictions, and the courses of spiritual physic which they led authorities to develop, can reconfigure the perceived content and significance of major events in Red Cross Knight's quest. Our perceptions will be sharpened if we adopt the terms employed in Paul Ricoeur's study of biblical symbols of fault, terms which can help to show that the processes which return Red Cross to spiritual health are contrived to transform objective states of "sin" into subjective awareness of individual "guilt."[65] The objective state is sin perceived from the deity's own perspective, a perspective from which humankind appears to be radically sinful because always living in violation of a sacred relationship of allegiance to God. This relationship is symbolized variously in the Old Testament – in the covenants, the conjugal metaphors, the events of Exodus that display all Israel wandering in the desert. Breaking the covenant, committing adultery, and wandering on a tortuous path become symbols that represent sin as complete, individual, and yet at the same time communal. The Lord's omnipotence and his omniscient perspective give sin an objective reality that transcends the individual sinner's conscious awareness of particular transgressions. But of course the sinner is also individually accused, in the Commandments, in the indictments of the prophets, and in the later accusations spoken by Jesus and Paul. Individual accusation seeks to arouse a subjective recognition of individual sinfulness, which aims in turn to disclose the hidden reality of objective and absolute sinfulness.

THE KNOWLEDGE OF FAITH

According to Pauline / Protestant paradigms of salvation, humankind can be rescued from its utter sinfulness only by faith. Like holiness, faith may appear, at first, too familiar a concept to warrant scrutiny. But for poets and readers attuned to doctrinal concerns, "faith" can suggest a variety of implications which seldom find their way into modern interpretations of Spenser's poems. Although there is some disagreement about its full range of features, Reformed descriptions of faith normally ascribe three characteristics to its possessors: an ever-increasing knowledge of the truths of the Bible, especially of the Gospel's merciful promises; a particular application of those promises to the believer himself; and a resilient assurance that God's good will enables the believer to persevere in grace.

The first of these, the knowledge necessary for salvation, can be reduced to a thumbnail definition,[66] but was commonly said to embrace all the articles of belief, explicit and implicit, contained in the scriptures and epitomized in the Apostles' Creed, the Lord's Prayer, and the Decalogue. Anyone familiar with the elaborate explications to which commentators submitted these documents will recognize at once that a faith which embraces all their implications must result from diligent study – and that this faith's immutable precepts can look different to different interpreters. A basic constituent of faith, therefore, is studiously acquired knowledge of an elusive object, "that eternal Verity which hath discovered the treasures of hidden wisdom in Christ."[67] If believers are to pursue this object, faith and reason cannot be so simply antithetical as Spenserian criticism has sometimes implied. Despite Luther's numerous, vociferous assaults on reason, even he allowed that "because faith comes through hearing and understanding the Word . . . reason – man's rationality in the broadest sense . . . [is] faith's indispensable tool." When regenerate, reason is "virtually absorbed into faith, becoming faith's cognitive and intellective aspects."[68]

The prominence of knowledge as a component of faith provides the basis for Protestant attacks on the Roman Catholic doctrine of implicit faith. As Beza puts this common polemical point, "the kingdom of God is not a kingdom of ignorance, but of faith, and consequently of knowledge . . . a man cannot believe that which he knoweth not."[69] But like all other objects of human intellect, knowledge that comes by faith can sometimes be enshrouded in impenetrable darkness. The knowledge of faith begins "here with a weak apprehension of things not seen." It can achieve only posthumous fulfillment in "the intuitive vision of God in the world to come."[70] Although it remains dark in comparison with the intuitive vision available to souls in bliss, however, true faith includes an element of unquenchable certainty.[71] Thomas Becon makes the point emphatically: "Faith is not only to know and believe, that the history of Christ is true, but faithfully to be persuaded, that all that ever Christ did, was done for thy sake, for thy sake, for thy commodity and wealth, for thy health and salvation." Becon's repeated "thy"s insist that every true believer must feel that Christ's merciful promise of salvation applies to him in particular. Unless it brings such assurance, faith is not "lively" and life-bearing but "dead" and potentially a sign of damnation.[72] Elaborating this point, Perkins declares that the application of Christ's promises to the self distinguishes the Elizabethan concept of faith from the Roman Catholic. The Catholics understand faith, Perkins says, to be "a general . . . faith, whereby a man believeth the articles of religion to be true. But we hold that the faith which justifieth is a particular faith, whereby we apply to ourselves the promises of righteousness and life everlasting by Christ."[73]

This reassuring attitude extends also to the doctrine of perseverance, which maintains that believers feel assured that true faith, once granted by grace, cannot utterly fail in them. According to the Elizabethan authorities who prevailed in the controversy occasioned in the 1590s by Peter Baro and William Barrett, this doctrine belonged to the Elizabethan Church's consensus at least from 1559 onward. But Baro and Barrett were reinterpreting texts upon which the consensus depended. Their "proto-Arminian" reading illustrates the instability of doctrinal formulas, and that their interpretation was suppressed illustrates with unusual forthrightness that stable readings often achieve their stability through overt political power.[74] The power in this case belonged to Calvinist authorities at Cambridge (William Whitaker and Robert Some, *inter alia*) as well as to Whitgift and Andrewes, who claimed to harbor no doubt that the verities established by authority of the Articles, the *Homilies*, the Prayer Book, and the Catechisms included the doctrines of assurance and perseverance.[75]

Official voices often sound definite on these matters but, as we have frequently noticed, comfortable doctrines can be qualified to discomforting degrees. Hooker, for instance, is eager to reassure believers that "where faith is entered, there infidelity is for ever excluded." From "infidelity, which is an inward direct denial of the foundation" of faith, God "preserveth [the believer] by special providence for ever."[76] But as the consolatory context of this assertion implies, the faithful can be temporarily ignorant of their own persisting belief in "the foundation." Like sin, faith and the movements of the Spirit that sustain it exist at depths beyond the reach of human consciousness. And clearly, therefore, the doctrines of assurance and perseverance do not preclude a phenomenon that could seem incompatible with them: not only can this assured faith vary in intensity, but as He sees fit, the Lord can afflict his chosen with temporary loss of conscious assurance. Though inaccessible to the consciousness of the believer at such times, true faith "is never so extinguished or snuffed out that it does not at least lurk as it were beneath the ashes."[77]

That faith can vary in degree, even to the point of becoming utterly unknown to the believer in whom it resides, testifies to the immediate omnipresent providence of God. For as Hooker says, the Lord grants faith and its assurance as gifts which never work "like a natural agent, as the fire doth inflame, and the sun enlighten, according to the uttermost ability which they have to bring forth their effects." On the contrary, God's wisdom limits "the effects of his power to such a measure as seemeth best unto himself. Wherefore he worketh that certainty in all, which sufficeth abundantly to their salvation in the life to come; but in none so great as attaineth in this life unto perfection."[78] According to Perkins' analysis, the degrees of faith that might at different times seem best to God range from a hidden or unconscious faith to the opposite extreme, "a full persuasion of the heart . . . that God loveth him, and that he will give to him by name, Christ, and all his graces pertaining to eternal life."

A prior stage in the development of faith Perkins calls "a little or weak faith." The description of this stage suggests how believers can best deal with the discomfort that arises from assurance that sometimes fails to reassure. For "weak faith" is marked by deficiencies either in knowledge of the Gospel or in the conviction that those promises apply to the believer. This faith "also hath power to apprehend Christ with his benefits, and to assure the very conscience thereof," but unlike its more powerful expressions, this weak faith lies "infolded . . . in the heart, as the leaf and blossom in the bud."[79] Perkins remarks elsewhere that the gracious author of scripture uses the term "belief" euphemistically, to describe the uninformed faith of the Samaritan woman (John 4) and of the apostles who, though ignorant as yet of most of the essentials of faith – Christ's death, resurrection, ascension, and kingdom – nevertheless are called believers because they are ready to accept Him as the Messiah and to adhere to His future teachings.[80]

The key here is a "teachableness, with the desire to learn" that results from an authentic motion of the Spirit. And since "faith rests not on ignorance, but on knowledge . . . not only of God but of the divine will,"[81] it mandates its own growth. Manifesting what has been perceived as their common concern "to elevate teaching, discussion, the rational element in religion generally, against the sacramental and ceremonial aspects,"[82] Protestants often insisted that faith cannot be true unless it shows marked (if unsteady) increase. The *Homilies*, for example, advocate a persistent searching of the scriptures,[83] and Calvin gives similar stress to faith's inherent educative impulse. Citing I Corinthians 13:9, he asserts that "we must constantly keep at learning" because we strengthen faith by eliminating "ignorance." Perkins insists that "God doth not despise the least spark of faith," on condition that "it by little and little, do increase, and men use the means to increase the same." More threateningly, he asserts that "the beginnings of grace" manifest in a weak faith "are counterfeit unless they increase." Along with one's experience of the call itself, one's "spark of grace" might "go out"; it must therefore be nourished "by the use of the word, sacraments, and prayer," and daily "stirred up by meditating, endeavoring, striving, asking, seeking, knocking."[84]

By such persistence, believers come at length to behold, with increasing frequency and in moments of increasing duration, a vision that even a weak faith allows them to glimpse: the glory of God "with uncovered face and no veil intervening." This vision inevitably has "such effect that [the faithful] are transformed into his very likeness [II Cor. 3:18]."[85] Explored in some detail, the orthodox Reformed concept of faith therefore promises comfort; once present, it will persist. Yet because the sensations and convictions people take as manifestations of faith can be temporary or illusory, the doctrine of faith, like that of holiness, presents a basis for anxiety as well as a motive for anxious striving to foster and extend one's faith, and so to make election sure.[86]

IMAGES OF HOLINESS

By transforming believers into "His very likeness," faith's vision of divine glory reshapes them into imperfect but legitimate images of Christ's holiness. And just as the theological concepts of sin are founded on biblical symbols, so too the sanctifying life of faith appears shadowed in familiar biblical images which (as we shall see) Spenser adapts to the purposes of his poetry. Faith's sanctifying potency is most conspicuously imaged in the pattern of Christ's own redemptive act, his death and resurrection. The manifold afflictions divine providence imposes, the effects of bearing "the cross," initiate the first phase of this pattern.

As Perkins puts it, "the right way to go unto heaven, is to sail by hell, and there is no man living that feeleth the power and virtue of the blood of Christ, which first hath not felt the pains of hell."[87] These pains are imposed partly by worldly tribulations, but the Gospels abet them by setting out a paradigm of psychic experience which the faithful necessarily undergo – and should also deliberately imitate. Explaining this implication of the Gospel narratives, Paul asks,

Know ye not that all we which have been baptized into Jesus Christ, have been baptized into his death? We are buried then with him by baptism into his death, that like as Christ was raised up from the dead by the glory of the Father, so we also should walk in newness of life . . . our old man is crucified with him, that the body of sin might be destroyed, that henceforth we should not serve sin. (Rom. 6:3–6)[88]

Baptism, the "sacrament of regeneration," as Protestant theologians persistently call it, here serves both to illustrate Paul's readers' mystical unity with Christ and to reassert the moral obligation which attends that union. The effects of baptism are to be reenacted throughout one's life by means of carefully cultivated psychological fluctuations, a state of affective dying and rising.

Experts in the cure of souls prescribe that this medicine be regularly self-administered through alternating doses of the Law, which chastises the Old Man, with applications of the Gospel's promises, which raise up, comfort, and sustain the New. Bradford advises that when his listeners' consciences feel "disquieted for fear of God's judgments against sin," they must call to mind those parts of the Gospel which offer "God's grace and eternal mercy." Conversely, when the conscience is disposed to lie "in quiet," it should be forcefully aroused: "then [in] God's name let her look on the law . . . thereby to bridle and keep down the old Adam, to slay that Goliath."[89] The new life wrought by faith therefore comprises a sequence of deliberately contrived inner deaths and resurrections, an alternation through which the believer can "put on the new man, which after God is created in righteousness, and true holiness" (Eph. 4:24).

This Pauline metaphor of clothing occupies a prominent place in Reformed treatments of holiness.[90] Its prominence is easily explained. Not only can the metaphor of "putting on" Christ project in a single image the dying and rising pattern of baptism, repentance, and sanctification; it also images both the predestined and the willed elements in the life of holiness. It presents holiness as an extrinsic, purely outward thing, a garment; yet men must labor to "put it on." To be "holy and without blame before [God] in love" (Eph. 1:4) means to be "clothed with Christ's righteousness" (Geneva gloss, 1587). Yet the writer often (Eph. 4 and 5) urges believers to strive to achieve holiness of life. By imputation, the faithful become righteous, with the first onset of saving grace. By energetic endeavor impelled by grace, which works through a cooperating will, they gain sanctity in increments slowly and haltingly accrued.

Treating the imagery of clothing in detail and introducing the related metaphor of arming, Henry Smith declares that Romans 13:14 ("Put ye on the Lord Jesus Christ") contains "the sum of the Bible." This image of clothing and its cognate image of arming ("put on the armor of light") imply, respectively, justification and sanctification, both gifts of Christ. The Pauline phrase "put on Christ" signifies that He "doth cover us like a garment . . . [which] hideth our unrighteousness with his righteousness . . . that the wrath of God can not find us." When conceived of as armor, on the other hand, Christ becomes men's protection in the active pursuit of holiness: "This garment is called an armor, because it defendeth us from all the assaults of the devil, the flesh, the world, the heat of persecution, and the cold of defection."[91] In a passage that will prove useful to readers who are puzzled by repetition in *The Faerie Queene*, Book I, Smith adds that in the course of individual human lives Christ is put on in a variety of ways and at a number of times. Notable among these times are, first, baptism; second, when we are "called and sanctified; that is, when [we] cast off the old man . . . and put on the new man which is regenerate in righteousness and holiness"; and, third, when we receive Holy Communion, "and are partakers of his body and blood, that is, the merits of His obedience and passion by Faith."[92] These interpretations of the Pauline symbols of clothing and armor represent Elizabethan / Reformed doctrinal norms – their Christological focus, their certainty that all righteousness flows from Him, and their acknowledgment that believers must nevertheless exert their wills and experience the sensations of strenuous exertion if they are to be holy: "They which labor to be righteous, and yet believe that Christ's righteousness shall save them, have put on Christ as Paul would have them."[93] Such believers understand that holiness finds appropriate expression in metaphors of the most intense varieties of human exertion: in the race of Hebrews 12 and the spiritual warfare of Ephesians 6.[94]

As I have suggested throughout this chapter, the entire complex set of ideas surveyed above – concerning holiness within the contexts established by sixteenth-century Protestant, especially Reformed, notions of predestination, grace, will, faith, law, and sin – can induce readers to construct passages of *The Faerie Queene* in ways that are both definite and variable. The informing presence of these ideas, however, does not result from the automatic effects of a static intellectual "background." The poem's theological content and meanings can be realized only by readers, who must themselves provide much of the doctrinal material this enactment requires. Readers are invited to supply and experience this doctrinal material sometimes in fairly direct ways. We are nudged by conspicuous scriptural allusions, dogmatic propositions, and personification allegories, or, more subtly, we are solicited to imagine horizons of implication evoked by sly semantic hints or unobtrusive scriptural echoes. Even modestly detailed knowledge of major tenets of sixteenth-century theology reveals an intricate interplay between complex and unstable doctrines, on the one hand, and, on the other, poetry whose altering meanings arise in part from the persistently shifting generic identities of successive passages. As I hope to show in the following chapters, the richly varying patterns of diction, imagery, allusion, character, event, and meaning that can form and reform in readers' minds as they move through *The Faerie Queene* characterize even those passages most likely to appear at first dogmatic, therefore univocal, and consequently (for many readers) oppressive or dull.

2

MULTIPLYING PERSPECTIVES

Many readers approaching *The Faerie Queene* for the first time dread the task before them, fearing that (as they have been told) Spenser is confronting them with an "allegory." If they were to enter the poem by way of the preliminary matters its earliest editions presented – title page for the volume, dedication page, title page for Book I, and Proem – these apprehensive souls would certainly be made alert for signs of allegorical implication. Yet their search for meaning would not be so confining, specifically focused, or simple as many readers' eager desire for control inclines them to make it. Beginning with its opening stanzas, the poem insistently presents too intriguing a range of generic features, and too great a variety of interests and values, to allow readers to feel oppressed by or altogether satisfied with simple equations like Red Cross = Holiness; Una = Truth; Dwarf = Reason.[1]

The impulse toward simplicity that often yields such equations is abetted by subtle mechanisms which tacitly prestructure readers' perceptions of the poem. Among the most powerful of these unnoticed mechanisms is the anachronistic prominence modern editions grant to Spenser's Letter to Raleigh. Although many twentieth-century readers understandably assume that the Letter has always appeared as a *preface* to *The Faerie Queene*,[2] the early editions never printed it before the poem – nor did they make it readily accessible elsewhere. In the 1590 quarto, the Letter must have been invisible to most readers, for it was buried between the end of the poem and the commendatory and dedicatory verses and errata. In the 1596 edition of the six-book *Faerie Queene*, the Letter was (for reasons about which we can only guess) omitted. In the first folio *Faerie Queene* of 1609, it remained absent; in the collected works of 1611, it at last reappeared, but was again tucked between the end of the poem and the commendatory and dedicatory verses.[3] Only with the eighteenth-century editions (Hughes' in 1715, Birch's in 1751, Church's and also Upton's in 1758) did the Letter begin to appear at the beginning of the poem.

Even if the Letter does represent an authentic formulation of Spenser's intentions, therefore, it could have influenced few actual readings.

Modern readings of Book I, however, are often guided from the outset by the Letter's announcement that Red Cross' armor *is* "the armor of a Christian man" of Ephesians 6. Readers are thus prepared in advance to seek allegorical meanings that display the characteristics ordinarily expected of theological discourse: clarity, stability, perhaps dullness, and an imperious intent to subsume or nullify other kinds of meaning. Readings guided by the preliminary materials of the early editions, by contrast, can more easily acknowledge that, like subsequent books, the Legend of Holiness represents a rich mixture of generic types, types which carry with them conflicting as well as complementary meanings, values, and rhetorical and poetic styles. The title pages of the 1590 and the 1596 volumes – "*The Faerie Queene*: Disposed into twelve bookes, Fashioning XII. Morall vertues" – announce the work's affiliations both with romance and with moral philosophy.[4] The title of Book I is rich in further generic indicators: "The First Booke of The Faerie Queene," it reads, "Contayning The Legend of the Knight *of the Red Crosse, or of Holiness.*" Reference to a queen of fairies alone predicts that readers will confront the magical and fabulous elements, and accompanying occasions for allegorical characterization and implication, normally associated with folklore and narrative romance. The titles of the volume and of Book I may also prompt readers to expect a variety of other, not altogether compatible, generic features, such as highly contrived symbolic settings; a world that values chivalric courage, prowess, and courtesy; characters whose accoutrements can both declare and conceal their identities, and so on. The proem to Book I, furthermore, indicates that Spenser writes in imitation of Virgil's epic and so is likely to incorporate (within a plot more unified than those characteristic of romance) themes of national history, identity, and destiny by describing the reestablishment of a nation which has been damaged or destroyed.

The opening passages of the work, finally, rich in biblical allusions that become still more insistent later on, extend the reader's preliminary sense of genre even further. Biblical allusions are likely to generate allegorical meanings specifically of the sort predicted by the subtitle "of Holinesse," a term emphasized by italics,[5] and repeated when the Argument to I.i refers to "The Patron of true Holinesse." Taken together, the multiple generic signals readers receive as they begin to encounter the poem prepare for a complex response. To be invited to explore "holiness" in conjunction with the varied possibilities of being and perceiving that moral philosophy, romance, and epic convey does not constitute an invitation to employ a simple religious idea to oversimplify human experience. We seem invited instead to confront experience in something like the (always limited) degree of multiplicity and complexity that human minds are capable of grasping. The author appears intent on offering alternative generic signals, clues that induce readers to construe the text by way of differing schemata or frames, and so to notice, project, and invest with significance different patterns of detail at different moments of perception.[6]

When we first enter the poem proper, its original preliminary materials help to ensure that non-religious elements can compete for the reader's attention on nearly equal terms with religious ones. What the poem provides at the outset is a pageant that repeatedly reannounces, through its vivid proliferating details, the generic foundation of the work as a whole, which is narrative romance. The construction of an exclusively theological interpretation for Book I therefore encounters multiple impediments, inhibitions that do not simply frustrate or discourage but, by means of scriptural allusions as well as semantic and grammatical ambiguities, incite further effort to achieve a controlling meaning for local passages and to anticipate the kinds of meanings to expect from the book as a whole. The prominence of romance features should guarantee, however, that most perceptions of the text will incorporate a vividly imagined world peopled with romance characters and suffused with romance mystery. Because of this richness, a reader's pursuit of theological meanings can generate as many alien associations as there are trees in Spenser's Wood of Error.[7] These complicating implications resist subordination, and they resurface persistently, much like the temporarily unattended patterns in Gothic tracery.

In this potentially fluid situation, the preeminence of romance features first becomes evident in the sequence of descriptions devoted to Red Cross Knight, Una, and her subservient dwarf. If we approach the poem without yielding preemptive authority to simple notions about the author's allegorical procedures, we can experience recurrent deceptions lurking within the comfortable familiarity of the opening lines. Spenser appears to present us at first, for example, with a merely generic knight, a palladin of the sort who typically provides focus for the events of romantic story: "A Gentle Knight" whose "mightie armes," we assume, have been battered by "many a bloudy fielde" in which he had himself gained victory in heroic struggle. Once we recognize how doggedly stereotypical the opening image is, the subsequent qualification ("Yet armes till that time did he never wield") delivers a sharper surprise than it otherwise can. By reversing established expectations, this line presents a puzzle that reinstates or reintensifies the search for allegorical implication. The history of this text's reception certainly confirms the persistence of that intensity – few editors decline comment. Yet nothing so far offered by the text justifies the usual editorial assertion that the armor actually is that of Ephesians 6, an allusion normally taken not only to be self-evidently there, but also and more importantly to be self-evidently self-interpreting.

For first-time readers who have not come to the poem by way of the Letter to Raleigh, the scrutiny elicited by line 5 is unlikely to be deflected away from the text toward an extrinsic Pauline allusion. Even though that allusion may be implicitly present in the perceptions of practiced readers of romance, and will become more or less quickly available to most, those who notice the puzzling quality of line 5 are likely to scrutinize the immediately succeeding details in search of interpretive clues. They are likely to note, among other possibilities, that the "angry steede" disdains "to the curbe to yield" and that the knight only "seemd" fit "for knightly giusts and fierce encounters." Is the horse (perennial symbol of bestial passion) safely under control, or does his disdaining "to the curbe to yield" imply that he is under uncertain government, from the beginning of the quest? Does the steed, because of its origins, suggest a Platonic opposition of reason to passion? Or will that opposition require revision in light of theological perspectives that count reason itself among the evils which must be overcome in quests for religious virtue? In short, the arrangement of materials in this stanza does not provide pat answers to set questions; it solicits engagement – enlivened attention to the reader's hermeneutic task, a task which is itself a defining feature of "romance."[8]

Such moments of engagement balance others that are equally important in reading the poem, moments of slackened attention induced by a tone of easy familiarity. Readers are invited to relax, for instance, when the final line closes stanza 1 (its pretense of completeness abetted by the leisurely pace of the Alexandrine) by referring to an apparently timeless world of unspecified chivalric "giusts" and "encounters." If indulged, this invitation to relax endows the opening of stanza 2 with a contrasting touch of mild but significant surprise: "But on his brest . . ." "But" slightly unsettles the sensation that we are reading ingenuous romance. "And" would have sufficed to imply that the knight's impresa, the "bloudie Crosse" on his breast, simply added further detail to an otherwise innocent description. "But," the conjunction which the poet apparently preferred,[9] hints that a conflict exists between the simply romantic or earnestly moral activities referred to at the end of stanza 1 and the subject introduced in stanza 2.

That mild tension prepares for a sequence of similar, individually unobtrusive but collectively emphatic subversions of expectations the text has invited us to form:

> But on his brest a bloudie Crosse he bore,
>   The deare remembrance of his dying Lord,
>   For whose sweete sake that glorious badge he wore,
>   And dead as living ever him ador'd:
>   Upon his shield the like was also scor'd,
>   For soveraine hope, which in his helpe he had:
>   Right faithfull true he was in deede and word   (I.i.2.1–7)

As emblem of the Lord who died once in order to live and send aid to His knights for ever, the bloody cross invites attention to the knight's identity as Christian warrior. Such an identity is sufficiently vague that readers might construe it in various ways. The cross to which the lines refer can evoke doctrinal ideas which suggest, for instance, that Christ's blood, now no longer literally but spiritually real and present, can continue to function as one of the effective sources of human holiness. So interpreted, this blood represents either Christ's merits applied to the faithful (imputed righteousness) or His virtues enacted in and by them (actual holiness of life). That is, such a process of reception translates the blood, accepted momentarily as metaphor for color ("a bloudie Crosse"), back into blood as a physical reality (that actually shed at the crucifixion) which can now symbolize, for knight and reader, a real spiritual presence. However the details of such a construction might be enacted, they will work dynamically and specifically to suggest that Christ's presence somehow belongs mysteriously to the knight's equipage and also to his person. Developing in close conjunction with the romance elements of the passage, the doctrinal implications will be too complex and indeterminate to result in a simple equation: Red Cross Knight = Holiness, but they will also be (for readers who are interested in theological ideas) somewhat too potentially specific to be relegated to an undefined "Christian significance."

In some way, this now dominantly religious construction implies, Red Cross possesses grace, which perhaps brings with it faith, hope, and love, the three theological virtues that comprise all others and are quietly registered in the phrases "right faithful," "sovereign hope," and "ever him adored."[10] Given later events, it is worth noting that Red Cross' devotion to Christ is here said to be earnestly self-conscious. The implied presence of this deliberate devotion and the virtues it entails point toward further implications that reside within the horizon of thematic ideas established by the Legend's title. If the knight's quest concerns holiness, then he must wear the "bloudie Crosse" in a particular way. He must have "put on" Christ, or must in some sense belong to that Lord (ch. 1, pp. 45-46, above). Some readers can be prompted to make this surmise by the mystifying collection of pronouns that pervade the stanza, grammatical elements that require too much sorting to allow easy assimilation.

Despite the variety of ways these lines might be construed, readers should encounter no special complication in the phrase "dead as living ever him adored," but the subsequent line provides a potentially more intractable puzzle, "Upon his shield the like was also scored." Whose shield? Red Cross', or his Lord's? Fleetingly, the text invites us to imagine Christ as a warrior. This possibility can be created in various ways for different readers by recollections of scriptural or apocryphal depictions of the Lord donning his armor (e.g. Is. 11:4–5; 59:16–18; Ws. 5:17–23), or of the heroic Savior of Revelation (e.g. Rev. 12:7[11]), or of iconographic traditions presenting Christ as chivalric knight, or of literary avatars like Langland's jousting Piers / Christ.[12] The next line allows us to reorient ourselves, however, and to feel comfortable with the notion that the shield belongs unambiguously to the romance hero, since only a human knight is likely to feel the hope "which in his helpe he had."

The transition to line 7, however, can unsettle one's confidence again, this time more emphatically: "For soveraine hope, which in his helpe he had: / Right faithfull true he was in deede and word." Who is true in deed and word? Confronted by another ambiguous pronoun reference, readers incline automatically to privilege the simpler implication favored by romance convention: these panegyric terms, we presume, describe the hero-knight's integrity. But another notion is likely to be superimposed on this simplicity. According to Protestant soteriology, believers can feel assured of salvation not because their own works merit anything but because Christ remains unshakably faithful and true to His promise of salvation to those who believe in Him. The Savior's fidelity to the faithful is a primary denotation of the "truth" exalted in the Bible (see, e.g. John 8:32), elaborated in liturgical and religious poetry (e.g. Chaucer's "Truth"), and intermittently embodied, in the Legend of Holiness, by Una. For readers able to trace the poem's less obtrusive allusions to the Apocalypse, Spenser's "right faithful true" will recall, as commentators have noted, the rider, "faithful and true," who dominates the scene at Revelation 19:11–16. Major Reformation commentators interpret this figure as Christ, termed faithful because "faithful, to his faithful. True in all his promises towards the godly and ungodly."[13]

Such scriptural and doctrinal associations can help constitute the meaning of Spenser's lines whenever the uncertain syntax of those lines induces readers to hesitate between interpreting the "he" in "Right faithfull true he was" as Red Cross or as "his dying Lord." Expectations oriented toward the discovery of theological meaning can realize either of these constructions, and will probably realize both, in rapid alternation. This alternation produces a striking and complex image of the Legend's announced theological subject, "Of Holinesse," for we "perceive" that Red Cross' first appearance in the poem represents the doctrinal idea that to be holy is to "put on" Christ, to exist by grace "in Him." The enigmatic commingling of pronoun references, that is, enables readers to experience something comparable to a photographic double exposure, a perception that merges Red Cross and his "dying Lord." This experience initiates questions, which later become persistent, about the puzzling relation of Red Cross Knight to the deity who renders human holiness possible. Problematic though that relation may be, the merger which the pronouns encourage readers to effect invites them to recognize that Red Cross must in some way participate in Christ. That possibility can alter readers' perceptions of the opening passage, not to mention their notions about its significance. To "see" Red Cross here as *in Christum* is very different from seeing him as a youthful, untried knight, about to fall into difficulty because he is inexperienced in the ways of the world's deceptions. The first perception, and the implications we will soon begin to explore, is theological; the second is moral or "humanistic."[14] These perceptions may overlap, but they belong to distinct discourses which, as we shall note below, can conflict as often as they cooperate.

For some readers, the doctrinal concept of participation, once recognized as applicable, may induce a thorough (re)reading of the armor Red Cross wears, allowing it to become the focus for a complex of religious meanings that will configure subsequent moments of reading. Interpreters who are interested in religious matters might know that scriptural references to the armor of God, of which Ephesians 6 is the most elaborate, locate that symbol in a context that invests it with a range of fairly specific doctrinal implications. In its opening passage, for instance, Ephesians presents an epitome of the Pauline doctrine of salvation, which includes the insistence that God "has chosen us in him, before the foundation of the world, that we should be holy" (1:4). "In him" introduces an idea which is central to the epistle and was also (as we have seen) central to a major strand of the Reformed Protestantism dominant in Spenser's England. If they are to attain holiness, according to this scheme, Christians must be incorporated into the "body of Christ." This incorporation justifies them, and enables them to cooperate with grace in order to achieve good works which, however holy, will be corrupted by the inevitable sinfulness of their human agents.[15]

If they interpret Red Cross' armor as a variant of the common scriptural metaphor for incorporation in Christ (ch. 1, pp. 45–46), readers can assign to it complex and various implications. They can see it as (1) symbol of the wearer's unassailable imputed righteousness, or as (2) symbol of his assailable and always-to-be-labored-for actual righteousness or "holiness," or (3) as both, actual righteousness giving reliable outward expression to imputed righteousness.[16] For readers who actualize such possibilities, Red Cross will appear from the outset to number among the chosen, one who has received his effectual calling and justification, and whose pursuit "of holiness" from I.i.1 onwards comprises spiritual battles of the sort that sanctification entails. Readers need not yet view the armor in light of scriptural contexts at all, however. We are free to view the knight's actions as purely human, sometimes heroic and moral efforts that can be measured against non-theological, "humanistic" criteria. Such criteria will yield positive evaluations. Doctrinal perspectives, by contrast, may detect the presence of sin, even in actions that can legitimately be termed "holy."

Readers who accept the knight's armor as prima facie evidence of his prior election and calling may associate with that assumption the idea of comfortable dependence. For a major emotional consequence of the doctrine of predestined election was thought to be a comforting degree of assurance, derived from the certainty that salvation rests on a foundation more reliable than the believer's own inevitably flawed works.[17] Readers who recall this effect of election and who "perceive" Red Cross as elect, may experience a reversal of expectations when they read the subsequent line, "But of his cheere did seeme too solemne sad." As a result of this reversal, Red Cross' sadness, commonly explained as an attitude appropriate to a youthful and untried knight, can yield a larger significance. It introduces a hint of insecurity which is not fully compatible with theological meanings the poem has encouraged some of its readers so far to perceive. If the knight exists in a state of conscious and true faith, possibly even "in Christ," then why should he remain "sad" to such a degree that the narrator feels impelled to comment?

Having raised the question, the narrator assures us that cowardice has nothing to do with it (2.9) and appears to revert once more to innocuous romantic narration. He tells of the knight's laudable devotion to a quest undertaken on behalf of Gloriana, laudable partly because Red Cross' priorities remain in their proper hierarchical order, "his dying lord" taking precedence over Gloriana: "her grace to have, / Which of all earthly things he most did crave." Despite this diligent acknowledgment of the superior claims of his ultimate Lord, Red Cross' state of mind, as described in the final lines of stanza 3, may also include some less-than-admirable attributes:

> And ever as he rode, his hart did earne
> To prove his puissance in battell brave
> Upon his foe, and his new force to learne;
> Upon his foe, a Dragon horrible and stearne.   (i.3.6–9)

Such aspiring self-assertion is entirely praiseworthy when viewed from perspectives supplied by romance or epic or, indeed, from what most of us would consider "normal" standards of judgment.

Viewed from perspectives that theology makes available, however, the passage also hints at negative possibilities – possibilities whose presence appears the more definite in retrospect, as subsequent moments of reading reshape memories of earlier ones. The pronouns again provide a key: the sequence of possessives ("his hart," "his puissance," "his new force") seems a shade too insistent, hinting that Red Cross might consider the new force he feels to be simply his own autonomous possession. However "normal" and "human" it might appear, even this slightly proprietary attitude toward one's capacity for achievement conflicts with what it means to "put on Christ," as the theologians discussed above have defined that action. Although doctrinal perspectives might rigorously identify fault in this way, however, they need not induce us sourly to censure Red Cross for what many Spenserian interpreters have inclined to call an attitude of "excessive self-reliance." Theological doctrine can enable us instead to see that the very eagerness which makes for successful opposition to evil may automatically require the participant in spiritual warfare to look forward a little too specifically to the glories achievable in battles "brave," where he can "prove his puissance."

Recognition of this possibility can activate and in part depend on the secondary implications of Spenser's artfully selected words. The *OED* reveals that "brave" can mean (as Spenserian editors usually remark) "courageous" and "splendid," but it may also imply "showy"; "prove" can denote (as is often said) "test," but it may also carry a histrionic implication, to "exhibit before the world." Because of the doctrinal implications available so far and the always potentially rapid alternation of generic frames, both the positive and the critical implications of this diction can become active – positive when our perceptions are guided by romance or epic attitudes, critical when theological perspectives dominate. Such alternatives will assert themselves with varying degrees of intensity at different moments for the same or for different readers. The critical implications will probably command more pronounced attention in retrospect, as successive moments of reading modify passages already encountered, newly subordinating some features, obliterating others, magnifying still others (in the recollected version of the text) to a bulk their immediate contexts did not appear to justify before.[18]

As we pass from the portrait of Red Cross to that of Una, to the threshold of the woods, a further ambiguity can become active. On learning that the knight wears a "bloody" cross on both his breast and his shield, readers sensitive to scriptural allusion might have perceived a reference to texts like II Corinthians 4:10: "Everywhere we bear about in our body the dying of the Lord Jesus, that the life of Jesus might also be made manifest in our bodies" (Hamilton, *FQ* I.i.2.2n). For many more readers, however, the details of Red Cross' costume could have sparked a recollection which scriptural statements like this had firmly associated with the very idea of wearing a cross. In Christian usage, "the cross" commonly denotes sufferings that represent divinely imposed tests and correctives. The New Testament insists that such mundane buffetings are inevitable features of the experience of the elect – inevitable, and a source of joy; for when suffered "for Christ's name" these torments become "certain marks . . . branded upon us by which God commonly designates the sheep of his flock . . . we are accounted worthy of God's kingdom, for 'we bear in our body the marks of our Lord and Master.'"[19]

However latent the idea of beneficial torment might be when we first hear of the crosses Red Cross Knight wears, that idea can begin to emerge as a persistent theme in stanza 6:

> Thus as they past,
> The day with cloudes was suddeine overcast,
> And angry Jove an hideous storme of raine

> Did poure into his Lemans lap so fast,
> That euery wight to shrowd it did constrain,
> And this faire couple eke to shroud themselves were fain.   (i.6.4–9)

The intrusion of "angry Jove" reasserts Spenser's readiness, already evident in the Proem, to employ classical gods and goddesses as symbols of authentic divine potency in a world conceived in explicitly Christian terms.[20] Yet even from the point of view of readers accustomed to translating classical vehicle into Christian idea (Jove = the Christian God's power), the "hideous" quality of Jove's sudden eruption can recall the violent caprice of gods like Virgil's angry Juno or Homer's implacable Poseidon. Jove brings into view epic qualities adumbrated in the Proem's announcement that its author is emulating the shape of Virgil's career and obeying the muses of history, or heroic poetry, or both at once.[21]

Jove's violence not only reasserts the poem's epic qualities and concerns; it also introduces a second generic modulation that will be sustained throughout the approach to Error's cave.[22] The first hint of that modulation is an echo of Lucretius or, still more likely, of Virgil's *Georgics* 2.325 ("Then the almighty father Heaven descends / Into the lap of his rejoicing bride / With fecund showers").[23] Readers who recognize the allusion, or who respond even semi-consciously to the notion of a deity-pervaded world of the sort the image suggests, will begin to conceive an idea akin to that which the *Georgics* embody in Jupiter. There "[h]e is Providence, the Zeus of the Stoics, who has ordained that man should have difficulties to overcome so as to sharpen his wits and keep him from degenerating into sloth."[24] This recognition is likely to lead in turn to the reflection that, in the *Aeneid* and subsequent epics, destructive or evil powers unwittingly serve designs of cosmic scale and benign purpose.[25] Taken together or separately, such meditations suggest that Jove's attack represents the onset of sufferings which will ultimately benefit the sufferer.

Still, recollections of Jove's anger do not simply dissipate. Even for readers inclined to adopt an attitude of providential optimism, the episode creates an effect that recurs throughout the poem, when its events imitate a feature of ordinary experience that seems always to conflict with religious interpretations of that experience. Although our misadventures might feel at first like accidents of a random world or intrusions of a hostile one, Christianity obliges its adherents to reinterpret such events as both deliberate and beneficent. Spenser's poem often mimes this experience by evoking ordinary secular responses to events, then invoking perspectives of the sort theology relentlessly employs to dislodge secular ones.

Once perceived and taken to be consequential, this dialectic between secular and theological ways of understanding can complicate and enliven our responses to the Wood of Error. Critics usually notice features which just one of the potentially applicable generic frames, moral philosophy, tends to highlight, and many of Spenser's interpreters have assumed that moral and theological interpretations are identical. Readings informed by knowledge of theology, however, would more likely view moral philosophy as a discipline that can overlap or complement the ethical requirements of revelation, but will often fall short of those requirements, or even contradict them. Lodowick Bryskett, for example, displays a typical sensitivity to moral philosophy's subordinate and limited sphere when he calls it "but the hand-maide of the doctrine of Grace."[26] This is an attitude Spenser could have shared, and one which some readers will have taken for granted. Of course, interpreters who grant moral implications unchallenged control over their responses to the Wood of Error are indulging in a legitimate act of selective attention of the sort reading normally entails. Yet this moral reading demands that we restrict our attention to an unusually narrow range of this setting's features – to potentially minatory details like "sommers pride," which excludes "heavens light," and the odd preponderance of "pathes and alleies wide, / With footing worne" (7.4, 7). Experienced readers of allegorical epic-romance will incline to suspect immediately that the wood conceals moral danger, as do its prototypes in Dante, Ariosto, and Tasso. That expectation proves accurate when Red Cross and Una discover Error's residence at the heart of the forest.[27]

The selective attention that supports this reading, however, can be confidently maintained only if we allow the "etc. principle" to exercise unqualified control over our perceptions. If we resist that inclination, we will find surprisingly little in the way of clear moral signals as we move through the opulent passages that lead toward Error. We do meet an abundance of features which can implicitly carry with them values normally associated with georgic poetry. For readers familiar with that kind, the most conspicuous georgic element in I.i, the tree catalogue (familiar, of course, from epic and other kinds as well),[28] can establish a more-than-usually inclusive alternative to the common moralistic readings of the passage:

> Much can they prayse the trees so straight and hy,
> The sayling Pine, the Cedar proud and tall,
> The vine-prop Elme, the Poplar never dry,
> The builder Oake, sole king of forrests all,
> The Aspine good for staves, the Cypresse funerall.
>
> The Laurell, meed of mightie Conquerours
> And Poets sage, the Firre that weepeth still,
> The Willow worne of forlorne Paramours,
> The Eugh obedient to the benders will,
> The Birch for shaftes, the Sallow for the mill,
> The Mirrhe sweete bleeding in the bitter wound,
> The warlike Beech, the Ash for nothing ill,
> The fruitfull Olive, and the Platane round,
> The carver Holme, the Maple seeldom inward sound.   (i.8.5–9; 9)

By virtue simply of being a detailed catalogue of natural phenomena which incorporates multiple references to human labor and social customs, the passage can be taken not simply to echo the Ovidian, Chaucerian, and other "sources" usually adduced, but to draw meaning from the larger contexts in which such lists typically flourish. In its expressions of admiration for the trees, Spenser's passage shares with 2.439–53 of Virgil's *Georgics,* and the georgic kind as a whole, a high valuation of the productive symbiosis of humankind's relationship – through the hard work of farming, woodcraft, harvesting of foods that appear without benefit of agricultural arts, and so on – with fecund Nature. This generic affiliation might readily have been noticed by sixteenth-century readers who had not yet been persuaded, as later readers have been, to limit the category "georgic" exclusively to close lexical imitations of Virgil.[29]

Recognition of the georgic element in this passage can help make Una's and Red Cross' condition thoroughly understandable to Spenser's readers, who tour this marvelous grove with them. Only after the Wood is revealed to be "of Error," will the passive voice of the phrase "led with delight" seem definitely to describe dispositions somewhat too pliable. In spite of this potential inference, as well as details like the cedars "proud" and the maple "seeldom inward sound," threatening moral hints remain, until then muted amidst the profusion of engaging details the setting offers.[30] Even if we assume that this landscape must, as romantic landscapes often do, externalize its inhabitants' interior state, most of the detail in Spenser's description of the wood seems designed to deflect the reader from moral reflection and to induce a positive valuation of the myriad activities that might engage anyone in the course of normal living.[31] An appropriate construction of the setting would be to take this very lack of insistent negative moral signposting, together with the neutral or positive valuation of nature and human industry, as the passage's most striking and significant feature. Past experience with threatening literary forests can make Spenser's wood meaningful precisely because it departs from a generic norm of romance or epic. Many elements of the Wood of Error conflict, that is, with expectations engendered by woods to which Spenserian commentators usually refer – like that of *Aeneid* VI, which obscures the golden bough; or the patently symbolic *selva oscura* of *Inferno* I; or the woods in which Ariosto's (more or less "furious") knights pursue Angelica; or that "forrest wyde," later in Spenser's own poem, "Whose hideous horror and sad trembling sound / Full griesly seem'd," into which everyone but Britomart "lightly follow[s] beauties chace" (III.i.14, 19).[32]

The engaging georgic distractions of Spenser's wood appear instead to imply a somewhat more complicated idea than that embodied in its antecedents. Spenser's wood implies that the world's manifold activities – which cannot be eschewed and which can make everyday living engrossing, authentically valuable, and beautiful – are the same things that make it spiritually dangerous. Not necessarily evil in itself, engagement in the world's business leads its participants to lose their way by inducing them to forget the purpose of the quest – achieved holiness – which, as Protestants defined it, provides experiential evidence of salvation. But – and here is where a generically adjustable reading differs from the univocal and usually censorious "moral" ones – a theological interpretation can acknowledge that such forgetfulness of ultimate purpose is part of the divine purpose. Loss of conscious devotion to the ultimate goal is unavoidable: anyone who becomes so distracted becomes entangled in sin, and sin is a condition necessary to the elect soul's predestined life of holiness.

Readers who notice the absence of conscious ill intent on the part of Spenser's hero and heroine can begin to recognize that another sharp incompatibility separates the rational and moral perceptions promoted by the genial georgic from perceptions prompted by theology. The imperceptibility of Red Cross' and Una's lapse into error, together with the benign nature of most of the attendant circumstances, constitutes a powerful reminder that theology imposes demands which are nothing less than absolute. This guarantees, in turn, that unavoidable and unconscious sin will be present in all finite creatures, in Red Cross, in Una, and in the reader.

For readers familiar with Protestant / Reformed theology, this doctrine can help determine perceptions of the knight's first combat, his battle with Error. The language which describes this battle draws attention to Red Cross' armor, and, as we have noted above, the armor can represent, among other things, the second variety or action of grace. This sanctifying grace will vary in effectiveness, either because the elect themselves fail to labor hard enough in cooperation with it, or because the Lord's benevolent knowledge of the elect soul's needs dictates varying increments of divine energy: "as long as the days of our warfare last . . . we are both subject to diminution and capable of augmentation in grace."[33] Providing a powerful illustration of the effects of a discipline (in Foucault's sense),[34] Protestant pastoral theology trained its adherents to discover the effects of grace in every event, however apparently mundane. Calvin illustrates this point by reference to experiences which many of us would now attribute to variations in adrenalin or biorhythms:

Whether you will or not, daily experience compels you to realize that your mind is guided by God's prompting rather than by your own freedom to choose. That is, in the simplest matters judgment and understanding often fail you, while in things easy to do the courage droops. On the contrary, in the obscurest matters, ready counsel is immediately offered; in great and critical matters there is courage to master every difficulty.[35]

Commenting on Ephesians 6:11, a text important to readers of *The Faerie Queene*, Calvin also registers his conviction that the second function of grace can be resisted: "God has furnished us with various defensive weapons, provided we do not indolently refuse what is offered. But we are almost all chargeable with carelessness and hesitation in using the offered grace; just as if a soldier, about to meet the enemy, should take off his helmet, and neglect his shield."[36]

From this perspective, the apparently spectacular carelessness Red Cross displays in the Orgoglio episode (I.vii) represents every believer's common fault. In the Error episode, his victory partakes more obliquely of similar failings, even as the text's epic and romance modulations invite us to engage sympathetically with him. For many of us, this invitation will become particularly forceful when the knight displays his eagerness to avoid "shame," his confidence in "vertue" (interpretable both as moral virtue and as strength), and his heroic attitude of "fire and greedy hardiment" (12.7–9, 14.1). These admirable qualities prevent the knight from heeding Una's warnings against rash confrontations with evil. And although many critics have read his assertion "Vertue gives her selfe light, through darknesse for to wade" as self-evidently a symptom of pride, others have noticed that it also echoes a tenet of proverbial wisdom hallowed by antiquity. In contexts construed with the help of romance perspectives, the knight's remark appears justifiable. If he behaves uprightly according to the code of Christian chivalry, how can the darkness of this cave damage him?

The tension some readers appropriately feel at this moment results from competition between perceptual and generic frames, which enable apparently antithetical options to seem equally true. Red Cross can be seen *both* as displaying some sort of sinful pride *and* as proceeding sensibly according to an ethic that requires accurate assessment of and confidence in whatever strength one possesses. If allowed to read in less restricted ways than an uncontested moral or overly simple theological schema determines, many interpreters will recognize that the knight's assessment, "shame were to revoke, / The forward footing for an hidden shade" (12.7–8), is not a patent symptom of arrogance. Such readers might also notice that Red Cross' comment gains validity because, remarkably, Una herself admits its truth. She identifies the place and the den ("This is the wandring wood, this *Errours den*") only after acknowledging that to act on her warning would be to incur "disgrace" (13.2–3). Readers who have not yet identified Una as "Truth" (a label which first appears in the Argument to I.ii), or who recognize that that theological idea only intermittently determines her activities, can also notice how lame her advice sounds at this point: "Yet wisedome warnes, whilest foot is in the gate, / To stay the steppe, ere forced to retrate" (13.4–5). In direct conflict with the reflexive desire for action which romance or epic expectations can activate here, "wisedome" recommends indecisiveness.

Yet however morally defensible or generically appropriate Red Cross' behavior might feel, deft irony implies that something is amiss in the course of the battle, where it soon becomes evident that the knight neither comprehends nor acknowledges the true source of his power. Although Red Cross expects that his virtue will provide light, the poem quietly informs us that it was the "glistring armor," not human virtue, which "made / A little glooming light," that could render Error's ugliness clearly visible (14.4–6). The light is a "little glooming" one, but it reveals the monster so "plaine" that even the forward "woman's shape" appears "most lothsom, filthie, foule, and full of vile disdaine" (14.6–9). Scholars often refer us to this monster's forebears, as if Error simply replicates an iconographic convention,[37] but it is possible also to see that

Spenser has transformed that convention. Whereas Error's iconographical ancestors are normally specious, attractive at least from the waist upwards, Error herself is so patently repulsive that readers who recollect the conventions might be struck, primarily, by this monster's puzzling divergence from the norm. Once perceived, the novel forthrightness of Error's self-revealing aspect requires an explanation. Theological perspectives can propose one: divine aid, manifest here as light from the armor, sharpens the knight's moral or spiritual vision; grace enables human intelligence to recognize that Error is clearly repellent.[38]

The light's "little glooming" feebleness implies, on the other hand, that Red Cross shares our own incompetence to comprehend this adversary any more deeply than to recognize its dangerous repulsiveness. As reported in stanza 15, the armorial illumination reveals Error's affinity with the "durtie ground," her labyrinthine shape, her "mortall sting," and her capacity to reproduce herself in a thousand disgusting shapes, details rich in theological possibility yet remaining partly opaque to discursive intelligence. This opacity both invites and justifies varied responses, as recent commentary demonstrates.[39] The knight's words have already revealed that he foresees a threat which "vertue" can adequately oppose, merely, that is, a physical danger ("vertue" as strength) or a moral one ("vertue" as ethical goodness). In subsequent stanzas, his conception of the struggle remains unchanged, though accumulating evidence implies that the danger transcends a merely ethical sphere.

A compatible interpretation of the light's simultaneous adequacy and feebleness arises if we recall that divine aid does not work like natural agents, which always exert as much energy as they inherently possess (ch. 1, p. 43, above). Despite the steady outward presence of its agents or symbols, "the grace of sanctification" supplies energy at voltages that vary, remaining always sufficient to enact the Lord's immediate purposes for particular recipients. Hence the armor, its glooming light here establishing Error's nature to be prolifically evil, will at times provide no illumination at all. The knight's imminent deception by Archimago and his readiness voluntarily to remove the armor in I.vii provide instances of this.[40] Especially when viewed from perspectives which such later episodes supply, Red Cross' conflict with Error seems to invite special attention to unpredictable variations in the assistance grace provides.

The episode's conclusion is at least outwardly successful for the knight, and his success occurs only partly because the armor provides him sufficient aid to see his enemy clearly. Acting as agent of higher authority, his companion must elicit the energy that brings victory:

> His Lady sad to see his sore constraint,
> Cride out, Now now Sir knight, shew what ye bee,
> Add faith unto your force, and be not faint:
> Strangle her, else she sure will strangle thee.   (i.19.1–4)

These lines raise a number of intriguing questions – about human beings as agents of grace, about the nature of identity and how it can reliably be discovered and displayed ("shew what ye bee"), about the relative contributions of powers which must be divinely provided (faith) and the human power that both "adds" them and deploys other, cooperating varieties of "force," and so on. Despite all the puzzles, two points seem clear: first, no single reading is likely to follow through on all the possibilities of response which this typically multivalent Spenserian text invites; and, second, readers who focus on the question of human capacity are likely to note that, in Una's view, both faith and force must combine to achieve the victory over Error. The divine does not simply supplant the human, Una implies, and human beings can somehow in her view choose to add faith, which Protestants normally define as an unmerited and uninvited gift of grace, to their force.

From the perspectives of Reformed theology, these implications are puzzling, at least on first glance. Guided by humanistic presuppositions, modern criticism has often perceived no complexity at all and been content to assume that Red Cross acts on the first half of the advice – he adds a dose of faith to his force.[41] This critical acquiescence in the doctrinally questionable may differ little from sixteenth-century readings of the sort likely to have been produced by the bemused nominal Christians, harboring Pelagian assumptions, who were the majority of Spenser's contemporaries.[42] But any informed Protestant construction of the passage would probably be more persistent. It would probably presume that faith must indeed account for any authentic human victory over evil. Readers adopting that presupposition could become puzzled, however, because the poem describes Red Cross' actions in words that seem emphatically to deny faith's presence. Hearing the injunction "add faith unto your force," the knight finds himself "in great perplexitie," in which

> His gall did grate for griefe and high disdaine,
> And knitting all his force got one hand free,
> Wherewith he grypt her gorge with so great paine,
> That soone to loose her wicked bands did her constraine. (i.19.6–9)

Red Cross does not, so far as the language indicates, mobilize or even sense the presence of his faith at all; instead, he feels anger aroused by

an insult to his warrior's self-esteem.[43] And although a theological reading will understandably become judgmental about this, it need not do
so to the degree "moral" interpretations often do when they attribute to
Red Cross an attitude of proud self-reliance.

Yes, from a theological perspective, pride is implicit and sin is emphatically present here, but theology allows us to recognize something
in addition to so clear-sighted an acknowledgment that the knight has
fallen into sin. We can also note that sin is often unconscious, that Red
Cross' reliance on what he takes to be his autonomous powers is a common misapprehension that heightens his vulnerability. When such powers begin to slacken, as they inevitably will ("His forces faile," 24.1–2),
he "can no longer fight." Only desperate fury remains:

> Thus ill bestedd, and fearefull more of shame,
>   Then of the certaine perill he stood in,
>   Halfe furious unto his foe he came,
>   Resolv'd in minde all suddenly to win,
>   Or soone to lose   (24.1–5)

The continuing influence of romance norms, which preclude fear of
physical harm as a permissible sensation for the hero, helps to secure
readers' sympathetic participation in Red Cross' actions. He is noble
when judged by the criteria of romance, of epic, and of broad cultural
norms that continue to dominate many attitudes toward combative behavior today. These social and literary codes so emphatically exclude
fear of physical harm and condone fear only of "shame" that sympathetic
engagement with Red Cross becomes difficult to resist. Unless it is forestalled by single-mindedly moral or overly simple theological perspectives, some degree of positive engagement will become, for many readers, an indelible feature of the episode.

If so, the readers' sympathy will not altogether disappear when their
sense of the mixture of locally dominant generic frames alters again. Insistently competing with romance and epic perspectives, the moral and
theological ones invite such a shift, enabling readers to notice that "halfe
furious" identifies Red Cross' motives with Error's own most conspicuous affective trait ("enraged," "fierce," "angry," 17.2, 6, 7; 18.2, 6).[44]
When Red Cross comes to share this emotion, his desperate anger violates standards established by the major literary and discursive kinds that
are simultaneously or sequentially active here – including romance, epic,
moral philosophy, and theology. Inviting readers to re-evaluate the "certaine perill," to perceive spiritual rather than physical or merely moral

danger, theology exerts the most extensive claims. Any hero so frustrated that he would rather lose suddenly than persevere in a combat with Error, identified broadly as an avatar of the rulers of the darkness of this world, has succumbed already to the enemy. The degree of Red Cross' submission remains vague or minimal from the point of view of moral philosophy. Protestant dogmatic and pastoral theology, however, would find that it represents "sin," any trace of which is damnable (ch. 1, pp. 37–40, above).

The "discovery" of such sinfulness in the knight's behavior will invite some readers to undertake a more particular scrutiny of the monster whose overt defeat can also be seen as its surreptitious victory. While romance expectations allow us to perceive as generically appropriate such bloody and graphic items as the vomit of undigested "lumpes of flesh" and "loathly frogs and toades," and could allow us to leave such things uninterpreted, theological interests would highlight the "bookes and papers," the blindness of the frogs and toads ("which eyes did lacke"), the "inky" color of the monster's spew (i.20). Theological perspectives encourage an interpretation of the sort commonly applied to biblical monsters, like the comparable ones that appear abundantly in Revelation. Such an interpretation suggests that the physical attributes of Error's offspring represent the "fleshliness" of heretical writings, their origin in human minds whose rational functioning itself betrays that it represents, by nature, "the flesh." Error's frogs and toads therefore embody an evil which humankind cannot avoid exacerbating by the mere exercise of the loftiest of human capacities – reason, which, used at its autonomous best, produces entangling discourses which prove mortal to those who develop and adhere to them (cf. ch. 1, p. 36, n. 45, above).

Portentous doctrinal themes of this sort can readily be perceived in a beast whose "huge long taile" is "in knots and many boughtes upwound, / Pointed with mortall sting" (i.15.2–4; 18). This monster, like its ancestors – the subtle serpent of Eden, the "crooked serpent" of Isaiah 27:1, and their descendent, the dragon of Revelation 12 – "is wonderful subtle, and can turn himself into folds infinite, that he may deceive, and keep the deceived in error."[45] And the entire clutch of interrelated beasts shares with Error's brood (which "creeping sought way in the weedy gras," 20.8) and the "spirits like frogs" of Revelation 16:13 (whose outward shapes declare their inward love of "earthly things") an affinity with "the durtie ground" (15.1). Such creatures recall the "frogs of Egypt raised out of the dust" who "cried out against God's verity"; and these frogs in their turn were often in Reformation times interpreted as agents of the pope, who "molest with talk the preaching of the gospel." In particular, they "molest" a central theme that Reformed theologians and Elizabethan churchmen found to be ubiquitous in the gospel – that salvation is achieved only through the unmerited gift of faith in Christ's merits ("the free deliverance, the Christian liberty").[46]

Since man in his natural state is, by Protestant definition, not simply sick but "dead,"[47] the romance narrative and its potential theological themes correspond neatly in the Error episode: to become enwrapped in this serpent's "endlesse traine" (18.9) is to suffer strangulation, to lose, that is, the breath that represents both physical life and the eternal life infused by the Spirit, a presence often (as both etymology and biblical precedent determine) symbolized by movements of air or water. Readers who interpret the armor as an emblem of imputed righteousness will recognize that Red Cross Knight is proof against a monster who embodies the very antithesis of life, a privation of being. This recognition makes sense of the otherwise surprising ease of the victory, here tacitly effected by a weapon that belongs to the knight's equipage. He "strooke at her with more then manly force . . . [and] raft her hatefull head." Epic and romance perspectives induce us to construe such words as conventional hyperboles: the blow is so strong that it surpasses the powers ordinarily available to men. Theological perspectives suggest, however, that "more then manly" bears literal force: grace directs and empowers the blow, making it transcend whatever the man himself might do.

Although readers can perceive that Red Cross wins by means of this transcendent force, the knight still betrays no consciousness that divine power achieves his victory. On the other hand, modern interpreters, persuaded that direct actions of grace, without resort to earthly instruments, account for all victories over evil, often show as little awareness that the knight's human faculties do play a part.[48] A somewhat more fully articulated theological perspective, which distinguishes between grace's two major functions as Reformed orthodoxy usually defined them, allows us to perceive clearly that the knight's will does play a part here. The same theological perspective also enables us to recognize something more. By forgetting the presence of grace and by supplying impure motives (anger and pride), Red Cross' mind and will not only contribute to a fundamentally good action; they also contribute a measure of sinfulness. Even while laboring to defeat a patent source of evil, those faculties corrupt the actions of grace with which they cooperate (ch. 1, pp. 36–37). Readers who perceive *both* the positive and the negative aspects of Red Cross' battle witness an act of "holiness" as the major Reformed doctrines of grace defined that idea. Such readers' double perception can allow them at once to acknowledge the flaws in Red Cross' performance and yet to join with Una in assessing the conquest of Error as proof that the knight is "well worthy . . . of that Armorie" in which he has "great glory wonne this day" (27.6).[49] Despite inevitable defects in actual holiness, Red Cross and every elect soul share, by imputed righteousness, in the eternal glory of Christ's absolute victory over evil.[50]

This construction appears to describe the episode's theological implications, as a Reformed reading might construe them, with some degree of accuracy, to solve its interpretive difficulties reasonably well, and to account for more of its details than interpretations usually do. Like all readings, however, this one rests on selective perception and subjective projection, and it remains open to retroactive reconstruction as readers encounter subsequent features of the text. The poem's next passage, in fact, challenges the interpretation I have just elaborated, especially the perception that Red Cross Knight has fallen into sin even as he achieves an act of holiness. In its patness of tone, the narrator's announcement of the battle's end implies absolute victory: "Now needeth him no lenger labour spend, / His foes have slaine themselves, with whom he should contend" (26.8–9). When Una compliments her champion, declaring him "well worthy" (27.5–7), the completeness of the conquest seems certain. Una contributes, that is, to an effect which is not least among the temptations Error embodies, "the temptation to assume that to vanquish her in martial combat is to become free of her power."[51] Earlier in the passage, however, Una urged not only that Red Cross employ a hero's strength, but that he also display something more elusive, his very identity: "Shew what ye bee." This demand initiates a movement that will reach its goal in canto x, in a rarely achieved and always ephemeral possibility of human experience as theology construes it, a moment of triumphant contemplation in which Red Cross learns his identity.

When the topic arises in canto i, the theological contexts suggest notions of identity that differ from any which modern readers might automatically adopt. During the Renaissance, it has been cogently argued, "fashioning" became widely current as a term "designating the forming of a self" conceived as "a distinctive personality, a characteristic address to the world, a consistent mode of perceiving and behaving."[52] The description accords readily with prevailing modern assumptions, and it is salutary to be reminded, by various recent theories that "de-center" the self, that so individualistic a conception is a construct especially fostered by the circumstances of modern capitalist cultures. A contrasting notion of selfhood has already been suggested in *The Faerie Queene* when, as we have seen, the knight's very investment in the armor, interpreted in the possessive sense "of God," can suggest that he is elect, and therefore worthy of wearing it. Even so generously interpreted, however, the armor implies that this worth, "imputed" and existing as a generous fiction endorsed by a gracious deity, is extrinsic to the wearer. If perceived primarily as "actual" holiness in which the human will cooperates, moreover, the virtue remains God's; the imperfections that mar achievement are particularly human, though the actor can be credited, as Red Cross much later says, with "good will" (II.i.33). From either perspective, the armor confers an identity that has little to do with "distinctive personality." The identity implied in Red Cross' case appears to be constituted instead by a diminishing of the individually human, which occurs when the separate existence is merged with that mysterious composite entity, the body of Christ.

Reformed eagerness to promote corporate and individual "discipline" led to the creation of mechanisms to foster the reshaping of individuals, by meticulous obedience to the divine will, into members of Christ.[53] There could of course be variety in roles and styles. But an overriding aim of individual disciplinary techniques was to discover a single foundation toward which all the prescribed behavior pointed. Although it could not earn increments of spiritual merit, obedience to divine law could manifest that yearned-for essence of human identity: "Thy good works . . . certify thee that the Spirit of God is in thee . . . and that all good things are . . . laid up in store against that day, when every man shall receive according to his deeds, that is, according as his deeds declare and testify what he is and was."[54] Remarking on the abundance of "the grace of God," Hooker asserts that "[w]e are by it that we are, and at length by it we shall be that we would."[55] This gradual achievement of "what we would be" requires diligent introspection and relentless striving. The *Homilies* urge listeners to study the mirror ("that glass") of divine prescriptions, specifically, this time, Paul's lists of works of the spirit and works of the flesh. "If thou see that thy works be . . . consonant to the prescript rule of God's word . . . then assure thyself that thou art endued with the Holy Ghost."[56] Your works have then shown "what ye bee."

Impediments more dangerous than Error abundantly populate the world in which Red Cross Knight must now undertake to secure his conviction that he possesses inalienably the divinely validated identity of which he has already given some proof. As he proceeds on that quest, knowledge of contemporary religious orthodoxies can aid readers to construct specific, alternative versions both of the ultimate goals of the effort and of its intervening stages. Like the poem's opening passages, its successive episodes invite readers to construct their responses from material mediated by persistently altering generic coordinates. Readers who accept that invitation soon find themselves constructing notions of evil that are more complex, more variable, and therefore more interesting than moral and theological allegories are normally expected to present.

3

CONSTRUCTING EVIL

Until he reaches canto x in the Legend of Holiness, Red Cross will be confronted by a relentless sequence of agents of evil. Readers meanwhile must face an equally relentless series of challenges to construct the significance of those agents. The building materials for our acts of construction are various, but from late in Book I, canto i, through the end of I.iii, the major quarries from which we are invited to draw those materials are dogmatic theology, the Bible, antimonastic satire, and expositions of divine law. While following the adventures that lead from Error to Lucifera, readers will find that perspectives drawn especially from Reformed orthodoxy can render their experience not only more various but also, paradoxically, more unified and inclusive than a less fully informed doctrinal interpretation enables it to be. By the time they emerge from canto iii, readers inclined to credit Reformed doctrines and to employ them in construing the full sequence of episodes – concerning Archimago, Sansfoy, Duessa, Fradubio, Abessa-Corceca-Kirkrapine, Archimago, and Sansloy – will have collaborated with Spenser's text in the construction of a powerful instrument of Tudor ideology. They will have found in the knight's and Una's sequence of opponents a frightening composite vision of the reprobate, a most terrifying "Other" whose characteristics good subjects of the Queen will earnestly seek to purge from their own lives.

As before, the text here demands active participation by inviting us, immediately after the death of Error, to revise what appeared to be secure responses. We have noted that Una's apparently unqualified praise for Red Cross Knight's victory over Error contributes to the tempting deceptiveness of the episode. Readers who perceive Una, at least for the moment, as romance heroine rather than metaphysical principle will suspect that she errs. Readers inclined to think of her as an embodiment of Christian ethical ideals could find in her overly simple praise of the knight a reminder that human perceptions cannot reliably judge what is spiritually good and what evil in actions outwardly good. From this second perspective, Una's assessment of Red Cross becomes ethically exemplary rather than objectively definitive. She judges in the way Christian law prescribes and scripture illustrates when its inspired authors employ the appellation "saints" or "righteous men" or "believers": "According to whose example of charitable judgment, which leaveth it to God to discern what men are, and speaketh of them according to that which they do profess themselves to be." In a word, "charity doth always interpret doubtful things favourably."[1]

After speaking as a generous but fallible fellow mortal, Una subsides into a still more submissive variation of her romance-heroine's role. She remains silent as Red Cross Knight adopts an attitude more explicitly self-absorbed than ever before: "That path he kept . . . forward on his way . . . He passed forth . . . he travelled, before he heard of ought" (I.i.28.3–9). These singular pronouns supplant the plurals which suggested mutual endeavor in earlier passages: "foorth they passe . . . they thus beguile . . . some end they finde" (8.1; 10–11).[2] Yet because Error has been subdued, it appears that the wandering wood can no longer perplex the protagonist, despite the self-isolating inclinations the pronoun shift has announced. He effects his own and Una's exit by following "one" straight, undeviating, path "beaten . . . most plaine" (28.3–5). This again sounds like unambiguous victory, a simple movement out of befuddling mazes into the straight and narrow of scriptural precedent.

Some readers, on the other hand, might notice that this path appears remarkably similar to the one that led directly to Error's lair. From the perspectives supplied by moral or theological allegory, it seems odd that the way out of error should so closely resemble the way in. The knight's selection of the approach to Error is described thus: "At last resolving forward still to fare . . . That path they take, that beaten seemd most bare" (11.1–3). Readers prepared to notice difference may focus on the contrast between "bare" (connoting heavy traffic) and "plaine" (connoting clear visibility). Once this difference is perceived, it can easily yield a simple allegorical interpretation: because he has defeated error, he can reverse his direction on the path that brought him to Error, and he can clearly perceive this reversal as the path of virtue.

Readers who notice no difference between the paths to and from Error, however, might construct a somewhat more complex theological meaning: the paths leading toward and away from confrontation with particular evils are fundamentally the same, for entanglement with error of many kinds is an essential feature of the way that leads the elect finally, and all the while, toward salvation. Although critics have often interpreted the assertion that Red Cross has "God to frend" (28.7) as evidence of unqualified divine approval of his defeat of Error, interpreters aware that the path toward salvation often corresponds to the way of sin may want to revalue that phrase. Both parts of the process of entanglement with and disentanglement from evil can equally offer evidence that one has "God to frend" (28.7). That divine friendship is signalled not just in the defeat of Error, but in the very sinfulness and spiritual blindness Red Cross Knight has subtly exhibited during the battle. Both Red Cross Knight's problematic triumph and his escape, that is, support the hypothesis that he numbers among the elect and is, from the outset, pursuing works of "holiness." If we were to overlook the knight's sinfulness, a Reformed theological point of view would find our construction an implausible fiction for, as we have seen (ch. 1, pp. 36–37, above), Reformed Protestantism insisted that humankind cannot achieve works of holiness without simultaneously sinning. As we have also seen, however, Tridentine theology would incline us to overlook or minimize symptoms of sin in order to discover an authentically good work in the Error episode. Many modern interpreters, even some who mean to be guided by Reformed doctrinal perspectives, have automatically and unawares adopted these Catholic assumptions when reading much of the Legend of Holiness.[3]

Besides enriching our potential responses to superficially routine events like Red Cross Knight's departure from the Wood of Error, doctrinal perspectives can draw attention more broadly to Spenser's extraordinary capacity to charge apparently innocent details with serious implications. Those straight biblical pathways which conventionally symbolize the pursuit of holiness always imply a definite goal, but Red Cross' single-minded adherence to an unbending path before he emerges from the wood contrasts with his behavior immediately thereafter, when "[h]e passed forth, and new adventure sought" (28.8). The search begins to sound newly random (30.2–4), like a freewheeling adventure characteristic of ordinary romance. The first encounter this search produces also includes some typical chivalric bluster for, on first hearing of the fictional villain whom Archimago describes, Red Cross assures us that "to all knighthood it is foule disgrace, / That such a cursed creature lives so long a space" (31.8–9). The fatuity of this comment will be especially apparent to readers who recollect that the knight's overriding obligation has received stress earlier in the canto, "Upon a great adventure

he was bond" (i.3), where "bond" implies a special burden of human
and religious obligation.

Readers inclined to favor a simple romance frame might overlook the
knight's errancy, however, and, encouraged or overwhelmed by the characteristic multiplicity of romance narrative, they might share something
of his forgetfulness of larger purpose. Humanistic or psychological perspectives can strengthen this temporary amnesia. Whatever he embodies elsewhere, Red Cross Knight from this point of view can simply represent vulnerable humankind, eagerly pursuing whatever reassurance his
frail ego can glean from modest successes. Theological perspectives, by
contrast, suggest that Red Cross bears out of the forest symptoms of the
overvaluation of his autonomous human force that became evident during his combat there. Having at least partly recovered his way after de-
feating Error, the knight promptly loses it again in a manner that suggests that he never actually extricated himself from the errors that the
serpent represented. Such reversals will recur during the succeeding
phases of Red Cross Knight's quest; he will learn to foresee and, imperfectly, to forestall them only in cantos x and xi.

Although the knight's new deviancy is obliquely suggested in I.i, it is
soon confirmed and rendered specific by the introduction of Archimago.
This evil genius's first encounter with Red Cross is alive with potential
ironic touches because the protagonist's responses to the tempter's gradually unfolding character can differ markedly from our own. It is true
that the traits which betray Archimago's duplicity can function, briefly,
to blur the reader's vision too, to make us share with Red Cross Knight
the experience of a morally ambiguous world. The ambiguity arises first
because Archimago enters wearing the aspect of a monk or hermit, and
because, in doing so, his costume parallels that of Una herself.[4] In Una's
portrait, the clerical costume functions in part to obscure her snowy
whiteness, metonymy for unearthly beauty, in part to express a special
degree of sanctity. Archimago's implied aims differ, though their difference is not immediately apparent:

> An aged Sire, in long blacke weedes yclad,
> His feete all bare, his beard all hoarie gray,
> And by his belt his booke he hanging had;
> Sober he seemde, and very sagely sad,
> And to the ground his eyes were lowly bent,
> Simple in shew, and voyde of malice bad,

> And all the way he prayed, as he went,
> And often knockt his brest, as one that did repent.   (i.29.2–9)

Having met his type before, readers conversant with Renaissance epic-romance might quickly suspect that this figure conceals some degree of fraud. Readers familiar with antimonastic satire, a generic modulation becoming conspicuous in these lines, would have extra cause for suspicion simply because the satiric treatments (common in Spenser's time) of monks, friars, and hermits represented them as figures of corruption, of hypocrisy, and of a false religion that values works more than faith.[5]

Many readers are likely to notice, too, that here the poem resists any easy assumption that the costume functions as exterior sign of good intentions. Una's black stole had marked her "As one that inly mournd: so was she sad, / And heavie sat upon her palfrey slow" (4.6–7). In Archimago's portrait, not only do the narrator's assertions become tentative ("so was she sad" becomes "Sober he seemde," and "Simple in shew") but the very accumulation of details – the bare feet, the book, the downcast eyes, the incessant prayer, and especially the gesture of self-conscious self-deprecation drawn from Roman Catholic liturgy, "and often knockt his breast," suggests histrionic intent. The knight and his lady remain oblivious to such hints of duplicity, and their oblivion reaches remarkable completeness when Archimago responds to Red Cross Knight's eager request for news of "strange adventures." The hermit's reply displays attitudes that, to readers applying Protestant theological perspectives, would constitute a forthright revelation of his nature:

> "how should, alas,
> Silly old man, that lives in hidden cell,
> Bidding his beades all day for his trespas,
> Tydings of warre and worldly trouble tell?
> With holy father sits not with such things to mell."   (i.30.5–9)

From the perspectives that Elizabethan Protestantism supplies, heavy irony attaches to the notion that a "holy father" ought to spend his life in uninterrupted penitential prayer "[b]idding his beades all day,"[6] and to the assertion that seekers after holiness have nothing to do with "warre and worldly trouble." From a point of view encouraged either by common sense or by romance, Archimago's refusal to "mell" with "warre and worldly trouble" might be admirable, but from a Protestant doctrinal perspective, his avoidance marks this hermit as representative of the fugitive, cloistered, and therefore specious virtues fostered by Catholicism. Archimago's habitation "hard by a forests side, / Far from resort of people, that did pas / In travell to and froe" (34.2–4) reinforces that association with what Protestants considered a self-indulgent religiosity, which is actually an expression of "faithlessness." Interpreted as spiritual combat, wars and worldly troubles constitute every Christian's proper business. Red Cross Knight and Una also fail to note that the tempter, having said he knows nothing of wars and worldly troubles, nonetheless can tell of a "straunge" (that is, a foreign) "man," who is also paradoxically a "homebred evill," "[t]hat wasteth all this countrey farre and neare" (31.2–4). Despite the seeming proximity of this vandal, as he is at first described, he abides (we soon learn) "far hence." Archimago's inconsistencies tell us, long before the poet chooses to do so outright, that this hermit could adopt "As many formes and shapes in seeming wise, / As ever Proteus to himselfe could make" (I.ii.10.3–4).

Although this duplicity can become rapidly apparent to many readers, Una and Red Cross Knight both remain naively trusting. For reasons the poet as yet declines to specify, his knight this time receives gratuitous light neither from the armor whose illuminating potency made Error's true nature visible, nor from the Lady who at times appears preternaturally wise. As we have seen (ch. 3, p. 57, above), the providential implications of the armor itself can suggest that even this refusal of divine aid argues that the Christian warrior has "God to frend." While most readers continue to anticipate Red Cross' eventual triumph, therefore, they will also anticipate that he must in the interim fall more deeply into error, under the influence of a figure who represents diabolic evil itself. Like all avatars of such evil, Archimago plays resourcefully upon, and intensifies, inclinations present already in the souls of his victims. He works in particular to propagate "the basic and radical ur-sin of Pride, usurping Godhead,"[7] and to disguise that sin, at first, as an impulse toward moral purity.

This disguise has often limited the perceptions of Spenser's interpreters. When Red Cross Knight awakes from erotic dreams to discover the false Una at his side, he feels understandable dismay. He also feels a less readily comprehensible emotion:

> And halfe enraged at her shameless guise,
> He thought have slaine her in his fierce despight:
> But hasty heat tempring with sufferance wise,
> He stayde his hand. (i.50.2–5)

Perhaps because this "hasty heat" is soon tempered, commentators have taken "halfe enraged" as a description of an innocent emotion.[8] Certainly, Red Cross Knight's reaction to the false Una can be read as evidence that he is a saint in embryo, a strict, well-meaning soul rightly angered that his lady is violating his lofty standards of behavior. Perhaps many readers will be inclined to join those who gloss this "fierce despight" as if it were justifiable and righteous indignation of a sort religion and moral philosophy, in some moods, can approve.[9] Yet anger of any sort would hardly dominate the sensations of most readers who might awaken to find the object of an amorous dream to be both present and eager. Red Cross Knight's implied difference from our more predictable response can be taken to indicate an amazing moral superiority.

This reading must suppress, however, the text's invitation to focus on the knight's temporary but nonetheless overtly homicidal intent. Simply to notice that he "thought have slaine her in his fierce despight" is to see Red Cross Knight's behavior, viewed from any perspective which most readers could consider normal, as extreme. Viewed from theological perspectives, however, the emotion becomes not merely worrying, but radically illegitimate. Divine law judges even momentary anger to be a serious sin. As Erasmus paraphrases it, the most familiar Christian pronouncement on the subject (Matt. 5:21–22) maintains that "what homicide is in the old law, the same in the new law is the vehement motion of the mind to be revenged. For the first degree of homicide is to be angry."[10] Such principles of Christian ethics invite the recognition that Red Cross Knight's "fierce despight" emerges from the easily angered pride he has tacitly displayed in combat with Error (i.19.6).

Red Cross Knight's reaction on seeing the false Una abed with her newly manufactured squire is still more obviously culpable:

> Which when he saw, he burnt with gealous fire,
> The eye of reason was with rage yblent,
> And would have slaine them in his furious ire,
> But hardly was restreined of that aged sire.   (ii.5.6–9)

Although humanistic perspectives might judge the knight, even here, to be sinless, the New Law would convict him of grievous offence, vengeful homicide, in intent though not in deed. As a direct result of receiving the fraudulent ocular proof of Una's falsehood, the knight's recurrent myopia deepens toward an advanced incapacity to distinguish truth from falsehood. Readers' perceptions, by contrast, remain less impaired, and not least among the insights available to us now is a revelation latent in the words "gealous fire" – words that strengthen an idea implied earlier, "In this great passion of unwonted lust, / Or wonted feare of doing ought amis" (49.1–2).[11]

This jealousy, as the knight's subsequent anguish implies still more clearly, is the green-eyed monster epidemic among human lovers of flesh-and-blood ladies:

> He could not rest, but did his stout heart eat,
> And wast his inward gall with deepe despight,
> Yrkesome of life, and too long lingring night. (ii.6.3–5)

A recognition of the erotic quality of Red Cross' symptoms invites retrospective reinterpretation of the dreams and visions that afflicted him earlier. They reflect not only the devil's outward soliciting but also what a psychological perspective would identify as repressed desires originating within the knight's soul. The surprise readers might feel on discovering, thus late and indirectly, that Red Cross Knight harbors a lover's physical desire for Una is seldom remarked, partly because romance norms make an amorous relationship between knight and lady almost obligatory, and therefore easily felt to have been implicit before. Theological perspectives, however, make Red Cross Knight's obliquely suggested love for Una problematic.

The Christianized Platonic contexts widely available in Spenser's time suggest that, although Truth's beauty has remained always under a veil, it has nevertheless captivated her champion's mind. As a beautiful woman and as embodied Truth, Una makes manifest the ultimate goodness that (according to Platonic commonplace) should, when perceived, wonderfully ravish the beholder with love of its beauty.[12] But, while he is moved by the appropriate object, Red Cross Knight's attraction itself, from the viewpoint of theology, betrays man's natural corruption: his love is tainted by unavoidable corruptions of the flesh. The intensity of Red Cross Knight's incipient desire appears above all in the vengefulness of his wrath, and in language which identifies injured pride as chief among the knight's motives for rage. Recalling the earlier moment when "his gall did grate for griefe and high disdaine" (i.19), the text now stresses that the knight wastes "his inward gall with deep despight" and rides away in impassioned frenzy, "borne" by his "light-foot steede, / Pricked with wrath and fiery fierce disdaine" (ii.8.3–4). The obtrusiveness of Red Cross Knight's recurrent feelings of "disdain" and "despight" betrays injured vanity as well as frustrated desire. Wrath and pride appear totally intermingled, furthermore, in the phrase "fiery fierce disdain." In this economical phrase, which blurs distinctions between sins, the text recalls a long-established conviction of Christian casuistry, that "ire is . . . executor to pride."[13] The poet's phrasing repeatedly indicates that in activating Red Cross' sexual jealousy, Archimago has also exacerbated an ingrained human susceptibility to "the basic and radical ur-sin of Pride." Subsequent movements of the narrative enable readers to develop this notion of the underlying interconnectedness of sins (see ch. 1, pp. 39–40, above).

Despite the poet's disingenuous "him chaunst to meete" (I.ii.12.5), readers may feel that there is nothing accidental in the knight's encounter, immediately after his will becomes his guide (12.4), with

> A faithlesse Sarazin all arm'd to point,
> In whose great shield was writ with letters gay
> *Sans foy:* full large of limbe and every joint
> He was, and cared not for God or man a point.   (12.6–9)

Having abandoned Una, Red Cross has himself committed infidelity, and his gigantic armed enemy is in part an accurate projection of his own current state.[14] Like a host of literary ancestors descending from Neoplatonic allegorizations of Polyphemos, this creature embodies the sensual pride that refuses to recognize divine authority.[15] The text invites us to notice Sansfoy's membership in this godless class by juxtaposing a line describing his huge size with one that stresses godlessness (12.8–9). By his implied rebellion, Sansfoy embodies the obverse of holiness, contemptuous disobedience that springs as surely from faithlessness as holiness does from faith.

Accordingly, Sansfoy fights "prickt," as Red Cross Knight has for several stanzas past, "with pride" (14.6) and wrath – "spurring so hote with rage dispiteous" (15.2). The ensuing battle piles up parallels between these opposites to show that in many respects they are the same – both "fell and furious" (15.4), both equally self-destructive, "[a]stonied with the stroke of their owne hand" (15.8), both comparable to "rams stird with ambitious pride" (16.1), both fiercely repaying "cuff with cuff" (17.3).[16] The fierce blow-for-blow vengefulness that dominates these proud antagonists becomes most obvious at their battle's climax. Red Cross answers a blow to the crest with a precise (and more successful) return:

> Who threat wondrous wroth, the sleeping spark
> Of native virtue gan eftsoones revive,
> And at his haughtie helmet making mark,

> So hugely stroke, that it the steele did rive,
> And cleft his head. (19.1–5)

The sources of Red Cross Knight's success are stated in puzzling fashion. Somehow vengeful anger leads to, is accompanied by, or finds itself mingled with, a resurgence of virtue – virtue that can be construed as natural power (virtú), moral purity, or both. Good and evil mingle in indistinguishable increments to achieve, in the destruction of Sansfoy, an unambiguously positive end.

As before, interpreters might perceive here the good works of the elect, whose victories always spring from the direct operation of "the Spirit of God" and nevertheless suffer corruption "of our flesh, that mingleth itself with them, in the doing by the way."[17] For readers who consider Una's absence especially significant, on the other hand, the word "native" can indicate that Red Cross' situation differs from the earlier one. Lacking the (perhaps mainly unconscious) impulses of faith that Una's companionship supplied in the battle with Error, the knight's reliance on autonomous natural capacities is more complete now. This transforms actions that could earlier constitute signs of election and the incremental achievements of sanctification into mere sins. By revealing in detail the similarities of Red Cross and Sansfoy, the poet has made this point. Working without grace, Red Cross Knight's deeds differ little from those of merely natural men, who can do nothing but sin, even when achieving moral victories (cf. ch. 4, p. 88, below). Few are likely to see Red Cross simply as a natural man, however. His devotion to Christ seemed too definite at the outset, and we have recently been informed that he is "the true Saint George" (I.ii.12.2). Nonetheless, he can for the moment represent the fearful condition of life without grace, or that still more frightening possibility imagined by Reformed theologians, life in which the light of faith has "gone out" and what seemed a true calling turned out to be a temporary alleviation of the reprobate's eternally punishable blindness (ch. 1, p. 43–44, above).

Without helping us settle this question, the text now hints that divine power is somehow present in the battle. When Sansfoy smites "with rigour so outrageous" upon Red Cross' crest, "That a large share [he] hewd out of the rest, / And glauncing downe his shield, from blame him fairely blest" (18.7–9), his helmet – some readers will recall its Pauline identification with "salvation" (Eph. 6:17), or "the hope of salvation" (I Thess. 58)[18] – suffers damage. Readers who bring to their reading such recollections of the Pauline panoply can recognize that Red Cross is quite literally "blest," by means of his shield of faith (Eph. 6.16). He is "blest" specifically from "blame," the word efficiently translating the literal narrative's physical wound into a sign of spiritual damage. Nor is the sword of God's word (Eph. 6:17) omitted, for "the steele" of that sword, piercing Sansfoy's "haughtie" helmet, is named as the immediate cause of his destruction. While Red Cross' "native vertue" aims to return vengeful blow for vengeful blow, his weaponry, implicitly the word of God and hope of salvation working unconsciously within, gives that effort a positive, spiritual effect.[19] Or so the text can be taken to mean. The description of Red Cross' combat with Sansfoy leaves the exact relations of grace and free will, and the actual state of the protagonist's soul, finally ambiguous.

Yet because Red Cross' shield and sword function, in the view of readers attentive to theology, as signs of an invisible power offering intermittent aid; because the extent of his natural human debility is as yet unknown to him; and especially because some of Sansfoy's leading characteristics now clearly infect the knight's own nature, Red Cross' victory is again Pyrrhic. His meeting with Duessa consequently brings to the fore impulses latent in what we have seen of the knight's passion for Una. Intensified expressions of those impulses are implied by the epic simile of I.ii.16:

> As when two rams stird with ambitious pride,
>   Fight for the rule of the rich fleeced flocke,
>   Their horned fronts so fierce on either side
>   Do meete . . .   (1–4)

The context of rams fighting for dominance over a "rich fleeced flocke" activates a secondary denotation of the word "pride," which can mean "sexual heat."[20] The doubleness of meaning suggests that individual sins all express the fundamental unity of sin. Or, as the combination of proud and erotic impulses in this episode suggests more precisely, individual sins express "the flesh," comprehensive symbol for all sins to which humankind is prone.

Duessa's suitability as prize of such contention is patent even to readers who might fail at first to notice her kinship with the purple-and-scarlet-clad harlot of Revelation 17. Like that scriptural ancestor, Duessa appeals brazenly to the physical eye, alluring her lovers by means of garish attire (ii.13.2–6). These attractions, intensified by "faire disport and courting dalliaunce," prove overwhelming, and the knight's eye of reason is seeled still more tightly by passion. He consequently remains impervious to the threatening religious significance of Duessa's costume and the autobiographical tale she tells (ii.22–25). As commentators have pointed out, that story implicitly represents her ignorance of the very substance of faith, Christ's resurrection.[21] Duessa unwittingly identifies herself, that is, as a more insidious equivalent of her former champion. Despite Red Cross' apparent victory over Sansfoy, both that "paynim" and his Duessa now secretly "possess" the victor.

The nature of Duessa's and of Sansfoy's combined possession of Red Cross is explored in Book I, canto iii, a section of the poem from which the knight remains altogether absent. Its content, apparently digressing from the major concerns of The Legend of Holiness, has drawn the attention primarily of scholars concerned with the poem's "historical" allegory, narrowly defined. A doctrinally informed interpretation, however, can find in I.iii a concentrated image of concerns that pervade the poem as a whole. Red Cross Knight's absence matters little to the construction of such an interpretation, so long as readers notice the generic signals that invite us to identify the canto as an instance of romance "entrelacement." In such a plot, events "are not juxtaposed; they are interlaced, and when we get back to our first character he is not where we left him as we finished his episode, but in the place of psychological state or condition of meaningfulness to which he has been pulled by the events occurring in following episodes written about someone else."[22] In effect, when Red Cross reappears in canto iv, we find him in the condition of meaningfulness to which he has been initiated by his infatuation with Duessa and which we can feel has developed in him during our separate sojourn in I.iii. The direction of that development becomes evident in the canto's dominant episode, Una's confrontation with Corceca, Abessa, and Kirkrapine.

The approach to Corceca's gloomy establishment bristles with ethical and theological signposts which a doctrinal construction can readily appropriate. That Una seeks her knight in a landscape fit for spiritual testing ("In wildernesse and wastfull deserts," 3.4; "through deserts wyde," 10.1) would be especially noticeable for readers who begin to perceive that landscape as a version of recurrent scriptural motifs which originate in the Exodus and its forty-year sequel. Readers who have already begun to see Una as a figure for the Church, an association for which her first appearance in the poem provides forceful evidence, will readily build their perceptions of this setting from materials such scrip-

tural antecedents provide. These materials also suggest an analogy between Una and the "woman clothed with the sun" (Rev. 12:1).[23] Although Spenserians have usually taken the implications of this allusion
to be self-evident, its conventional interpretations in Reformation times
can prove illuminating. This familiar biblical figure of the church is
"clothed with the sun" in Revelation, Protestant readings maintain, because she has "put on Christ"; the Savior has consequently become her
"light, [her] life . . . [her] righteousness . . . [her] ornament and
beauty."[24] Like the tribulations of her Old Testament types, this woman's
desert exile in Revelation 12 constitutes a sanctifying exercise designed
to instill unshakably faithful dependence, and loyal, if necessarily imperfect, obedience to God's law.[25]

These scriptural contexts enable us to find significance both in Una's
initial solitude and in her eventual discovery of a path worn by "peoples
footing . . . / Under the steepe foote of a mountaine hore"
(I.iii.10.5–6).[26] This anomalous evidence of heavy traffic in the desert
can strengthen the possibility that readers will construe the episode
against the complex of meanings associated with Israel's post-Exodus
sojourn. Like the wandering track Israel followed in Numbers, and like
subsequent roads modelled on it – in the Sermon on the Mount (Matt.
7:13), in Error's wood (I.i.11), and in the approach to Lucifera's gates
(I.iv.2) – this beaten way threatens a concealed and as yet unspecified
destruction. In the context of its scriptural analogues, moreover, the
contrast between road and mount can emerge as a detail that invites
scrutiny. Both steep and old, the mountain can indeed suggest "that
upon which Moses received the law, by which covenant Abessa and
Corceca still conduct their lives."[27] Because it stresses, as sixteenth-century Lutheranism did, the discontinuity of Old Law and New Law, however, this interpretation can be joined by an alternative possibility which
Reformed orthodoxy provides.[28] Although Reformed theologians and
preachers could also stress the differences between the Old and the New,
they frequently emphasized continuity, as Christ did when He insisted,
in a setting that purposefully recalls Sinai, that He had come not to
abrogate the Law but to fulfill it (Matt. 5:17–19). Readers guided by
this sense of the Law's essential continuity may well perceive that
Spenser's mountain recalls not only Sinai but also that similarly feature-
less, abruptly introduced, and more approachable mountain on which
the New Law was promulgated (Matt. 5–7) and brought to light the
deepest implications of the Old.

In one of its aspects, the mountain in Matthew 5 is steeper than Sinai, for the New Law made conspicuous a theme somewhat obscure in the Old: believers cannot hope to obey the demands God's law imposes (ch. 1, pp. 37–38, above). The reader who assimilates Spenser's mountain to its scriptural antecedents will therefore recognize that despite their inaccessibility to human striving, such mountains must be scaled, not skirted.[29] Travellers who follow this lowly wilderness road are failing or refusing to undertake an obligatory ascent whose achievement offers spiritual insight and whose steepness symbolizes moral and spiritual exertion. Like Old Israel wandering in the desert, the denizens of Una's wilderness cling to the earthbound and the low, and like Old Israel, they can do nothing else: "Certainly they shall not see the land, whereof I swear unto their fathers" (Num. 14:23). Such reflections could induce readers to reflect, increasingly as they move through canto iii, on the idea of reprobation, the most terrifying spiritual condition Protestantism imagines. Even before meeting the residents of Spenser's wilderness, readers attuned to Reformed perspectives may foresee that a predestined and at the same time stubbornly willed literalism prevents this desert's residents from entering into the Promised Land (Num. 14:20–29; 26:64–65; 32:10–11). This recognition can produce divergent responses, ranging from the pleasure of recognizing comforting doctrines renewed by literary treatment, to anxiety about one's own possible reprobation, perhaps even to anger at a theological system that seems, to "humanist" sensibilities, cruel.

Such diversity of response will most likely recur as the narrative proceeds, for our introduction to the desert's inhabitants intensifies the focus on reprobation. This happens when Una overtakes a "damzell" (only later named "Abessa") "slow footing her before" (10.8). Spenserians have often argued that, because she carries a water vessel, this figure ought to remind us of the Samaritan woman who meets Christ at Jacob's well (John 4). This perception can be confirmed, retrospectively or on rereading, by an increasingly sturdy conviction that the episode of Corceca and Abessa as a whole concerns issues similar to those raised by Christ's appearance at Jacob's well. Because of its location in a developing complex of water imagery which suggests the inadequacy of Jewish rituals of purification (the "waterpots" at the miracle of Cana, John 2) and of the inferiority of baptism by water as opposed to baptism by the Spirit (John 1:33), water from Jacob's well represents in John's treatment of it the radical insufficiency of Jewish and of Samaritan religion. Torah is analogous to physical water because its concerns are predominantly external, matters chiefly legal and ceremonial. Unless Christ is accepted as its ultimate meaning, John implies, Torah remains a superficial, temporary, and partial remedy for spiritual thirst.[30] By contrast, Christ announces that he brings an intrinsic cure for this thirst: "whosoever drinketh of the water that I shall give him shall never . . . thirst: but the water that I shall give him shall be in him a well of water, springing up into everlasting life" (John 4:14). The Samaritan's reply, "Sir, give me of that water, that I may not thirst, neither come hither to draw," displays a fixation on the literal. The Samaritan exhibits an exegetical literalism that accompanies fleshliness of a more commonplace sort: she has had five husbands and now dwells with a man "who is not her husband." Her thoroughgoing adherence to the "flesh" parallels leading characteristics not only of her own tribe but of the erring Israelites who could not see the water-yielding rock and the manna as evidence that the Lord demands and deserves total trust, absolute dependence, and undivided fidelity. Abessa's Spenserian setting and her scriptural prototype therefore predict that she will manifest the spiritual myopia and rebellious appetite exhibited by Moses' stubborn and stiffnecked people.

But the parallel between Abessa and the Samaritan woman, which Spenserian interpreters often accept wholesale, is partial. The Samaritan is not hopelessly addicted to the world; she implicitly rejects the water of Jacob's well in favor of the offered living water. Transformed (in Erasmus' genial paraphrase) from "a sinful Samaritan . . . [to] as it were an apostle,"[31] she abandons her water pot, returns to the city, announces her hope that the stranger at the well is "the Christ," and leads others to meet him. Abessa likewise discards her "pitcher," but she does so with less grace:

> seeing by her side the Lyon stand,
> With suddaine feare her pitcher downe she threw,
> And fled away: for never in that land
> Face of faire Ladie she before did vew,
> And that dread Lyons looke her cast in deadly hew.
> (I.iii.11.5–9)

Whereas her Samaritan ancestress gradually came to perceive Christ's true nature, Abessa feels unqualified terror. She appears destined to remain always beyond the sphere of grace.

Although critics often discuss only the first line of the description ("seeing . . . the Lyon," 11.5),[32] the ensuing lines (11.7–9) reveal that

Abessa fears *both* Una and her companion, "for . . . never . . . Face of faire Ladie she before did vew, / And that dread Lyons looke." For readers who have activated even a few of the possible connections between Spenser's episode and its nexus of scriptural antecedents, Una and the lion together can be perceived to "stand for" Christ by assuming his place in this redaction of the biblical narrative. Of course, readers' political or ecclesiological interests would have Una and her protector also represent "the Church supported by royal power,"[33] but a doctrinal construction can find in them a subtle version of a paradox that pervades Christian revelation generally and finds its supreme embodiment in the Messiah himself – at times the gentle Savior, at others the fearful Pantocrator who will eventually come to judge both the quick and the dead. This divine exemplar incarnates the awe-inspiring power of Christianity's doctrines, simultaneously or in sequence, both to terrify and to allure.[34] Fleeing *both* the dread lion's look and Una's supernatural beauty, Abessa responds readily enough to the fearful elements of Christian revelation, but the Gospel's comforts are unknown to her, or prove frightening in themselves. The ignorance commentators consistently ascribe to Abessa can therefore be redefined more precisely as ignorance and even fear of the New Testament's comforting promises, which demand a frightening surrender, especially of the illusion of individual competence and autonomous participation in matters concerning salvation.

Abessa's sensory deficiencies are inherited from the mother to whose protection she flees: "And home she came, whereas her mother blynd / Sate in eternall night" (3.12). Readers familiar with the norms of antimonastic satire can recognize that Corceca practices a routine of ascetic devotion that reflects the austerities and ritual observances of the monastic orders, as they were ungenerously represented, that is, in Protestant polemics. Una finds both Corceca and Abessa

> In darkesome corner pent;
> Where that old woman day and night did pray
> Upon her beades devoutly penitent;
> Nine hundred Pater nosters every day,
> And thrise nine hundred Aves she was wont to say. (iii.13.5–9)

Earlier sections of canto iii have prepared especially for this, Corceca's enslavement to a self-punishing effort to employ the rituals of religion as if they constituted a kind of black magic that can produce salvation through obsessive repetition of prescribed incantations.[35] The idea that chiefly unites the earlier allusions to Numbers and to John with Corceca's behavior is the pathetic or (depending on the reader's allegiances) the vexing, the tragic, or the serio-comic bondage of figures who adhere to things of this world and to the Old Law without being granted the capacity to recognize worldly things as signs and to see the merciful Christ as the Law's essence. As her physical blindness indicates, Corceca lacks any hint of the grace that endows recipients with capacity for sacramental and typological understanding, the capacity which provides a hermeneutic grounding for faith.[36] This lack suggests the most obvious point about Corceca: her name, as Upton noted, alludes to Paul's reference to sinners "whose understanding [is] . . . darkened, being alienated from the life of God through the ignorance that is in them, because of the blindness of their heart" (Eph. 4:18; cf. Rom. 1:21).[37] Reformed theology often took this text as a description of "human nature," corrupt in its every faculty, whether physical, emotional, or mental. The passage therefore applies "to all those whom the Lord has not yet formed again to the uprightness of his wisdom and justice."[38] Paul is describing, that is, the "natural man" – a category of which many, but not all, are reprobate. The reprobate are doomed to live without God's grace and consequently to suffer not only lack of any hope for salvation but impairment even of the capacity to employ their natural faculties in positive ways.[39] Despite the limited sphere of Corceca's activity in the narrative, such doctrinal attitudes enable readers to perceive that her name comprises the impressive variety of evils her religion will be shown to countenance (the sacrilegious robbery and fornication of Abessa and Kirkrapine, iii.18), those she will shortly indulge in herself (vengefulness through slander, iii.22–23), and those her spiritual kin (Error, Night, Ignaro, among others) more actively dramatize.

Without the grace to see God's wisdom clearly, the Israelites were susceptible to idolatry, and although Corceca worships no palpable idols, she shares that ailment in its extended sense. As Tyndale explains, "thou mayest commit as great idolatry to God, and yet before none outward image, but before the image which thou hast feigned of God in thine heart." "Yea," he adds, when worshippers undertake

ceremonies and sacrifices (the meaning and signification lost, and the cause forgotten, which God ordained them for) to flatter and please God with the gloriousness of the deed in itself, and to purchase aught of him for the costliness or properness of the present; what other [make] they of God in their imagination, than a child, whom, if he cry or be displeased, men still with a puppet, or if we will have him to do aught, make him an horse of a stick, or such like?[40]

Corceca exhibits a case not of open but of "colored atheism," the sort promoted "by the very religion of the Church of Rome," which may "rightly acknowledge the unity of the Godhead in the Trinity of persons: yet so, as by other necessary consequences, partly of their doctrine, and partly of the service of God, they overturn that which they have well maintained." Any religion that "makes the merit of the works of men to concur with the grace of God . . . overthrows the grace of God."[41] For a reading informed by Protestant doctrines, this would be the gravest consequence of Corceca's exaggerated revival of Old Law formalism.

A closely related but still broader subject of canto iii is humankind's "overweening arrogance [which] would pass the deity through our sieve."[42] As reflected in Corceca's establishment, monasticism offered a conspicuous sixteenth-century manifestation of this endemic disease suffered by the Israelites, the Samaritans, and the unregenerate. All of these categories worship God "in the similitude of the image of a corruptible man, and of birds, and fourfooted beasts, and of creeping things" (Rom. 1:23), in any shape desire happens to propose. This ample idea seems readily perceptible in *The Faerie Queene* I.iii, but it also seems apparent that this meaning will be fully as much a construction of the reader as it is a discovery of meaning "in" the text. Unless readers actualize some of the potential connections between Spenser's text and its scriptural antecedents, and recognize the presence of antimonastic satire as we have done in the foregoing paragraphs, they will see in the Corceca episode chiefly what many readers have taken it self-evidently to be: a "historical" episode containing a gratuitous satiric attack on a Catholic institution that had not existed in England for decades, or disguised satire of English bishops' misappropriation of church properties – through impropriation of lands, absenteeism, and related abuses.[43]

For readers who seek to discover large-scale implications and formal unity in the poem, *Faerie Queene* I.ii–iii has had much to offer so far. And at the end of canto iii, human nature's total perversity receives climactic expression, when Una and Archimago (now masquerading as Red Cross Knight) confront Sansloy. As this fierce hooligan's shield proclaims, Sansloy symbolizes anarchic opposition to law, and law, as many of Spenser's earliest readers would have learned to understand it, existed in a hierarchy of manifestations: divine, natural, rational, and human.[44]

Yet in this episode, Sansloy's anarchic urgency to violate all laws – a defining condition of the reprobate "who abandon themselves to all manner of iniquity" – drives him to act less as a figure of outright anarchy than as a potent embodiment of "malice and revenging will."

This vengefulness becomes evident when Sansloy approaches "with hastie heat" (iii.33.2), burns "in fire" (34.3) when he sees the red cross on the disguised Archimago's chest, and overthrows him in a flurry of aggression compounded mainly of pride and wrath: "But that proud Paynim forward came so fierce, / And full of wrath" (35.1–2; 36.1–3). Sansloy's proud wrathfulness, mirrored in a "loftie" steed that gnaws its bit "for anger," serves a conspicuously pagan code of familial vengeance:

> "Lo there the worthie meed
> Of him, that slew Sansfoy with bloudie knife;
> Henceforth his ghost freed from repining strife,
> In peace may passen over Lethe lake,
> When morning altars purgd with enemies life,
> The blacke infernall Furies doen aslake:
> Life from Sansfoy thou tookst, Sansloy shall from thee take."
>
> (iii.36.3–9)

Although lust possesses him too (41.7), Sansloy's attempted rape of Una is itself presented as an extension of what the poet soon depicts as "fierce revenging Wrath" (iv.33.1; cf. iii.43.9, "his rage is more of might"; 44.5, "he enrag'd with rancor") mingled with the desperate, sadistic ego-assertion that constitutes one of the most powerful motivations of rape:[45]

> He now Lord of the field, his pride to fill,
> With foule reproches, and disdainfull spight
> Her vildly entertaines   (43.5–7)

Sansloy's arrogant lawlessness can be seen ultimately as a vengeful appropriation of the *lex talionis*, an inversion of the essence of divine law, which is represented here by the self-denying charity of Una's love for Red Cross.

From the vantage provided by this final episode, therefore, *The Faerie Queene* I.iii can be construed as a carefully unified argument for obedience to complementary levels of established law. Sansloy's adherence to a distorted law of vengeance, together with the brute desire expressed in his attack on Una, reveals his kinship with Corceca, Abessa, and Kirkrapine. By differing means – magical ceremonies, burglary, rape, violent revenge – each of the canto's evil agents seeks to manipulate or subdue the religious Truth that Una intermittently represents. All the figures of evil which the text of I.iii invites readers to construct collectively represent recurrent anthropocentric efforts to corrupt or destroy God's law in its varying manifestations – natural (the lion destroyed by Sansloy),[46] divine (perverted by the monastics), and human (broken by Kirkrapine and Sansloy). So interpreted, the canto becomes a satisfying aesthetic object, and for that reason it can also be viewed, as I suggested at the beginning of this chapter, as a powerful agent of reigning orthodoxies. Like the evil agents introduced in earlier cantos, those in I.iii constitute a composite vision of an especially terrifying Other whom "good" readers, those susceptible to the fashioning Spenser's poem at times seems prepared to impose on them, will fashion themselves against.

4

ACHIEVING SIN

As we have seen, Red Cross Knight's spiritual condition has been very much at issue in *Faerie Queene* I.iii, for those readers, at least, who accept the invitation to construe its episodes as instances of romance entrelacement. The ensuing cantos, I.iv–v, demonstrate more directly that sin's manifold social and political consequences are already active in the knight. The rudely disdainful lady who presides at the beginning of I.iv can recall Red Cross' own earlier penchant for "disdain" and its more active variant "despight" (I.i.19.6, 50.3; ii.6.4, 8.4). These implied similarities adumbrate what will be our major preoccupations in exploring I.iv–vi, cantos that bring Red Cross to the point of collapse. This portion of the narrative juxtaposes theological ideas – concerning human nature, sin, providence, and predestination – with a diversity of literary genres, especially chivalric romance, court satire, allegorical pageant, epic, and pastoral idyl. These varied materials can help us construct a more than usually inclusive and coherent assessment of Red Cross Knight's potentially damnable defects and, more obliquely here, of his yet unrealized spiritual resources.

Although commentators often resist the idea that Red Cross is infected by the sinfulness that Lucifera and her house represent,[1] the knight's attitude toward the vainglory of her court includes a moralistic element which some theological perspectives would judge to be culpable:

> Yet the stout Faerie mongst the middest crowd
> Thought all their glorie vaine in knightly vew,
> And that great Princesse too exceeding prowd,
> That to strange knight no better countenance allowd. (I.iv.15.6–9)

The generic modulation which court satire persistently supplies in this canto (e.g. "Some frounce their curled haire in courtly guise, / Some prancke their ruffes . . . each others greater pride does spight," 14.7–9) identifies Lucifera's palace at this point as an image of the petty conflicts and fierce mutual emulation that characterized Renaissance courts. This recognition invites readers to applaud Red Cross' inclination to remain aloof, as we might applaud Guyon's refusal to wed Philotime (*FQ*

II.viii.43–50), or Colin Clout's *(Colin Clout's Come Home Again)* or Wyatt's rejection of courtly luxury, pretense, and hypocrisy ("Myn Own John Poyntz").

Yet just at the moment when we feel inclined to grant the knight unqualified approval, we might also notice that his aloofness itself springs from injured vanity and that he applies standards of judgment which are entirely courtly and chivalric, in a word, "knightly" (15.7), not moral or in any way religious. "Stout" can mean "proud," and this stout pride need not represent simply a righteous sense of injured merit. *Their* mere courtiers' vainglory, the knight assures himself, is vain, unlike his own chivalrous pursuit of honor. In contrast to the exclusively human standards which Red Cross applies, theological perspectives could induce us to consider him as a well-meaning soul whom "virtue" has afflicted with a subtle form of sin. His location "mongst the middest crowd" may therefore suggest that he has joined Lucifera's household in spirit as well as in body.

Doctrinal constructions of the passage, however, are capable not only of extending the spiritual indictment against Red Cross; they can also soften readers' judgments of him. Reformed moral theology could read Red Cross' place and attitudes as indices of damnable sin and yet recognize that the impulse toward morality is conscious, the sin unconscious. We can therefore respond positively to limited achievement while also acknowledging its limitations: this is an authentically "good knight" (I.iv.37.7)[2] whose chivalrous sense of self leads him to avoid Lucifera's pageant: "Him selfe estraunging from their joyaunce vaine, / Whose fellowship seemd far unfit for warlike swaine" (37.8–9). The generic affiliations of the passage can reinforce our sense of the knight's goodness, for the initial moments of the pageant (16–17), might induce readers to expect an experience familiar from civic rituals, court entertainments, and progresses that typically sought to reinforce devotion to established authority by presenting it as agent of transcendent power.[3] For readers who anticipate such a ritualized occasion when Lucifera "for her coche dothe call" (16.2), the ensuing allegory of the seven deadly sins will constitute a surprising return to a contrasting set of conventions.

Despite his refusal to join a pageant in which Lucifera's prominence at beginning and end (iv.17, 37) symbolizes the paradoxically unitary multiplicity of evil (ch. 1, pp. 39–40), Red Cross continues to betray affinities both with her and with wrath, the vice adjacent to her and to her coachman, Satan himself. The portrait of "fierce revenging Wrath"

(33.1), whose location in the pageant indicates its intimate psychological, moral, and metaphysical relationship with the very pride of Lucifer, embodies a congeries of angry symptoms we have glimpsed, and soon will see more directly displayed, in Red Cross Knight. As has happened before, the knight declines overt alliance with this patent evil but abruptly falls when it reappears in improved disguise. For just at the end of Lucifera's pageant, another of Red Cross' enemies (and images) arrives in the person of Sansjoy:

> Enflam'd with fury and fiers hardy–hed,
> He seemd in hart to harbour thoughts unkind,
> And nourish bloudy vengeaunce in his bitter mind.   (iv.38.7–9)

Obviously, this creature represents a joyless sadness akin to despair, as interpreters often say. Readers engaged by theological ideas, however, may feel impelled to consider more exactly why joylessness should have as its most conspicuous trait the intense vengefulness that appears in all Sansjoy's actions.

As first presented in I.iv.38.3–9, Sansjoy seems to represent not any obvious joylessness, but vengefulness in essence, seeking (like characters in Renaissance revenge plays) any occasion to unleash a spontaneously escalating animosity. This inclination toward essential vengefulness subtly links Sansjoy with Red Cross Knight, for the two soon begin to act the same. Their kinship becomes especially apparent, for example, after the indecorous tussle at court (39–40), when "th'angry" Red Cross Knight and Sansjoy exhibit identical mental and emotional responses: "with harts on edge, / To be aveng'd each on his enimy" (43.3–4).

During her nocturnal visit to Sansjoy, Duessa's machinations throw further light on the interrelations of anger, revenge, and joylessness when she seeks to reinforce her newest champion's chronically wrathful mood. As has happened to her before, Duessa speaks subtle, unwitting truth while telling bald-faced lies about a pathos-ridden romance with Sansfoy:

> For since my brest was launcht with lovely dart
> Of deare Sansfoy, I never joyed howre,
> But in eternall woes my weaker hart
> Have wasted, loving him with all my powre,   (iv.46.5–8)

Duessa's liaison with faithlessness, in short, automatically joined her to the utter joylessness of "eternal woes." Doctrinal perspectives help to explain Duessa's condition, for as Protestant theologians frequently insisted, joylessness is as certainly linked to faithlessness as joys are to faith. Once Christ, the substance of faith, becomes clouded by false doctrine, "traditions of men, and depraving of scripture," as He has in the religion Duessa represents, "there is no rest, quietness, security, or spiritual pleasure . . . but only tediousness." By contrast, "Christ pure, and sincerely received, is to man a joy unspeakable, and a most bright and joyful light."[4] For Paul (speaking in phrases supplied by Erasmus and his English translators), the grace that brings true faith makes believers "glad, lusty, cheerful and true hearted unto God and to all creatures."[5] Duessa's visit to Sansjoy, calculated in part to assure her alliance with whomever emerges as victor, obliquely dramatizes a psychological condition that her role as religious symbol has already guaranteed. Her religion of the flesh, which values the physical and exalts the autonomy of human will, assures her of "eternal woes" in the hereafter and a temporal version of those woes in this life. Red Cross' combat is with all of this – a complex of evils whose symptoms he himself already displays.

Some of these symptoms begin to become apparent in the qualities of the prize for which the knight now competes. Both knights prepare to fight, with angry vindictiveness, for Sansfoy's shield, a symbol of Aveugle's (Blindness') familial honor and of the conventional chivalric victor's individual "glory." Sansjoy

> to him leapt, and that same envious gage
> Of victors glory from him snatcht away:
> But th'Elfin knight, which ought that warlike wage,
> Disdaind to loose the meed he wonne in fray,
> And him rencountring fierce, reskewd the noble pray.   (iv.39.5–9)

Spenser's commercial diction ("ought," "wage," "meed"), which modulates at "noble pray" to suggest something more paradoxical and predatory than commerce, indicates that both knights view Sansfoy's shield as symbol of an earth-bound variety of honor, which seeks nothing higher than human admiration. Lucifera aptly terms this honor "gay chivalree." Though pride and wrath may be the knights' immediate motivating passions, they both manifest the less conspicuous and emphatically material desire for this cheapened variety of honor.

The unobtrusive presence, in this desire, of "cupidity," the corrupt desire which Christian theology has persistently considered to be sin's root,[6] reasserts the idea that everyone, elect or reprobate, participates in every variety of sinfulness. To be "in sin," Spenser's diction suggests, is to share a condition symbolized by Lucifera's vain pageant, in which the

seven grand categories represent – for interpreters who bring to their
reading some familiar theological and literary conventions or scriptural
number symbolism – sin's potentially infinite variety.[7] As Spenser's depiction of Red Cross Knight invites readers to see, to be "in sin" is a
condition that exists quite independently of the sinner's consciousness
of his sinfulness (see ch. 1, pp. 39–40). The poetry implies this, for
instance, when Sansjoy and Red Cross part for the night and some cun-
ningly inclusive plural pronouns involve both the "good" and the evil
knight in the comprehensively sinful "joyaunce" of the court:

> So been they parted both, with harts on edge,
> To be aveng'd each on his enimy.
> That night they pas in joy and jollity,
> Feasting and courting both in bowre and hall;
> For Steward was excessive Gluttonie,
> That of his plenty poured forth to all;
> Which doen, the Chamberlain Slowth did to rest them call.

(iv.43.3–9)

This veneer of "joyaunce" masks the comprehensive sinfulness which
altogether precludes the restful "joy" that, as we have seen, Reformed
(and Erasmian) theology views as a direct consequence of faith. Gluttony and Sloth replace healthy conviviality here and, as the artful chi-
asmus of line 6 shows, lechery lurks partly unseen, "courting . . . in
bowre."[8] Despite whatever efforts we might make to assume that Red
Cross avoids such activity, our minds cannot easily exempt him from
the area of reference to which the stanza's plural pronouns extend. Along
with his already hinted pride and wrath, the knight of holiness now seems
covertly and unconsciously to be implicated in sin, in that term's most
comprehensive sense. While he resides in Lucifera's house, her pageant
inhabits his soul.

The prominence of pride and vengeful wrath in both knights' prepa-
rations for combat, plus the more obliquely hinted sins of the night
before, renders problematic the commentary that Spenser's narrator provides for the battle itself. Elaborating the implications of Red Cross
Knight's epic epithet ("good"), the narrator insists on the hero's virtue:

> The noble hart, that harbours vertuous thought,
> And is with child of glorious great intent,
> Can never rest, untill it forth have brought
> Th'eternall brood of glorie excellent: (v.1.1–4)

It is possible that these lines exuberantly express "the Renaissance faith that well-knowing leads to well-doing,"[9] and so can effectively engage readers' enthusiasm for the victory of "right" as romance and epic normally define and celebrate it. Yet the immediately ensuing description of Red Cross Knight's nocturnal yearnings might give the same readers pause:

> Such restlesse passion did all night torment
> The flaming corage of that Faery knight,
> Devizing, how that doughtie turnament
> With greatest honour he atchieven might;   (v.1.5–8)

Voluminous medieval and Renaissance discourses on honor demonstrate that virtue in action can indeed give birth to something which Spenser's contemporaries could consider literally an "eternal brood of glory." This lasting offspring of virtue results from actions deemed virtuous by the Lord Himself; as Christian ethical precepts relentlessly imply, such deeds bring to their human agents true glory, which is by definition the approbation of God.[10]

These orthodox notions, if present for readers as an implicit horizon of the ringing phrase "th'eternall brood of glorie excellent," will jar somewhat with implications perceptible in later phrases in the stanza. The knight's intentions are driven by "restlesse passion," a term doctrinal perspectives do not allow us easily to translate as zeal for the glory to be won in battle against God's enemies. As the recurrent satiric modulations of the canto have reminded us, Red Cross Knight now resides in an altogether worldly setting, having earlier exiled himself from Una, symbol of the community within which believers must fight if any of their endeavors are to become authentically holy. Recollections of earlier battles will induce some readers to notice that Red Cross' resolve resides in his "flaming corage," which has been the persistently ireful heart of a man who now devotes his sleepless night to planning a "doughtie turnament" dedicated to his own "greatest honour" (v.1.7–8).[11]

As we move closer to the combat, an expansive epic simile suddenly broadens our perspective on the subsequent action:

> At last the golden Orientall gate
> Of greatest heaven gan to open faire,
> And Phoebus fresh, as bridegrome to his mate,
> Came dauncing forth, shaking his deawie haire:
> And hurld his glistring beames through gloomy aire.   (v.2.1–5)

Phoebus' cheerful rising can (re)establish the predominance of theological perspectives by reminding readers that divine illumination, dispersing the gloom of evil, presides over the impending battle. Hamilton's notes (*FQ* I.v.2) draw attention to this passage's origin in Psalm 19:4–5. It is important to recognize too that this psalm celebrates the beneficent providence that, through the workmanship of the heavens and of divine law, provides error-dispelling light to sinful men.[12] And as we saw in chapter 1 (pp. 39–40, above), this psalm also lent authority to Protestant discussions of the inevitability and the extraordinary pervasiveness of unconscious sin. Phoebus' jollity manifests, therefore, in a canto in which joylessness is the salient enemy, what for Protestantism constituted humankind's ultimate source of joy, a comforting trust in benevolent providence and the salvation it guarantees to the elect. Only through his alliance to this power, visible to readers in the knight's "sunbright armes" (2.8), can Red Cross attain joy that surpasses the artificial pleasures provided by Lucifera's court: "There many Minstrales maken melody, / To drive away the dull melancholy" (v.3.4–7; 4.4–6). Whatever his current sinfulness, Red Cross' sunbright armor, if construed as evidence that its wearer is securely "clothed with the sun" (cf. ch. 1, pp. 45–46; ch. 3, pp. 83–84, above), will assure readers that he is finally invulnerable to the assaults of Sansjoy.

Of course, this invulnerability would be ultimate, not immediate. As in the engagement with Sansfoy, the contrasts between antagonists here are balanced by telling similarities. Overtly, the narrator stresses opposition. The Saracen longs for "bloud and vengeance"; the knight fights "all for prayse and honour" (v.7.3, 6). Twice we hear the summary judgment: "So th'one for wrong, the other strives for right" (8.1; 9.1). And yet, available theological perspectives invite readers to notice that "prayse and honor" are adequate synonyms for only a limited kind of "right," and the rhetoric and action of the battle make the antagonists' similarities more apparent than their differences. The combatants differ chiefly in the techniques and relative superiority with which they perform otherwise identical actions.[13] Both the hero and his antagonist assail each other "with greedy force" (6.6), a phrase suited to betray the sinful soul's ingrained cupidity. Red Cross, "fiers, and full of youthly heat" (7.4), displays characteristics that match Sansjoy's "wrathfull fyre" (10.2) and also bespeak sin's grounding in the self-asserting self-love that gives birth specifically to ire. The weapons which both combatants use are "instruments of wrath and heavinesse" (6.5), "heavinesse" denoting here the sadness and grief Sansjoy personifies (*OED*, s.v., "heaviness," I, e). The increasingly obvious bestiality of the knights becomes still more complete when Sansjoy is compared to a dragon, Red Cross to a griffin "seized of his pray" (8.2).

On the other hand, readers might focus their construction of the phrase on "griffin" rather than "pray." Because, as some commentators have noted, the griffin combines features of both lion and eagle, it can represent Christ's inseparable union of divinity and humanity, as it does in *Purgatorio* xxix.108. Read in the light of Reformed doctrines of holiness, this symbol can acquire a new aspect that makes it an appropriate emblem for Red Cross. Because he is human, the knight is radically sinful and at the same time enclosed in armor which represents both an inalienable imputed righteousness and the source of authentic divine power to move toward holiness of life (ch. 1, p. 46, above).[14] If readers supply it, this exalted parallel will serve partly to provide a sense of irony as details of the battle continue to stress the mutual bestiality of both the griffin (Red Cross) and his enemy, the dragon (Sansjoy). Each monster fights for "ravine" (8.5) which, though in some sense rightfully the griffin's, scarcely constitutes a noble prize. "Rightfull ravine" implies that this prey is suitable to beasts.

The prizes in themselves, the shield of faithlessness and a lascivious lady, remind us that the conditions under which spiritual battles are fought can transform a conquest good in itself, the defeat of Sansjoy, to indubitable sin. This can account in part for the ambiguous character and ironic manner of the battle's violent climax:

> Soone as the Faerie heard his Ladie speake,
>   Out of his swowning dreame he gan awake,
>   And quickning faith, that earst was woxen weake,
>   The creeping deadly cold away did shake:
>   Tho mov'd with wrath, and shame, and Ladies sake,
>   Of all attonce he cast avengd to bee,
>   And with so'exceeding furie at him strake,
>   That forced him to stoupe upon his knee   (v.12.1–8)

As a (by now) familiar application of doctrinal perspectives has led us to expect, these lines express the ambiguity of motivation that characterizes all human achievement. Red Cross appropriates the encouragement that Duessa intended for Sansjoy and, driven by a complex of sinful impulses, recovers from the spiritually death-dealing effects of Sansjoy's staggering blow (11.6).

Perspectives which theology can bring to the poem invite us to perceive that "quickning [i.e. spiritually life-giving] faith" is the independently active subject of the sentence's predicate "the creeping deadly cold away did shake." Faith's presence, unconscious to the knight, is announced by means of a coordinating conjunction: "*and* quickening faith" rather than the more predictable "*because.*" Faith's arrival dissipates the enervating effects of joylessness, the "creeping deadly cold" that fore-runs spiritual death. Even the hypocritical agents of a false church can become instruments of grace directed toward the elect and, in Red Cross' case, an unconscious accession of true faith coincides with Duessa/Fidessa's reminder that promised rewards follow success in battle: "Thine the shield, and I, and all." Having received gracious divine rescue, Red Cross allows his own conscious intentions to sully the purity of his victory. He is "mov'd" "with wrath, and shame, and Ladie's sake" to gain revenge by means of a furious blow: "he cast avengd to bee, / And with . . . exceeding furie at him strake" (12.5–6). The objectively good action of destroying Sansjoy becomes subjectively sinful, a paradox made powerfully clear in the knight's cruel boast over his prostrate foe (6.2):

> "Goe now proud Miscreant,
> Thy selfe thy message doe to german deare,
> Alone he wandring thee too long doth want:
> Goe say, his foe thy shield with his doth beare."   (v.13.1–4)

After Sansjoy disappears into a magical cloud (13.6), Duessa has much ado to quench what she rightly judges to be Red Cross Knight's "flame of furious despight, / And bloudie vengeance" (14.4–5). The knight's "furious despight" compels him to seek through the blinding mist "with greedie eye" to bathe his sword "in bloud of faithlesse enemy" (15.2–3). Taken as a whole, Red Cross' behavior in and after the battle reveals him now to be a committed subject of Lucifera. This newly overt commitment abruptly receives ritual expression:

> he goeth to that soveraine Queene,
> And falling her before on lowly knee,
> To her makes present of his service seene:
> Which she accepts . . .
>   and by her takes the knight,   (v.16.1–4; 6)

Red Cross' obeisance to Lucifera and his acceptance of a place in her coach constitute no new and sudden reversal, as scholars sometimes imply when they assume that the knight has somehow authentically renewed his faith in order to conquer Sansjoy. For the reading we have developed here, the knight's overt alliance with Lucifera provides vivid ritual confirmation of implications that most of his recent deeds have implied.

At the same time, Lucifera's new ability to engage Red Cross' direct service might be taken to manifest the insidiousness which theology attributes to the temptations of pride. Having failed to tempt him earlier with courtly pastimes, which had seemed vain "in knightly view," the tempters accommodate themselves to their victim's particular weakness. Here they satisfy Red Cross' "knightly view" with all the ego-inflating ceremonial that adorned Tudor recreations of medieval chivalric pageantry (I.v.3–6).[15] Now that Lucifera's pageant has assumed the aspect of a "triumph," the traditional reward of military conquest, Red Cross readily joins it.

Although physical luxury is conspicuous among his rewards (I.v.17), Red Cross' new allegiance to Lucifera promises not to cure but to "beguile" (17.8) the rankling "griefe and agony" wrought by Sansjoy's blows. When darkness approaches, Duessa sets out to revive the source of Red Cross' pains by visiting Night, whose first-named attribute, "deadly sad," links this matriarch of evils to the chronically "sad" Red Cross. Night's sad visage, antipathetic to "Phoebus chearefull face" (20.1–2), befits the gloom of a shadowy cavern (20.4) whose topography at once discloses its occupants' affective and metaphysical kinship with Error and Corceca and Abessa, not to mention Sansjoy himself. In a craftily comic recognition scene (27), there appears the first of many allusions to Virgil which establish the epic modulation that pervades this passage: night's "O welcome childe whom I have longd to see" echoes the effusive greeting which Anchises gives his son in *Aeneid* 6.257–58.[16]

When Duessa's descent to the underworld begins (I.v.30), we reach a series of passages that transparently imitate Aeneas' similar descent and supply a continuous ironic perspective for Duessa's journey. As A. C. Hamilton has clearly seen, Spenser's version of this descent constitutes a deliberate and comprehensive parody of Virgil's. In Spenser's redaction, "the adversary, not the aged priestess of Phoebus, makes the prophecy of woe; and the great mother of the hero's adversaries, not the hero's sire, reveals the hero's destiny."[17] As usual, however, Spenser's redaction transforms the earlier text in more ways than one. His partial imitation of Virgil's famous lines on the ease of descending to Hell and the difficulty of return (*Aeneid* 6.126–31) illustrates this:

> there creature never past,
> That backe returned without heavenly grace;
> But dreadfull Furies, which their chaines have brast,
> And damned sprights sent forth to make ill men aghast.   (v.31.6–9)

Virgil's original passage reads:

> A few, whom Jupiter
> has loved in kindness or whom blazing worth
> has raised to heaven as gods' sons, returned.[18]

Spenser's reworking of the lines adds the point that Furies and "damned sprights" are permitted or deliberately sent to work divine justice in the world. And Spenser omits the notion that "blazing worth" (*ardens virtus*) allows return from the underworld and raises one *ad aethera*. Spenser's excision of *ardens virtus* enables Night's underworld the more easily to enforce a theme essential to the idea of holiness as Reformed perspectives can induce readers to create that idea. Human worth can provide no escape from this hell.

This theme becomes more apparent and more elaborate when the underworld itself is revealed to be a subterranean extension of the House of Pride. The notorious sinners imported from Homer, Virgil, and Ovid (v.35) suggest this, since most of them – Ixion, Tantalus, Tityus, Typhoeus, and Theseus – in one way or another committed sacrilegious attacks on one or all of the Olympians. The Danaids, whose murder of their husbands constitutes an indirect attack on divine order,[19] belong definitely if less clearly in this hubristic company. So too does Sisyphus, long considered an emblem of perpetually toiling, self-frustrating ambition. Having observed these exempla, readers will understandably begin to anticipate the yet unannounced goal of Duessa's epic descent – some fitting demonic counterpart of Odysseus' Tiresias, Aeneas' Achises, Bradamante's Melissa, and Carlo's and Ubaldo's provident and venerable seer. Or, since we have recognized this inferno to be a dungeon for the proud, we may with reason expect to meet some version of Satan himself, comparable to the embodied pride that inhabits the very abyss of Dante's hell.

Any of these expectations, induced by recognition of the passage's epic modulation, will induce a sense of bathos when we have finally "come unto the [underworld's] furthest part" (v.36.4). We there confront not a titanic evil figure but a pathetically isolated one: in "a Cave ywrought by wondrous art, / Deepe, darke, uneasie, dolefull, comfortlesse," we

find "sad Aesculapius farre a part / Emprisond . . . in chaines remedi-
lesse" (36.4–8). The bathos raises questions. Why Aesculapius? Why
the emphatic point that his cave is the product of "wondrous art," which
results in so demoralizing a string of attributives? And why does "sad"
Aesculapius' epithet pointedly ally him with Night, Red Cross, Sansjoy,
and the entire "sad house of Pride" (53.9)?

The final question points toward a reading which Reformed doctrines
suggest. Aesculapius' appropriateness as a figure for one central aspect
of the very devil himself becomes apparent through a superficially innocent digression, a narrative of the legend of Hippolytus. Aesculapius
has been condemned, we are reminded, for resurrecting a conspicuously
virtuous devotee of Diana, "a jolly huntsman"

> That wont in charet chace the foming Bore;
> He all his Peeres in beautie did surpas,
> But Ladies love as losse of time forbore: (v.37.2–4)

After Hippolytus' "members chast" (38.7) have been "scattered on every mountaine" and then brought by "Dianes meanes" to Aesculapius,
they receive new life "by his art" (39.8). That the chaste and virtuous
Hippolytus appears to have merited special treatment matters nothing
to avenging Jove, who judges Aesculapius' action an encroachment on
divine prerogative and

> unto hell did thrust him downe alive,
> With flashing thunderbolt ywounded sore:
> Where long remaining, he did alwaies strive
> Himselfe with salves to health for to restore,
> And slake the heavenly fire, that raged evermore. (v.40.5–9)

The inset narrative casts Aesculapius in the figure of one who would,
by his own "art," resurrect others and himself. This does cast him in the
role, as has been noted, of a "false Christ" (42.6).[20] But the interpretation we are developing also implies that Aesculapius embodies Red Cross
Knight's own deepening affliction. As Spenser presents him, Aesculapius
provides a classical image of the central belief promoted by Roman
Catholic dogma as Protestants interpreted it and as the Decretals of Trent
in fact described it – that believers' works can contribute something toward their own salvation. Both the knight and the frustrated physician
suffer a sadness that torments everyone who depends for deliverance on
human "art." This sadness afflicts all who inhabit Lucifera's household,
including those, like Red Cross Knight, whose spiritual residence there

is unconscious, and whose conscious dedication is to strive for "right."

The notion that a single, monolithic evil underlies all sins' manifold variety is suggested repeatedly in Lucifera's establishment. It is implied most elaborately in the pageant of sins, but it recurs in the testimony of the dwarf's nameless informants who obliquely disclose that the inhabitants of this prison are guilty, not of pride alone, but of all the deadly sins:

> Of whom he learned had in secret wise
> The hidden cause of their captivitie,
> How mortgaging their lives to Covetise,
> Through wastfull Pride, and wanton Riotise,
> They were by law of that proud Tyrannesse
> Provokt with Wrath, and Envies false surmise
> Condemned to that Dongeon mercilesse   (v.46.2–8)

Hamilton provides the revealing comment that "riotise" *is* the life of Idleness, and that if "wanton" (line 5) comprises gluttony and lechery, all the deadly sins are included in the stanza. Consequently, to fall to pride is to fall to "sin" in its uniform yet variously manifested and invariably damning essence. Incapable of any truly worthy act, much less of self-deification, humankind can contrive its own damnation in a thousand ways (51.9). Implicit in this perception is the judgment, later explicitly stated in Spenser's poem, that "if any strength we have, it is to ill" (I.x.1).

This doctrine may help to explain why the "donghill of dead carkases" that Red Cross sees as he makes his escape can stand as a "spectacle," that is, a special sign or token of that "sad house of Pride" (53.8–9). This spectacle embraces not only the house's dungeons but its architectural glitter as well. The dead carcasses, metaphors for the spirit's eternal death, present both the timeless essence and the temporal end of pride as it is manifested in Lucifera's markedly courtly milieu and the historical courts it satirizes. The power of this vision casts a gloomy light over Red Cross' escape, made, as we have noted, at the urging of his companion the dwarf. The common assumption that the dwarf symbolizes "reason" finds support here, if we limit that allegorical label to something narrower than usual: reason reduced simply to self-preserving wariness. The knight flees because he fears an outcome comparable to that of the prisoners: "he no lenger would / There dwell in perill of like painefull plight" (52.3–4). This seems reasonable enough, judged

by ordinary human standards, but theological measures require more –
fear of offending "his dying Lord" by breaking His law. Red Cross'
departure therefore promises no actual escape from the spiritual dan-
gers of pride, as becomes ironically evident when he makes his exit "by
a privie Posterne." This aperture contrasts, appropriately enough, with
the wide gate and broad way by which one enters Lucifera's castle. If it
were to provide a less furtive exit, leading past less conspicuously minatory terrain than the dunghills it here traverses, this postern might represent that "strait gait" which Redcrosse's good intentions normally lead
him to seek. But this little parody of the strait gate and narrow way
suggests that Red Cross has been granted a merely temporary reprieve.

The opening of *The Faerie Queene* I.vi invites us, moreover, to reinterpret this reprieve as an action of gracious providence, employing prudential reason as its almost comically inept instrument:

> As when a ship, that flyes faire under saile,
>   An hidden rocke escaped hath unwares,
>   That lay in waite her wrack for to bewaile,
>   The Marriner yet halfe amazed stares
>   At perill past, and yet in doubt ne dares
>   To joy at his foole-happie oversight:
>   So doubly is distrest twixt joy and cares
>   The dreadlesse courage of this Elfin knight,
> Having escapt so sad ensamples in his sight.   (I.vi.1)

Often in epic, and elsewhere in The Legend of Holiness, winds that
propel mariners safely through perilous waters can be read as agents of
benevolent divine presence.[21] The mariner in this epic simile embodies
humankind's own contribution to his providentially charted voyage. And
although the human agent contributes vaguely and unreliably, by way
of a "fool-happie oversight," to his own steerage, only divine guidance
enables him to evade spiritual disasters which are often too subtle for
human perception. Readers who perceive this amusingly presented providential implication at the opening of I.vi are likely to scrutinize subsequent passages for further instances of increasingly direct divine interventions into Red Cross' affairs. Left largely to his own devices in the
previous two cantos, he appears capable only of "fool-happie" progress
toward any goal that theology would judge to be positive.

Subsequent episodes in I.vi, moreover, prepare readers who are attuned
to theological meanings for Red Cross' enervation and his collapse be-

fore Orgoglio in I.vii. The main action of I.vi begins with Sansloy's renewed assault on Una (I.vi.4.6–9). Although he looks directly on Truth,
the "angels face" that "As the great eye of heaven shyned bright" (I.iii.4.6–
7), Sansloy remains impervious to her meaning.[22] This imperviousness,
together with his lustful vengefulness and anarchic energy suggest, further, that we might now view this reprobate (ch. 3, p. 88, above) as a
representation of a still broader category, "natural man." As Reformed
doctrine delineated him, the natural man is capable of behaving worse
than any "mad beast," likely to commit "every evil thing for which Paul
condemns all nature" (e.g. Rom. 1:24–32; 3:10–20). They are only
prevented from doing so because God "restrains by throwing a bridle
over them only that they may not break loose, inasmuch as he foresees
their control to be expedient to preserve all that is."[23] In a canto that
will frequently invite readers to reflect on the mystery of degrees of grace,
Sansloy embodies the partially restrained congeries of evil impulses that
manifest humankind's natural depravity.

Sansloy's demonic act of violent presumption supplies the narrator's
occasion to return, more explicitly now, to the mysteries of providence.
Having asked how the heavens can witness this assault "and hurle not
flashing flames upon that Paynim bold," the narrator proceeds to demonstrate that the heavens incline, on the contrary, to work in indirect if
nevertheless wondrous ways. Instead of staging an overpowering divine
intervention, the heavens put Una's rescue into the most unlikely hands
of "Faunes and Satyres," creatures who appear to inhabit an idyllic world
of innocent pleasure and *otium*, "dauncing in a rownd, / Whiles old
Sylvanus slept in shady arber sownd" (I.vi.7.8–9; 13.5–9).[24] This transition introduces a delightfully fanciful instance of the Lord's inclination to employ the foolish and weak things of the world to confound
the powerful and the wise (I Cor. 1:27).

Una's new protectors replace and improve on the lion, her purely natural ally, for, although they are half goat, they are also half human.[25] Their
human elements being free of civilized evils, they respond to Una in a
way that recalls the lion's behavior. Like him, they pity her "unhappie
state." They also respond, but with somewhat fuller consciousness, to
her transcendent beauty: "All stand astonied at her beautie bright" (9.8).
Because they see this beauty unveiled (9.3), they can clearly recognize
something worthy of devotion in it. They can even share Una's sorrows:

> The salvage nation feele her secret smart,
> And read her sorrow in her count'nance sad;

> Their frowning forheads with rough hornes yclad,
> And rusticke horror all a side doe lay,
> And gently grenning, shew a semblance glad
> To comfort her, and feare to put away,
> Their backward bent knees teach her humbly to obay.

The innocent, spontaneous admiration and sympathy of the "salvage nation" ("They all as glad, as birdes of joyous Prime . . . about her daucing round, / Shouting, and singing all a shepheards ryme," 13.5–7) dramatizes an instinctive responsiveness to the law of nature.[26] The sylvan creatures' generous natural impluses induce gestures of reverence, "their backward bent knees," which "teach [Una] humbly to obay" by calming her fears. The canto's action has progressed, at this point, from representing Sansloy's lawless violation of all law, to an idyllic pastoral scene, rich in classical creatures and references, in which the natural law of love reigns supreme.

Natural law's supernatural source also becomes manifest in the canto. Viewed first as a "mirrhour rare" (15.6) of divine Truth, Una appears next as a mythological embodiment of love that paradoxically unites Venus' sensuous attractions with a disarmed, approachable version of Diana's immaculate purity:

> old Sylvanus selfe bethinkes not, what
> To thinke of wight so faire, but gazing stood,
> In doubt to deeme her borne of earthly brood;
> Sometimes Dame Venus selfe he seemes to see,
> But Venus never had so sober mood;
> Sometimes Diana he her takes to bee,
> But misseth bow, and shaftes, and buskins to her knee. (vi.16.3–9)

Sightings of such Venus/Diana figures recur in Spenser's works (e.g., II.iii.21–31; III.i.43, 46; vi.18; IV.vi.19–20), though here an unusual emphasis falls on the ways a particular perceiver construes the vision. For theologically oriented readers of Spenser's poem, to view Una as Venus/Diana may be to recognize that divine love can actually be experienced in the sublunary realm, where it becomes manifest as an ardor that miraculously and beautifully fuses antithetical qualities. But for Sylvanus, whose perceptions are guided by categories that his classical and mythological world provides, the paradoxical fusion remains imperfect. He can apprehend Una's double valence only in alternating and successive moments of perception. This limitation may symbolize natural reason's incompetence to imagine, much less to achieve, a love which is at once passionate and pure. Spenser's mingling of romance and theological discourse enables him to depict such a love in Una's devotion to Red Cross Knight, an attachment that directly embodies *caritas*, "for his love, and for her owne selfe sake, / She wandred had from one to other Ynd" (vi.2.6–7; cf. 32.1–6).[27]

Despite an auspicious beginning, the sylvans soon display limitations that prevent them from forming a comparable personal attachment which manifests religious devotion. They seek first to worship Una herself and, being dissuaded, they turn "her Asse . . .[to] worship fayn" (vi.19.9). These actions exhibit a touching but hopelessly ignorant devotion, which aims (as an erudite pun implies) toward truth that lies forever beyond the satyrs' grasp.[28] Although their god Sylvanus might be identified with Pan ("All"), the text offers little evidence to support the notion that these sylvans approach, even remotely, the full degree of knowledge about God which human reason might attain without the aid of direct revelation. The scriptural analogue many readers could find relevant here, I think, is Romans 1. Because the sylvans see Una's face unveiled, they enjoy an unusual opportunity to perceive, reflected in a created thing, "the invisible things of [God]." By worshipping Una, then the ass, they change "the glory of the incorruptible God to . . . the image of a corruptible man . . . and fourfooted beasts" (Rom. 1:20–23).

Despite their natural kindness and the sympathetic humor with which the poet treats them, Reformed theological perspectives would most likely induce readers to assign the fauns and satyrs to the category of souls for whom there can be no excuse (Rom. 1:20), and also no hope of salvation. Tension between the characteristic values of idyllic pastoral and those of theological discourse becomes especially intense at this moment in the canto. Reformed theology can consider the gentle and well-meaning but incorrigible sylvans decisively reprobate, like the Cambridgeshire villagers whom Greenham had had to give over as "intractable and unteachable" (Introduction, pp. 11–12, above). Readers who bring to bear on this passage the Catholic doctrine of implicit faith might be more optimistic, but the sylvans seem incapable of advancing even to the point of being "prepared to embrace as true whatever the church has prescribed" (ch. 1, p. 43, n. 79). Still, even as theological perspectives predict for Una's rescuers an eternal exclusion from grace, the pastoral and romance modulations of the episode solicit a combination of sympathy and nostalgia. Some readers, perhaps all, will feel that these sympathetic creatures' plight is tragic. Though the fauns and satyrs seem to be willing and decent, the divine will has apparently abandoned them either, as a Protestant reading would suggest, to damnation, or, as Catholic perspectives could predict, to the milder but still painful exile of Limbo.

Una's escape from these eager but feckless pupils obliquely attributes their exclusion from grace to its ultimate source, providence, which again becomes the canto's focus:

> It fortuned a noble warlike knight
> By just occasion to that forrest came,
> To seeke his kindred, and the lignage right,
> From whence he tooke his well deserved name   (vi.20.1–4)

Like the pilot's "fool-happie oversight" and the fauns' and satyrs' fortunate rescue of Una, this "chance" event has a discernible secondary cause, its "just occasion" in Satyrane's desire to visit the nation from which he sprang. Although "he had in armes abroad wonne muchell fame, / And fild far landes with glorie of his might" (20.5–6), Satyrane's return exemplifies sturdy adherence to a familiar classical virtue, Virgilian *pietas*.

> evermore it was his manner faire,
> After long labours and adventures spent,
> Unto those native woods for to repaire,
> To see his sire and ofspring auncient.   (vi.30.1–4)

The thoroughgoing classical cast of the episode as a whole aids readers to consider Roman *pietas* – duty to country, family, and gods – as one of the canto's potential topics.[29] Despite the fame he has achieved in human society, Satyrane does not disdain his rustic paternity and "native woods." His visits seem to manifest an inherited capacity for love based on likeness of nature, love similar to that which the satyr-nation earlier showed toward Una. In fact, Satyrane's genealogy, reported in a striking passage often overlooked or thoroughly rewritten by critics' perceptions of it, provides no reason to expect that this expatriate woodlander could attain to the nobility evident in his moral integrity and record of lofty achievement. Satyrane was conceived when his mother Thyamis ("passion"), daughter of Labryde ("turbulent" or "greedy"), was raped by a satyr, who held her for some time "captive to his sensuall desire" (I.vi.22–23). In short, Satyrane's paternal origin is a lawlessness comparable to that embodied by Sansloy at the canto's beginning, and it is to the father who embodies these passions in his "native woods" that Satyrane regularly returns (I.vi.30). Reformed theological perspectives can therefore induce us to perceive in Satyrane's recurrent returns to the forest a symbol of everyman's inescapably bestial origins and impulses. Satyrane's maternal inheritance reinforces such a reading. He descends, on the mother's side too, from a desperate expression of desire: the rape occurred while Thyamis sought urgently to "serve her turne" (22.3) on her wayward spouse, Therion ("wild beast"), who was at the time in hot pursuit of "other game and venery" (22.5).

Just before hearing Satyrane's inauspicious myth of origin, nonetheless, we learn that he has become a paragon of virtue:

> Plaine, faithfull, true, and enimy of shame,
> And ever lov'd to fight for Ladies right,
> But in vaine glorious frayes he litle did delight.   (vi.20.7–9)

Clearly Satyrane has inherited and been able to improve upon the ingenuous good nature of Spenser's satyr-kind. And he has done this to such a degree that his character explicitly recalls Red Cross', as it had appeared, "right faithful true," at the beginning of the poem. Yet the pagan ethos of I.vi invites us to understand "faithful" and "true" (at first) in restricted, social and moral senses.

This line of reasoning appears to support the argument that Satyrane's lineage reveals him to be a creature altogether of the order of nature, one whose virtues are to be considered natural products of inherent goodness.[30] As we have seen, however, Reformed theology can support a somewhat different construction: only by means of grace can natural capacities function naturally, and only through grace can authentic virtue be achieved. Such theology suggests that we should read Satyrane's nobility, which contrasts absolutely with anything he might inherit from his natural progenitors, as a consequence of the grace that has radically altered his nature. In the context of I.vi, his story illustrates in a new way that "eternall providence exceeding thought" frequently mocks the "wit of mortall wight" by eliciting goodness from places that human reason considers least promising. Satyrane's virtue is itself miraculous, inviting surprise and wonder at processes that lie beyond reason's ken. This marvel is increased by the account of Satyrane's childhood, dominated by a fiercely impetuous desire to subdue brute nature to his will (vi.25–27):

> And for to make his powre approved more,
> Wyld beasts in yron yokes he would compell;
> The spotted Panther, and the tusked Bore,
> The Pardale swift, and the Tigre cruell;

> The Antelope, and Wolfe both fierce and fell;
> And them constraine in equall teme to draw.
> Such joy he had, their stubborne harts to quell,
> And sturdie courage tame with dreadfull aw,
> That his beheast they feared, as a tyrans law.   (vi.26)

Having learned already that Satyrane has become not only "plaine, faithfull, true" as well as famed in "far landes with glorie of his might" (20.6), readers are likely to focus on details like the imposition of "yron yokes" that require beasts to forgo their natural antipathies and in "equall teme to draw." This activity then comes to represent a civilizing process generically akin to those undertaken by the earliest agents of civility, Orpheus and Amphion, whose songs civilized "stony and beastly people" symbolized by stones and beasts.[31]

Nevertheless, this imposition of order on bestiality is itself devoted to the proving of self to oneself and to others: "to make his powre approved more," where "approved" denotes "proved, demonstrated,"[32] and Satyrane is himself "fearelesse, and . . . fell" and of "horrid vew" (25.1, 3). His domination of the beasts, which can be seen (from a humanistic perspective) to dramatize an impulse toward civilization, can become (from a theological viewpoint) a war not of flesh against spirit but of flesh against flesh. In terms that echo Red Cross Knight's impulse toward prideful self-display in I.v, Satyrane's transition to the human realm betokens an advance toward worthy achievements. Yet such advances remain as always inextricably rooted in the desire to display oneself to and among enemies:

> and then his courage haught
> Desird of forreine foemen to be knowne,
> And far abroad for straunge adventures sought:
> In which his might was never overthrowne,
> But through all Faery lond his famous worth was blown.
> (vi.29.5–9)

Against this background, Satyrane's crowning achievement is his recognition, his *anagnorisis*, of Una. His already achieved virtues indicate that Satyrane has attained the highest levels of wisdom available to humankind in the absence of revelation.

The promise of less ambiguous achievement appears when Satyrane's already moral manner of life receives outward reinforcement from Una, who here most evidently represents what the theologians call the church, a "means of grace." Una's presence promises to transform Satyrane's miraculous, admirable, but so far merely moral rectitude into conscious faith. Satyrane heeds Una's "wisdome heavenly rare," compares her words with her deeds ("And when her curteous deeds he did compare, / Gan her admire," 31.3–4), and consequently "learnd her discipline of faith and veritie" (31.9). Like More's Utopians, Satyrane begins as a pagan who lives by the highest ethical standards to which non-Christian culture, and elect individuals before their calls, can aspire. When Christian revelation arrives, he takes to it as an end toward which he had long unwittingly inclined.[33] So now Satyrane's familial *pietas* is supplanted by a higher piety (33). In abetting, "with courage stout and bold," Una's escape from the satyrs, Satyrane tacitly obeys a commandment of her "discipline of faith and veritie." He joins those who "forsake houses, or brethren, or sisters, or father, or mother, or wife . . . for [Christ's] name's sake" and who consequently bid fair to "inherit everlasting life" (Matt. 19:29; cf. Mark 10:29).

The way to salvation always entails at least apparent reversals, however, and in a miniature reprise of Red Cross Knight's early confrontation with a specious hermit, Satyrane and Una happen upon

> A wearie wight forwandring by the way,
> And towards him they gan in hast to ride . . .
> But he them spying, gan to turne aside,
> For feare as seemd, or for some feigned losse
>
> (vi.34.3–4; 7–8)

This figure's behavior can tantalize readers as effectively as it does Satyrane and Una: "more greedy they of newes, fast towards him do crosse." Like Duessa's coyness, the "weary wight's" evasiveness creates an appetite, and with it an inclination to believe.

The devil's skill at enlisting in his service even people of good will becomes conspicuous during the interchange between this pilgrim, eventually revealed to be Archimago, and Una and Satyrane. As in his earlier appearance, the disguised tempter's replies to Una and to her protector's questions are rife with inner contradictions. At first he can offer no "[t]ydings of warre, [or] of adventures new" (36.2–3). Within a moment, however, he can relate in grim detail a story of two knights whom he has witnessed "this day" "arraung'd in battell new" (38.4). The immediate result of this tale is a flurry of regressive actions on the part of Satyrane. Hearing that the combatant who has supposedly slain Red Cross Knight "hence doth wonne / Foreby a fountaine . . . / Washing his bloudy wounds" (39.7–9), Satyrane marches forth "in hast," and Una finds herself once again temporarily abandoned by a rash defender (40.2–3). Arriving "whereas that Pagan proud," soon identified as Sansloy, "him selfe did rest, / In secret shadow by a fountaine side" (vi.40.5–6), Satyrane accosts him with "fowle reprochfull words," preliminary evidence that Satyrane's abandonment of Una entails a return to his childhood eagerness for dominance. The reproaches he selects, though conventional in chivalric romance, have by now acquired special significance in Spenser's narrative. A combination of proud self-assertion, vengeful wrath, and exaggerated accusation, Satyrane's speech invokes the ethos of Sansjoy:

> Arise thou cursed Miscreaunt,
> That hast with knightlesse guile and trecherous train
> Faire knighthood fowly shamed, and doest vaunt
> That good knight of the Redcrosse to have slain:
> Arise, and with like treason now maintain
> Thy guilty wrong, or else thee guilty yield.   (vi.41.1–6)

Although Spenser has revealed this miscreant's identity to the reader (40.7–8), Satyrane has heard only that he slew Red Cross in a combat that found both "arraung'd in battell new, / Both breathing vengeaunce, both of wrathfull hew" (38.4–5). Satyrane's impassioned attachment to Una's cause leads him here to exaggerations we can feel to be extreme, given the evidence so far available to the speaker.

Sansloy himself points this out, and does so in terms which provide a forceful reminder that he is an enemy who ought to be combated (I.vi.42). Yet in this just combat, Satyrane's emotions and motives tarnish his endeavors in ways that become especially perceptible in the imagery of the battle. As was the case in earlier combats in *The Faerie Queene*, opposed warriors are presented in ways that insist on their likeness. Both are "furious and fell" (43.1); both "fell revenge pursue" (44.1); both alternate between moments of frenzied combat and periods of rest that serve to renew their fierce intensity (45.2–4); both are described by means of an unflattering epic simile: "As when two Bores with rancling malice met, / Their gory sides fresh bleeding fiercely fret" (44.4–9). While undertaking what is objectively a skirmish in the grand cosmic war of good against evil, Satyrane becomes, subjectively, as malicious and vengeful as the boar to which he is compared.

The spiritual similarity of the combatants becomes still more evident in a striking visual image, when "with their drerie wounds and bloudy gore / They both deformed, scarsely could be known" (45.5–6). Deformity here provides a variant expression of the privation of being that,

by Augustinian definition, evil essentially is. Satyrane has as surely lost
the "form" of man here as had Fradubio (I.ii.33.3).[34] And yet, in the
midst of this dehumanizing, spiritually destructive battle, Spenser urges
us to see that Satyrane's lawless motives are not unmixed with loftier
matter. When Una arrives, "that proud Sarazin," betraying once more
the double nature of his pride, is "burnt in his intent" (15.7):

> he gan revive the memory
> Of his lewd lusts, and late attempted sin,
> And left the doubtfull battell hastily,
> To catch her, newly offred to his eie   (vi.46.2–5)

When Satyrane interrupts this renewed assault on Una (46.7–8; cf. 42.3),
Sansloy's angry words invite us to see that Satyrane is now dramatizing
caritas in action and has become, from the natural man's point of view,
a Christian fool: "Most sencelesse man he, that himselfe doth hate, / To
love another" (47.5–6). In the midst of his corrupting battle, therefore,
Satyrane can be dimly yet definitely viewed as a defective imitator of
Christ, devoting himself to another's cause. On the loftiest plane, that
is, Satyrane's last moment in *The Faerie Queene*, Book I, presents an image
of Law's essence, *caritas*, locked in eternal struggle with a demonic negation of all law.

Alternatively, that unresolved combat can remind us of "the inadequacy
of unaided human nature,"[35] inadequacy to overcome evil without special intervention from on high. Tridentine Catholicism could agree with
Protestantism's insistence that human nature needs grace if it is to combat evil – though some versions of Catholic theology could then proceed to interpret Satyrane's behavior before his alliance with Una as
preparation for grace, his subsequent works as actual contributions to
his salvation. Protestant readings would be more likely to perceive that,
by calling attention at its end to Satyrane's continuing need for special
grace, *The Faerie Queene* I.vi concludes with an image that presents holy
action as it must always appear in this life. Having received the call that
enabled him to accept Una's "discipline of faith and veritie," Satyrane
will nonetheless always achieve sin, even while pursuing his most charitable actions. So construed, the concluding chivalric image of *The Faerie
Queene* I.vi provides a conception of holiness that is at once humbling
and approachable. That image soon receives extended elaboration; it
does so, that is, for readers who accept the subsequent cantos' invitations to construct a detailed version of Christian heroism.

5

RECONSTRUCTING HEROISM

Interpreters who bring to their reading a relatively well-articulated knowledge of theological doctrine can, as we have seen, construe *The Faerie Queene* I.iv–vi as a sustained exploration of the darker implications of predestinarian theology, concluding in the Satyrane episode with the cheering possibility that grace may at any moment effect a miraculous transcendence of natural limits. In I.vii–viii, such readers will find material from which to extend this hint of metaphysical optimism, optimism which is contained and tempered by a resurgence of scriptural allusions that can be read as reaffirmations of Reformed theology's broadest doctrines. For readers bringing such doctrines to bear on Spenser's text, the heroism illustrated in these cantos can appear worthy of imitation, totally dependent on unpredictable effusions of grace, and markedly ephemeral. The image of this appealing yet fragile heroism will soon appear fully formed in Arthur. The declining fortunes of Red Cross Knight meanwhile provide a variety of perspectives from which that heroism can be clearly perceived.

Apparently innocent details near the end of I.vi can help to prepare us for the knight's disastrous encounter with Orgoglio. The most notable of these details links Red Cross with Sansloy, the "pagan proud" who could recently be found "foreby a fountaine" where "him selfe did rest" (39.8; 40.5). Ten stanzas later on, we find Red Cross Knight in a similar condition and topography:

> whereas he wearie sate,
> To rest him selfe, foreby a fountaine side,
> Disarmed all of yron-coted Plate   (vii.2.6–8)[1]

For many readers, the implied comparison between Sansloy and the weary Red Cross will lend support to commentators' often-repeated assertion that Red Cross' behavior exhibits pridefulness. His removal of the symbolic armor signifies presumption, the argument runs, because by that action he forgoes what has been his best defense, having become overconfident as a result of successive triumphs over Error, Sansfoy, and Sansjoy.[2] The argument seems to become irrefutable when Red Cross succumbs to a character whose allegorical label, we learn at vii.14, means "pride." Though widely accepted, this reading depends on a strictly limited selection of details from the text. Our last glimpse of Red Cross stressed the knight's sadness: "Yet sad he was . . . And yet more sad" (vi.2). Readers who recall this dejection would be prepared to note that it is complemented and deepened now, a full canto later, by the one explicit assessment of his mood at the beginning of I.vii. The knight is said here to be not exultant but exhausted: "he wearie sate . . . Disarmed all of yron-coted Plate."

This oddly dismissive description of the knight's armor certainly could indicate his ignorance of its value,[3] but the phrase can also communicate a sense of oppressive weight. And this oppressiveness can induce us to infer that the knight's usual means of defense, transformed into a wearying burden, now lays him open to danger. This point receives support when the "wofull Dwarfe" takes up his fallen master's "forlorne weed . . . His mightie armour . . . His silver shield . . . His poynant speare . . . The ruefull moniments of heavinesse" (vii.19). This "heavinesse" denotes the mood of onlookers who might view the weaponry of a fallen warrior, no doubt; but the word can also deftly imply the Reformed theological notion that helped us to construct and explain the knight's conflict with Sansjoy (ch. 4, p. 95, above): an unbroken "tediousness" will eventually weigh down anyone for whom conscious devotion to Christ is lost in "traditions of men" that induce him to seek salvation in himself. And for the elect, grace itself, symbolized by the knight's now oppressive armor, sometimes imposes that deprivation of "rest, quietness, security, [and] spiritual pleasure."[4]

The armor's weight suggests that this is the burden which drives the knight to seek escape, not through the violent anger that Sansjoy exhibits, but through a more seductive diversion:

> He feedes upon the cooling shade, and bayes
> His sweatie forehead in the breathing wind,
> Which through the trembling leaves full gently playes
> Wherein the cherefull birds of sundry kind
> Do chaunt sweet musick, to delight his mind   (vii.3.1–5)

The conventional attributes of a *locus amoenus* here, like those of its prototypes in Ariosto, Tasso, and elsewhere, suggest comprehensive immersion in gratifications of sense.[5]

Joyless because overburdened by spiritual labors which he does not comprehend and at which he can never succeed, Red Cross turns to sat-

isfactions which can be had at lower cost. The situation that immediately thereafter develops in this luxurious garden might be characterized by Greenham's remark that "prosperity is a drunkenness" from which
the Lord awakens us "by inward temptations and outward crosses . . .
lest we should lose the experience of our knowledge and faith in Christ,
and seek some easier kind of life for flesh and blood."[6] Red Cross seeks
escape from spiritual tribulation in an illusory paradise that promises,
precisely, "some easier kind of life for flesh and blood."

Images of bathing provide an index of the knight's progressive apos-
tasy. At first, he "bayes" his forehead in the wind; shortly, reunited with
Duessa, he "bathe[s] in pleasaunce of the joyous shade"; finally, "goodly
court he made still to his Dame, / Pourd out in loosnesse on the grassy
grownd" (7.1–2). The full consequences of removing the armor become
apparent now, for Red Cross has as emphatically lost the "forme of man"
as Fradubio and Satyrane did earlier (ch. 4, p. 113, above). "Pourd out,"
Red Cross Knight has become mysteriously united in substance with
the spring from which he drank. That spring provides occasion for an
etiological myth that explains the protagonist's accelerating spiritual
decline. Though it is pointedly Ovidian in content and tone, Spenser's
redaction of Ovid's narrative of Salmacis invites doctrinal interpretation,
especially because the nymph's story incorporates an intriguing divergence from its source. The nymph in *Metamorphoses* is notorious for
refusing ever to interrupt her leisure to join Diana's hunt.[7] Spenser's
nymph has been an energetic participant in that hunt, but having become "quite tyr'd with heat of scorching ayre" she has "[s]at downe to
rest in middest of the race" (5.3–4).

The knight falls into bondage, precisely, when he tires in a race that
recalls and parallels Diana's hunt, symbol of chastity's destruction of
bestial vices. Significant implications of Red Cross' and the nymph's
shared behavior are suggested by the words "in middest of the race."
For some readers, this phrase will echo a conspicuous instance of the
Bible's recurrent description of the pursuit of holiness as a race: "Let us
run with patience the race that is set before us, looking unto Jesus the
author and finisher of our faith, who for the joy that was set before him,
endured the cross . . . Consider therefore him . . . lest ye should be
wearied and faint in your minds" (Heb. 12:1–3). This admonition to
make Christ the source of perseverance during the wearying struggle
includes a reminder that sufferings can themselves be signs of divine
favor: "despise not the chastening of the Lord . . . for whom the Lord

loveth, he chasteneth." He designs this chastening to enable all believers to complete Red Cross Knight's quest: "that we might be partakers of his holiness." And after the chastisement has ended, it will renew for "them which are thereby exercised," the capacity for joy which the knight has lost, "the quiet fruit of righteousness" (Heb. 12:5–11).[8] Readings that relate this scriptural context to Spenser's passage would infer that Red Cross' otherwise unexplained weariness arises because he has lost sight specifically of "his dying lord." Failing to "consider Him," Red Cross becomes "wearied and faints." As we shall see more clearly below, the knight's weariness is exacerbated by failure to recognize that worldly suffering supplies evidence of spiritual health: "For whom the Lord loveth, he chasteneth." Of these possibilities "the gentle knight" remains characteristically "unweeting" (vii.6.1).

Red Cross requires a dramatic awakening, and receives it when Orgoglio's eruption into the poem re-establishes the apocalyptic as one of the narrative's contributing kinds. Allusions to John's Apocalypse have been intermittently visible before. The word "intermittently" warrants emphasis, to counteract a habit of overstatement which the Book of Revelation appears to inspire among literary scholars engaged in its study. From early in twentieth-century Spenser studies, Revelation has so often been counted among the most important influences on Spenser's Legend of Holiness that recent work often takes the view for granted. Reconsideration of apocalypse as a kind, and re-examination of the content of John's book and of the responses it typically received during Elizabethan times, can provide grounds for fresh perceptions of climactic episodes of Red Cross Knight's quest. Readers whose constructions of *The Faerie Queene* we are most concerned to trace (Introduction, p. 18) would be likely to possess a notion of the apocalyptic that is akin to the version I am about to present.

As characterized in recent literary studies, apocalypse is often reduced to only one of its many features: a concentration on the Last Judgment and the social and political turmoil expected immediately to precede that promised end. This assumption that eschatology is Revelation's predominant concern appears so natural to twentieth-century interpreters of Spenser that, for most, the idea hardly warrants a second thought.[9] This idea can dominate readings of the Legend of Holiness when they receive compelling formulations like that of Patricia Parker, whose argument gains force in part because it so accurately states unexamined assumptions shared by most readers. Having listed major features of *Faerie Queene*, Book I, that derive from Revelation, Parker concludes that the entire collection of episodes, characters, echoes, and allusions suggests "conclusion and consummation," that this establishes a powerful expectation of apocalyptic finality, and yet that

[i]n the very Book most remarkable for its sense of an ending, the end turns out to be less like the Apocalypse than the romance *Odyssey*, where Ulysses, after twenty years of wandering, returns to tell Penelope that he must set out again . . . The traditional function of Apocalypse is to portray the enemy as already defeated, in a vision of the end which places us outside the monsters we are still inside.[10]

To re-examine Revelation is to discover the usefuless of recognizing a distinction between "apocalypse" as the name for a genre and "apocalypse" as shorthand for "apocalyptic eschatology."[11] As apocalypse (the genre) was established by numerous Jewish, Intertestamental, and early Christian texts, and developed in later periods, it embraced a great deal more than the eschatological prophecies to which ordinary usage reduces it. Apocalyptic texts could be vehicles for the revelation of a great variety of mysteries, including "learned material on angelology, meteorology, geography and astronomy . . . The genre was designed to achieve many ends, only some of which should be properly called apocalypticism in the sense of apocalyptic eschatology."[12]

That John's Apocalypse was true to type in its readiness to accommodate and transmit teachings of broad scope, and that this aim overshadowed the book's concern with eschatology, seemed self-evident to prominent interpreters in Spenser's era. Energetic English Reformers like Bale, for instance, present as axiomatic the view that Revelation is "[t]he very complete sum and whole knitting up . . . of the universal verities of the bible."[13] For Bullinger, too, the chief aim of Revelation was not to depict the end of the world and the Last Judgment but to propagate central doctrines of Christianity.[14] When John does treat eschatology, such Reformed commentators believe, he employs it more to induce an anticipation of closure than to depict its actual achievement. On this view, the strangely repetitious, overlapping, seemingly endless disasters recorded in Revelation always insist on the reverse of Parker's formulation: Apocalypse provides a vision of the monsters we remain still inside, which will certainly be defeated – perhaps soon, but not yet.[15]

In readings guided by views like these, Revelation's commentators can hardly be said to focus chiefly on political history, the future of the

Church, or visions of achieved closure and consummation.[16] The commentators are more accurately described as insisting that the book propagates doctrines which apply at all times and in all places, relevant "no less unto us, than if now the bearer entering into the church, should deliver these letters unto us." In Revelation, as a typical formulation has it, "we shall see, as it were in a table set before us, what the true and right doctrine of the church is . . . [and also] what the false and corrupt doctrine."[17] Although the teachings will (in this reading) be consistent, the order in which they are presented and the historical matters that accompany or manifest them will not appear in temporal or logical sequence. The segments of teaching and event never form a continuous narrative in the way that modern epitomes, unlike Renaissance ones, imply that they do or should.[18]

In the view of Reformed commentators, Revelation displays a different kind of continuity. For them, Reformed doctrine speaks through every syllable of John's Apocalypse, a book which supports the theses that human nature ("the flesh") is thoroughly corrupt even in its highest faculties; that salvation must therefore be received through faith and the predestined grace that brings it; that belief in human merit is the most insidiously corrupting error promoted by the emissaries (especially by monks, friars, and papal legates) of Roman Catholicism; and that divine providence always determines earthly events in ways that benefit, however mysteriously, the Church and its individual members.[19] Readers who entertain expectations of such large-scale doctrinal meaning in Revelation can carry those expectations with them to places in Spenser's poem that invoke features of apocalypse or directly echo John's Apocalypse.

Orgoglio brings apocalyptic implications into I.vii when he bursts upon the scene just as Red Cross and Duessa have undertaken to become, in a literal sense, one flesh. The timing of this monster's apparition helps bring doctrinal perspectives into play. To lie with Duessa is at once a literal act of sensual self-indulgence and a symbol of adulterous betrayal of humankind's due relationship to God, the bond metaphorically expressed (e.g. in Jeremiah 2–6) as conjugal love, and dramatized in Revelation's presentation of the Bride of the Lamb.[20] Like the conjugal metaphor, the armor of Ephesians 6 symbolizes (ch. 2, pp. 54–55, above) every elect soul's right relationship to Christ, and Spenser here again brings this symbolic armor into prominence. Having earlier in this passage cast off those grace-created gifts of sanctification that human will has the power to reject (ch. 2, p. 62, above) – the shield of faith, breastplate of righteousness, helmet of salvation, and the rest – Red Cross now forgoes the girdle of Truth, which represents, Latimer and other commentators say, "a restraint or continence" preventing "lechery or other sinfulness." This girding must be "in the heart."[21]

As Latimer's permissive phrasing suggests, Red Cross' action represents humankind's radical evil, "sin" in the absolute, unitary sense. The act implies on the one hand a fracturing of the soul's spiritual relationship to God, and hence sin as negation; at the same time, it represents sin's positive, captivating energy. Fornication is an especially appropriate metaphor for the nature of sin because the sexual drive can so readily seem at once to be deliberately willed and yet involuntary. In some ways a phallic image, the giant embodies Red Cross' aroused sexual desire,[22] but Orgoglio is also an external oppressor and a minister of divine justice.

Although Red Cross arrived at the spring in a state of weariness, his liaison with Duessa has brought on this energetic onslaught from a complex symbolic beast whose name means "pride." On reaching I.vii.10, in fact, interpreters can legitimately begin describing Red Cross as proud. In vii.7, the knight has made a sexual conquest, and the spiritual consequences of that victory are suggested by Orgoglio's phallic features, which imply that Red Cross, too, exults "through presumption of his matchless might." Having conquered by means of the flesh, Red Cross is at the same time conquered by it. He is overcome by his own sensual impulses, and also by an exceptionally dangerous mental characteristic of "the flesh," the desire to win paradise by embracing a religion made in the image of his own mental and emotional preferences. This is the broadest theological implication of the knight's sexual liaison: he has married himself to a religion of outward ceremonies that attributes merit to good works and so embodies everything that the evil demons of Revelation also represent. In this sense, readers can perceive Orgoglio as a more than usually specific embodiment of "the knight's fallen state,"[23] for Red Cross' condition here reflects the arrogant impotence of natural man.

Yet to Red Cross' consciousness, only the enemy's potency is apparent: the knight feels "haplesse, and eke hopelesse," and

> all in vaine
> Did to him pace, sad battaile to darrayne,
> Disarmd, disgrast, and inwardly dismayde,
> And eke so faint in every joynt and vaine,

> Through that fraile fountaine, which him feeble made,
> That scarsely could he weeld his bootlesse single blade.
>
> (vii.11.4–9)

Having discarded his sources of strength, Red Cross now feels not only "sad" but "hapless," fated to fail. For the first time, he explicitly shares the reader's awareness that his efforts are "all in vaine." He experiences the desperate sadness of undertaking solitary battle while having "departed from grace given," as the Thirty-Nine Articles describe that condition (Article XVI). The isolation registered in the reference to "his bootlesse single blade" can be taken to refer most specifically to the absence of that grace which alone can make the knight's weapons effective. When "single" in that sense, even the elect soul's possession of the sword of the word remains useless. In short, Red Cross suffers the pangs felt by the elect whenever God withdraws his influence and they consequently feel as if they might number among the reprobate ("dis-made").[24]

As a result of these manifold deficiencies, Red Cross readily succumbs when Orgoglio strikes:

> so maynly mercilesse,
> That could have overthrowne a stony towre,
> And were not heavenly grace, that him did blesse,
> He had beene pouldred all, as thin as flowre:
> But he was wary of that deadly stowre,
> And lightly lept from underneath the blow:
> Yet so exceeding was the villeins powre,
> That with the wind it did him overthrow,
> And all his sences stound, that still he lay full low.   (vii.12)

Calamity once again coincides with the workings of providence, whose unwavering kindness, throughout what appears to be a history of relentless disaster, remains a dominant theme of the apocalyptic kind. Grace – whose blessing, Elizabethan doctrines would urge readers to perceive, operates *through* the knight's wariness ("heavenly grace, that him did blesse . . . But he was wary" 12.3–5) – allows him to avoid the annihilation of being "pouldred all," reduced to the dust that is any completely "disgrast" man's essence (cf. 14.3). Because Red Cross has fallen so far from grace, his wariness is most appropriately seen not as a consequence of the grace which enables cooperation in works of holiness but as the limiting grace that prevents believers from falling into irrecoverable sinfulness.[25] The wind that fells the knight at once parodies and represents, here at vii.12 and at vii.9, the Holy Spirit.[26] As God's active agent in the world, His Spirit directly undertakes not only the punishment but also the rescue of sinners; functioning as a collateral effect of Orgoglio's blow, its power brings about Red Cross' fall.[27]

Having fallen to this power, Red Cross lies "still . . . full low." He suffers a sudden paralysis that images more emphatically than ever before the spiritual torpor into which he had already lapsed in Duessa's company. Having often infirmly "stood," a posture the Pauline text enjoins ("Take unto you the whole armor of God, that you may be able to . . . stand," Eph. 6), he has declined, as we have seen, to supinity, "poured out in looseness."[28] Red Cross' earlier myopia and hardness of hearing now become total when Orgoglio's blow stupifies him – "all his sences stound" (12.9). The knight can now be seen as an image of spiritual death, humankind's natural condition as Protestants conceived of it. The "slombred sencelesse corse" of vii.15.6 precisely represents this nature. Having fastened on this image as a significant detail, readers would have difficulty seeing Red Cross as an instance of human nature as (some versions of) Catholic doctrine perceived it: comparable to a prisoner who "if the Holy Ghost do but untie his bands, and reach him His hand of grace, then can he stand of himself, and will his own salvation, or anything else that is good." Reformed Protestants, by contrast, saw human nature as "not only sick and weak, but even stark dead: which cannot stir though the keeper untie his bolts and chains, nor hear though he sound a trumpet in his ear." Those dead in sin have no power whatever "to move or stir; and therefore [they] cannot so much as desire or do anything that is truly good of [themselves]" until God supplies "the spirit of grace to quicken and revive [them]: and then being thus revived, the will beginneth to will good things at the very same time, when God by his spirit first infuseth grace."[29] As we shall see, the Protestant notion of being "dead in sin" can help us interpret crucial elements of Red Cross Knight's further progress, including the metaphors that describe his condition after I.vii.15, the possibilities and the limits of Arthur's liberation of him in viii, and the nature of the support which Mercy supplies in x.[30]

Although he first arrives on the scene appearing as an amalgam of signs that overtly denote various forms of pride, Red Cross Knight's gigantic antagonist soon begins to acquire political dimensions that can bring historical allegory to the fore. His alliance with Duessa initiates this transformation, and his imprisoning of Red Cross' "corse," "in a Dongeon deepe . . . without remorse" (vii.15.7, 9), elaborates it. In Orgoglio's dungeon, Red Cross enters a prolonged spiritual torpor analogous to that into which the temporal powers of Europe had fallen during (as Protestants viewed it) the dark age when Kirkrapine had license to plunder with impunity (iii.16–18). Red Cross' captivity symbolizes, that is, not only the individual sinner's bondage to the sin in his members but also England's collective enslavement both to sin and, as commentators have often said, to sin's outward ministers.

Enslavement to these human ministers of evil becomes the primary concern of the passage when Orgoglio makes Duessa "his deare," and she begins overtly to resemble "great Babylon, the mother of whoredoms" (Rev. 17:5):

> He gave her gold and purple pall to weare,
> And triple crowne set on her head full hye,
> And her endowd with royall majestye   (vii.16.3–5)

The giant next augments Duessa's power over men's bodies as well as their souls, and the text suggests that the alliance between Orgoglio and Duessa is designed specifically to inspire terror:

> Then for to make her dreaded more of men,
> And peoples harts with awfull terrour tye,
> A monstrous beast ybred in filthy fen
> He chose, which he had kept long time in darksome den.
>   (vii.16.6–9)

At the end of the beast's portrait, deliberate terror again receives stress from rhythm, rhyme, and the Alexandrine's last word:

> Upon this dreadfull Beast with sevenfold head
> He set the false Duessa, for more aw and dread.   (vii.18.8–9)

To an interpretation constructed from the perspectives of Protestant ecclesiology, this stress on the "awfull terrour" imposed on "peoples harts" can represent the dread of literal harm to person or property which arose when the religious authority of Rome entered into tyrannical alliance with political power. Clearly, too, English readers who desired further reform of the national church could perceive and apply the images of Duessa and her beast differently than would interpreters eager to preserve the Church of England's recently and still uneasily established structure. Those images could readily represent Catholicism in the eyes of both categories of readers; they could also represent, for the frustrated reformer, the coercive power of the imperfectly reformed Elizabethan

Church itself. And for members of both parties, the alliance of Duessa and beast could represent a less historically specific theme: that political power corrupts whatever church comes to possess it – a theme to which Dante had given powerful, similarly apocalyptic expression (*Purgatorio* 32.110–60).

Beyond these constructions, moreover, Duessa's dominance over "the beast with sevenfold head" (Revelation 17), which she later employs as if it were a war-horse, figures an idea that will move some readers from ecclesiology and political history back toward dogmatic theology. Placed as she is, Duessa embodies the claim that human powers can manage and control sin. More effectively than any of its other mechanisms of ideological domination, the Roman Church's claim to possess the power to forgive or withhold forgiveness – to bind or to loose this beast by preaching themselves (as Luther, Tyndale, and other Protestant polemicists put it) rather than Christ – brought the populations of Europe into bondage to the Pope's coercive law: "And peoples harts with awfull terrour tye." That the beast can also represent sin, in something like the complexity and extensiveness which Reformed theology ascribed to sin, becomes evident in an impressive epic simile:

> that renowmed Snake
> Which great Alcides in Stremona slew,
> Long fostred in the filth of Lerna lake,
> Whose many heads out budding ever new,
> Did breed him endlesse labour to subdew   (vii.17.1–5)

Thus described, the hydra/Hercules allusion offers an epitome of the experience of moral striving that Red Cross Knight has so far undergone. Sin's infinite variations place it beyond the control of human consciousness and moral effort.

The hydra simile enables readers to perceive doctrinal truth here by revealing that Red Cross' situation is at once comparable to but also significantly different from Hercules' struggle with the hydra. The conventional hydra had many heads – in Ovid, a hundred of them – and when destroyed, each head yielded two still fiercer replacements.[31] "But this same Monster much more ugly was; / For seven great heads out of his body grew" (17.7). Just why seven heads should make this monster uglier than its many-headed progenitors momentarily puzzles the mind. One way to resolve the dissonance is to interpret the number in scriptural terms, for the Bible frequently employs seven to indicate a complete array, or simply an enormous number.[32] This recognition can bring affiliated doctrinal perspectives into play, and these recall that each of the seven sins produces multifarious offspring and arises from a single unitary source. The monster is uglier than Alcides' victim because its seven heads represent, in Spenser as in Revelation, sin's infinite variety, which can never be subdued, not even by "labour" which is literally "endlesse."[33]

As a descendent of Job's Leviathan and a conflation of the dragon and the beast of Revelation 12–13, Spenser's beast represents anew the Satanic root of all sin:

> His tayle was stretched out in wondrous length,
>   That to the house of heavenly gods it raught,
>   And with extorted powre, and borrow'd strength,
>   The ever-burning lamps from thence it brought,
>   And prowdly threw to ground, as things of nought
>
> (vii.18.1–5)

Although interpreters can readily attach political and historical implications to the scriptural monsters to which these lines allude, the scholars of Geneva had no doubt that the dragon of Revelation 12:3–4 represents above all "the devil, and all his power." Authoritative Reformed interpretations of the passage focus on such general doctrinal meanings to the exclusion of the political or narrowly sectarian. Even outspoken puritans like William Fulke, for example, join other major commentators in interpreting the stars in Revelation as ministers, including those who teach true doctrine, who become corrupt and are dragged to earth by the dragon's tail, which represents the seductive "lust of earthly things."[34]

The conspicuous apocalyptic modulation of such passages can induce readers to share Red Cross' sensation of overburdened hopelessness. Construed as symbols of gigantic, impalpable, metaphysical antagonists, the knight's enemies are far more overpowering and insidious than the Pope, or Philip of Spain, or other temporary human avatars of evil. The invitation to construct an apocalyptic version of fundamental conceptions of evil prepares the way for an equally apocalyptic emphasis on fundamental notions of human capacity. And when Arthur first enters the poem, we can perceive how specifically Spenser's reconstruction of heroism derives its identifying features from the evil possibilities delineated by Red Cross Knight's collapse.

From his first appearance, Arthur's harmonious relations with higher powers receive special stress. He comes – to transfer to him an apocalyptic description that Spenserians have so far granted only to Una – "clothed with the sun" (cf. ch. 3, p. 84, above). This perception is likely to occur to readers who recognize that the scriptural "woman clothed with the sun" represents holy people, individually or collectively, clothed with Christ, as are all who wear the Christian armor: "His glitterand armour shined farre away, / Like glauncing light of Phoebus brightest ray" (vii.29.4–5; cf. ch. 1, pp. 45–46, above). Arthur's panoply appears to reflect the cheering illumination of the sun, symbol of the Son. This sign of the hero's ultimate allegiance becomes at once more personal and more historically specific because the lights on Arthur's armor include not only the sun but also subordinate luminaries that reflect in smaller compass the ultimate glory: his bauldric "shynd, like twinkling stars, with stons most pretious rare" (29.9).

> And in the midst thereof one pretious stone
>   Of wondrous worth, and eke of wondrous mights,
>   Shapt like a Ladies head, exceeding shone,
>   Like Hesperus emongst the lesser lights   (vii.30.1–4)

Though national and personal ties are more limited, the loving service of Gloriana/Elizabeth and the service of God coexist without strain. Such implications will be especially likely to occur, at any rate, to readers who have learned to read Revelation as contemporary authorities read it.[35]

The same implications, which express an ideological proposition favored by the Tudors, would also reassure interpreters who were comfortable with the Elizabethan *status quo*. But these implications precede a surprising modulation of tone which theological perspectives might induce less politically comfortable interpreters to scrutinize carefully. This tonal shift is effected by the description of Arthur's helmet:

> His haughtie helmet, horrid all with gold,
>   Both glorious brightnesse, and great terrour bred;
>   For all the crest a Dragon did enfold
>   With greedie pawes, and over all did spred
>   His golden wings: his dreadfull hideous hed
>   Close couched on the bever, seem'd to throw
>   From flaming mouth bright sparkles fierie red,
>   That suddeine horror to faint harts did show;
> And scaly tayle was stretcht adowne his backe full low.   (vii.31)

For readers prepared to assimilate the hero's armor to its Pauline antecedents, these lines present Arthur's "helmet of salvation" in a shape that

both surprises and potentially carries its own commentary. For interpreters thinking in genetic terms, of course, the dragon-helmet might
recall a variety of antecedents: the chimerae on Turnus' shield in *Aeneid*
(7.785–86)[36], Arthur's helmet in Geoffrey of Monmouth,[37] or the dragon
on Soliman's helmet in *Jerusalem Delivered* (19.15). Literally, of course,
all of these express the military utility of fierce-looking armor when it is
turned against "faint hearts." This threatening monster – despite its
"dreadfull hideous hed" throwing "from flaming mouth bright sparkles
fierie red" which inspires "suddeine horror to faint harts" – has been
considered defensive and enervated because its "scaly tayle was stretcht
adowne his backe full low."[38] Perceived together with the dragon's other
attributes, however, that stretching tail can contribute an effect of insidiously dangerous reach, and so reinforce the likelihood that the
dragon-helmet expresses a terrifying aspect of the power Arthur represents, a divine power which inherently inspires salutary terror. Embedded in, even crowning Arthur's helmet, the source of this terror can be
seen as a salient part of this elect man's best defense and of his "hope of
salvation." In a remarkably novel way, Arthur's helmet invites the recognition that the old serpent himself plays a necessary role in humankind's individual and collective salvation. The dragon must somehow
belong to the spiritual equipment that believers put on when grace enables them to don the whole armor of God.

This seems a curious paradox, but various doctrinal explanations suggest themselves. Some readers might recall, for instance, that sin works
through the divine law itself: "I once was alive, without the law: but when
the commandment came, sin revived, But I died . . . Sin, that it might
appear sin, wrought death in me by that which is good, that sin might
be out of measure sinful by the commandment" (Rom. 7:9–13). In light
of interpretations current in Elizabethan England, this Pauline assessment of sin's capacity to exploit even God's law to achieve corrupting
purposes helps to explain the nature of the bondage from which Arthur
will rescue Red Cross Knight.[39] Interpreting Romans 7, Thomas Becon
points out that although "sin is always in us . . . it is as though it were
buried or asleep. For it disquieteth us not, it vexeth us not, it tormenteth
us not." We consequently continue to heap up sins to burden us further. "But then that thunderbolt . . . the law of God striketh the conscience . . . then beginneth sin . . . to wax alive again, so that now we
begin to know, how mighty a thing sin is, which taketh God away from
us, and casteth us down headlong unto the Devil and hell fire."[40]

This comparison of the law to a thunderbolt is not gratuitous. As Becon also points out, "thunder and lightning and smoke" accompanied the promulgation of the law on Mount Sinai because the law's properties are similar to those phenomena: "it worketh effectiously in the heart, to terrify and fear, and to drive a man to desperation."[41] Sin's action through the law is absolute, for it engenders a condition which Becon, like many Roman Catholic theologians, calls "contrition," and "where true contrition is, there is no other thing, than the kingdom, power, and regiment of sin." Where sin does its work through the law, making itself "known to be sin indeed," it reveals that the law's demands are infinite: when "of one sin infinite sins are made [and] the sinner can find no rest . . . there . . . floweth nothing out of that, but plain desperation."[42]

These reflections can endow with new meanings – or at least newly specific ones – some conspicuous features of the monster which Arthur arrives to combat. The earthquake to which Orgoglio is repeatedly compared ("That all the earth for terrour seemd to shake," vii.7; cf. vii.9, viii.8.9),[43] as well as the thunderbolt that explicitly links Orgoglio with divine judgment ("As when almightie Iove in wrathfull mood, / To wreake the guilt of mortall sins is bent, / Hurles forthe his thundring dart" viii.9.1–3), can now be seen not simply as expressions of unspecified "apocalyptic" implications, or as judgments against the knight's indulgence in the sins of sloth and lechery. These earthquakes and thunderbolts can be read as signs of the immediate, actual, terrifying presence of divine judgment, at those moments of crisis when God's law devastates individual sinners by engendering in them an overpowering sense of their radical sinfulness.

That this ultimately salvific recognition is brought home to Red Cross Knight by a monster which represents "the radical ur-Sin" of pride makes doctrinal sense: sin, working through the law, brings such recognitions about. The hellish depth ("all a deepe descent, as darke as hell," viii.39.8) and completeness of the affliction Orgoglio imposes on Red Cross ("O who is that, which brings me happy choyce / Of death" viii.38.3–4) reflect, moreover, the condition that the Pauline text and Becon's Elizabethan reading have described for us. In captivity to Orgoglio, Red Cross is completely dominated by "the kingdom, power, and regiment of sin," a condition that could induce some readers to re-evaluate their earlier assumption that the knight had been called and justified before his quest began. He appears now either as an image of natural man, awaiting his foreordained calling, or as an image of the deepest fall from grace which the regenerate can experience. Such at least are alternative meanings which Reformed doctrines might induce readers to locate in Red Cross' imprisonment when Arthur's helmet or related details suggest the relevance of the Pauline axiom that "the strength of sin is the law" (I Cor. 15:56).

The symbolism of Arthur's helmet can also imply the positive side of the Pauline formula: "[T]he Law entered thereupon that the offense should abound: nevertheless where sin abounded, there grace abounded much more" (Rom. 5:20). The Spenserian stanza describing the threat built into Arthur's helmet is balanced, with comparable promptness, by a stanza whose mood conveys a tone of untrammeled joy,[44] the quality Red Cross has long since lost:

> Upon the top of all his loftie crest,
>   A bunch of haires discoloured diversly,
>   With sprincled pearle, and gold full richly drest,
>   Did shake, and seem'd to daunce for jollity,
>   Like to an Almond tree ymounted hye
> On top of greene Selinis all alone,
>   With blossomes brave bedecked daintily;
>   Whose tender locks do tremble every one
> At every little breath, that under heaven is blowne.   (vii.32)

The stanza offers a pastiche of symbols employed elsewhere in the Legend of Holiness. His "loftie crest" atop the "haughtie helmet," "ymounted hye" recalls emotional and spiritual elevations, mostly errant or delusional ones, experienced by many figures earlier in the book. These trembling locks recall, too, the trembling leaves of the trees that were Fradubio and Fraelissa (I.ii.28.5) and of the grove in the earthly paradise (I.vii.3.3) in which Red Cross met with spiritual catastrophe. But here the joyful tone of the poetry precludes threatening implications, and the sensitivity to "every little breath, that under heaven is blowne," recalling breezes and winds prevalent earlier in I.vii, suggests receptivity to the influence of the omnipresent Spirit.[45] This interpretation is strengthened by the iconographic almond tree, whose description dominates the stanza. Scholars appropriately relate this symbol to Aaron's rod, which "brought forth buds, and brought forth blossoms and bare ripe almonds" (Num. 17:8).[46]

Theologically informed readings might discover still further implications in Arthur's symbolic panoply. In the battle against Red Cross' captors,[47] Arthur's shield is his decisive weapon, and commentators convincingly identify it as Paul's shield of faith, "wherewith ye may quench all the firie dartes of the wicked" (Eph. 6:16). But because faith is a complicated thing, and because Arthur faces a carefully particularized enemy, Spenser's presentation of the shield suggests that a specific aspect of faith might be at issue here. Like Una's face – and Moses' on his return from the mount – the shield wears a veil, "ne might of mortall eye be ever seene" (33.1–2). "Mortal eye" registers a significant ambiguity: mortal (carnal or merely human) vision cannot apprehend the objects of faith, which are the "the ground of things, which are hoped for, and the evidence of things which are not seen" (Heb. 11:1); conversely, the eye that does receive power to look on the objects of faith can no longer be accounted merely "mortal," destined for the second death (damnation).

To eyes rendered perceptive by grace, the shield represents the substance of faith, and it does so, first of all, by its unity. Like Una it is "one" in its indivisibility and purity.

> all of Diamond perfect pure and cleene
> It framed was, one massie entire mould,
> Hewen out of Adamant rocke with engines keene,
> That point of speare it never percen could,
> Ne dint of direfull sword divide the substance would. (vii.33.5–9)

In contexts a doctrinal reading supplies, the very material of the shield, "adamant rocke," implies that Arthur's defense is faith, specifically, in Christ. Rock is of course a familiar symbol of Christ in scripture, and faith in Him is the rock upon which the Messiah founds His church in Matthew 16:18.[48] The Geneva gloss makes this point directly: "Upon this rock," the commentators say, means "upon that faith whereby thou hast confessed and acknowledged me: for it is grounded upon an infallible truth." Once Arthur's shield is thus understood to symbolize the ultimate source of light rather than that light's planetary subordinates, readers will find no hyperbole in the observation that "so exceeding shone his glistring ray, / That Phoebus golden face it did attaint" (34.6–8). If that be the case, the following construction seems plausible: the less overpowering but still impressive light reflected by the armor as a whole is comparable to Phoebus' light ("like glauncing light of Phoebus brightest ray," 29.5), and so might be taken as a symbol of the divine glory as it appears refracted and diminished in actual, inherent, and imperfect holiness. The uncovered shield, however, represents the divine glory unmediated, a direct intuitive vision made possible and rendered transcendently potent by the grace that justifies.

Understandably then, the shield's light provides a kind of vision that cannot suffer delusion:

> all that was not such, as seemd in sight,
> Before that shield did fade, and suddeine fall:
> And when him list the raskall routes appall,
> Men into stones therewith he could transmew,
> And stones to dust, and dust to nought at all;
> And when him list the prouder lookes subdew,
> He would them gazing blind, or turne to other hew.   (vii.35.3–9)

These wondrous properties, and those listed in the previous stanza, may seem fanciful when applied to so weighty a conception as Christian faith. But the passage wittily illustrates Spenser's ability to remain true at once to the vehicle of his romantic fiction and to the tenor of doctrinal implication. Petrification as literal event is common in folklore, but by Spenser's time it had also been adapted to subtle uses, as in Dante's *Inferno*, where Medusa represents terror that culminates in despair (*Inf.* 9.56–57). This terror is embodied most forcefully in the Law whose vengeance speaks from every level of the abyss that engulfs the pilgrim in the *Inferno*. Nearer Spenser's time, Natalis Comes interprets Niobe's metamorphosis as a collapse into despair occasioned by the loss of mortal goods, from whose possession she had contracted her notorious case of heaven-defying pride.[49] As Spenser describes Arthur's shield here ("when as monsters huge he would dismay, / Or daunt unequall armies of his foes," 34.2–3), however, Arthur's power to employ his shield is most immediately comparable to Perseus' use of Medusa's head in *Metamorphoses* V.175–40. Perseus' enemies there can aptly be described as "raskall routes." So construed, the mythic counterparts of Spenser's passage constitute analogies to the earliest action that faith undertakes in the human soul, which is to destroy inflated self-esteem. As Luther put it in phrases provided by his Elizabethan translator, "when thou beginnest to believe thou doest learn withall, that all things in thee are altogether blameworthy, sinful, and damnable."[50] Belief in the validity of divine law achieves this necessary effect of faith.

Arthur dramatizes this effect when he carries his victories to their ultimate conclusion, turning his victims, petrified by fear, "into dust, and dust to nought at all." The shield produces first a paralyzing terror akin to despair; it then reduces proud enemies to what they in essence are, dust, ashes, "nought at all." This sequence, first paralysis then reduc-

tion to nullity, foreshadows with precision the effect that Arthur's shield
has on Orgoglio and his beast, both of whom find themselves "with
gazing blind" (viii.19, 20), then completely obliterated. In the end,
Orgoglio is dramatically turned "to other hew," a shape that shows his
essence to be "nought at all":

> But soone as breath out of his breast did pas,
> That huge great body, which the Gyaunt bore,
> Was vanisht quite, and of that monstrous mas
> Was nothing left, but like an emptie bladder was.   (viii.24.6–9)

Having followed the shield's description carefully, we can recognize
that Spenser's concluding remarks on it juxtapose the materials of
Arthurian romance playfully against the passage's doctrinal implications.

> Ne let it seeme, that credence this exceedes,
> For he that made the same, was knowne right well
> To have done much more admirable deedes.   (vii.36.1–3)

The lines invite readers who have been pursuing a doctrinal interpretation to expect to hear the Lord named outright, but Spenser returns
puckishly to his narrative's Arthurian base: "It Merlin was." Within a
few lines, however, a central doctrinal point of the armor passage becomes readily perceptible. When Arthur died, we are told, the Faerie
Queene brought shield, and sword, and armor "To Faerie lond, where
yet it may be seene, if sought" (I.vii.36). Since grace provides power to
seek the virtues these weapons represent, he who seeks will inevitably
find them.

At the beginning of *The Faerie Queene* I.viii, the nature of Arthur's impending battle is introduced by means of a stanza that carries consider-
able theological import. The narrator mimes the pattern dramatized with
increasing frequency in his narrative: he begins in a state of helpless
gloom about even the "righteous" man's propensity to sin: "Ay me, how
many perils doe enfold / The righteous man, to make him daily fall?"
Yet the narrator's occasion for this resigned dismay describes only half
of the affective pattern that faith engenders. Gloom would prevail "Were
not, that heavenly grace doth him uphold, / And stedfast truth acquite
him out of all." Though he falls daily, the righteous man nevertheless
remains righteous because grace, by means of the Saviour who is Truth,
"acquites" all "righteous" men by imputing His righteousness to them.
For readers who interpret the passage this way, "stedfast truth" will be

obliged to undergo a sudden gender transformation when romantic narrative again takes precedence over theological reflection. Line five suddenly invites us to reidentify "Truth" with Una, who sometimes embodies features of that vast set of theological notions (the Lord's own fidelity to his promises; His wise governance of the universe; His wisdom as revealed in scripture, etc.) operating through a character who can represent a church that possesses the capacity to help "acquite" believers of their unavoidable guilt. Earlier, Una led a lamb (I.i.4.9), thereby expressing visually the church's function to bring Christ to elect souls, who are assured of His grace yet always in need of its immediate support. Now Una leads Arthur, a prince who intermittently conforms to the image of Christ.[51] Only because he does in some sense conform to that image can Arthur rescue Red Cross from torments imposed both by "his owne foolish pride" and "weakness."

Heroic endeavor, not spiritual conformity to the Savior, is the prince's salient attribute as his battle with Orgoglio begins:

> his mightie shild
> Upon his manly arme he soone addrest,
> And at him fiercely flew, with courage fild,
> And eger greedinesse through every member thrild. (viii.6.6–9)

In at least one forceful reading, these words have been taken simply to replicate the ambivalence evident in the earlier presentations of Red Cross' battles (fierce, "eger greedinesse" propels defenders of truth). So construed, this passage implies that "the general point [is] that man's spiritual resources inevitably partake of his earthly, sinful nature."[52] From perspectives Protestant readers could bring to bear on the passage, this would be an acceptable interpretation, assuming of course that the phrase "man's spiritual resources" is recognized as shorthand for spiritual resources which grace provides. Yet the perspectives made available by Tudor Protestantism can also draw attention to subtle differences as well as similarities between passages that describe the behavior of Arthur and Red Cross Knight.

A potentially significant difference is that Red Cross Knight's symbolic weaponry remained nearly invisible in descriptions of his earlier battles, but Arthur's symbolic shield receives primary emphasis here. Because it is so conspicuous, the shield can be seen to impart righteous force to the powers exerted by its bearer's "manly arme." Since Arthur combats enemies who do not mirror his own appearance, actions, or emotions (as Sansfoy, Sansjoy, and Orgoglio mirror those of Red Cross),

Arthur's fierceness and sharp greediness carry less obvious suggestions that he is tainted (as Red Cross is) by what he combats. Above all, perhaps, Arthur's "greediness" contrasts with that of the early Red Cross because the prize sought is neither a "rich-fleeced flock" (Duessa) nor a trophy of perhaps moral but chiefly self-promoting chivalric conquest (Sansfoy's shield). Arthur fights at the request of a distressed maiden to liberate a fellow servant of Gloriana.[53]

In other significant ways, Arthur's combat with Orgoglio differs markedly from those in which Red Cross has engaged. Not only does the passage avoid confusing the combatants' identities, as occurs in Red Cross' earlier battles; it also involves Arthur sparingly in the action described. Arthur's enemies, who receive most of the poet's attention, bring to the battle traits that have recurrently characterized Red Cross Knight: "Therewith the Gyant buckled him to fight, / Inflam'd with scornefull wrath and high disdaine" (I.viii.7.1–2). Unlike Red Cross in his earlier heroic endeavors, Arthur is "wise and warie,"[54] his vision undiminished by pride or its attendant rage and "disdaine." He consequently avoids the vain self-assertion, epidemic among conventional heroes of epic and romance, that accepts any confrontation with powerful opposites, no matter what the odds: "Ne shame he thought to shunne so hideous might" (8.1). Pride's blinding fury and inherent myopia contribute to a self-destructive impotence that becomes decisive in battle against so adroit an opposite as Arthur:

> The idle stroke, enforcing furious way,
> Missing the marke of his misaymed sight
> Did fall to ground   (viii.8.2–4)

This "misaymed" stroke transmutes Orgoglio to unwitting "villein" in a way that exploits the secondary connotations of the word ("peasant," "country labourer," *OED*): "with his heavie sway / So deepely dinted in the driven clay, / That three yardes deepe a furrow up did throw" (8.4–6).

This image of earthiness and impotence is soon contested by an epic simile that compares Orgoglio to "almightie Jove" when that deity

> in wrathfull mood,
> To wreake the guilt of mortall sins is bent,
> Hurles forth his thundring dart with deadly food,
> Enrold in flames, and smouldring dreriment   (viii.9.1–4)

The simile indicates, most obviously, that Orgoglio acts as minister of divine judgment, punishing sin. And as the blow initiates Orgoglio's own demise (viii.10), its further contribution to providential beneficence appears through an audacious allusion. "[W]ith blade all burning bright" (10.5), Arthur sets about Orgoglio's destruction and, after his blow falls, "Large streames of bloud out of the truncked stocke / Forth gushed, like fresh water streame from riven rocke" (10.8–9). By fatally wounding humankind's evil nature – "Puft up with emptie wind, and fild with sinfull crime" (vii.9.9) – the sword of God's word releases the fresh ("living") stream, just as Moses the lawgiver had released an identical stream from the rock in the desert (Num. 20:11). That rock typified faith in Christ, and Spenser's monstrous image of evil, Orgoglio himself, thus becomes a startlingly novel *figura Christi*. More precisely, by recalling the water that was a type of the blood released when Christ's body was lanced on the cross, Orgoglio embodies the Old Man, humankind's evil nature ("*native* might," 10.7), defeated during the crucifixion.

In Spenser's fiction, Orgoglio's death wins the release of Red Cross Knight, an event presented as a new birth ("now three Moones have changed thrice their hew . . . Since I the heavens chearefull face did vew," viii.38.6–8). A Protestant doctrinal reading can consequently interpret this release in one of two ways: as the birth of the New Man in an elect soul now first receiving his calling and justification; or as a dramatic rebirth of the New Man in an elect soul already called and justified but since fallen deeply into sin. Readers inclined to adopt assumptions compatible with those of Tridentine Catholicism could also see this event as the birth of the New Man, but would interpret that as the beginning of justification viewed as a process in which the knight's will cooperates (see ch. 6, p. 157, below) to achieve salvation in his ensuing spiritual struggles. Any of these constructions predicts, in turn, that Red Cross will hereafter display not only marked improvements in his spiritual condition but also the weaknesses that the New Man, especially when very new, always exhibits relative to the established and never entirely defeated Old: " 'The old man' is like to a mighty giant, such a one as was Goliath; for his birth is now perfect. But 'the new man' is like unto a little child, such a one as was David; for his birth is not perfect until the day of his general resurrection."[55]

Although Arthur, here and in the rescue of his squire (viii.15), pursues the most charitable of heroic actions, he too appears to be a site for continuing struggle between the Old Man and the New. He falls before Orgoglio, in a *peripeteia* which should discourage readers growing confident that this hero "stands for" grace or stands as a "Christ figure" in any simple and consistent way. When Orgoglio raises his "hideous club," the lines' ambiguous "that" (interpreted first as demonstrative pronoun, then as subordinate conjunction) indicates in rapid succession that the weapon is made of oak and that its power is great enough to destroy the strongest of oaks: "And at his foe with furious rigour smites, / That strongest Oake might seeme to overthrow" (viii.18.5–6). The blow fells Arthur, like "strongest oak," with ease:

> The stroke upon his shield so heavie lites,
> That to the ground it doubleth him full low:
> What mortall wight could ever beare so monstrous blow?
>
> (viii.18.7–9)

The language invites us to compare Arthur's fall with Red Cross' earlier one by adding that when Arthur lies "full low," Orgoglio raises "on high" his "weapon huge," "For to have slaine the man, that on the ground did lye" (19.8–9). When Red Cross was overthrown, he "lay full low," and Orgoglio at one point "[h]is heavie hand he heaved up on hye, / And him to dust thought to have battred quight" (vii.12.9, 14.2–3).

At this point, despite the obvious differences between them, the ultimate hero shares the fallen knight's spiritual supinity. The ironies of viii.19 argue that the rhetorical question put at the end of viii.18 ("What mortal wight . . . ?") may be answered with conviction: no "mortall wight" can escape falling to the collection of human evils epitomized in Orgoglio. A greater power must intervene:

> And in his fall his shield, that covered was,
>   Did loose his vele by chaunce, and open flew:
> The light whereof, that heavens light did pas,
>   Such blazing brightnesse through the aier threw,
>   That eye mote not the same endure to vew.
> Which when the Gyaunt spyde with staring eye,
> He downe let fall his arme, and soft withdrew
> His weapon huge   (viii.19.1–8)

Arthur's fall unleashes his true strength, by a "chaunce" which announces more emphatically than ever that divine foreordination guides events which human perceptions are likely to assign to accident.

As a result of this "chaunce," the monster receives an overwhelming blast of illumination, and with "staring eye" "read[s] his end / In that bright shield" (viii.21.4–5). This shattering insight renders him senseless, like the beast at viii.20 and like Red Cross Knight at vii.15, but such stupifaction may carry with it the beginnings of true illumination: "As where th'Almighties lightning brond does light, / It dimmes the dazed eyen, and daunts the senses quight" (viii.21.8–9). "Th'Almighties lightning brond" enlightens in part by destroying, and the experience narrated here concerns the beginnings of true faith, in people in whose minds and hearts Orgoglio always necessarily dwells. To interpret the episode in this way is to make sense of the intriguing detail which observes that Orgoglio has "*read* his end / In that bright shield." In scripture and in theology, mirrors frequently function as symbols of Christ and of the Word in general, but most often of God's demanding law (cf. ch. 1, p. 39).[56] Calvin compares "the Word itself . . . [to] a mirror in which faith may contemplate God," but this mirror "rather blinds and stuns," when the reprobate gaze upon it. Such destructive power is displayed in Orgoglio's sudden debility, "for since that glauncing sight, / He hath no powre to hurt, nor to defend" (viii.21.7). Orgoglio's final appearance, bereft of head and breath "like an emptie bladder" (24.9) aptly expresses the essence of what faithful Christians are to know themselves by nature to be: empty and yet filled with evil nonetheless.

The giant's death does not free Red Cross Knight automatically. The exact nature of his imprisonment is now embodied in Ignaro, whose particular ignorance identifies him as both an unwitting jailer ("keeper," 31.7) and an equally unwitting potential liberator:

> And on his arme a bounch of keyes he bore,
> The which unused rust did overgrow:
> Those were the keyes of every inner dore,
> But he could not them use, but kept them still in store.
>
> (viii.30.6–9)

Since the keys are plural in number, and since they do not open the dungeon of the castle (37.4–5), the usual gloss relating this passage to Revelation 9:1, where the fallen angel receives "the key of the bottomless pit" and immediately employs it, would probably occur to few readers. Matthew 16:19 is the more obvious allusion. Although Ignaro's keys have now rusted through disuse, they once represented, as the Geneva gloss on Matthew's text helps us to see, "the word of God," or, more specifically, Christ's delegated power to unlock the liberating wisdom of that word.[57] Red Cross' keeper retains no trace of the life-sustaining hermeneutic skill originally disseminated but now (Protestants relentlessly argued) hoarded by the church in Rome, which seeks to keep it "still in store."[58]

If Ignaro presents the Law's literal sense, as is often said, therefore, he does so in a most limited way. He cannot represent the Law's power to make men conscious of sin and to afflict them with guilt; his ignorance is more absolute than that. Together with the rusty keys, Ignaro's repeated disavowal ("He could not tell") bespeaks a befuddled inability even to recognize one's own sinfulness. Having broken Gods' law, egregiously, with Duessa, Red Cross can recognize in only a comparably befuddled, general, and consequently debilitating manner that he has broken divine interdict. He therefore suffers pangs from which there can be no issue except a generalized and overwhelming despair. In bondage within the prison over which Ignaro presides, Red Cross has not yet reached the point at which law can teach him to trace sin's operations within his own soul. Consequently, on hearing Arthur's call, intended "to weet, if living wight / Were housed therewithin, whom he enlargen might" (viii.37.8–9), Red Cross can perceive only the imminent fulfillment of a now deeply rooted death-wish:

> "O who is that, which brings me happy choyce
> Of death, that here lye dying every stound,
> Yet live perforce in balefull darkenesse bound?" (viii.38.3–5)

The knight's bondage does not appear to have taught him the important doctrinal lesson that in himself he is nothing.[59] What he has learned is as yet more rudimentary than that; he has discovered his extreme susceptibility to domination by evil forces and impulses.

This powerful negative insight requires positive support, and when Una somewhat tactlessly dwells on Red Cross' self-"berobbed" state, his chronic possession by Sansjoy reasserts itself:

> The chearelesse man, whom sorrow did dismay,
> Had no delight to treaten of his griefe;
> His long endured famine needed more reliefe.   (viii.43.7–9)

These lines declare also that Red Cross' hearing remains impaired, for Una had concluded her speech with an expression of faith in providential benevolence to come, "good growes of evils priefe" (viii.43.6). Red Cross hears only the preceding stress on his ill fortune. And although Arthur next begins by emphasizing the positive possibilities latent in Red Cross' recent experience, the apparent consolation ends with an observation as sobering as it is bathetic:

> th'onely good, that growes of passed feare,
> Is to be wise, and ware of like agein.
> This dayes ensample hath this lesson deare
> Deepe written in my heart with yron pen,
> That blisse may not abide in state of mortall men.   (viii.44.5–9)

If we take Arthur's comment on "blisse" to refer both to temporal happiness and to accompanying sensations of spiritual exaltation and security, it provides an apt conclusion to an episode concerned with the pervasive and subtle destructiveness, and the inevitable destruction, of pride and its victims. The gloom of this summary conclusion is hardly relieved at all by Arthur's subsequent encouragement to "take to you wonted strength, / And maister these mishaps with patient might" (viii.45.1–2). "Mishaps" seems a ludicrous understatement, and "might" and "wonted strength" have so far in the the Legend of Holiness meant, at best, power to commit well-intentioned sins.

Such perceptions, critical even of Arthur, diverge of course from the norm. Persuaded that Arthur must here stand beyond reproach as the book's most complete representation of its titular virtue, some readers will find no place in their constructions for details that register his limitations.[60] As we have seen, Arthur's behavior in I.vii and viii reveals him to be genially cheerful, generous-spirited, energetically charitable, and far more adept than Red Cross at cooperating with grace in battle with sinful opposites. Arthur has also, however, fallen before Orgoglio's violence and so displays his own persisting need for grace. Though he acts as an instrument of grace in that combat, at viii.45 he discredits himself as embodiment of it, or even as theological truth's consistent spokesman. He commends force and reason to a knight who has been victimized by his efforts to employ force and reason.

Yet in recommending these powers, and doing so with a disarming simpleness that is an element of his charm, Arthur recommends the only defenses which mortals can possess, and which they know beforehand will always fall short of perfection. After completing a magnificent achievement, this hero's capacity for misunderstanding of his own role and of the spiritual issues at hand implies a good deal about heroism as the Legend of Holiness invites readers to construct it. This heroism is a quality as attractive as it is imperfectly resident in the corrupting channels grace has selected for its use. It is a paradox of power and weakness, a paradox that always most loudly testifies to the power of the transcendent force on which it utterly depends. Read in this way, episodes often treated as expressions of historical allegory focus instead on fundamental doctrines of Reformed theology. And as a consequence, they carry weightier ideological force than more limited, partisan sorts of allegory can support.

6

DISCOVERING HOLINESS

On the assumption that Arthur has brought grace and heroism into the Legend of Holiness, commentators often treat its climactic episodes as if their meanings were transparent. And it is true that Red Cross gradually comes to seem less perplexed by his world, now a place in which simple personifications sometimes declare their unproblematic identities forthrightly. As in the poem's earlier phases, however, a reasonably detailed awareness of sixteenth-century doctrines can reveal that even the Legend's concluding episodes illustrate the instability of available doctrinal contexts and the variability of their potential applications. In the final three cantos of Book I, doctrinal complexity intensifies in part because ecclesiology now joins dogmatic theology as a dominant concern. This new emphasis on the church, the community that fosters holiness, will become most visible in the sequence of pedagogues and comforters who minister to Red Cross Knight in I.x, and it will remain conspicuous in the knight's battle with the ultimate dragon in I.xi and his admission to Una's family in I.xii.

Spenser lays the foundation for those cantos, however, in I.ix, in the knight's confrontation with Despair. The events interposed between Red Cross' redemption from Orgoglio's dungeon and his rehabilitation in I.x reveal that his recovery has been partial. Although he has been redeemed from bondage to an overpowering embodiment of pride and has seen falsehood unmasked, Red Cross remains "weake and wearie" (ix.20.9). This is a condition Una perceives, though the knight himself feels thoroughly revived and readers have been invited to share his misguided optimism: the formerly "weake captive wight," we are assured, "now wexed strong" (ix.2.3). Una's perception of the knight's concealed weakness is reported immediately after we are reminded that his real source of strength lies in a will far greater than his own. He is "her chosen knight" (ix.20.5), a description in which the ambiguous reference of the epithet allows readers to perceive that Red Cross can legitimately be considered "chosen" not solely by Una, but by the divine will. Events in I.ix reveal that, despite the resurgence of grace which Red Cross experiences in I.viii, he remains unsteadily unconvinced of his election. The knight's spiritual privation is fully exposed by Despair, whose potent rhetoric effectively plunges Red Cross into an emotional hell comparable to that in which Orgoglio had confined him.[1] Comparable, but not the same; for, as we have noted, the knight earlier appeared overwhelmed by a powerful apprehension of his sinfulness but incapable of comprehending it. Some readers would be able to recognize in Red Cross a condition of which sixteenth-century spiritual counselors were well aware, a generalized variety of "grief" induced "by something unknown to us and uncertain." As I mentioned ealier (Introduction, pp. 17–18, above), such "blind griefs," as Richard Greenham labeled them, were assigned varying causes by the diverse disciplines of the day. Pastoral theologians like Greenham ascribe such distresses to the aims of a "secret providence" determined to correct some of "God's children . . . who either never knew God, or else had but a general knowledge of him."[2]

To cure such ailments, the sufferers must first be brought "to the sight of sin, as to some cause of their trouble . . . and so draw out of them the confession of some several, especial, and secret sin." Like modern analysts, the sixteenth-century pastor not only constructed a narrative that constituted the patient's disease while seeming simply to describe it; he also practiced a hermeneutics of suspicion to counter the manifold deceptiveness of the human psyche. His discovery of the special and secret sin is impeded at every turn by the infinite "deceivableness of the heart," which leads many to know vaguely about sin and yet leaves them helpless: "they either cannot descry several sins, or they will not be brought to acknowledge their secret sins: whereof the one proceedeth of the ignorance of the law of God, and the other of self-love."[3]

Both of these motives – defensive self-love and ignorance of the law – can be perceived in Red Cross Knight. He certainly demonstrates his blindness "to the true meaning of the texts cited."[4] But Greenham's perspectives might also induce some readers to think, paradoxically, that this most insidious tempter in fact speaks truth, rendering articulate the causes of Red Cross' chronic yet latent infection. Despair inadvertently realizes divine law's primary purpose, which is to convince believers of their damnable sinfulness by bringing specific individual sins to detailed conscious knowledge. This pattern becomes visible as Despair speaks, at first, in general terms: "The lenger life, I wote the greater sin, / The greater sin, the greater punishment" (ix.43.1–2) but then gives his accusations a powerfully individual turn:

> Thou wretched man, of death hast greatest need,
>   If in true ballance thou wilt weigh thy state:
>   For never knight, that dared warlike deede,
>   More lucklesse disaventures did amate:
>   Witnesse the dongeon deepe, wherein of late
>
>   . . . .
>
>   Is not enough, that to this Ladie milde
>   Thou falsed hast thy faith with perjurie,
>   And sold thy selfe to serve Duessa vilde,
> With whom in all abuse thou hast thy selfe defilde?
>
> (ix.45.1–46.9)

Despair's repeated "thou" insists on special familiarity. His reprise of specific acts of wrongdoing induces acute remorse because he interprets them as symptoms of the knight's infinite and incorrigible corruption:

> Why then doest thou, O man of sin, desire
>   To draw thy dayes forth to their last degree?
>   Is not the measure of thy sinfull hire
>   High heaped up with huge iniquitie,
>   Against the day of wrath, to burden thee?   (ix.46.1–5)

Like "the word of God," Despair's speech feels sharper to Red Cross "than any two-edged sword" which "entreth through, even unto . . . the joints, and the marrow, and is a discerner of the thoughts and the intents of the heart" (Heb. 4:12):[5]

> The knight was much enmoved with his speach,
>   That as a swords point through his hart did perse,
>   And in his conscience made a secret breach,
>   Well knowing true all, that he did reherse,
>   And to his fresh remembrance did reverse
>   The ugly vew of his deformed crimes,
>   That all his manly powres it did disperse,
>   As he were charmed with inchaunted rimes   (ix.48.1–8)

Despair's rhetoric has the precise effect which pastoral theology ascribes to divine law, which can begin to cure "our festred sores" because God has made it "as sharp as the two-edged sword, piercing the very closest and most unsearchable corners of the heart, which the Law of Nature can hardly, human laws by no means possible, reach unto."[6] Voicing accurate accusations, but also speaking as a diseased psychological condition[7] induced by unavoidable human failings and exaggerated by errant (unconsciously Pelagian) doctrine, despair endeavors through the law itself to transmute the sinner's recognition of his sinfulness into a particularly self-destructive manifestation of pride.

So dangerous a temptation demands exceptional aid, and Red Cross here receives it from Una. Her intervention seems contrived to suggest that Red Cross Knight is saved not by reason and experience, which Arthur has recommended (viii.45), but by a faith for which Una advances no argument whatever. This absence of any appeal to reason is the more apparent because this rescue follows immediately upon a section of the poem easily recognizable (especially, e.g., at ix.41) as debate, a genre favored by Renaissance humanists.[8] This induces us to expect that superior dialectical skills will provide the knight's victory. As theology itself invariably seeks to do, however, Una fundamentally alters the nature of the discourse; exhortation and assertion replace argument:

> In heavenly mercies hast thou not a part?
> Why shouldst thou then despeire, that chosen art?
> Where justice growes, there grows eke greater grace (ix.53.4–6)

The previously vacillating knight's ready acceptance of so simple an assertion of dogma implies that reason at this crucial point has little to do with the matter.[9] Red Cross escapes Despair because something super-rational has enabled him to believe, at least for the moment, that he enjoys a "part" in "heavenly mercies." His subsequent actions appear to express a decisive inner alteration: the exhortation "Arise, Sir knight arise, and leave this cursed place," is followed abruptly by the laconic: "So up he rose, and thence amounted streight" (ix.53.9–54.1).

Of course, Una's doctrine does not cure Red Cross' affliction. It is all very well to be told, and momentarily to believe, that God's "equall" eye can wink away the sins of his chosen, but it is quite another thing to remain convinced that He has chosen to do so for oneself. Reformed theology could endow this distinction between general and personal knowing, as we have seen, with frightening implications. Whether readers locate the all-important divine call before the beginning of Red Cross Knight's quest, or at the moment when Arthur rescues him from Orgoglio's prison in I.viii, or at the end of I.ix when he appears consciously to accept the doctrine of predestined election, some will be aware that that event can be illusory, no matter how real its symptoms might appear to be.

Before the call that has eternally been written into the Lord's schedule for temporal events, even the elect "wander scattered in the wilderness common to all; and they do not differ at all from others except that they are protected by God's especial mercy from rushing headlong into the final ruin of death."[10] When the call arrives, it might turn out to be only "the general call, by which God invites all equally to himself through the outward preaching of the word." The deity envisioned by Reformed theology, infinitely superior to merely human notions of fair dealing, can simply "hold . . . out" the general call to the reprobate "as a savor of death . . . and as the occasion for severer damnation." More frighteningly, even "special" calls, "which [God] deigns for the most part to give to the believers alone, while by the inward illumination of his Spirit he causes the preached Word to dwell in their hearts," the Lord may grant to some people "only for a time." It is perfectly possible that he will later "justly [forsake] them on account of their ungratefulness and [strike] them with even greater blindness" (cf. ch. 1, pp. 43–44, above).[11] Such possibilities add urgency to the desire to perform introspective exercises that can discover reliable evidence of one's own election.

Locating such evidence is Red Cross Knight's task when he visits the House of Holiness in *The Faerie Queene* I.x. It is probably best to pause at the threshold of the House of Holiness to notice how insistently its features and presentation invite readers to construct a variety of potentially incompatible meanings. If we come to the poem expecting it to refer to theological doctrines that are simple, stable, and therefore predictably self-interpreting, evidence of complexity cannot be perceived. But if we acknowledge that established dogmas comprised unresolved contradictions as well as deliberate ambiguities, the House of Holiness can assume novel aspects, offering surprises that beget and reward active mental engagement. It too participates in a broad humanist effort to employ reading to provoke active thought rather than to instill unquestioned ideas.[12] A politically oriented response to I.x. can also perceive forceful illustrations of the poem's contribution to the cultural work of securing the positions of newly dominant groups by rewriting features of the Roman Catholic past.

This rewriting can become visible immediately. For readers who notice features that make the House resemble an exemplary monastic institution – the total dedication to prayer and charity (x.3), the locked door "warely watched night and day," the Porter "with lookes full lowly cast" (5), and so on – the transitions from one interior setting to the next will require persistent and active revision of expectations. Having entered what appeared to be a monastery, we find ourselves in something more like an aristocratic household, "the Hall" rich in "rare courtesie." We then traverse a set of educational facilities, two of which are explicitly "schoolhouses," the third a "darksome lowly place" more monastic in cast than the others (x.18, 24–25, 32). We then enter upon a "ready path" (33.9; 35.5) that turns out not to be ready at all but cluttered with "bushy thornes, and ragged breares" (35.3). It leads first to a "holy Hospitall" which suggests, once again, a monastery because it is peopled by "Bead-men." But this place violates the expectations aroused by that term, by parading a set of figures engaged in unrelenting, active relief of human suffering: "Their gates to all were open evermore . . . And one sate wayting ever them before, / To call in commers-by, that needy were and pore" (36.6–9). The Beadmen's activities are so varied that readers cannot easily hold on to the impression that these monk-like figures are isolated from the larger community by monastic or hospital walls (36–45). More strikingly, the House of Holiness as a whole abandons the idea of a walled enclosure with which it began. It does this so completely that readers normally think of the canto's later setting, the Mount of Contemplation, as a clearly separate place. Any perceived partition between Mount and House must be supplied by readers, however, for Spenser's language does not explicitly divide the trio of towering visionary mountains (x.49, 53, 55) from the earlier sequence of settings that the House comprises.

The ever-dilating outlines of the House of Holiness help to explain its paradoxical history of reception: its meanings are said to be transparent, but it has received contradictory interpretations.[13] Its initial monastic aspect, together with its much-discussed "beadmen" and their systematic pursuit of good works, has led interpreters to believe that Spenser opposed the doctrine of justification by faith. Others, more urgently partisan, argue that "Spenser did not believe the ideals of monastic life to be evil in any way." Still others find irreconcilable doctrinal self-contradictions embedded in the canto – evidence either of the author's deliberate pluralism or of his equally deliberate reluctance to resolve (rather than merely to call attention to) a mysterious truth of the human condition.[14]

Despite such fundamental differences, most of these interpreters would agree that the opening stanza presents one of the least ambiguous dogmatic assertions to appear in Spenser's works:

> What man is he, that boasts of fleshly might,
> And vaine assurance of mortality,
> Which all so soone, as it doth come to fight,
> Against spirituall foes, yeelds by and by,
> Or from the field most cowardly doth fly?
> Ne let the man ascribe it to his skill,
> That thorough grace hath gained victory.
> If any strength we have, it is to ill,
> But all the good is Gods, both power and eke will.   (x.1)

This opening pronouncement implies that dogmatic theology may so dominate the canto that its content and generic characteristics will approximate those of unmodulated theological discourse. Now, some readers might think, we can know for sure that "Spenser" meant us to construe the poem according to the most unrelenting of "Calvinist" perspectives. After all, the final line of x.1 derives authority from its origin in Philippians 2:13, "it is God which worketh in you, both the will and the deed, even of his good pleasure."

The drift of the entire stanza, reinforced by another Pauline echo many readers will discern in lines 6–8 ("For by grace are ye saved through faith, and that not of your selves: it is the gift of God, not of works, lest any man should boast himself," Eph. 2:8–9), seems totally antivoluntarist.[15] Most interpreters have understandably taken Spenser's apparent insistence on the absolute power of God and the correspondingly absolute human debility as the sole and obvious point of x.1.9. Many have also considered self-evident the idea that "this stanza gives a drastic account of human frailty: more than any other in Book I it invites the term 'Calvinist.'"[16] The stanza appears less stable when readers recall some of the doctrines we examined earlier. The immediate context of Philippians 2:13 itself constitutes a scriptural source of ambiguities that recurrently appear in Reformed doctrines of free will (see ch. 1, pp. 30–31, above). As many readers might know, the immediately preceding line (Phil. 2:12) urges believers, in the familiar phrasing of the King James Version, to "work out your own salvation with fear and trembling."[17] The passage appears to be self-contradictory: "It is God which worketh in you" (Phil. 2:13), but yet "work out your own salvation" (Phil. 2:12). The contradiction can be clarified by attending to the term which Spenser's text places in the emphatic last foot of his stanza's concluding alexandrine: "both power and eke *will*."

Despite variations in detail and in larger theological assumptions, the history of reception of Philippians 2:13 – as recorded in works by Augustine, Aquinas, Calvin, and major Elizabethan authorities – displays remarkable consensus on two points. First, unless it possesses some degree of volition, no faculty can rightly be called a "will." Second, the "good" will under discussion is not God's own immediate executive function; it is the renewed human will through which His grace works.[18] These points seem equally applicable to the term with which Spenser's stanza concludes. Most readings take x.1.9 to refer generally to all "the good" in the world or the cosmos, and presume that the power and will in question are, directly, God's. Another legitimate construction of the lines – suggested by the context of spiritual warfare in which "grace," not "skill," yields victory, and retroactively confirmed by the long exploration of good works in canto x – would run something like this: if we have any strength of our own, it invariably pursues evil; but all the good which we have (and we do have some), including both our power and our very desire to seek good, ultimately belongs to God.

Readers who make this guess about the literal meaning of the text might also pause to consider how the will, which somewhat furtively recovers a legitimate and positive existence in the stanza's last line, can coexist with the overpowering grace asserted earlier. Such readers are likely to adopt a pattern of reasoning that is, by now, familiar to us. Spenser's lines (x.1.6–7), they might reason, like their original in Philippians, preclude human self-congratulation by crediting all good works to the divine "grace," not the human "skill," that gains "victory" in spiritual warfare. Spenser's lines nonetheless attribute to human wills that have been renewed by grace the capacity to cooperate with deity in the performance of good works. As we have seen, Reformed theologians would term such works, specifically, acts of "holiness." Despite a high degree of consensus about the meaning of the Pauline lines that authorize Spenser's stanza, fundamental differences of opinion appear when theologians take up the question of whether acts of the renewed human will are meritorious. As we have noted before, post-Tridentine Catholicism and some pre-Tridentine strands of it consider good works impelled by grace working within the human soul to be sinless, part of the process of justification.[19] For Reformed theologians, such works contribute to the process of sanctification, and although they are accurately termed "holy," those works are shot through with sin.

That both Roman Catholic and Protestant doctrines grant human will a role in the performance of good works suggests solutions for interpretive puzzles which commentators have often discovered in *The Faerie*

Queene I.x. The Protestant idea that "holiness" involves both the cooperative achievement and the sinful corruption of works that nonetheless remain "holy" suggests a way to reconcile features of the text that are at first sight incongruous. The monastic elements of the House, its seven beadmen in particular, need not imply the heresy of "works-righteousness" that Protestants believed to be embodied in monastic devotion. That is, the beadmen may not prove, as Virgil Whitaker asserts, that Spenser contradicts himself by denying the possibility of human participation in good works in stanza 1, but then "shows a fondness for good works which is in line with the conservative preference for Catholic ways . . . [and] clearly implies that the works have 'merit.'"[20]

Nor need figures like the beadmen support the conclusion that, as Paul Alpers says, "everything humanly valuable we see in the first two-thirds of canto 10 derives its sanction from the realm of grace, not of nature," and that "[t]here is no way of reconciling, in a single structure of judgment" statements that seek to legitimize human striving for admirable achievement in the human sphere with the demands of grace.[21] Features of the text that (for Whitaker) imply merit and (for Alpers) problematically assert the claims of human effort can be transformed by readers' perceptions into metaphoric expressions of differing versions of orthodoxy. Nothing prevents readers of Catholic or unselfconscious Pelagian leanings from reading merit into the knight's actions in I.x, or readers of humanistic biases from remaining puzzled by the canto's apparent contradictions. If the House of Holiness is viewed as a metaphoric representation of Protestant doctrines of holiness, however, *The Faerie Queene* I.x will be found to embody the overall implication that works in this world are important, admirable, eagerly to be pursued, and yet contribute nothing to justification.[22]

Readers who perceive the inhabitants and features of the House of Holiness as signs of grace's justifying presence will often find their attention drawn to affective concerns. As we have seen, the pursuit of holiness was thought to have important emotional consequences. This conviction would draw attention to the point that a central function of the House and the practice of holiness is specifically to "cherish" Red Cross Knight (x.2.7). Una delivers him to Celia's dwelling so that he "chearen might, / Till he recovered had his late decayed plight" (2.8–9). The possibility of gaining this "cheer," a word that neatly combines implications of nourishment and "cheering up" (*OED*), implies that the chronically "sad" knight's capacity for joy may at last be realized.

A Protestant actualization of this anticipated reading could build upon materials current in works of practical divinity. A fine instance of this genre, Greenham's *Treatise of Blessedness*, argues that the Reformed sequence of causes (the "golden chain") of election yields blessedness *in this life* by providing authentic "assurance," the obverse of that "vaine assurance of mortality" rejected by Spenser's narrator at x.1.2. Reliable intellectual and emotional support derives from the "assurance of faith . . . wrought by the word preached." This true assurance has many effects, including "peace of mind": "this peace causeth joy, joy being accompanied with security, security working in love, love laboring with a care to please God . . . from whence issueth a desire of welldoing to others." As Greenham develops the idea, the potential relevance of all this to a comprehensive doctrinal construction of the House of Holiness becomes clearer. The "instrumental cause" of the bliss that assurance brings, he points out, is "partly within us, as *faith*, and partly without us, as the word and the appurtenances accompanying the same, as prayer, the sacraments, the discipline of the Church." Together with the inward illumination of God's Spirit (the "formal cause" of beatitude), our active use of these instruments "so [applies] the promises of God to our proper and peculiar comforts, that it sealeth us up to the Lord, affording a certain testimony to our hearts, that we have not in vain received the good spirit of God."[23]

What Greenham does in this passage and elsewhere is to demonstrate that the "good works" which are constantly described in Protestant doctrine as providing experiential evidence of one's election ("a certain testimony") need not be limited to outward acts of charity toward the poor, sick, and helpless. Popularizing the notion that "good works" include a broad range of activities – study, introspection, repentance, contemplation, and the outward works of worship ("prayer, the sacraments, the discipline of the church")[24] – Elizabethan catechisms normally present lists of holy works that mark one as a "good Christian." These lists can sound like descriptions of Red Cross Knight's progress through the House of Holiness: the good Christian "maketh the body subject to the spirit with the moderate use of eating and drinking. He exerciseth himself in godly meditations, in reading the Holy Scriptures, in offering up prayers and thanks continually to God. He succoreth the poor members of Christ."[25] Elizabethan pastoral theology regularly counts such actions as these among "the sweet and sure signs of election." Even backsliding can qualify as such a sign, for it supplies evidence of a salubrious "conflict of the flesh and spirit."[26]

An awareness that a great variety of activities belonging to holy living can qualify as "good works," and hence constitute sources of assurance, can transform our reading of I.x. Among the newly conspicuous features of the canto is joy, the mood which Protestant conceptions of "holiness" incline readers to anticipate as a consequence of assurance. Once our guiding presuppositions incline us to notice it, that emotion pervades the canto. Zeal, a "francklin faire and free," entertains the newcomers with "comely courteous glee" (6.4–6), and Reverence, a "gentle Squire, / Of milde demeanure, and rare courtesie," provides a new and measured "sadness" to complement zeal (7.3). When Caelia herself, at once a kindly woman and a personification of grace, greets Una, "[h]er hart with joy unwonted inly sweld" (8.8). The ambiguous reference of "her" allows both readings – "Caelia's" and "Una's" – and so expresses the reciprocity normal to charitable joys. After Una's first interview with Caelia, the mood of cheering entertainment reasserts itself "with all the court'sies" that Caelia can devise "to shew her bounteous and wise." Grace makes her nature and presence visible through acts of human courtesy, a Renaissance portmanteau virtue here reworked into an expression of generosity of spirit ("bounty") joined to wisdom. The social elements of the House of Holiness – not only its extremely deferential Reverence (who "knew his good to all of each degree" 7.5), but what readers could justifiably perceive as its promotion of the manners of courtship by transforming them into "simple true" manifestations of grace – suggest how powerful the ideological impact of Spenser's theological allegory can become.[27]

Inspiring all these cheerful good manners is Charissa, whose literally absent but spiritually present spouse's potency accounts for the "multitude of babes" (31.1) which represent her fertility. As the poet's own term indicates, they are, strictly speaking, not children but "pledges" (4.9), both of mutual love between human spouses and of that which links each faithful soul to Christ. The Savior's generosity allows the faithful to see their own good works as "pledges" that He has granted them the grace which saves. This is how the productive love Charissa embodies can make one's election sure. To the ever-anxious question "[h]ow shall I see my faith?," Tyndale replies, "I must come down to love again, and thence to the works of love, ere I can see my faith." By works of "brotherly charity," the Tudor homily declares, we "certify our conscience the better that we be in the right faith."[28] That good works provide tangible evidence of assured salvation suggests a way to understand why, once his conscience has been "cured" by Patience, Red Cross must be delivered directly to Charissa with the aim "[h]imselfe to chearish, and consuming thought / To put away out of his carefull brest" (29.5–6). A healthy self-love becomes the necessary foundation for love of others, and acts of charity will assure the actor of God's inalienable love for him.[29]

Before concentrating on acts of charity, however, Red Cross must be treated by Caelia's elder daughters. Fidelia provides the first of a series of educative experiences which the knight undergoes in the canto, and his matriculation into her "schoolehouse" (18.4) looks at first as if it will lead to *the* central moment toward which an allegory of Protestant religious experience would appropriately move. The very preeminence of the doctrine *sola fide* predicts that Fidelia will be incontestably dominant. So too does the imagery that makes her, on first view, comparable to the unveiled Una of I.iii – "Like sunny beames threw from her Christall face . . . like heavens light" (x.12). This imagery invites readers attuned to the contributions of Revelation to compare both Una and Fidelia to that book's similarly illumined angels, who were normally interpreted as symbols for Christ Himself.[30] Fidelia's radiance suggests that she possesses and communicates the very wisdom of the Savior. As embodied here, that wisdom wears a more formidable aspect than it does in Una.

Dread, in fact, is the sensation Fidelia most effectively communicates:

> in her right hand bore a cup of gold,
> With wine and water fild up to the hight,
> In which a Serpent did himselfe enfold,
> That horrour made to all, that did behold;
> But she no whit did chaunge her constant mood:
> And in her other hand she fast did hold
> A booke, that was both signd and seald with blood,
> Wherein darke things were writ, hard to be understood.   (x.13.2–9)

Fidelia's dark meanings receive commentary when she assumes another role that makes her formidable in yet another way. She becomes a professor, or rather a schoolteacher, of theology:

> Faire Una gan Fidelia faire request,
> To have her knight into her schoolehouse plaste,
> That of her heavenly learning he might taste,
> And heare the wisedome of her words divine.

> She graunted, and that knight so much agraste,
>   That she him taught celestiall discipline,
>   And opened his dull eyes, that light mote in them shine. (x.18.3–9)

This image of Faith as pedagogue accords with the view that faith includes an imperative to learn.[31] A Protestant reading would most likely emphasize that the learner is here "agrast," and interpret the word to mean that it is grace which drives believers "to hear the heavenly learning" and enables them to comprehend it. So grace-dominated a reading also calls attention to an aptly chosen preposition: the light that opens "dull eyes" shines not "into" but "in" them. Although it normally employs human teachers and ministers of the sacraments, for whom Fidelia can stand as allegorical embodiment, faith must always also work from within as a function of the Spirit.

Having long followed Red Cross Knight's frustrated search for reliable guidance amidst the world's dissembling appearances, readers may by now expect to share the illumination Fidelia brings. When she ascends her pedagogical chair, the anticipated revelation begins:

> And that her sacred Booke, with bloud ywrit,
>   That none could read, except she did them teach,
>   She unto him disclosed every whit,
>   And heavenly documents thereout did preach,
>   That weaker wit of man could never reach,
>   Of God, of grace, of justice, of free will,
>   That wonder was to heare her goodly speach:
>   For she was able, with her words to kill,
>   And raise againe to life the hart, that she did thrill.   (x.19)

An immediate function of grace, faith at last empowers Red Cross' reason to penetrate the otherwise impregnable barrier that separates the realms of nature and grace.[32] She teaches "every whit."

Just at this point, when readers might expect to share the ultimate illumination, we receive a mere list: Fidelia speaks "Of God, of grace, of justice, of free will." For some readers, this line will be opaque. For others, automatically treating these general terms as screens onto which favored doctrines can be projected, the line can feel richly revealing. The poem discloses all by revealing nothing but the key words of an outline. Spenser thus makes available the sensation of revelation, and preserves that revelation's status *as* revelation: we simply hear what a "wonder" it is to listen to faith's voice. To suggest the degree of variability that Fidelia's list allows, we need only recall how elaborately terms like "grace," "jus-

tice," and "free will" – much less "faith" itself – were interpreted in theological writings authorized in Spenser's England.[33]

Whatever the precise content of her theology, Fidelia forcefully recasts
her protégés' lives in the pattern of Christ, their archetype, by employing words that can "kill, / And raise againe to life the hart, that she did
thrill" (x.19.8–9). Red Cross affectively enacts this alternately dying
and rising pattern when, for the first of three occasions in the canto, he
is said to achieve "perfection":

> The faithfull knight now grew in litle space,
>   By hearing her, and by her sisters lore,
>   To such perfection of all heavenly grace   (x.21.1–3)

At last, Red Cross Knight has reached the invulnerability which complete possession of "all heavenly grace" must unerringly confer. But we
soon learn that true perfection eludes the knight's grasp; it seems instead to renew his suicidal yearnings:

> Greev'd with remembrance of his wicked wayes,
> And prickt with anguish of his sinnes so sore,
> That he desirde to end his wretched dayes:
> So much the dart of sinfull guilt the soule dismayes.   (x.21.6–9)

How can "perfection of all heavenly grace" issue so immediately in another attack of suicidal guilt?

One answer may be that among the diverse consequences of faith, as
Perkins says, is to oblige the believer "to sail by hell" (see ch. 1, p. 45).
In Taverner's less colorful phrases, this means that faith includes an element of despair: "faith despairing of her own proper powers and fixing
her eyes upon the Lord's goodness, is the thing that getteth us forgiveness of our sins, righteousness, and everlasting life."[34] The doctrine of
sanctification precludes closure, in lives actual or fictional, and each time
the poet assigns "perfection" to Red Cross, or anything that sounds like
a fully actualized spiritual health, the idea is shortly retracted.[35] To
mitigate the distress faith brings, "wise Speranza gave him comfort
sweet," for example, "And taught him how to take assured hold / Upon
her silver anchor" (22.1–3). "Assured hold" on hope implies unshak-
able confidence, the certainty which Reformed conceptions of faith include under the label "assurance" (ch. 1, pp. 42–43). But readers who
feel any confidence in the knight's assurance will soon experience another reversal: within five lines, Red Cross is "disdeining life, desiring
leave to die."

Such relapses move Una to ensure that the knight will more consistently heed her appeal "himselfe to chearish" (x.29.5–6). She will let him see his faith, which means that he must, as Tyndale puts it, "come down to love again." He does so in x.29–34, for Red Cross here meets Charissa, who will finally establish the assurance he is now prepared to receive. Only when schooled by *caritas*/Charissa does Red Cross with full consciousness know

> Of love, and righteousnesse, and well to donne,
> And wrath, and hatred warely to shonne,
> That drew on men Gods hatred, and his wrath   (x.33.4–6)

This new competence in well-doing suggests that Red Cross can now achieve salvation: "From thence to heaven she teacheth him the *ready* path" (33.9; emphasis added). The Charissa passage can be taken to imply not only that one can fulfill the demands which divine law imposes; it might also hint that charitable works win heaven. The stanza invites a voluntarist, "Pelagian," or post-Tridentine Catholic reading.

By acts of selection and projection, readers are free to sustain such a reading, though in ways which Spenser makes typically complex. The complexities begin to arise immediately, for the "ready path" to heaven soon appears strewn with impediments, blockages which Charissa apparently foresees when she provides an "auncient matrone" to guide Red Cross Knight's "weaker wandring steps":

> Her name was Mercie, well knowne over all,
> To be both gratious, and eke liberall:
> To whom the carefull charge of him she gave,
> To lead aright, that he should never fall
> In all his wayes through this wide worldes wave,
> That Mercy in the end his righteous soule might save.   (x.34.4–9)

Readers susceptible to Protestant implications could discover in these lines solid evidence that the knight's works cannot gain salvation in any direct way. Charissa, whose reciprocal nature allows her to represent at once the love believers express toward one another and the love God extends to humankind, provides, in Mercy, a correspondingly Janus-faced figure.[36] For Mercy, representing, first, the Lord's disposition to be "gratious, and eke liberall" toward sinful humankind, embodies the very "spring-head of . . . justification." She also embodies the mercy which believers show, in turn, to fellow mortals.[37]

Acting as figure of divine liberality, Mercy embodies the generosity that imputes saving righteousness to Red Cross and so prevents any irrevocable fall into sin. In this sense, it can accurately be said that "he should never fall / In all his wayes through this wide worldes wave"; Protestant doctrines of salvation reveal that closure has always already been achieved. Yet Mercy also sustains the knight's efforts to win increments of actual holiness:

> And ever when his feet encombred were,
> Or gan to shrinke, or from the right to stray,
> She held him fast, and firmely did upbeare,
> As carefull Nourse her child from falling oft does reare.   (x.35.6–9)

On the one hand, Red Cross' salvation is assured; on the other, it is impeded because the faithful must cooperatively labor and therefore must sin. Spenser's language allows a precise application of Reformed dogma here, for it enables readers to preserve a distinction between perfect, imputed righteousness on the one hand, and holiness of the imperfect, sanctifying kind. This second righteousness can be perceived in the image of the "carefull Nourse," which implies that believers do contribute to their sanctification – to the halting degree that an unsteady child contributes to the first steps its parents enable it to take. This image, which Erasmus (in controversy with Luther) employed to argue that believers make some real if feeble contribution to their salvation, suggests how readers might sustain a voluntarist interpretation of the images of striving which the canto presents. They need only assign those images to the process of justification, understood as some medieval theologians (including St. Thomas) and the Tridentine decrees defined that process.

On the other hand, readers bringing Protestant perspectives to bear could strengthen their case by noting a striking contrast between this image of Red Cross as feeble infant aided by the "careful nourse" and the comparable earlier moment when the knight could contribute to his rescue in no way at all. Functioning in a way that suggests the arrival of the grace of justification, Arthur there

> found the meanes that Prisoner up to reare;
> Whose feeble thighes, unhable to uphold
> His pined corse, him scarse to light could beare,
> A ruefull spectacle of death and ghastly drere.   (viii.40.6–9)

For Protestant readings, this action can portray the moment of calling, when justifying grace takes irresistible hold on an elect soul that has so far remained "dead in sin" (cf. ch. 5, p. 123, above). The contrast with this earlier episode can heighten a reader's sense that it is appropriate for Mercy "eftsoones" to take Red Cross "unto an holy Hospitall" where "seven Bead-men," having "vowed all / Their life to service of high heavens king" enact that vow by "spend[ing] their dayes in doing godly thing" (x.36.1–5). As Williams and Alpers have rightly observed, the beadmen's seven kinds of labors express *caritas* working through sympathy directed toward fellow "images of God in earthly clay" (39.7). Taking seven to imply completeness (ch. 5, p. 125), readers might think of Red Cross as totally instructed in every variety of charitable works that Mercy ("of their order she was Patronesse," 44.8) and Charissa ("their chiefest founderesse," 44.9) move people to undertake. Surely now, we might foresee, Red Cross has at last gained the capacity to "see his faith" registered in a multitude of outward actions that bespeak true devotion and rightly ordered love.

This implication of total achievement leads to another announcement that Red Cross has reached perfection:

> Shortly therein so perfect he became,
> That from the first unto the last degree,
> His mortall life he learned had to frame
> In holy righteousnesse, without rebuke or blame.   (x.45.6–9)

Such a statement can readily support a Catholic reading, for nothing forbids us from viewing this perfection in works of "holy righteousness" as a collaborative process in which believers can earn increments of merit that are so pure ("without rebuke or blame") that they contribute toward justification. Just as readily, however, Protestant readers can interpret this perfection as complete only by way of imputation. For in the next effort at moral striving, which treats contemplation as an extension of the exertions personified in the beadmen, human power proves inadequate:

> That hill they scale with all their powre and might,
> That his frayle thighes nigh wearie and fordonne
> Gan faile, but by her helpe the top at last he wonne.   (x.47.7–9)

"Gan faile," meaning "did fail," suggests a defect too serious to be compatible with the ascription to the knight of meritorious righteousness.

Such a recurrence of fault indicates that Red Cross needs a still more reliable source of assurance than good works can supply, however comprehensive those works might be. In the final episode of I.x, he therefore undergoes a visionary experience that can finally moderate the chronic sadness which makes him vulnerable to despair. The poet embodies this ultimate spiritual state in a hermit:

> And eke a litle Hermitage thereby,
> Wherein an aged holy man did lye,
> That day and night said his devotion,
> Ne other worldly busines did apply
>
> . . . .
> Each bone might through his body well be red,
> And every sinew seene through his long fast:
> For nought he car'd his carcas long unfed (x.46.4–7; 48.5–7)

Like other residents of the House of Holiness, Contemplation can be construed as a personification of one recurrent but not monopolistic feature of every righteous soul's life. His primary work might best be described as "meditation" (46.9).

Readers open to the possibility that individuals could exemplify the true Christian life even within monastic orders,[38] but convinced that monasticism normally fostered corrosive spiritual and social evils, can readily "see" in this figure a congenial meaning. Contemplation certainly can be viewed, as some have claimed, as evidence of Spenser's nostalgic admiration for a medieval religious institution. Protestant interpreters, however, can construe this monastic figure as a striking metaphoric representation of a quite different kind of religious dedication, which Reformed Christianity itself prescribed. As Peter Martyr explains the relevant attitude, people must be both active and contemplative: "Aristotle treateth severally of civil life and function, and also of life contemplative . . . that whosoever aspireth to felicity, may know, that he is not able to obtain the same, except in an excellent sort he be partaker of both these estates of life." If we are able, we must be active, but when leisure serves "then we [are] to be occupied with great pleasure in the contemplation of divine and human things; that so these actions, which in kind seem to be diverse, may help one another."[39] Just as contemplation should be undertaken at appropriate moments in one's day, so too it can find place in the cycles of life: if people "may endure the travails of their mind and body, and by their calling are bound six days in the week . . . to follow the same," they are not to emulate "a widow of fourscore and four years, living in contemplation," for whom such behavior is appropriate.[40] A reader possessed of such attitudes, and predisposed to understand Spenser's Contemplation in light of them, would be likely to note that he makes both "God and goodness" the subjects of his meditation. He acknowledges and explores the ethical obligations that follow from accurate apprehension of deity. Appropriately, therefore, Contemplation urges Red Cross to return to the world until he has completed a life of heroic endeavor, "when thou famous victorie hast wonne, / And high emongst all knights hast hong thy shield" (60.5–6).

The climax of the episode and of the canto provides further support for readers who have begun to see Contemplation as a Reformed revaluation of the very idea of contemplation.[41] However ready such readers might be to transform Contemplation into a symbol of thoroughly Protestant beliefs and practices, however, their responses are likely to be conditioned in part by pre-Reformation norms. Spenser's description of this "aged holy man" makes such expectations difficult to avoid, for Contemplation looks like a specialist in mystical exercises of the kind that could provide direct access to divine mysteries:

> Great grace that old man to him given had;
>   For God he often saw from heavens hight,
>   All were his earthly eyen both blunt and bad,
>   And through great age had lost their kindly sight,
>   Yet wondrous quick and persant was his spright,
>   As Eagles eye, that can behold the Sunne   (x.47.1–6)

Approaching the highest mount, under the guidance of this visionary, readers will most likely anticipate experiences akin to "the transports of contemplation," as mysticism describes them. In such contemplation, "all intellectual operations should be abandoned" and one confronts directly the "'absolute and unchangeable mysteries of theology [which] are deeply hidden, according to the superluminous darkness of instructive silence.'"[42]

Readers harboring anticipations of this kind have a surprise in store. Not only do we find ourselves confronted not by a vision but by another long, narrow, arduous climb (x.55.2); we also find that after this final labor the promised vision lies beyond the narrator's powers of expression ("Too high a ditty for my simple song," 55.7). What hints of description we do receive are drawn from comfortably familiar images: Red Cross sees "a goodly Citie"

> Whose wals and towres were builded high and strong
> Of perle and precious stone, that earthly tong
> Cannot describe, nor wit of man can tell   (x.55.4–6)

To be sure, these images derive authority from the scriptural passages they selectively echo (Rev. 21:10–21), but Spenser's text presents little even of the visualizable features of Revelation's city. The poet requires us to recollect most of the holy text's very words if those words are to contribute to our perception of the revelation toward which his language gestures. This treatment of the vision seems designed to make clear that the revelatory consequences of reading such scriptural passages are, literally, "too high" for "earthly tong"; grace alone gives such reading the character of revelation. As their varied inclinations prompt them, readers may complete the fragmentary vision Spenser provides with materials drawn from Revelation itself, or from Bonaventura, or Dante, or other visionaries less tentative than the author of *The Faerie Queene*.

Yet the idea that the process of contemplation ends not in a mystic's ineffable rapture but in confrontation with an (as yet) uninterpreted holy text, again invites readers to interpret Spenser's "Contemplation" in ways compatible with Protestant doctrines. The influential prayers and meditations of John Bradford, for example, even those meditations whose announced topics predict contact with ultimate spiritual realities, end not with visions but with quotations of scriptural texts which themselves obliquely describe visions.[43] Moreover, this reformer's meditations illustrate not only a characteristic deferral of the visionary; they also display the corresponding rationalistic quality of Protestant prescriptions concerning meditation. The aim is to "set our minds on work, about the cogitation of things heavenly . . . and so debate and reason about the same, that our affections may thereby be moved to love and delight in, or to hate and fear, according to that which we meditate on." The affections are to be engaged too, of course, but to a degree that, by contrast with medieval and later Catholic conceptions of the ultimate goal of human "cogitation of things heavenly," would appear subordinate to the analytical processes of reason.[44]

To Red Cross Knight's bland overall vision of the city, Spenser adds details that render it still less like a Bonaventura's or a Dante's efforts to evoke apprehension of the ineffable. The perception Red Cross receives is downright homely:

> As he thereon stood gazing, he might see
> The blessed Angels to and fro descend
> From highest heaven, in gladsome companee,
> And with great joy into that Citie wend,
> As commonly as friend does with his frend.   (x.56.1–5)

If this depiction of happy comradery stands as the climax of Red Cross' seemingly endless ascent into the mountain range of holiness, it does so by stressing something which has been quietly present throughout the canto. From its courteous outset, holiness' "house" has been notable for "gladsome companees" in which allegorical personifications, whether of virtues, divine graces, or states of the human mind, can also represent people who generously aid, teach, console, and in other ways enable fellow mortals "themselves to chearish." This "gladsome" milieu suggests something of the fundamental nature of the church, a true community of the faithful, as the Legend of Holiness invites readers to conceive of it.

The heavenly city which Contemplation envisions provides this conception of the church with lofty validation. This community turns out, as x.57.1–4 insists ("Hierusalem that is . . . that God has built / For those to dwell in, that are chosen his, / His chosen people"), to be a domesticated and cheering institutional embodiment of predestined election. If social historians' descriptions of contentious human relations in the sixteenth century are accurate,[45] or if we simply recall images of courtly emulation and backbiting in Spenserian episodes like Lucifera's house – and their explosive and demoralizing re-emergence in the denizens of Philotime's court (FQ II.46–47), in Ate (FQ IV.i.19–30, 47), and above all in the Blatant Beast (FQ VI.iii.24–27, xii.38–41) – we can view this canto's identification of beatitude with unfeigned fellow-feeling as a compensatory wish-fulfillment. As he will do elsewhere in his works, Spenser's narrator laments the modern absence of such feeling at I.ix.1,[46] where he celebrates the knights' readiness in genuine friendship and mutual praise, "friendly each did others prayse devize," as an expression of the "[g]oodly golden chaine, wherewith . . . noble minds of yore allyed were."

The stress on humane community intensifies, paradoxically it seems, as we approach the moment many feel to be climactic in the canto and the book, Red Cross' discovery of his identity (x.60–61). Commentators who treat this event as climactic often assume it to be unproblematic, but the knight's discovery of his identity occurs at a moment that can cause puzzlement, when Contemplation concludes his argument that Red Cross must continue in active service to Cleopolis' "sovereign Dame":

> And thou faire ymp, sprong out from English race,
> How ever now accompted Elfins sonne,

Well worthy doest thy service for her grace,
To aide a virgin desolate foredonne.
. . . .
Then peaceably thy painefull pilgrimage
To yonder same Hierusalem do bend,
Where is for thee ordaind a blessed end:
For thou emongst those Saints, whom thou doest see,
Shalt be a Saint, and thine owne nations frend
And Patrone: thou Saint George shalt called bee,
Saint George of mery England, the signe of victoree.

(x.60.1–4; 61.3–9)

Contemplation urges a life that combines secular service and contemplative withdrawal. The service is devoted specifically to the knight's nation and to his queen. Sainthood implies both national affiliation and an expression of the knight's "ordaind . . . blessed end." Red Cross' "self" emerges when displayed in a name and a narrative that reveal neither his unique separateness nor any mystic's separation from the world. Both name and narrative bespeak instead his inextricable involvement in overlapping communities – the British nation, the community of saints, and, as both name (*geos*, earth) and narrative of origin (x.66) emphasize, the earth, the community of creatures whose material substance continues to announce a basis for humility shared by all humankind, saints and plowmen, elect and reprobate.[47]

Having "seen" his faith in canto x's elaborate image of the works of holiness, Red Cross has at last fulfilled Una's earlier exhortation, "shew what ye bee" (I.i.19.2; ch. 2, p. 65, above) and so can be said to have found himself ("himselfe . . . to find," x.68.1). As a result, he can respond to Una's subsequent prescription: "strive your excellent selfe to excell" (xi.2.7). He does this in I.xi, by being "conformed" with increased steadiness to that image in which "we all behold as in a mirror the glory of the Lord," and as the canto proceeds he is "changed into the same image" (II Cor. 3:18).[48] This transformation is symbolized by actions that compare the knight's new struggles to those of "his dying lord." When he enters battle with the dragon, Red Cross begins patently to bear the cross. The dragon's fiery breath burns his face,

And through his armour all his bodie seard,
That he could not endure so cruell cace,
But thought his armes to leave, and helmet to unlace.

(xi.26.7–9)

The knight's former defense becomes the chief agent of his agony, a point made both here and at 27.8–9. As in Orgoglio's dungeon, the knight despairs, "death did he oft desire" (28.4). Because it is so thorough-going, the defeat can be read as anticlimactic repetition, or as Red Cross' sudden reversion to the status of "unregenerate man" or to a condition of "mortal sin." Each of these positions is maintained in Carol V. Kaske's influential article on the canto, and each is persuasive so long as non-Reformed theological conceptions of sin and of grace supply the interpreter's materials for construing the text.[49]

Reformed perspectives can construe this battle as an instance of struggles that the regenerate must undergo throughout their lives as they combat the very essence of evil. Often the immediately supplied measure of grace will suddenly be reduced and the diabolic will temporarily triumph (ch. 1, p. 43). At this trying moment in Red Cross' battle, when the divinely supplied armor becomes the agent of insufferable pain, faith can regard even so agonizing a reversal as a direct function of grace. Some readings might also specify the mechanism of that grace more narrowly, seeing the tormenting armor as a symbol of those gifts of grace (the law, perhaps, working through despair) which, laboring to destroy the Orgoglio within, torment the conscience so terribly that even the faithful yearn for release from obligation.

That the sufferings which dragon and armor together impose are manifestations of grace can be readily confirmed, by readers convinced that divine activity is omnipresent. Taking advantage of the knight's pain, the dragon supplies the immediate impetus for Red Cross' collapse into a post-lapsarian version of the "well of life," into which "the knight backe overthrowen, fell" (xi.28.8–9, 29.9, 30.9). The knight's movement is completely involuntary. Suffering imposed by grace working through evil drives him "unweeting" (29.2) to a source of gracious healing, a "springing" (29.3) or "living" well (31.6). As the familiar scriptural origins of these metaphors imply,[50] the well represents grace, most broadly defined as the source of eternal life and, as Reformed interpreters would maintain with special vigor, the immediate impetus of all the secondary means (e.g. sermons, sacraments) which help to confer that life upon preordained recipients.

Readers who interpret the well as broadly as this can rest satisfied with a conclusion like that proposed by Hume, who follows Tuve: both the well and the tree in I.xi symbolize "Christ's doctrine and Christ himself" rather than the more specific baptismal or eucharistic implications for which many commentators have argued.[51] Readers who seek greater detail in doctrinal implication, however, might notice a series of adjustments in the poetry – adjustments that might impede the persistent inclination to limit the well to a symbol of baptism, as many have done.[52] Baptism counteracts original rather than actual sin, but Spenser's well can perform other functions too: "For unto life the dead it could restore, / And guilt of sinfull crimes cleane wash away" (30.1–2). Protestant theology often saw the raising of the dead as a metaphor for conversion, the moment when someone "dead in sin" is suddenly possessed by an onset of justifying grace. We might, then, be dealing here with a symbol of conversion.

Yet this well can also heal the sick:

> Those that with sicknesse were infected sore,
> It could recure, and aged long decay
> Renew, as one were borne that very day. (xi.30.3–5)

Having defined justification as a prolonged process that involves varying degrees of merit, post-Tridentine Roman Catholic readers could interpret the raising of the dead *and* the healing of the sick as undifferentiated moments in that process. Protestant doctrines, by contrast, would be more likely to suggest that this well's capacity for healing the sick is a symbol of sanctification, the amelioration of wounds suffered by people who, like Red Cross Knight, have already been raised from the dead (i.e., called and justified) and yet remain in need of frequent reinfusions of grace.

Either version of the episode soon meets with an apparent reversal of the sort the poem has long since prepared us to expect, for the knight appears, incongruously late in the narrative, to undergo baptism. At sunrise, Red Cross "upstarted brave / Out of the well, wherein he drenched lay." Like a newly rejuvenated eagle, "this new-borne knight to battell new did rise" (xi.34). The experience has much heightened Red Cross' effectiveness in battle (35.6–8), and as usual, the narrator can list possible explanations but cannot assign definite causes:

> I wote not, whether the revenging steele
> Were hardned with that holy water dew,
> Wherein he fell, or sharper edge did feele,
> Or his baptized hands now greater grew;
> Or other secret vertue did ensew;
> Else never could the force of fleshly arme,
> Ne molten mettall in his bloud embrew (xi.36.1–7)

The passage seems to insist that some supernatural power made the human equipment ("revenging steele," "molten mettall," "force of fleshly arme") newly capable of damaging the dragon. This in itself suggests that we are to perceive here an impressive expression of Protestant "holiness": powers of grace here work with human instruments to diminish evil. This interpretation seems eminently plausible, though again, nothing precludes a Catholic / Pelagian reading: Christ's virtues infused into the knight enable him to achieve meritorious actions in the process of justification.

But why the more specific possibility that "his baptized hands now greater grew"? A point worth stressing, because interpreters have so consistently overlooked it, is that the hands are not said to be *newly* baptized. Although the idea that the knight's baptism might occur so late in the narrative appears anomalous, readers need not retreat directly to the generalizing position (held by Tuve, Kellogg and Steele, Hume, and others) that the well can only represent very general theological meanings, like Christ, His grace, and His doctrine. This interpretation does provide a valid construction of the episode, especially because some leaders of the Elizabethan church held that "Christ doth truly and presently give His own self in His sacraments."[53] But the sacraments were also more widely thought to have psychological consequences, divine concessions to human insecurity: "if our mind be not confirmed on every side, it wavereth."[54] Elaborating the commonplace metaphor of the seal, Jewel asserts that "[a]s princes' seals confirm and warrant their deeds and charters, so do the sacraments witness unto our conscience that God's promises are true and shall continue for ever."[55]

For readers possessed of them, such ideas can help make sense of the overall movement of Spenser's narrative. Working in I.xi with spiritual learning and experience acquired in I.x, Red Cross displays the capacity to locate, recognize, confront, and combat ultimate evil. At crucial moments during the battle, predictably, he requires further aid. What he receives is the kind of renewal and reassurance provided specifically by sacramental ministrations. Guided by Protestant norms, readers can feel it to be appropriate that these sacramental elements appear after the self-conscious training in faith and Christian life which Red Cross received in canto x. First and repeatedly, one must hear the preached word, then see, hear, feel, and taste its confirmation at the celebration of the sacrament. Whatever differences concerning the "real," specific, and immediate effects various theologians might attribute to the sacraments,

Reformed Protestants normally also viewed them as visible and tangible reminders, reassuring "signs," and "seals" of saving truths.[56] The imperative inherent in faith itself always impels the faithful to know these truths, in ever-increasing depth and detail (ch. 1, pp. 43–44, above). And as Protestants conceived of it, faith, like sin, always transcends consciousness and remains at work even when the faithful cannot detect its presence in their souls (ch. 1, pp. 42–43, above). In light of these doctrines, it makes sense, first, that the knight, like the eagle to which he is compared, "marveiles at himselfe" when "new-borne" he rises "to battell new" (34.8–9); second, that his wonder should occur after an immersion that offers no hint of conscious attentiveness to anything so abstract as doctrine ("he drenched lay," 34.2); and, third, that this whole miraculous recovery could be construed not only as a rebirth wrought generally by grace, but more particularly by a reinvigoration of the effects of the knight's own baptism.

The final option here could occur most readily to readers aware that "baptism doth represent unto us our profession, which is to follow the example of our Savior Christ, and to be made like unto him, that as he died and rose again for us, so should we which are baptized die from sin, and rise again unto righteousness."[57] Although infants are usually the direct recipients of this sacrament, it is not only a once-for-all experience. It must also be regularly renewed. Tyndale puts it this way: "In our baptism we receive the merits of Christ's death through repentance, and faith, of which two baptism is the sign; and though when we sin of frailty after our baptism, we receive the sign no more, yet we be renewed again through repentance and faith in Christ's blood." The effects represented by baptism, then – repentance and faith – are recurrent sources of renewal in the Christian life, and they are fostered by the important memorial functions of the baptismal rite: "that sign of baptism, ever continued among us in baptizing our young children, doth ever keep us in mind [of repentance and faith], and call us back again unto our profession."[58] For a reader who recalls this doctrine, which was incorporated into the Elizabethan baptismal liturgy,[59] Red Cross Knight's "baptized hands" can "now greater grow" without undermining the assumption that he had been baptized long before I.xi.

His baptismal renewal initiates another movement in the Christological dying-and-rising pattern of Red Cross Knight's experience in I.xi. That archetypal pattern is itself reiterated in individual believers who, as Tyndale implies, and as Nowell puts it, "use" their baptism, constantly renewing its effects by dying to sin through repentance and rising to new belief and obedience through faith.[60] Spenser's text can easily accommodate such implications, and it can do so with a striking degree of originality that the mingling of theological discourse and chivalric-romance narrative makes possible. The knight's new strength, for example, results in increasingly terrible opposition by the dragon, and his "mortall sting his angry needle shot / Quite through his shield, and in his shoulder seasd, / Where fast it stucke, ne would there out be got" (38.5–7). This will surprise readers who take the shield quite simply to represent "the shield of faith," described in Ephesians. Yet as we have seen before, agonies imposed by sin are often functions of grace, and faith itself breeds both guilt for sin and desire to oppose it. Moreover, faith can admit intrusions of unbelief, even into the hearts of the elect, who can never lose their faith but may often appear to do so.

Unbelief. . . does not mortally wound [believers] with its weapons, but merely harasses them, or at most so injures them that the wound is curable. Faith, then, as Paul teaches, serves as our shield [Eph. 6:16]. When held up against weapons it so receives their force that it either completely turns them aside or at least weakens their thrust, so that they cannot penetrate to our vitals.[61]

Weakening rather than deflecting the dragon's death-yielding sting, Red Cross' shield of faith allows sin to inflict wounds that are curable and, like the downward movement in repentance, medicinal (x.39).

This invasion by sin results in newly energetic belligerence by the regenerate Red Cross, which in turn prompts another diabolic assault: the dragon "did fiercely fall / Upon his sunne-bright shield, and gript it fast withall" (xi.40.8–9). Protestant interpreters can view the ensuing struggle as an especially meticulous representation of the synergy characteristic of human "holiness." The dragon's fierce onslaught "forst [Red Cross] to retire / A little backward for his best defence" (45.2–3). This tactical retreat, deliberate in a way the previous fall (x.28–29) and his actions in earlier battles were not, registers a degree of progress in the conscious pursuit of holiness. So too does the narrator's unusually forthright admission that this second fall is providential: "eternall God that chaunce did guide" (45.6). Working together, human decision and divine arrangement precipitate a fall into the balm flowing from the "tree of life." The tree has "great vertues," giving "happie life to all, which thereon fed, / And life eke everlasting" (46.5–6). Balm flows from this tree

As it had deawed bene with timely raine:
Life and long health that gratious ointment gave,
And deadly woundes could heale, and reare againe
The senselesse corse appointed for the grave.
Into that same he fell: which did from death him save. (xi.48.5–9)

The significance of this tree and its balm have provoked understandable disagreement. Here as elsewhere differing possibilities made available by the variations within Elizabethan Protestant theology allow differing perceptions to arise from the same data. With Tuve, Hume, and
others, for instance, readers might settle on details that signal the broadest
of doctrinal possibilities.[62] For such readers, the tree symbolizes, essentially, Christ, His doctrine, and His grace. A little more detailed attention to relevant doctrines, however, can induce others to notice a number of potential distinctions. Yes, the tree yields beatitude ("happie life
. . . And life eke everlasting") and so must represent, most broadly, Christ
and his grace. Yet the imagery of balm, once selected as a significant
detail, can support a more specific meaning. Although "Christ" means
"anointed," as Nowell points out, the Savior was not anointed with "oil,
such as they used at creation of kings, priests, and prophets in old time,"
but with a "much more excellent oil; namely, with the most plentiful
grace of the Holy Ghost."[63] Such an identification, of the oil with the
gifts of the Holy Spirit, whose very name implies sanctification, would
appear altogether appropriate to Red Cross' situation and needs. Because it can resurrect "the senselesse corse appointed for the grave"
(48.6–9), the balm that anoints Red Cross can certainly be identifiable
as the grace that saves. But the balm also gives "long health" and heals
"deadly woundes" (48.6–7). This less thoroughgoing capacity implies
grace's other major function, its power to sanctify those already justified and called. Although it "did from death him save," therefore, the
balm also supplies continuing aid of the sort sanctification requires. As
readers move through the passage, they can recognize that sanctification is the balm's chief function – during this part of the narrative, for
this particular protagonist.

This observation implies, in turn, that Red Cross does not "become"
Christ.[64] He receives a new access of spiritual strength, an infusion of
the Spirit that makes him more holy, and therefore more "conformable"
to or more fully "incorporated" into the Savior. The battle's three-day
duration and the knight's repeated rising-and-falling pattern signal his
conformity to Christ. And the imagery of feeding on the tree of life –

"For happie life to all, which thereon fed, / And life eke everlasting did befall" (46.5–6) – can initiate a eucharistic reference which will condition some readers' responses to the balm which Spenser's tree exudes. Readers who possess some information about the eucharist can see that those effects are identical with the spiritual consequences of that sacrament as leaders of the Elizabethan Church and other Reformed churches described them. "By worthy [sic] receiving" the sacrament, Bradford explains, "we get by faith an increase of incorporation with Christ and amongst ourselves who be His members."[65] Like other originators of basic Elizabethan doctrines and liturgy, Bradford treats the eucharist as a major source of assurance and of reassurance, of the bolstered confidence that enables the world's Red Cross Knights to triumph over evil. An easily constructed reading of the knight's victory, therefore, could perceive the balm as symbol of the eucharist's power to strengthen assurance, to foster the confidence that Red Cross displays in his final victory. A compatible construction would focus on the idea of incorporation into Christ, a condition also increased by participation in the sacramental elements of religious life.[66] To view the knight as incorporated into the body of Christ is to recognize, first, that Red Cross' victory here derives from and recalls Christ's resurrection as a once-for-all triumph over evil, and yet, second, that Red Cross' victory remains at the same time merely a human triumph in a battle which must be waged again and again.

This reading accounts for the language that appears to attribute the knight's victory directly to divine power, to the weapon rather than to its human employer: "The weapon bright / Taking advantage of his open jaw, / . . . his life bloud forth with all did draw" (53.5–9).[67] The same reading accounts for the language that emphasizes the newly confident knight's energetic contribution to the outcome. The dragon "rusht upon him with outragious pride," but the knight "him r'encountring fierce, as hauke in flight, / Perforce rebutted backe" (53.3–5). A construction that notices both divine participation and human energy would see, therefore, a climactic achievement of "holiness" in the knight's victory. This is how Una's praise describes it: "Then God she praysd, and thankt her faithfull knight, / That had atchiev'd so great a conquest by his might" (55.8–9). Commentators have acutely pointed out that "his" modifies both "God" and "her faithfull knight." That double reference marks Red Cross as a hero of "holiness," one who contributes to a real but temporary defeat of evil by using his grace-renewed will to cooperate with grace.

If our long progress from Despair through the House of Holiness to this moment of knightly victory demonstrates anything with certainty, however, it is that such interpretations always remain optional. Readers will find meaning in such details of language if texts invite them to do so and if they themselves choose to do so. Many have seen the ambiguity of "so great a conquest by his might" (55.9) as giving all credit, without qualification, to the deity. Others will legitimately find meritorious synergy implied in the phrase, or, as I have just done, they can find synergy that does not merit, but rather signifies, election. Still others can overlook such niceties altogether and move on to enjoy in the lively narrative of the battle (which I have just interpreted nearly into invisibility), the buoyantly victorious conclusion to a romance narrative that has become too engaging on its own terms to clutter with theological speculation. This last group will find much that pleases them in I.xii, and all readers inclined to look for them can locate intriguing potential connections between holiness and the less overtly doctrinal virtues explored in subsequent books of *The Faerie Queene*.

7

"SPENSER" AND DOGMATIC MUTABILITY

To read the final canto of the Legend of Holiness while convinced that readers will variously construe theological contexts as well as Spenserian texts is to oppose prevailing currents. Established views of this canto presuppose that religious allusions dictate not only which passages of I.xii are significant, but what significance to find in them.[1] The allusions usually noted are important to any theologically grounded response to the text, but if we grant them single-minded attention we will fail to notice other intriguing features of the canto. Some of these features reveal the canto's remarkable appropriateness as a transition to subsequent books of *The Faerie Queene*. It will be helpful therefore to reread parts of I.xii, noticing various implications its surprising generic variety suggests. We will then be prepared to glance at a few ways in which the theological perspectives explored in earlier chapters of this book can inform responses to later, less persistently theological sections of Spenser's grand poem.

Knowledge of sixteenth-century doctrines of holiness can much modify our expectations of I.xii. Few readers interpreting Red Cross Knight's climactic battle as a triumph in the struggle for "holiness" as sixteenth-century Protestant theology defined it would expect that the knight's pursuit of that virtue had actually reached closure, an expectation readers either discover, we are often told, or feel disappointed when they do not.[2] Some doctrinally informed readers certainly might join modern scholars who perceive an analogy to the Harrowing of Hell when the imprisoned king and queen and their subjects emerge from "the brazen gate, / Which long time had bene shut" and proclaim "joy and peace through all his state" (I.xii.3).[3] If we view the release of Una's parents as an unmodified replication of the Harrowing, we may also expect the prisoners in *The Faerie Queene* I.xii to enter into beatitude, or at least into an earthly version of the communion of saints which Red Cross admired on the Mount of Contemplation.

Although some readers resort to the "etc. principle" and so actually

perceive a representation of that mystical fulfillment in I.xii, the poem
supplies material that might complicate their perceptions.[4] The early
passages of I.xii are remarkable not for visions of the afterlife but for
ceremonial display of political and social hierarchy. We watch a proces-
sion – King and Queen, followed by "sage and sober Peres," then "tall
young men," then "comely virgins," then "the fry of children young,"
and finally "all the raskall many. . . Heaped together in rude rablement"
(xii.5–9). The "raskall many" are granted an elaborate description:

> Some feard, and fled; some feard and well it faynd;
> One that would wiser seeme, then all the rest,
> Warnd him not touch, for yet perhaps remaynd
> Some lingring life within his hollow brest,
> . . . .
> Another said, that in his eyes did rest
> Yet sparckling fire, and bad thereof take heed;
> Another said, he saw him move his eyes indeed. (xii.10.1–4; 7–9)

And so on, as "diversly themselves in vaine they fray" (11.7) for another
full stanza. The dragon is dead; the community is released from his utter
dominance; but its people remain as rich in peccadilloes as most Christian conceptions of sin and human nature consider humankind inherently to be. Here the people compete to top one another's assessments
of the most superficial of all questions that might be asked about the
beast ("Is it *really* dead?"). By engaging in this comic competition, they
make Red Cross' great victory over evil an occasion to indulge an amusingly familiar impulse toward competitive vanity. As we have seen, a
more exalted social set indulge themselves similarly in Lucifera's castle
(I.vi.14). Once noticed, this intrusion of social satire into the fabric of
I.xii can bring back to earth a canto in which transparent allegories of
the mystical marriage of Christ and His church might have begun to
overwhelm other perceptions.

Red Cross himself soon joins the "rablement" in exhibiting the native
recalcitrance of the flesh. As critics have noted, the knight's retelling of
his adventures "[f]rom point to point" (15.8) omits a central point, his
dalliance with Duessa. The omission reveals a capacity for self-protec-
tion which fair-minded readers are likely to consider normal. But another evasion occurs in the very passage meant to atone for it, when Red
Cross places most blame on Duessa's skill at deception and reserves for
himself only the degree of fault attributable to generic human weakness:

> Who by her wicked arts, and wylie skill,
> Too false and strong for earthly skill or might,
> Unwares me wrought unto her wicked will,
> And to my foe betrayd, when least I feared ill.   (xii.32.6–9)

The excuse sounds lame, and Red Cross needs the help Una instantly supplies. She shores up his self-excusing version of the story, attributing everything to "that false sorceresse," who "onely . . . did throw / This gentle knight into so great distresse" (33.7–9). Truth here departs from truth, but her readiness to overlook Red Cross' sin is perfectly suited to the human situation: she seeks to allay a father's understandably aroused suspicions of her suitor.

Una's past generosity makes this instance feel perfectly predictable, and the local dominance of non-allegorical generic features (social satire, romance false-accusation scene) invites readers to escape the rigors of relentless allegorization. Yet this invitation is often stymied by the insistence with which commentators, following Upton, see (xii.39, for instance) allusions to the marriage song of the Lamb and the Church (Revelation 19.6–7). A reader construing the book in ways informed by a slightly wider range of scriptural texts could easily notice the more direct allusion to Revelation 19.7–8, which occurs at I.xii.22. There Una appears prepared for her betrothal, clothed like the bride of the Lamb:

> All lilly white, withoutten spot, or pride,
> That seemd like silke and silver woven neare,
> But neither silke nor silver therein did appeare.   (xii.22.7–9)

This last line forthrightly demands allegorical interpretation. In Revelation, the bride is clothed, according to the Geneva version, in "pure fine linen and shining," a material the biblical author himself immediately decodes: "the fine linen is the righteousness of saints" (Rev. 19:7–8). Protestant interpreters construe this righteousness either as imputed or actual righteousness, as Bullinger illustrates: commenting on the garment ("of clean or pure silk" in his version), he associates the bride's clothing with Paul's recurrent reminders "that we should put on the Lord Jesus," and he exhorts us to "beautify ourselves with the works of charity . . . of righteousness, chastity, and temperancy."[5] As usual in Revelation, then, the bride personifies the church in a way which implies that she herself, along with all her individual members, needs to put on Christ by undertaking good works. Such a construction recognizes that the Savior's own power (the gratuitous source of good works) is present here, symbolized by the garment. And this recognition can help readers who bring biblical contexts to their reading of Spenser to perceive that Red Cross and Una do not represent the bride and the Lamb. Their behavior in I.xii displays the inconsistency characteristic of people who need grace, and must always labor to wear the Lamb and His virtues more completely.

The allusive association of Red Cross with Christ also implies that the knight now actually enjoys a measure of beatitude, which the elect can fully experience only after death. Various features of the knight's final appearance in *The Faerie Queene*, Book I, suggest in fact that his incorporation into Christ enables him to participate in the final stage of the "Protestant paradigm of salvation," glorification (ch. 1, p. 28). Reformed conceptions of this stage inclined toward Calvin's view that "[r]egeneration is . . . a sign that, even though we have to wait till the final consummation of the Kingdom for our full share in the resurrection of Christ, nevertheless, this resurrection life has already begun to exert its power within us, and here and now we participate in it."[6] Divine music, which becomes audible after Una's father's court engages in its series of ancient Roman nuptial observances (xii.37–38), initiates such anticipations, sounding

> through all the Pallace pleasantly,
> Like as it had bene many an Angels voice,
> Singing before th'eternall majesty,
> In their trinall triplicities on hye;
> Yet wist no creature, whence that heavenly sweet
> Proceeded, yet eachone felt secretly
> Himselfe thereby reft of his sences meet,
> And ravished with rare impression in his sprite.   (xii.39.2–9)

The music validates this marriage, indicating that the bond between Una and Red Cross warrants a direct manifestation of divine favor. The last line, 39.9, also implies that the song performs a gentle version of the irresistible conquest described in the final line of Donne's "Batter my heart" – "Nor ever chast until thou ravish me." Spenser's milder description of divine ravishment appears in the effect Una's presence exerts on Red Cross Knight:

> Great joy was made that day of young and old,
> And solemne feast proclaimd throughout the land,
> That their exceeding merth may not be told:

> Suffice it heare by signes to understand
> The usuall joyes at knitting of loves band.
> Thrise happy man the knight himselfe did hold,
> Possessed of his Ladies hart and hand,
> And ever, when his eye did her behold,
> His heart did seeme to melt in pleasures manifold.

> Her joyous presence and sweet company
> In full content he there did long enjoy   (xii.40.1–41.2)

Readers invited to understand "by signes" the "usuall joyes at knitting of loves band," and who include in their perceptions anything whatever of "pleasures manifold" that make the heart "seeme to melt" may for the moment forget that this is a betrothal rather than a consummated marriage. The diction of amatory poetry and the idea of enjoying "full content" seem more appropriate to consummation than anticipation.

The necessity of postponement has been repeatedly made clear (xii.18; 19.9), however, and a reader's suspicion that Red Cross cannot possibly feel "full content" can coexist with the notion that his condition represents something beyond natural possibility. Still, marriage and sexual consummation often serve as metaphors for, perhaps even intimations of, such absolute fulfillment. At this final moment in the poem, therefore, it would be possible to conclude that Red Cross' sensations represent his entering not into humankind's typically imperfect pleasures, but into bliss – pleasures that satisfy, finally. "Glorification" is what Reformed theology could induce readers to find imaged here. "Yet," Spenser must inevitably emphasize, anticipations must not be confused with actualities: "swimming in that sea of blisfull joy, / He nought forgot, how he whilome had sworne, / . . . Unto his Farie Queene backe to returne" (xii.41.5–7).

Readers who follow Red Cross out of Book I into the wider world of Faerie will often meet passages that invoke perspectives explored in the Legend of Holiness. If any general rule about theological implications in Books II–VI can be applied with confidence at such moments, that rule will need to be undogmatic. It will go something like this: moments of achieved fullness of knowledge or virtue, repeatedly shown to crumble at the very instant of their announced "perfection" in I.x (ch. 6, above), then shown to require repeated shoring up during their active exercise in I.xi and their verbal reconstruction in I.xii, remain similarly elusive and ephemeral throughout *The Faerie Queene*.

In later books, however, those moments of achievement also become more difficult to view as credible traces of the benign if sometimes threatening providential order that appears to govern events in Book I. As they read *The Faerie Queene* II–VI, interpreters inclined toward providentialist optimism must work harder to sustain their version of the poem and the world it claims to mirror. Skeptical versions both of the world and of the poem, meanwhile, can find abundant materials on which to work. Whether readers apply theological perspectives in ways that support or undermine belief, however, those perspectives can complicate and enrich rather than reduce the experience of reading.

We can glance now at only a few passages that illustrate this point, episodes which I will not restrict to "vision" cantos.[7] Although I shall deliberately give more time to Book II than to the other books, a degree of randomness governs the selection of materials that follow here. This reflects my conviction that theological "contexts" for reading *The Faerie Queene* are things readers create when Spenser's text has somehow provoked or invited or simply not precluded their doing so. Often, such contexts find their way into our reading as affiliates of a prior conception of "Spenser" (see Introduction, p. 2). The hermeneutic circularity of this process can become conspicuous in scholarly discussions of the transition from the Legend of Holiness to that of Temperance.

Having determined that Spenser was a "protestant poet," Anthea Hume can appropriately also argue that "the poem possesses a unified frame of reference and that its protagonists all share the same Christian status." This consistency provides the foundation for more specific points of interpretation: that "Spenser's choice of a narrative structure composed of a sequence of linked quests allows for a clear analysis first [i.e., in Book I] of justification *sola gratia* and then of the successive virtues one by one," and that subsequent books are marked by "Spenser's unselfconscious acceptance" of the "established doctrine" that "*after* justification the regenerate human will could turn towards goodness and co-operate with God in the process of moral development."[8] Once established as a presupposition of subsequent reading, this strong, usefully organizing schema provides interpretive consistency.

If Guyon "starts at the point at which [Red Cross] leaves off"[9] and the poem's "protagonists all share the same Christian status" as "saint," then of course Guyon's disturbance by the concupiscible passions in the early cantos of the Legend of Temperance will be perceived as minimal.[10] Overt challenges to the virtue in which he specializes can hardly disturb a knight whose status is the same as Red Cross', who has become a successful protégé of the sequence of formidable professors who inhabit Celia's house. If we presuppose Guyon to be so very well prepared as Red Cross has become, we will readily perceive him to be but briefly "inflam'd with wrathfulnesse (II.i.25)" when Archimago deceives him at the opening of Book II. He can honestly be seen as subject there and throughout the opening five cantos only to "those normative tendencies to passion which the temperate or continent man must learn to bridle."[11]

Readers aware of the complexities and contradictions of sixteenth-century Protestant doctrines are likely to find this view of Guyon and his relation to Red Cross somewhat too neat. At the beginning of Book II, the text can seem to dramatize not an easy "taking up the baton" but a sequence of actions in which allegory darkens toward enigma. In the canto's opening stanzas, Guyon appears unwilling to embody Temperance. Told of an anonymous knight's rape of a "virgin cleene" (i.10.4), Guyon becomes "halfe wroth" (11.1), and shortly "with fierce ire / And zealous hast away is quickly gone / To seeke that knight" (13.1–3). He persists in this unreflecting anger even after realizing that he knows the putative rapist, and knows him to be a "right good knight" who had won glory in "[t]h'adventure of the *Errant damozell*" (19.8). Following this preparation, readers may conclude that Guyon's readiness to become "inflam'd with wrathfulnesse" (25.8) and even to attack without formal challenge and with "fierce saliaunce, / And fell intent" (29.6–7) registers something darker than a normal tendency toward passion.

Readers accustomed to viewing ethics as a limited domain that resides within the superior and more extensive territories of moral theology might draw a parallel between Guyon and the Red Cross whom we have followed through Book I: Guyon's emotions here transform well-intended actions into sin. Guyon himself appears to express this judgment of his first action in Book II; when he suddenly halts his "saliaunce" and cries:

> Mercie Sir knight, and mercie Lord,
>   For mine offence and heedlesse hardiment,
>   That had almost committed crime abhord,
>   And with reprochfull shame mine honour shent,
>   Whiles cursed steele against that badge I bent,
>   The sacred badge of my Redeemers death,
>   Which on your shield is set for ornament   (i.27.1–7)

Once he recognizes his redeemer's "badge," Guyon can again reason clearly and behave temperately. An appropriate doctrinal inference appears to be that reason can function rationally, and the person can behave virtuously, only when faith holds sway within the soul by way of the "perpetual aid and concurrence of grace" (see ch. 1, p. 32, above). The palmer, who at last overtakes Guyon, appears to embody a rational power that is more consistently so aided than Guyon is. Perhaps because palmers, by definition, have visited the holy land and seen some version of the Jerusalem that readers glimpse at *Faerie Queene* I.x.55–57, this "aged guide" knows Red Cross instantly and perfectly: as "soone as on that knight his eye did glance, / Eft soones of him had perfect cognizance" (31.2–5).

Like earlier achievements of perfection in *The Faerie Queene*, this "perfect cognizance" soon evaporates, in the view, at least, of readers prepared to assess the palmer's extemporaneous panegyric in light of Protestant views of human endeavor:

> Joy may you have, and everlasting fame,
>   Of late most hard atchiev'ment by you donne,
>   For which enrolled is your glorious name
>   In heavenly Registers above the Sunne,
>   Where you a Saint with Saints your seat have wonne:
>   But wretched we, where ye have left your marke,
>   Must now anew begin, like race to runne;
>   God guide thee, *Guyon*, well to end thy warke,
> And to the wished haven bring thy weary barke. (i.32)

This description of Red Cross Knight's achievement appears to credit him with *winning* salvation: "hard atchiev'ment . . . donne / For which" his name is enrolled among the saints; he has "wonne" his place among them. Predisposed to view the palmer as the book's authoritative allegorical voice, commentators sometimes take this remark as reliable description.

Red Cross' rejoinder, however, can be seen to contain not simply a self-effacing redirection of praise but an important doctrinal correction:

> Palmer, (him answered the *Redcrosse* knight)
>   His be the praise, that this atchiev'ment wrought,
>   Who made my hand the organ of his might;
>   More then goodwill to me attribute nought:
>   For all I did, I did but as I ought. (i.33.1–5)

If "this atchiev'ment" is taken to include the achievement of salvation, not simply the literal completion of the dragon-slayer's quest, then the statement corrects the palmer's implication that Red Cross has earned salvation. God's might has done that, and Red Cross can accept credit only for "goodwill." To deserve even that much credit in the view of readers adopting Reformed theological principles, however, the knight's idea of "goodwill" must include a set of tacit qualifications: this good will is, at the moment of justification, a newly created human faculty which replaces the natural man's will and cooperates with grace in achieving good works; it can accept credit only for imperfect cooperation; and that cooperation merits no part of its possessor's foreordained, eternal reward. Readers possessing fairly detailed knowledge of contemporary doctrines can easily perform these mental adjustments. Readers adopting common-sense Pelagian or deliberate Catholic views will still more easily grant God most of the credit, and yet reserve some for Red Cross too.

Both constructions of the palmer's and the knight's conflicting statements express, in part, the recurrent conflict between theology and ethics which is staged in Spenser's poem. From the perspective of morality, for which the palmer speaks, Red Cross Knight's achievement was finite; it is completed; and it merits reward. From the theological perspective adopted by Red Cross, the task is infinite, never completed in this life, and (assuming his principles are Protestant) without any trace of merit. Once perceived in Book II's opening stanzas, this tension between the sometimes complementary but often conflicting perspectives of theology and ethics will help readers to construct both the content and the significance of other major episodes in the Legend of Temperance.

Especially from a Reformed theological point of view, Guyon has "like race to runne" not in the sense that he begins where Red Cross left off, but in the sense that he too undertakes good works that grace alone makes possible. His works of temperance represent a specific focus within the pursuit of that comprehensive virtue which Protestant moral theology named "holiness." Guyon's titular virtue might be said, then, to represent by synecdoche the virtue which Red Cross has pursued – a pursuit for which the metaphor of the race, like the metaphor of combat, stands as a salient Pauline symbol.[12] Recurrently, however, Guyon's own and his rational palmer's views of the world in which they strive display a sometimes troubling, sometimes comic ignorance of larger systems of meaning. Spenser's characters meticulously observe "decorum," in the rhetoricians' sense, and in *The Faerie Queene*, Book II, decorum requires that both the palmer and Guyon exhibit the blindness which theology often attributes to rational and moral perspectives (ch. 2, pp. 58–59, above).[13]

The always potentially playful Spenserian narrator sometimes exhibits his characters' blindness. Especially when viewed in the light of Guyon's rash assault on Red Cross Knight, the narrator's apparently innocent description of the palmer's role seems to oversimplify:

> his blacke Palmer, that him guided still.
> Still he him guided over dale and hill,
> And with his steedie staffe did point his way:
> His race with reason, and with words his will,
> From foule intemperance he oft did stay,
> And suffred not in wrath his hastie steps to stray. (i.34.4–9)

As the insistent "still. / Still" helps us notice, the palmer's guidance was available before, as it now is after, Guyon has displayed his extreme anger at Red Cross. The rational virtue this palmer represents can only imperfectly and often retroactively restrain "will" from intemperance, wrath, and other evils that have inner and even unconscious spiritual dimensions. Unless practitioners of morality are illuminated and animated by the immediate activity of grace, as the palmer is when he recognizes Red Cross Knight, the unconscious dimensions of sin and the imperfection of reason's control will burst into view.

The imperfections of rationally directed temperance are registered when Guyon confronts the spectacle of Mortdant and Amavia. In recounting her story to Guyon, Amavia reports that Mortdant had fallen to Acrasia's fleshly temptation, and that Amavia had "wrapt [her] selfe in Palmers weed, / And cast to seeke him forth through daunger and great dreed" (II.i.52.8–9). Wearing this disguise, she performs an effective impersonation of Guyon's palmer, for she not only looks like a palmer but becomes Mortdant's tutor in temperance:

> through wise handling and faire governance,
> I him recured to a better will,
> Purged from drugs of foule intemperance:
> Then meanes I gan devise for his deliverance. (i.54.6–9)

Working through rational persuasion as Guyon's palmer does, Amavia achieves a cure; she returns Mortdant not to the sort of "good will" Red Cross has achieved but to "a better will" than that Acrasia had fostered in him. What Amavia cannot provide is the "deliverance," for which she then sought to devise means. Her effort to do so results in Mortdant's death when Acrasia's charm proves mortal. It does so, significantly, just at the moment when the victim mixes water with wine, enacting a veritable emblem of temperance, "So soone as Bacchus with the Nymphe does lincke" (i.55.6).[14]

Guyon's first response to Amavia's death expresses again the capacity for warm, even volatile fellow-feeling he showed earlier toward the supposed victim of ravishment: he "could uneath / From teares abstaine" (56.5–6). His second response seems to miss the point:

> Then turning to his Palmer said, Old syre
>   Behold the image of mortalitie,
>   And feeble nature cloth'd with fleshly tyre,
>   When raging passion with fierce tyrannie
>   Robs reason of her due regalitie,
>   And makes it servant to her basest part:
>   The strong it weakens with infirmitie,
>   And with bold furie armes the weakest hart;
> The strong through pleasure soonest falles, the weake through smart.
>
> (i.57)

This argument may be valid enough on its own ethical terms. Perhaps the dominance of passion over reason does provide an image of much that is true of mortal experience. Perhaps – though the concluding generalizations may sound convincing as a result rather of their aphoristic tone than of their content – the strong soonest fall to pleasure, the weak to pain. But while this pat antithesis seems to make moral sense of Amavia's suicide and of Mortdant's earlier imprisonment, it takes no notice at all of Mortdant's death, which resulted from drinking water from the fountain *after* Amavia's tutorials on temperance had returned him to a better will and freed him from immediate imprisonment to Acrasia. This most specific illustration of "mortalitie" seems in pressing need of explanation.[15]

By evading this interpretive conundrum and enunciating instead a general moral aphorism ("the strong through pleasure . . . "), Guyon manifests blindness to issues that are too deep, theology would maintain, for reason's and morality's reach. Temperance does not free one from death, physical or spiritual: the temperance achieved by Mortdant[16] results from *ama-vi[t]a*, love of life, which can trigger the self-preserving energies that rescue some people, sometimes, from indulgence in self-destructive pleasures. Because moral discipline can effect such real if partial rescues, we may consider Amavia's teachings to be both good and inviting emulation by readers of a poem that aims to "fashion" those readers in "vertuous and gentle discipline." The moral commonplace subsequently enunciated either by Guyon or the palmer in II.i.58 (the ambiguous pronoun at 58.1 allows either) seems therefore generally true of the "pleasure" and "smart" mentioned at II.i.57.9. Yet it also seems unsatisfactory as a concluding meditation on the events just recounted:

> But temperance (said he) with golden squire
> Betwixt them both can measure out a meane,
> Neither to melt in pleasures whot desire,
> Nor fry in hartlesse griefe and dolefull teene. (i.58.1–4)

But, an attentive reader might object, Amavia did just what the palmer would do to measure out a mean, and her ministrations led Mortdant smack into Acrasia's death-inflicting trap. The inadequacy of this concluding observation on the episode is soon matched by Guyon's incapacity to cleanse the babe's hands: "He washt them oft and oft, yet nought they beene / For all his washing cleaner" (ii.3.5–6). In short, Guyon's ministrations seem as inadequate as Amavia's own. Some of the stains blood symbolizes are too deeply in grain to respond to the virtue he represents.[17]

As critics have often said, the bloody hands represent humankind's inherent sinfulness. Temperance will not cleanse such guilt though, like the nymph from whom this fountain originated, it can protect temperate people from the cruder sorts of pollution:

> For it is chast and pure, as purest snow,
> Ne lets her waves with any filth be dyde,
> But ever like her selfe unstained hath beene tryde. (ii.9.7–9)

Temperance can also reduce conflicting passions, as Medina does, for instance, when she imposes moments of order on the never-ending strife of her sisters and their lovers (II.ii.13, 27–28, 38). Clearly, temperance can combat some very fierce opposites, but only if its possessor follows rules established by rational self-discipline. Guyon's efforts to quell violent passions, for instance, can actually work against him – result in "his manly face" being "bruze[d]" – until the analytic powers of reason teach him accurately to identify his enemy's nature and genesis. At II.iv, that enemy

> is *Furor*, cursed cruell wight,
> That unto knighthood workes much shame and woe;

> And that same Hag, his aged mother, hight
> *Occasion,* the root of all wrath and despight.   (10.6–9)

This is sound moral interpretation: if analyzed in social and political terms, occasion might truly be "the root of all wrath." Yet that only holds true from the point of view of an ethic that deals with matters less radically inward than sin. Yes, Furor will yield to the reasoned discipline that begins by controlling Occasion:

> With her, who so will raging *Furor* tame,
> Must first begin, and well her amenage:
> First her restraine from her reprochfull blame   (iv.11.1-3)

But having asserted and then demonstrated this efficacy of this method (iv.12–15), the narrative promptly illustrates that all humankind are "children of wrath" in so deep a sense that reasoned principle can never hope to control them on its own. The illustration occurs in the story of Phedon (II.iv.16–36), which presents so decisive an instance of the limits of temperance that it almost produces comedy out of extraordinary violence. In this episode, Phedon tells his horrific story: that his friend Philemon persuaded him of his beloved Claribell's infidelity; that this threw Philemon into "horrour and tormenting griefe" wrought by the "wound of gealous worme"; that he murdered Claribell at the very instant when she subsequently appeared to him; that he experienced "hellish fury" on discovering that Philemon had lied about Claribell; that he poisoned Philemon for it; that he then sought to murder Claribell's maid; and finally that he was overtaken and mercilessly beaten by Furor. Having presented this litany of horrors, Phedon finds himself treated to a pair of lectures which assert that temperance can prevent such difficulties:

> Then gan the Palmer thus, Most wretched man,
> That to affections does the bridle lend;
> In their beginning they are weake and wan,
> But soone through suff'rance grow to fearefull end;
> Whiles they are weake betimes with them contend:
> For when they once to perfect strength do grow,
> Strong warres they make, and cruell battry bend
> Gainst fort of Reason, it to overthrow:
> Wrath, gelosie, griefe, love this Squire have layd thus low.   (iv.34)

All Phedon need have done, the Palmer advises, is deprive his violent passions of leisure in which to develop. Never mind that his vindictive jealousy exploded full blown into homicidal action so extreme that readers could be tempted to dismiss the story as improbable fiction – if every day's news were not proving such improbabilities to be quotidian fact in contemporary society.

The bathetic effect of the palmer's lecture intensifies as a result of the silly word-games that constitute its peroration:

> Wrath, gealosie, griefe, love do thus expell:
> Wrath is a fire, and gealosie a weede,
> Griefe is a flood, and love a monster fell   (iv.1-3)

This windy irrelevance consumes the entire stanza, but that does not prevent Guyon from topping it in the next:

> Unlucky Squire (said *Guyon*) sith thou hast
> Falne into mischiefe through intemperaunce,
> Henceforth take heede of that thou now hast past,
> And guide thy wayes with warie governaunce,
> Least worse betide thee by some later chaunce.   (iv.36.1–5)

"Least worse betide thee"? Phedon's story, illustrating in extreme form humankind's capacity for unmotivated malice and treachery (Phedon), for half-witting collusion in one's own self-deception, and for murderous obsession (Philemon), has discredited in advance any notion that mere "intemperaunce" caused those events, or that "warie governaunce" could have forestalled them. For reasons too deep for moral analysis to comprehend, people collaborate with occasion and willfully seek to become victims and agents of furor (see II.v.16–24).

When Pyrochles has demonstrated this by unbinding Occasion and is being pitilessly beaten by Furor later in Book II, a recurrent attribute of temperance comes to the fore. The palmer dissuades the always susceptible Guyon ("greatly moved at [Pyrochles'] plaint," v.24.1) from rescuing Pyrochles because

> He that his sorrow sought through wilfulnesse,
> And his foe fettred would release agayne,
> Deserves to tast his follies fruit, repented payne.   (v.24.7–9)

Clearly, temperance is not to be confused with charity. Like the self-protecting waters of the nymph-fountain that will not cleanse others' stains (ii.9), disciplined agents of temperance seldom turn outwards to help others combat the overwhelming gravitational pull of the flesh. In preventing Guyon from aiding Pyrochles, the palmer helps to distinguish temperance from the deeper virtue that would employ Guyon's human susceptibilities to drive him to a deeper generosity.[18]

The palmer similarly asserts the boundaries of temperance at other points in Book II, most conspicuously perhaps in its last four lines. Having been reviled by the man who would return to swinish state, Guyon comments:

> See the mind of beastly man,
> That hath so soone forgot the excellence
> Of his creation, when he life began,
> That now he chooseth, with vile difference,
> To be a beast, and lacke intelligence.
> To whom the Palmer thus, The donghill kind
> Delights in filth and foule incontinence:
> Let *Grill* be *Grill*, and have his hoggish mind,
> But let us hence depart, whilest wether serves and wind.   (xii.87)

It would be silly to fault these speakers for their reluctance to engage in debate with so unprepossessing an opposite as Grill. Yet it is worth noticing that the paired concluding speeches imply conflicting views of human origin and possibility. Guyon ascribes an "excellence" (apparently) to this Grill's original human birth; yet he also paradoxically refers to "the mind of beastly man" in a way that sounds generic rather than individual. The palmer echoes this second implication; "the donghill kind" suggests that some are "by kind" incorrigible.

There may be a trace of the moralist's occupational inclination toward smug superiority in this judgment. A reader inclined to apply Protestant notions of causality to such reflections could easily, however, share the palmer's dismissive view because people who actively resist moral rectification, as Grill does (xii.86.6–9), provide more than usually perspicuous evidence of their reprobation. As Reformed dogma insists, however, such people also willingly "choose" the viciousness to which they are predestined, and are appropriately left to work out their own damnation. Here the palmer's dismissive view could be taken – if theological ideas of predestination, grace, and will help to constitute readers' perceptions of the passage – to represent current ecclesiological policies. The national church and (with less hesitation) its puritan critics would both exclude the incorrigible from their flocks.[19]

But the palmer is no theologian; he is a moralist somewhat more reliably grace-and-reason-governed than the knight is himself. This evaluation of him receives especially convincing support in the middle of Book

II, from the passages that precede and follow Guyon's confrontation with Mammon. At the beginning of this much-debated episode, Phaedria has separated the palmer from Guyon, a deprivation the narrator compares to an experienced navigator's loss of a "steadfast starre" that had directed his course. The navigator resorts to "his card and compas . . . The maisters of his long experiment" and continues confidently on his voyage, "Bidding his winged vessell fairely forward fly" (vii.1):

> So *Guyon* having lost his trusty guide,
> Late left beyond that *Ydle lake*, proceedes
> Yet on his way, of none accompanide;
> And evermore himselfe with comfort feedes,
> Of his owne vertues, and prayse-worthy deedes.
> So long he yode, yet no adventure found,
> Which fame of her shrill trompet worthy reedes:
> For still he traveild through wide wastfull ground,
> That nought but desert wildernesse shew'd all around.   (vii.2)

It is possible to hear "[t]he tone of approval grow[ing] fainter as [this] stanza unfolds" and the pilot is "replaced by a traveller who feeds himself with comfortable memories of his own virtuous achievements."[20] But some readers might recognize in the same stanza an equivalence which the words literally assert. "So Guyon" indicates that Guyon is behaving like the pilot. The "experiment" of both the seasoned pilot in the previous stanza and the increasingly experienced warrior of temperance in this one provide sound guidance through territories suited to spiritual and moral testing. The memory of good deeds can also supply confidence that one has grace, which is difficult to sense directly.[21]

Like the experiential knowledge of election Red Cross gained in the House of Holiness, this "experimental" source of stability sustains Guyon throughout the sequence of temptations. His success cannot, however, be perfect. His resources, to some degree directly impelled by grace, will exhibit human shortcomings, and critics have been perceptive in discovering expressions of pride – the Legend of Holiness has demonstrated that such sin will be inevitable and often unconscious – even in Guyon's "correct" moral opposition to Mammon's temptations:

> Regard of worldly mucke doth fowly blend,
> And low abase the high heroicke spright,
> That joyes for crownes and kingdomes to contend;
> Faire shields, gay steedes, bright armes be my delight:
> Those be the riches fit for an advent'rous knight.   (vii.10.5–9)

As Mammon remarks, such effusions identify Guyon as a "Vaine glori-ous Elfe." Engaged in conflict with Mammon, the knight manifests in his desire for higher things an impulse to set the value of one's own de-lights a bit too high, "for crownes and kingdomes to contend."

Such a conclusion, however, need not become censorious. Instead, we can perceive once more that Guyon runs a race like that of Red Cross. He is *simul iustus et peccator*, at once (as a Calvinist view would deter-mine) extrinsically righteous and intrinsically sinful or (as an Augustin-ian reading might maintain) partly righteous and partly sinful (see ch. 1, p. 33, n. 34, above). Guyon's imperfect achievement against Mammon manifests a limited, local effect of the perfect achievement that "his Re-deemer" has graciously supplied. This way of construing the situation enables readers to account for the Christological analogy in the canto without attempting to see in Guyon, as some have done, a reiteration of the Savior's unique and comprehensive rejection of world, flesh, and devil.[22] To see Guyon as repeating Christ's triumph would require, es-pecially for Protestant interpreters, the attribution of infinitely too much credit to a human agent. On the other hand, we need not go to the opposing extreme, totally rejecting "any resemblance between Guyon and Christ."[23] If the episode's "desert wildernesse" (vii.2.9) setting for some readers suggests the analogy between Guyon's and Christ's temp-tations, and the "three dayes" duration of the "hardie enterprize" con-firms that analogy (vii.65.6), such readers can "see" that Guyon has re-mained immune to Mammon's overt temptation because the knight shares in his Redeemer's unique victory.

That Guyon did not achieve the victory himself and that he requires perpetual support by grace is made clear when he breathes in "the vitall air" and collapses, "all his senses . . . with deadly fit opprest" (vii.66.9). Because it is "deadly," the fit suggests that the grace of sanctification, which sustained Guyon during his three-day trial, has been attenuated. As when Red Cross' armor fails to provide the illumination or the pro-tection it can at other times supply (e.g. I.xi.26, 38), Guyon is now left to represent what humankind in itself essentially is, "dead in sin." The point is reinforced by other characters' insistence on calling Guyon, even if they know he is alive, a "slombred corse," an "outcast carkasse," the "dead," and similarly flattering circumlocutions (viii.11.7; 13.4; 14.9; 15.2,3,9; 16.4; 23.9; 27.4,8; 28.4,5,6; 29.7; cf. ch. 5, p. 123, above). What deprives all these descriptions of accuracy, apart from Guyon's lit-eral survival, is the persistent (though now outwardly invisible) presence of that deeper inalienable grace which justifies. This power has placed Guyon on the track where he can run a race like Red Cross Knight's. And this grace, its presence symbolized by the angel's care, here resides silently within the soul. In order to effect behavioral manifestations, it employs in II.viii two less exalted instruments, first the palmer, then Prince Arthur.

While delegating to the palmer the task of supplying immediate aid, the angel nonetheless attests to his own perpetual presence, delegated to him in turn by highest authority:

> The charge, which God doth unto me arret,
> Of his deare safetie, I to thee commend;
> Yet will I not forgoe, ne yet forget
> The care thereof my selfe unto the end,
> But evermore him succour, and defend
> Against his foe and mine: watch thou I pray   (viii.8.1–6)

Given this ultimate source of the knight's safety "evermore," readers will not be surprised to learn that the immediate instrument of his rescue is an "armed knight" whose character is defined by his possession "of bold and bounteous grace" (viii.17.5). It will feel comparably appropriate that the palmer instantly recognizes this new arrival in Book II as "the prowest knight alive, / Prince *Arthur*, flowre of grace and nobilesse" (18.3–4), and addresses him as a "hope of helpe, and timely grace" (25.6). That this source of gracious aid to others always himself requires extrinsic support appears in the ensuing battle. For when Pyrochles seeks to use Arthur's sword against him, "The faithfull steele such treason no'uld endure, / But swarving from the marke, his Lords life did assure" (30.8–9). Readers who correlate this passage with the armor of Ephesians 6 will recognize that the sword, described as "faithfull steele," represents Arthur's possession of the Word. They will also acknowledge that such individual human faith belongs to the equipment the Lord provides to his chosen; it also "assures" their "life," in the mundane and the spiritual senses of both words. Throughout one's life-long battle against spiritual enemies, this absolute equipment assures victory, but only lesser implements need be employed in the immediate engagement. Hence Arthur defeats Pyrochles and Cymochles, who represent moral faults, with Guyon's sword, provided by the palmer and guided by divine blessing (40.1–4; 45.2; 52.9). The dazzling shield necessary to match Orgoglio at I.viii.18–19 remains covered in II.viii (17.7; 38.3). Arthur also displays in this combat a surprising degree of anger, ex-

pressed through an epic simile that manifests both overwhelming power and ferocity: "As salvage Bull, whom two fierce mastives bayt, / When rancour doth with rage him once engore . . . So rag'd Prince *Arthur*" (viii.42.1–8). The prince's own desire prevents him for a time from strik-
ing Pyrochles effectively, for that opponent carries Guyon's shield, "Whereon the Faery Queenes pourtract was writ" (43.3). This hesita-tion occasions a wound inflicted by Cymochles, the embodiment of lustful desire; it is a damaging blow, which "pierced to the skin . . . [and] made him twise to reele, that never moov'd afore" (44.8–9).[24] The vic-torious hero in Book II exhibits impurities identical to those he com-bats, and he does so more emphatically now than he did in battle with Orgoglio (cf. ch. 2, p. 66; ch. 5, pp. 134–35, above). This perception strongly invites readers who bring Reformed theological perspectives into play to recognize that Arthur is effecting a victory, essentially, of holi-ness – expressed through the limited sphere of moral victory over a pair of portmanteau passions, lust (Cymochles) and wrath (Pyrochles). This impressive triumph secures Arthur's association with grace, an associa-tion that never approaches steady equation (Arthur = grace).

The Arthur/grace connection is conspicuously asserted at the moment when Arthur destroys Pyrochles, for the evil brethrens' deaths prompt Guyon's immediate recovery (viii.52–53). With his usual warmth of emotion ("His hart with great affection was embayd," 55.2), Guyon thanks Arthur for his "[m]ost gratious ayd," asks "[w]hat may suffise, to be for meede repayd / Of so great graces," and joins Arthur in "goodly purpose . . . Of kindnesse and of curteous aggrace" (55–56). The re-peated use of "grace" in such varying senses can be taken to imply that the kind of divine grace which sanctifies human behavior produces an array of moral and social traces. It makes Arthur gracious in manner as well as motive, and it reawakens the gracious mannerliness of Guyon. It is fitting, therefore, that their union of "curteous aggrace" directly precedes their arrival at the house of Alma, "the flowre of grace and chastitie" (II.ix.4.3), whose establishment and person figure forth the soul and body in pristine condition. In Alma, grace tempers all mental and physical functions, creating harmonious relations between elements, organs, faculties, and emotions.[25]

Alma's intricately harmonious cooperation between physical and spiri-tual, natural and divine – cooperation neatly captured in the near-oxy-moron "native grace" (ix.1.8) – is rendered more than usually secure at the end of II.xi. There Arthur destroys Alma's primary opponent,

Maleger, a fierce, powerfully physical yet paradoxically insubstantial embodiment of the Pauline "body of this death" (xi.20–23). To reinforce the safety of Alma, Arthur needs only to undertake half of the bipartite task of sanctification as symbolized in baptism. He does so by throwing Maleger into a "standing lake," an action that recalls the death of the old man as that death is represented by sprinkling or immersion in the English baptismal rite. Arthur's action symbolizes, that is, the destructive first half of any experience of spiritual renewal, which always includes both a death and a rebirth, as in baptism.

Guyon's action against Acrasia might then be taken not just to follow, but to follow from Arthur's defeat of Maleger. The death of "the body of this death" precedes the purging of the more limited evils. From this perspective, the achievement of a quest for temperance represents, here even more directly than before, a specific moment in the comprehensive pursuit of holiness. And like all victories in that quest, it will be flawed. Guyon's achievement of temperance can continue to be "like" Red Cross' "race" even though, or rather because, it is flawed by the imperfections temperance seeks to combat. Guyon feels lust,

> Now when they spide the knight to slacke his pace,
> Them to behold, and in his sparkling face
> The secret signes of kindled lust appeare   (xii.68.4–6)

and in the very act of destroying his Book's ultimate locus of intemperance, his actions become intemperate:

> But all those pleasant bowres and Pallace brave,
> *Guyon* broke downe, with rigour pittilesse;
> Ne ought their goodly workmanship might save
> Them from the tempest of his wrathfulnesse   (xii.83.1–4)

We need to undertake forceful acts of selection and projection to construe this "tempest of his wrathfulnesse" as simply identical with the notion of "just" dispassionate anger allowed and even commended by moral theology. A theologically grounded reading of the stanza can perceive instead that Guyon corrupts the good works he performs, and yet remains a true colleague of the knight of holiness. That neither the knight nor the palmer perceives flaws in their achievement provides a final reminder that temperance is a limited virtue. Temperance plays an important role in the poem's and the culture's project of fashioning human character.[26] Yet Book II's persistent ironies imply that temperance can be more effective, and perhaps even more generous, when its proponents recognize its limitations and acknowledge its status as a subsidiary manifestation of holiness.

In later books of *The Faerie Queene*, tensions between the overt aims of apparently moral actions and their covert motives or attendant circumstances develop more often, become more severe, and therefore resist the reconciliations which doctrinal perspectives can provide in Books I and II. Prince Arthur, whose activities in Book II reassert his role as instrument of grace, becomes a conspicuous register of this increasing tension in Books III and IV. At the beginning of III, Guyon addresses him in a significantly punning way: "good Sir *Guyon*, deare besought / The Prince of grace, to let him runne that turne" (III.i.5.1–2). While asking literally for the favor to be allowed first turn in the imminent combat, Guyon also implies that Arthur somehow acts in a higher sense as "prince of grace." When Guyon is defeated by the disguised Britomart and angrily seeks to take revenge on her, the prince plays an easily foreseeable role, helping establish human "accord . . . with that golden chaine of concord tyde" (12.7–8). This event provokes the narrator to pronounce a panegyric on the "goodly usage of those antique times, / In which the sword was servant unto right" (III.i.12–13).

Despite the apparent security of a knot so tied by the assistance of grace, and so guaranteed by antique custom, this new accord crumbles in a moment. Florimell bursts upon the scene, and all the knights save Britomart ("whose constant mind, / Would not so lightly follow beauties chace," i.19.1–2) join the lustful "Foster" in pursuit of her. Although they also aim to "reskew her from shamefull villany" (18.5), both Arthur and Guyon display a mixture of motives:

> Full of great envie and fell gealosy,
> They stayd not to avise . . .
> But all spurd after fast . . .
>   in hope to win thereby
> Most goodly meede, the fairest Dame alive   (i.18.2–8)

The power of beauty to sidetrack any well-meaning hero is, of course, an appropriate topic for a legend devoted to chaste love. Yet Spenser develops Arthur's pursuit of Florimell in a way that can be as unsettling to the Book's often overtly Neoplatonic and Christian themes as it is comically good-humored in tone. Both the unsettling and the humorous possibilities begin to be felt here, when the knights, impulsively viewing Florimell as a "goodly meede" for which to compete, "lightly" set off to "follow beauties chace." The sexual connotation of "light" (wanton, loose) sounds perfectly apt.

This connotation grows more apparent when Guyon and Arthur reappear nearly four cantos later, still hot on Florimell's trail. The "Foster," being pursued by Timias, has altogether disappeared from their mental horizons as these "two great champions did attonce pursew / The fearefull damzell, with incessant paines" (III.iv.46.2–3). Understandably, she has recognized the change in personnel but not in motivation among her pursuers, and so directly "from them fled" as they "each . . . assay, / Whether more happie were, to win so goodly pray" (46.4–9). Having declined in her pursuers' eyes from "meed" to "pray," Florimell seems to be obeying a shrewd impulse when "she no lesse the knight feard, then that villein rude" (50.9). Arthur himself, and the narrator too (50.1–3), seek to persuade Florimell and the reader that no harm is meant. But a Chaucerian note of comic innuendo has by now become audible: on seeing Florimell far off, Arthur "gan . . . freshly pricke his fomy steed," and his reassuring words sound like those of a suitor: "Full myld to her he spake, and oft let fall / Many meeke wordes, to stay and comfort her withall" (48.2, 8–9).

When night closes in and Arthur must try to sleep, he suffers still more evidently a lover's torment:

> But gentle Sleepe envyde him any rest;
> In stead thereof sad sorrow, and disdaine
> Of his hard hap did vexe his noble brest,
> And thousand fancies bet his idle braine
> With their light wings, the sights of semblants vaine:
> Oft did he wish, that Lady faire mote bee
> His Faery Queene, for whom he did complaine:
> Or that his Faery Queene were such, as shee   (iv.54.1–8)

So much for eternal devotion. When morning arrives, both Arthur and his horse exhibit the effects of a night spent in the impassioned frustration of "restlesse anguish and unquiet paine":

> He up arose, as halfe in great disdaine,
> And clombe unto his steed. So forth he went,
> With heavie looke and lumpish pace, that plaine
> In him bewraid great grudge and maltalent:
> His steed eke seem'd t'apply his steps to his intent. (iv.61.5–9)

Such Chaucerian comedy jostles genially but forcefully against Book III's recurrent, direct, and (it often seems) earnest expressions of Neoplatonic notions about love.[27]

Although scholars who follow Ellrodt's restrictive definitions might continue to think that Neoplatonism hardly affected *The Faerie Queene*,[28] others will often feel otherwise. In Book III, invitations to apply Neoplatonic ideas can be especially detailed. At the beginning of III.iii, for example, the narrator invokes:

> Most sacred fire, that burnest mightily
> In living brests, ykindled first above,
> Emongst th'eternall spheres and lamping sky,
> And thence pourd into men, which men call Love;
> Not that same, which doth base affections move
> In brutish minds, and filthy lust inflame,
> But that sweet fit, that doth true beautie love,
> And choseth vertue for his dearest Dame,
> Whence spring all noble deeds and never dying fame   (st. 1)

Such passages – this one continues for three stanzas – assert with remarkable directness a number of Neoplatonic propositions: that the universe is created and sustained by love, that what true lovers desire is not intercourse but beauty and the begetting of beautiful deeds, that individual human loves are inspired and directed by heavenly power.

A primary consequence of such propositions is to present Britomart's love and its eventual result, Elizabeth's dynasty, as products of benevolent divine planning: "The fatall purpose of divine foresight," which Love "doest effect in destined descents" (III.iii.2.5–6; 3). Merlin soon repeats this politically charged theme: "Most noble Virgin," he calls Britomart, "that by fatall lore / Hast learn'd to love, let no whit thee dismay" (iii.21.6–7). Dismay is needless, in the magician's judgment, because Britomart's descendents will include "[r]enowmed kings, and sacred Emperours" who will revive the "feeble Britons . . . and mightily defend . . . Till universall peace compound all civill jarre" in the reign of Elizabeth (iii.23). The subsequent narrative of Britomart's progeny comprises, as interpolated chronicles normally do, an appalling sequence of violent conflicts, beginning with Artegall's death.[29] That painful but blandly reported event is recorded immediately after we read of the birth of Britomart's son (iii.28.6–9). As in this moment of joy followed by immediate loss, glorious victories alternate with ghastly defeat in the ensuing chronicle, and these defeats extend into the Britons' long bondage to successive conquerors: Norwegian, Saxon, Danish, and Norman (iii.29–47).

Although it could no doubt stir minds predisposed toward patriotism, the brief subsequent panegyric celebrating the coming of the Tudors and of Elizabeth's reign seems also quietly to contradict itself. Under Elizabeth, "sacred Peace shall lovingly perswade / The warlike minds, to learne her goodly lore" (iii.49.3–4) yet the "royall virgin" who presides over this peaceful scene is memorialized not for her pacific but for her military achievements. She

> shall
> Stretch her white rod over the *Belgicke* shore,
> And the great Castle smite so sore with all,
> That it shall make him shake, and shortly learne to fall. (iii.49.6–9)

After his praise of a peace so bellicose in character, Merlin's conclusion seems perfectly apt:

> But yet the end is not. There *Merlin* stayd,
> As overcomen of the spirites powre,
> Or other ghastly spectacle dismayd,
> That secretly he saw   (iii.50.1–4)

Taken as a whole, the glorious history that Merlin offers as part of an unproblematic providentialist argument ("the fates are firme . . . Yet ought mens good endevours them confirme, / And guide the heavenly causes to their constant terme," iii.25.6–9) requires of the listener a resilient act of faith.[30]

Only such an act will so improve the chronicles that they can be construed as witnesses to a divine goodness whose ends should unquestioningly be furthered. That process of improvement must at every point qualify the events described. "Well, yes," the reader must persistently project upon what the text provides, "history is full of terrible events. But those evils result from human sin; happiness results from devotion to benevolent divine purpose, only part of which appears in this history; the cosmos expresses divine love; and divine love toward humankind will providentially bring so much good out of evil that the world's darkness can be read as necessary to the beauty of the overall design."

The sheer abundance of ideas and qualifications that must supplement or be used to discount the historical material in III.iii illustrates something crucial about religious perspectives in *The Faerie Queene*, especially Books III–VI: sturdy religious constructions of these books have been and can still be achieved, but for readers who are susceptible at all to

variations in the generic and other textures of the poem, a high level of
energy and great mental resourcefulness must sustain religious constructions. In Book III, the notion of a loving providence and its capacity to
guide and secure human affections is always put to the test, gently comic,
as in Arthur's pursuit of Florimell, or coarsely and unsettlingly so, as in
the tale of Malbecco (III.ix–x) and that of the Squire of Dames
(III.vii.47–61). If readers expect to emerge from Book III with an optimistic view of its world's metaphysical principles, they will need to
adopt an attitude Britomart recommends:

> if that heavenly grace some good reliefe
> You send, submit you to high providence,
> And ever in your noble hart prepense,
> That all the sorrow in the world is lesse,
> Then vertues might, and values confidence,
> For who nill bide the burden of distresse,
> Must not here thinke to live: for life is wretchednesse.
>
> (xi.14.3-9)

No matter how unrelieved the "wretchednesse" we perceive in the poem,
that is, we must employ its rare occasions of "good reliefe" to construct
an optimistic Christian-Neoplatonic reading of the whole. By adopting Britomart's stubbornly providentialist outlook, we can do this, and
so find especially "good reliefe" in the Garden of Adonis and the original ending to Book III. Such opportunities allow resilient and optimistic readers to construe the Legend of Chastitie as a celebration of divine
harmony, which is sometimes made available to human experience in
married love.[31]

That Britomart's victory over Busyrane represents an act of grace rather
than human skill can easily be inferred, for example, from her own minimal contribution to the combat. The limits of her contribution receive
repeated emphasis: she enters Busyrane's castle by means of a power,
metaphorically associated with divine intervention ("as a thunder bolt,"
III.xi.25.6), which she neither understands nor controls; she passes her
time in the castle caught up in uncomprehending puzzlement, wonder,
or neutral observation ("That much she muz'd, yet could not construe
it / By any ridling skill, or commune wit," xi.54.4–5; cf. 50.4–6; 53.3–7;
xii.29.1–2; 42.4–5); and she overcomes Busyrane with a single blow
(xii.33–34). As in Una's decisive exhortation to Red Cross Knight at
the end of I.ix (see ch. 6, p. 145) there is nothing in Britomart's actions
that can explain her success. Her very presence carries talismanic power,

and magic can easily function as a symbol of grace.[32]

As readers move beyond the boundaries of the 1590 *Faerie Queene*, they will need to expend still greater energy if they are to sustain doctrinally determined meanings. The text often seems to invite such readings, then to subvert or at least to test them with extraordinary rigor. They will survive the test most easily for readers already convinced (consciously or otherwise) that the aim of interpretation is to discover meanings intended by "Spenser," that that author's dedication to orthodox conceptions "Of God, of grace, of justice, of free will" (I.x.18.6) remained firm, and that such complex and ambiguous terms have readily ascertainable content.

In *The Faerie Queene*, Book IV, for example, readers working on such assumptions can again interpret Arthur as a symbol of God's grace, providentially bestowed. When the Prince appears in IV.viii.19, the poem invites a specific recollection of Book I and the symbolic meanings Arthur acquires there. Finding Aemylia and Amoret, who are at this point enervated victims of Lust, Arthur immediately recognizes their need for strong medicine. He employs it to cure Amoret:

> Eftsoones that pretious liquour forth he drew,
>   Which he in store about him kept alway,
>   And with few drops thereof did softly dew
> Her wounds, that unto strength restor'd her soone anew.
>
> (viii.20.6–9)

Readers prepared to correlate this passage with I.ix.19.3–5 (Arthur's "liquor pure . . . That any wound could heale incontinent"), or to construe Arthur more generally as agent of grace, can easily view the liquor as a symbol of that divine power. Readers might also link this liquor with specifically sacramental symbols, like the well of life in I.xi. This well, as we have seen (ch. 6, p. 167), can refer specifically to the sanctifying functions of grace, effects that result from renewal of the believer's baptism. Taken together, such associations identify what has cured Amoret. They also bring into this episode of Book IV a horizon of doctrinal implications developed in Book I and extended in II and III. Among those implications is the idea that instruments of grace, being human instruments, are imperfect.

This idea can temper our expectations of the hero, enabling us to reconcile Arthur's own apparent failures – his fall to Orgoglio, which occasions the "chance" rescue by the uncovered shield, his genial but bathetic moralizing about Red Cross' imprisonment, and so on – with his role as divine instrument.   In Book IV, Arthur's resuscitation of Amoret and Aemylia renews that role.   So too does his overnight stay with them at the residence of Sclaunder, which occasions a paean to the "antique age" when human innocence was equivalent, the narrator avers, to that which Isaiah foresaw and the Messiah brought into the world, and brings into human souls: "The Lyon there did with the Lambe consort" (IV.viii.31.1–5; cf. Isaiah 11:6).   Set against this lofty background, Arthur's behavior in the next canto effects a violent contrast.   In a weirdly gruesome action, he fixes Corflambo's severed head back onto his body; makes the corpse "so to ride, as it alive was found" (IV.ix.4.9); gains entrance to the castle; frees the prisoners; and takes possession of the place:

> Then gan they ransacke that same Castle strong,
>   In which he found great store of hoorded threasure,
>   The which that tyrant gathered had by wrong
>   And tortious powre, without respect or measure.
>   Upon all which the Briton Prince made seasure,
>   And afterwards continu'd there a while,
>   To rest him selfe, and solace in soft pleasure
>   Those weaker Ladies after weary toile;
> To whom he did divide part of his purchast spoile.   (ix.12)

Enjoying the spoils of victory may be admissible in most circumstances, but the stanza insists not only on the ladies' indulgence in "soft pleasure," but also on the "tortious powre" that accumulated the means to that pleasure and the generosity with which Arthur shares it.

   Although "for more joy" he frees Paeana to join his company in "feast and frollicke," she understandably "grieved was for losse both of her sire, / And eke of Lordship, with both land and fee" (ix.13.1–7) – in addition to losing the love of the Squire of Low Degree.   Here again, Arthur deploys "well wonted grace" (14.1).   This time, the term refers to his mannerly persuasiveness, a feature readily perceivable as symptom of the deeper grace that provides all human gifts.   In this case, the prince's grace functions as effectively as always: he persuades Paeana that her ill-humor detracts from her beauty – "she it all did mar with cruelty and pride" (14.9); and he persuades the Squire of Low Degree to marry her, in return for Arthur's generous grant of "lordship during life" of "all her land" (15.8).   The result is perfection:

> From that day forth in peace and joyous blis,
> They liv'd together long without debate,
> Ne private jarre, ne spite of enemis
> Could shake the safe assuraunce of their state.   (ix.16.1–4)

As in the previous canto, Arthur brings about a miraculously complete happiness, this time an utter marital bliss secure from all outward threats. This time, too, the prince works his miracle not through sacramental liquor, but through a combination of actions that include grotesque deception, force, confiscation, transference of property, and (finally) persuasion. The improved deportment to which he persuades Paeana is equivalent to total and cheerful acquiescence in whatever her male conqueror and his friends decide for her. Anything less cooperative would amount to those especially disfiguring blemishes on her femininity, "cruelty and pride."

That these actions are said to manifest, specifically, Arthur's "well wonted grace" might give pause even to an interpreter who feels assured of "Spenser's" commitment to sixteenth-century Protestant orthodoxies. What limits does grace impose on instruments as favored as Arthur has persistently been? Does the theological view that the best of humankind, cooperating with grace, inevitably becomes (as Polonius would phrase it) "a little soiled i' th' working" suffice to explain away the unsettling features of this passage? Perhaps theological perspectives can do this, as long as they draw reinforcement from an allied set of attitudes – about the proper disposition of stolen goods, the properly subordinate place of women, the priority of property in marriage settlements, and so on.

Such readings can certainly be sustained. The history of reception of *The Faerie Queene* demonstrates that interpreters can achieve the degree of selectivity and supply the additions required to sustain untroubled, optimistically "moral" readings.[33] Interpreters inclined to notice the frequent moments when theological ideas appear to be invoked but also to collide with material native to other genres and discourses, however, will need to perform their readerly ("writerly," some would say) tasks of selection and projection with great energy if they are to achieve comparably optimistic constructions. This seems to be as true of Books V and VI as it is of IV. The hero of Book V, Artegall, for example, has never enjoyed popularity among Spenser's interpreters. In his case, of course, the book's titular virtue predicts severity, and Artegall begins earning an appropriate reputation in the course of Book IV. He first appears bearing a shield which we are never told he abandons: "His word, which on his ragged shield was writ, / *Salvagesse sans finesse*" (IV.iv.39.8–9). Along with extraordinary effectiveness in combat, he displays an exceptional inclination toward vengefulness, even when he has suffered no wrong (IV.v.9.1–6; vi.11.4–6). Thus associated with the rough vengefulness necessary to law's executors, Artegall fits easily into the violent if "civilizing" company of Bacchus, who "with furious might / All th'East . . . did overronne," and Hercules, "[w]ho all the West with equall conquest wonne" (V.i.2).

A positive reading of Artegall and his fellow ministers of justice (including Mercilla) requires an especially powerful source of validation, and can only with difficulty forgo the sanctions of theology. Theological sanctions, of course, would have been more readily supplied by readers comfortable with their places in Spenser's England than by those suffering various degrees of alienation. Comfortable readers will be most ready to ascribe stabilizing significance to passages that derive Artegall's justice, however accommodated to and therefore corrupted by its mundane sphere of activity, from the purity and benevolence of the divine mind itself. Artegall's training by Astraea, goddess of original innocence and justice on the earth (V.i.5–11), helps to activate readers' predispositions to view the knight's justice as derived from God's. Artegall's sword's "perfect metall . . . Tempred with Adamant" and his armor's impenetrability (V.i.10) can, for readers of strong memory and theological interests, associate Artegall's armor with the grace-given equipment worn by his half-brother Arthur (I.vii–viii). This connection would become the more significant for readers who notice that the Faery Queene chose Artegall for this quest "For that to her he seem'd best skild in righteous lore" (V.i.4.9). The theological valence of "righteous" implies a connection, perhaps a degree of equivalence, between divine and human law.

For readers who activate these theological contexts early in Book V, later passages would appear to present the same idea more explicitly and elaborately. A commonplace of the age maintained that "law" denoted, ultimately, an immutable and indivisible pattern, coextensive with the providential order generated by the divine mind itself. This grand unified pattern of regulation was often said to appear to human observers as a hierarchy of partial manifestations – those which Hooker's memorable passage explains:

That part of [God's eternal law] which ordereth natural agents we call usually Nature's law; that which Angels do clearly behold and without any swerving observe is a law Celestial and heavenly; the law of Reason, that which bindeth creatures reasonable in this world, and with which by reason they may most plainly perceive themselves bound; that which bindeth them, and is not known but by special revelation from God, Divine law; Human law, that which out of the law either of reason or of God men probably gathering to be expedient, they make it a law.[34]

Such ideas help produce meanings discoverable in passages which maintain that

> th'hevens themselves, whence mortal men implore
> Right in their wrongs, are rul'd by righteous lore
> Of highest Jove, who doth true justice deale
> To his inferiour Gods, and evermore
> Therewith containes his heavenly Common-weale:
> The skill whereof to Princes hearts he doth reveale. (V.vii.1.4–9)

The system of ideas to which both Hooker's and Spenser's passages belong also maintained that equity plays a divine role, "that they both," equity and justice, that is, "like race in equall justice runne" (V.vii.4.9). In discussions of this sort, "equity" is often synonymous with the fundamental Christian law of charity.[35]

Such exalted notions of law can render insignificant, for some readers, the testing of orthodoxy that other readers will discover everywhere in the Legend of Justice. Among those who are sensitive to the testing will be any who recognize that theological materials in the book jostle uncomfortably against recurrent representations of political and social history. In V.ix, which most insistently presents Mercilla's (and hence Elizabeth's) court and person as the ultimate human habitation of divine and human law,[36] readers sensitive to the conjunction of theology and history will be particularly struck by the image of Malfont. This poet, who dared to speak an opposite vision of Mercilla ("he falsely did revyle, / And foule blaspheme that Queene for forged guyle," 25.4–5) has been "adjudged . . . by law" (25.3) to have his tongue nailed to a post adjacent to the presence chamber itself. The merciless power embodied throughout the book by Talus ("Immoveable, resistlesse, without end," i.12.7), the "dreadlesse might . . . [and] powre" recognized to be "the right hand of Justice truely hight" (iv.1.9), here inhabits Mercilla's court in an excruciatingly graphic way.

That power often receives equally unsettling dramatization in the
Legend of Justice. In V.ix, the case against Duessa becomes convincing
to the wavering Arthur, who is "inclined much unto her part" (46.3),
only when the prosecutor, Zele, calls a surprising trump witness. This
turns out to be "that old hag of hellish hew, / The cursed *Ate* . . . Who
privie was, and partie in the case" (47.3–5). Readers who recall anything of this figure's earlier activities and thematic scope ("even
th'Almightie selfe she did maligne . . . For all this worlds faire workmanship she tride, / Unto his last confusion to bring," IV.i.30) and her
Iagoesque capacity to employ circumstantial evidence to stir destructive passions (IV.i.47–50) might be forgiven for feeling some surprise.
Why does Mercilla's (and therefore the Lord's) case against Duessa depend so directly on this figure of diabolic duplicity and anarchism? Does
the prosecutor's readiness to employ Ate suggest anything about his next
sequence of witnesses – Murder, Sedition, Incontinence, Adultery, and
Impiety (V.ix.47–48)? These personifications, as artificial as they are
vague, can of course be taken as general names for specific actions of
Duessa/Mary. But they might also imply that the case is won through
demagoguery, a piling-up of fictions generated by the mal-speaking of
zeal, agent of the royal power that controls all tongues.[37] Scrutinized in
some detail, the episode translates only with effort into the view that
"Mercilla administers both justice and equity," and so presents a complete and laudable vision of justice.[38]

Subversive suspicions arise readily in Book V because its content often juxtaposes theological ideas against thinly veiled representations of
political history. The egalitarian giant provides a frequently discussed
further instance, one that repays attention to scriptural allusions.
Artegall's appeal to "the unmoving principles that guide the cosmos,"[39]
it is helpful to note, follow immediately upon his rhetorical question
that criticizes the giant's presuming to judge rightly of "things unseene"
("Of things unseene how canst thou deeme aright?" V.ii.39.1). Readers
who recognize this allusion to the familiar definition of faith ("the ground
of things, which are hoped for, the evidence of things which are not seen,"
Heb. 11:1) are likely also to notice that what Artegall then pronounces
is itself a credo – a recitation of the official Elizabethan view, rich in
references to Romans 13, to Job, and to comparable places, precisely of
things unseen: "He maketh Kings to sit in soveraity; / He maketh subjects to their powre obay" (41–43).

When Talus shoulders the egalitarian giant from his rock, one inference might be that violence, and only that, is what determines the legitimacy or illegitimacy of conflicting versions of things unseen. Such a subversive inference becomes difficult to escape if readers notice that the giant's rationale for his project of reshaping the political and social order incorporates convictions that the narrator himself has espoused (Book V, Proem).[40] That surprising coincidence can signal the presence of unresolved contradictions, perhaps within the author's own intentions, and this would impede easy adoption of some characteristic articles of interpretive faith. Faith about the author's intentions ("Artegall voices Spenser's own convictions, religious and political") or about Spenser's earliest readers ("Elizabethans would recognize their own convictions in the Christian ideas Artegall enunciates") must be employed to secure readings that find in *The Faerie Queene*, Book V, unambiguous representations of orthodoxy.

As always, my argument here does not aim to discredit one kind of reading in order to establish its opposite. My goal remains to bring to consciousness some of the processes that normally determine readings in general, and doctrinally grounded interpretations of *The Faerie Queene* in particular. As we move toward the end of *The Faerie Queene*, these processes can be observed with special clarity in the events on Mount Acidale. Colin's glorious vision in that delightful place, in fact, provides an appropriate occasion to conclude this study, which has begun to notice in its later pages what theological perspectives can not contribute to readings of Spenser as well as what they can. For Colin's vision appears at once to claim for itself the status of truth and to disclaim that status. Its setting is a place of complete fulfillment, where "Ne ought there wanted, which for pleasure might / Desired be, or thence to banish bale" (VI.x.8.5–6). This completeness, the *locus amoenus* convention from which the setting develops, and the identity of its producer Colin (poet of love's frustrated yearnings in *The Shepheardes Calender*) – all these features can prompt readers to view the dance of damsels and Graces as pure fantasy, a wish-fulfilling fiction of perfect satisfaction. The alluring, ephemeral vision that Colin conjures up focuses in the end on his own "Shepheards lasse," the object of his own desire. The instrument that evokes her turns out to be the masculine-suggestive "bagpipe" (x.18.5).

Yet if the song appears, on such evidence, simply to conjure up escapist fictions engendered by desire, it is also true that poets' visions often claim to image the highest truths. Like divine grace, the Graces presented here "to men all gifts of grace do graunt," and they do so only on their own initiative: "none can them bring in place, / But whom they of them selves list so to grace" (x.15.4–5; 20.4–5).[41] Still, when Colin launches into his full-fledged iconographic exposition, readers might notice that the interpretation arrives *ex post facto.* The poet here assumes the role of interpreter, quite different from that of the maker himself. He undertakes to satisfy the desire of Calidore's discursive intelligence, which impelled him to break in upon, and so destroy, the artifact itself ("resolving, what it was, to know," 17.8). And as interpreter, Colin specifies, fixes, or, more accurately, reconstructs that elusive artifact as an image of the sources of all human goodness and accomplishment. The circumstances of Colin's hermeneutic exercise draw attention to the factitiousness of the meanings it discovers.

Nonetheless, readers familiar with the traditions explored in Wind's treatment of Botticelli's *Primavera,* and ready to accept Colin as "Spenser's" sincere spokesman, can easily consider the vision and its commentary a serious assertion that "all gracious gifts . . . Which decke the body or adorne the mynde" derive from the Grace that is always one, and is often dimly reflected in the fictions of poets (23.1–2; 24).[42] Perhaps nowhere else in Spenser's works do we find a passage that invites contrasting interpretations so clearly, presents poetry as so thoroughly elusive an object of interpretation, and yet acknowledges the certainty that it will nonetheless be subjected to the reader's will to interpret. Colin's reading of his own art illustrates the irreducible paradox of poetic art as many in Spenser's age perceived it. The poet's imagination might truthfully "bod[y] forth / The forms of things unknown," and yet it might still more often simply fabricate satisfactions to match preexisting desire: "Such tricks hath strong imagination / That, if it would but apprehend some joy / It comprehends some bringer of that joy."[43] The energies symbolized by Colin's "bagpipe" would understandably drive his conscious powers to apprehend his beloved as the source of ultimate satisfaction and joy. Colin's commentary enables Calidore to comprehend her as avatar of the divine origin which Neoplatonism and Christianity insist on perceiving as the hidden source of all joy.

The later books of *The Faerie Queene* demonstrate with special clarity that deliberate, even willful, socially motivated constructions of meaning – like those exhibited in the interchange between Colin and Calidore – represent what readers must do in order to discover certainties in the works of Spenser. Such an assertion does not at all discredit the meanings those readers find in his richly varied works. As the preceding pages have sought to show, the process by which reading finds what it wills both repays study and helps determine what study discovers – in the assertive works of theologians (and literary scholars) as well as in the more accommodating productions of poets.

NOTES

INTRODUCTION: READING THEOLOGY / READING THE FAERIE QUEENE

1 Hayden White, "Historical Pluralism," *CritI* 12 (1986), 484.

2 In *Edmund Spenser: Protestant Poet* (Cambridge University Press, 1984), Anthea Hume's explications of Spenser's works both arise from and yield evidence for her thesis that "The religion to which [Spenser] adhered throughout his life was a fervent Protestantism which requires the label 'Puritan' during [the 1570s]" (p. 9). John N. King's *Spenser's Poetry and the Reformation Tradition* (Princeton University Press, 1990) presents interpretations grounded in the belief that Spenser adhered to "the progressive Protestant movement to continue the process of church reform" and to a "normative . . . Elizabethan theology" (pp. 9,11). For Stephen Greenblatt's statement of Spenser's dominant intention, see *Renaissance Self-Fashioning: From More to Shakespeare* (University of Chicago Press, 1980), p. 174; for John D. Guillory's, see *Poetic Authority: Spenser, Milton, and Literary History* (New York: Columbia University Press, 1983), p. 27.

3 The primacy of guesses in interpretation is acknowledged by authorities who occupy opposite ends of a major theoretical spectrum. See Stanley Fish, *Is There a Text in This Class? The Authority of Interpretive Communities* (Cambridge, MA: Harvard University Press, 1980), esp. ch. 13, pp. 311–12; and E. D. Hirsch, Jr., *Validity in Interpretation* (New Haven and London: Yale University Press, 1967), p. 170.

4 A useful recent discussion of the hermeneutic circle, and of ways to escape the isolating circularity it can impose, appears in Paul B. Armstrong, *Conflicting Readings: Variety and Validity in Interpretation* (Chapel Hill: University of North Carolina Press, 1990). On the helpful idea of the "heteronomous" mode of existence of texts, see chapter 2; the quoted phrase is from p. 21.

5 Ibid., pp. 12–16.

6 Berger's remark appears in " 'Kidnapped Romance': Discourse in *The Faerie Queene*," *Unfolded Tales: Essays on Renaissance Romance*, eds. George M. Logan and Gordon Teskey (Ithaca and London: Cornell University Press, 1989), p. 208. There are, of course, notable exceptions to this widespread inattention to the reader's role in Spenserian interpretation. In addition to Paul J. Alpers' *The Poetry of "The Faerie Queene,"* (Princeton University Press, 1967), see, e.g., Maureen Quilligan, *The Language of Allegory: Defining the Genre* (Ithaca and London: Cornell University Press,

1979), ch. 4, "The Reader," esp. pp. 255–60.

7 See esp. Louis Adrian Montrose, "The Elizabethan Subject and the Spenserian Text," *Literary Theory / Renaissance Texts*, eds. Patricia Parker and David Quint (Baltimore and London: The Johns Hopkins University Press, 1986), p. 305. By "the *textuality of history*," Montrose points out, new historicism emphasizes "the unavailability of a full and authentic past, a lived material existence, that has not already been mediated by the surviving texts of the society in question – those 'documents' that historians construe in their own texts, called 'histories,' histories that ineluctably and incompletely construct the 'History' to which they offer access."

8 Armstrong, *Conflicting Readings*, chs. 1–2, places salutary emphasis on the role of belief in acts of interpretation.

9 E. H. Gombrich, *Art and Illusion: A Study in the Psychology of Pictorial Representation*, 2nd edn (Princeton University Press, 1961), esp. Part III.

10 Ibid. See also Gombrich's *The Sense of Order: A Study in the Psychology of Decorative Art* (Ithaca: Cornell University Press, 1979), esp. pp. 115–16. Cf. P. N. Johnson-Laird, *Mental Models: Towards a Cognitive Science of Language, Inference, and Consciousness* (Cambridge, MA: Harvard University Press, 1983), esp. ch. 9. A useful sociological treatment of the idea of perceptual "frames" appears in Erving Goffman, *Frame Analysis: An Essay on the Organization of Experience* (Cambridge, MA: Harvard University Press, 1974), e.g. ch. 1, "Primary Frameworks."

11 Ulric Neisser, *Cognition and Reality: Principles and Implications of Cognitive Psychology* (New York: Freeman, 1976), pp. 54–57.

12 Gombrich, *Art and Illusion*, figs. 181, 182; pp. 217–19; the quotation is from p. 219. Examples of this process "bring home to us that it is our search for meaning, our effort after order, which determines the appearance of patterns, rather than the structures described by mathematicians," Gombrich, *The Sense of Order*, p. 147. Cf. *Art and Illusion*, p. 242.

13 Gombrich, *The Sense of Order*, pp. 157–58; 131; 146–47.

14 Neisser, *Cognition and Reality*, pp. 71–72.

15 Gombrich, *Art and Illusion*, pp. 219–21. Cf. *The Sense of Order*, p. 89.

16 Iser's theory is most fully elaborated in *The Act of Reading: A Theory of Aesthetic Response* (Baltimore and London: Johns Hopkins University Press, 1978). Pages 115–26 describe processes closely analogous to the ones Gombrich examines. Iser's book as a whole provides a helpful theory of how both the givens of texts and the activities of readers produce readings. To this model of reading, however, should be added an awareness that "the reader," as Iser conceives of that entity, needs to be considered in relation to the constituting functions of political and economic structures and discursive codes. See, for instance, Fredric Jameson, *The Political Unconscious: Narrative as a Socially Symbolic Act* (Ithaca: Cornell

University Press, 1981), p. 22, and Montrose, "The Elizabethan Subject." For related and useful discussion of feminist reservations about Barthes', Foucault's, and Derrida's erasure of authors, see Cheryl Walker, "Feminist Literary Criticism and the Author," *CritI* 16 (1990), 551–71.

17 Renaissance theories of poetry did indeed focus, as Jane P. Tompkins argues, "on response conceived as action or behavior." See "The Reader in History: The Changing Shape of Literary Response," *Reader-Response Criticism: From Formalism to Post-Structuralism*, ed. Jane P. Tompkins (Baltimore: Johns Hopkins University Press, 1980), pp. 206–7. Yet the period's impressive body of applied criticism – commentaries on ancient poetry and the Bible – displays a constant and central concern also with "response conceived as meaning." Erasmus' *On Copia of Words and Ideas [De Utraque Verborum ac Rerum Copia]*, trans. D. B. King and H. D. Rix (Milwaukee: Marquette University Press, 1963), for example, a standard guide for Renaissance schoolmasters, helped perpetuate the age-old view that "in all the creations of the ancient poets, allegory is found, either historical. . . or theological. . . or scientific. . . or moral. . . " and that it is the reader's obligation to uncover such meanings (p. 70). For an idea of how this kind of point might typically have been made, or ignored, as teachers labored to make their pupils fluent in Greek and Latin, see Anthony Grafton and Lisa Jardine, *From Humanism to the Humanities: Education and the Liberal Arts in Fifteenth- and Sixteenth-Century Europe* (London: Duckworth, 1986), esp. pp. 113–15.

18 The search for "consistent interpretations" of whole works cannot, of course, be attributed to all readers at all times. See, e.g., Terry Eagleton, *Literary Theory: An Introduction* (Minneapolis: University of Minnesota Press, 1983), p. 81, and Jonathan Culler, *On Deconstruction: Theory and Criticism after Structuralism* (Ithaca, New York: Cornell University Press, 1982), pp. 33–35.

19 Iser, *Act of Reading*, pp. 108–12 quotation from p. 111. See also pp. 115–26, and cf. Quilligan, *Language of Allegory*, pp. 229 and 235, on the effects of revision and "retroactive qualification" in reading Spenser. Because the human mind can attend consciously to only a limited number of details at any given moment, the full range of expected further details will be present only implicitly, as a "horizon" of typical continuations. On the useful notion of "horizon," see E. D. Hirsch, Jr., *Validity*, p. 72, and Maurice Merleau-Ponty, *The Primacy of Perception, and Other Essays on Phenomenological Psychology, the Philosophy of Art, History, and Politics*, ed. James M. Edie (Evanston: Northwestern University Press, 1964), p. 15.

20 In *Kinds of Literature: An Introduction to the Theory of Genres and Modes* (Cambridge, MA: Harvard University Press, 1982), pp. 60–73, Alastair Fowler offers a helpful treatment of "the generic repertoire," literary fea-

tures that induce readers to make generic assignments. See also Rosalie L. Colie, *The Resources of Kind: Genre-Theory in the Renaissance*, ed. Barbara K. Lewalski (Berkeley: University of California Press, 1973), p. 8.

21 Such shifts are best described as effects of "generic modulation," in the sense Fowler establishes in *Kinds of Literature*, pp. 60–72 and 106–7: "Modes have always an incomplete repertoire, a selection only of the corresponding kind's features, and one from which overall external structure is absent." Recent books that emphasize generic mixing in *The Faerie Queene* include, among others, Peter Conrad, *The Everyman History of English Literature* (London: Dent, 1985), ch. 8, "Spenser's Garden," esp. p. 60; Guillory, *Poetic Authority*; and King, *Reformation Tradition*.

22 Fowler, *Kinds of Literature*, p. 24. Cf. Gombrich, *The Sense of Order*, pp. 2–5, 110–14.

23 The range of possibilities is especially extensive because readers must organize their progress through the poem by means of guesses even about its genre, for generic identities, like meanings, are as much constructed as found. On this point, see Stephen Greenblatt, "Murdering Peasants: Status, Genre, and the Representation of Rebellion," *Representing the English Renaissance*, ed. Stephen Greenblatt (Berkeley: University of California Press, 1988), p. 13; and David Bleich, "Intersubjective Reading," *New Literary History* 17 (1986), 407–8. Bleich is drawing on Ralph Cohen, "The Attack on Genre," and "The Regeneration of Genre," The Patten Lectures, Indiana University, 24–25 September 1984.

24 Iser, *Act of Reading*, pp. 70–71, 96, 118. Cf. Montrose, "The Elizabethan Subject," p. 305.

25 A. G. Dickens, *The English Reformation*, rev. edn (London: Collins, 1967).

26 Christopher Haigh, introduction to *The English Reformation Revised* (Cambridge University Press, 1987), pp. 6–7. See also John Guy, *Tudor England* (Oxford and New York: Oxford University Press, 1988), pp. 294–95.

27 Haigh, "The Church of England, the Catholics and the People," *The Reign of Elizabeth I*, ed. Christopher Haigh (Athens, GA: University of Georgia Press, 1985), p. 196.

28 Ronald Hutton, "The Local Impact of the Tudor Reformations," *English Reformation Revised*, pp. 114–38. Quotations from pp. 114, 121.

29 Hutton, "Local Impact," pp. 124–25. D. M. Palliser, "Popular Reactions to the Reformation During the Years of Uncertainty, 1530–70," *English Reformation Revised*, p. 107, provides some useful reflections on the Reformation's progress: "It should occasion no surprise that the reception of Protestantism, like that of any new belief or ideology, had an uneven impact; making its way in a complex society divided by rivalries between individuals, families, social groups and entire communities, it was almost certain to become entangled with existing dissensions."

30 J. J. Scarisbrick, *The Reformation and the English People* (Oxford: Blackwell, 1984), see especially ch. 7, "Survival and Revival of the Old Faith," and p. 141. On Grindal, see pp. 141, 147. See also Eamon Duffy, *The Stripping of the Altars: Traditional Religion in England c. 1400–c. 1580* (New Haven and London: Yale University Press, 1992), ch. 17, esp. pp. 569–81.

31 Patrick Collinson, "The Elizabethan Church and the New Religion," *Reign of Elizabeth I*, p. 176. See also Christopher Haigh, "The Recent Historiography of the English Reformation," in *The English Reformation Revised*, p. 28, and D. M. Palliser's "Popular Reactions to the Reformation During the Years of Uncertainty," *English Reformation Revised*, pp. 102–3.

32 Christopher Haigh, "The Church of England, the Catholics and the People," *Reign of Elizabeth I*, pp. 212–13. Haigh's primary authority is Margaret Spufford, *Contrasting Communities: English Villagers in the Sixteenth and Seventeenth Centuries* (Cambridge University Press, 1974), pp. 327–28.

33 Collinson, "The Elizabethan Church and the New Religion," *Reign of Elizabeth I*, p. 173. And, in the same volume, Christopher Haigh, "The Church of England, the Catholics and the People," p. 213.

34 Collinson, *The Religion of Protestants: The Church in English Society, 1559–1625* (Oxford: Clarendon Press, 1982), ch. 5, "Popular and Unpopular Religion," esp. p. 202; cf. "The Elizabethan Church and the New Religion," p. 173. Keith Wrightson, *English Society 1580–1680* (New Brunswick, NJ: Rutgers University Press, 1982), pp. 204–5, cites similar complaints by William Perkins, who also registered his distressed awareness of a pervasive Pelagianism. Many ordinary people, he says, believed " 'that if they have a good meaning, and doe no man any hurt, God will have them excused both in this life and in the day of judgement'."

35 Cf. Hooker, who remarks that men are so inured to thinking of salvation as a reward, and the idea of reward so firmly "presuppose[s] such duties performed as are rewardable," that "[o]ur natural means . . . unto blessedness are our works nor is it possible that Nature should ever find any other way to salvation than only this." The true way to salvation, through unmerited grace, "could never have entered into the heart of man as much as once to conceive or imagine, if God himself had not revealed it extraordinarily," *Of the Laws of Ecclesiastical Polity*, intro. Christopher Morris, 2 vols. (London: Dent, 1907), I.11.5; I, 206.

36 Collinson, "England and International Calvinism, 1558–1640," *International Calvinism, 1541–1715*, ed. Menna Prestwich (Oxford: Clarendon Press, 1985), pp. 214–15. Collinson's essay draws useful material from C. M. Dent, *Protestant Reformers in Elizabethan Oxford* (Oxford University Press, 1983), pp. 1–2, 91–102.

37 Alister E. McGrath, *Iustitia Dei: A History of the Christian Doctrine of*

Justification, 2 vols. (Cambridge University Press, 1986), II, p. 34.

38 John T. McNeill, *The History and Character of Calvinism* (1954; rpt. Oxford University Press, 1967), pp. 201-3. In *John Calvin: A Sixteenth-Century Portrait* (New York: Oxford University Press, 1988), pp. 230–31, William J. Bouwsma presents "two Calvins, coexisting uncomfortably in one historical personage," a "philosophical" versus a "rhetorical" Calvin.

39 McGrath, *Iustitia Dei*, II, ch. 6, sections 22–24, esp. pp. 34, 36–9. McGrath cites Bullinger's *Decades* (157b). For an emphatic statement to the opposite effect – that justification *is* imputed – see Bullinger, *The Decades of Henry Bullinger*, trans. H. I., ed. Rev. Thomas Harding, 4 vols., Parker Society 7–10 (1587; Cambridge University Press, 1849), IV.iv; I, p. 46. I cite this edition of the *Decades* throughout, and will as here provide both the sermon numbers (Decade IV, sermon iv) and the volume and page number.

40 Quotation from John Calvin, *Institutes of the Christian Religion*, ed. John T. McNeill, trans. Ford Lewis Battles, 2 vols. (Philadelphia: Westminster Press, 1960), 3.21.5; II, p. 926. For the text of the Elizabethan article, see Philip Schaff, ed., *Creeds of Christendom*, 3 vols. (1897; Grand Rapids, MI: Baker Book House, 1977), III, p. 497.

41 *The Commonplaces of Peter Martyr* (London, 1583), AA6^r; see also John Patrick Donnelly, S. J., *Calvinism and Scholasticism in Vermigli's Doctrine of Man and Grace* (Leiden: Brill, 1976), pp. 174–78. On Hooker's views, see W. Speed Hill, "The Evolution of Hooker's *Laws of Ecclesiastical Polity*," *Studies in Richard Hooker: Essays Preliminary to an Edition of His Works*, ed. W. Speed Hill (Cleveland and London: Case Western Reserve University Press, 1972), pp. 117–58.

42 *Paraphrase*, II, Ei^r; Bii^v.

43 Collinson, "England and International Calvinism," p. 218.

44 Even the decrees of the Council of Trent, often assumed to be models of dogmatic univocality, can appear much less stable to a reader attentive to their eclectic origins. One such reader asserts that it is impossible to speak of "'the Tridentine doctrine of justification' as if there were one such doctrine." See McGrath, *Iustitia Dei*, II, pp. 80–97, esp. 85–86. For an illuminating discussion of pre-Reformation debates on free will, assurance, justification, and other such concepts, see Heiko Augustinus Oberman, *Masters of the Reformation: The Emergence of a New Intellectual Climate in Europe*, trans. Dennis Martin (Cambridge University Press, 1981), ch. 6.

45 The commonplace is repeated, e.g. by Alan Sinfield, *Literature in Protestant England, 1560–1660* (Totowa, NJ: Barnes and Noble, 1983), p. vii, quoting A. G. Dickens, *The English Reformation*. For an effort to describe the identity of the sixteenth-century Church of England as both

distinctive and uniform, see John N. Wall, *Transformations of the Word: Spenser, Herbert, Vaughan* (Athens and London: University of Georgia Press, 1988). Wall maintains that its "distinctive character inheres in the fact that the English Reformation was primarily a liturgical reformation" (p. 3).

46 In *Faith by Statute: Parliament and the Settlement of Religion 1559* (London: Royal Historical Society, 1982), Norman L. Jones provides a lucid delineation of the contending parties and a persuasive reinterpretation of the contentions that made strategic ambiguity obligatory.

47 H. C. Porter, *Reformation and Reaction in Tudor Cambridge* (Cambridge University Press, 1958), Part III, esp. ch. 14, "Grace and Predestination: the Doctrine Established by Authority."

48 Nelson Goodman and Catherine Z. Elgin, "Interpretation and Identity: Can the Work Survive the World?," *CritI* 12 (1986), 564–75.

49 Richard Greenham, *The Works of the Reverend and Faithful Servant of Jesus Christ* (London, 1612), K5^v–K6^r.

50 Similarly co-creative activities could have produced quite different results if the physician were of another sort – like the remarkable minister of the Church of England and "astrological physician" Richard Napier, whose eclectic healing techniques derived not only from pastoral casuistry but also from angelic and natural magic, astrology, witchcraft, folk ritual, and Galenic and Paracelsian medicine. See Michael MacDonald, *Mystical Bedlam: Madness, Anxiety, and Healing in Seventeenth-Century England* (Cambridge University Press, 1981), esp. chs. 1 and 5.

51 The quotation is from Richard Strier's *Love Known: Theology and Experience in George Herbert's Poetry* (University of Chicago Press, 1983), p. xi.

52 "September," *The Shepeardes Calender,* "*The Yale Edition of the Shorter Poems of Edmund Spenser,*" eds. William A. Oram, Einar Bjorvand, Ronald Bond, Thomas H. Cain, Alexander Dunlop, and Richard Schell (New Haven and London: Yale University Press, 1989), p. 151. I use this edition of *The Shepheardes Calender* throughout.

53 Interpreters seeking "historical allegory" in this passage end up agreeing more or less explicitly with Paul E. McLane, *Spenser's "Shepheardes Calender": A Study in Elizabethan Allegory* (Notre Dame, IN: Notre Dame University Press, 1961), p. 167, who has "no solution to offer for . . . the dog Lowder's being so fooled by the disguised voice of the Wolf that he opened the door of the sheepfold." An eye for scriptural analogues will produce a reading like King's, *Reformation Tradition,* p. 45: "Although the specific details of the incident remain enigmatic, Diggon's narrative styles Roffy as a type of the Good Shepherd, Christ."

54 Patrick Cullen, *Spenser, Marvell, and Renaissance Pastoral* (Cambridge, MA: Harvard University Press, 1970), p. 66.

55 In "The Moral Eclogues," *Revisionary Play: Studies in the Spenserian Dynamics* (Berkeley: University of California Press, 1988), p. 311, Harry Berger, Jr., interprets the episode as an instance of "Spenser's feeling for hayseed gullibility."

56 Hume, *Protestant Poet*, p. 38, takes the former position; she quotes the second from Nancy Jo Hoffman and cites earlier versions of this reading offered by H. S. V. Jones and Hallett Smith.

57 Cf. Lynn Staley Johnson, *"The Shepheardes Calender": An Introduction* (University Park and London: Pennsylvania State University Press, 1990), p. 75: guided by Boethius rather than Reformed doctrines of grace, Johnson makes the compatible point that "Hobbinol is right about human nature, but wrong in assuming that struggles against evil are useless just because they are fought by men whose strength and forebearance can never be equal to the task."

58 For E. K.'s assertion, see *Shorter Poems*, p. 102. Cullen, *Renaissance Pastoral*, pp. 44–45n, describes the reception history that has often found an absolute moral opposition between Piers and Palinode. For a version of the debate about Spenser's denominational allegiance as reflected in "Maye," see King, *Reformation Tradition*, pp. 35–42.

59 William Nelson, *The Poetry of Edmund Spenser* (New York and London: Columbia University Press, 1963), p. 46.

60 In *Rhetoric, Prudence, and Skepticism in the Renaissance* (Ithaca and London: Cornell University Press, 1985), Victoria Kahn makes this important point about humanist uses of literature: "the work of art is seen less as an object than as reflecting a certain process or activity of judgment" (p. 39).

1 HOLINESS: CONSENSUS, COMPLEXITY, CONTRADICTION

1 A note on theological sources: because I am not concerned with "sources" or immediate influences on the author's views, I do not limit citations in this chapter to theological works accessible to Spenser before he published *The Faerie Queene*. Alert readers of my text will note, however, that late-sixteenth- and early-seventeenth-century authorities like Greenham, Hooker, and Perkins, several of whose major works were published only after 1590, were all at work well before that date.

2 See esp. "the law of holiness," Lev. 17–23.

3 As will occasionally be the case, I cite here the 1587 edition of the Geneva Bible, which contains much more extensive commentary than does the more readily available 1560 edition. Hereafter, where biblical quotations and citations appear in my text, they will refer to the 1560 edition except when noted otherwise; and (as with all other early editions of prose works)

I have modernized the spelling.

4 Useful introductions to the concept of holiness and its scriptural backgrounds appear in *The Jersualem Bible*, "Index of Theological Topics in the Footnotes," s.v. "holiness"; *The New Catholic Encyclopedia*, s.v. "holiness"; and *The Encyclopedia of Religion and Ethics*, s.v. "sanctification." See also Michael Lieb, *Poetics of the Holy: A Reading of "Paradise Lost"* (Chapel Hill: University of North Carolina Press, 1981), ch. 1.

5 For an illuminating illustration of the way cultic notions of holiness could become metaphors for moral and spiritual cleanliness, see Lancelot Andrewes, *A Pattern of Catechistical Doctrine*, "*The Works of Lancelot Andrewes*," ed. J. P. W., 6 vols. (1854; New York: AMS Press, 1967), VI, p. 69.

6 On the image of God as holiness, see John Calvin, *Institutes of the Christian Religion*, trans. Ford Lewis Battles, ed. John T. McNeill, 2 vols. (Philadelphia: Westminster Press, 1960), III.iii.9; I, p. 601. Cf. *Institutes*, I.xv.4 and II.viii.51. On God's grandeur and generosity, see *Institutes*, I.xvi.1–2; III.xii.1–2; III.xxiv.5; cf. Exod. 19:16. Except where otherwise noted, further citations of the *Institutes* refer to Battles' translation. For readers' convenience, I include book, chapter, and section numbers, followed by volume and page numbers when the reference is sufficiently specific.

7 The process that tended to lose sight of the comforting half of this double emphasis began shortly after Calvin's lifetime, and although that transformation in emphasis did occur, it has been exaggerated by modern literary scholars. On some of the directions of change (e.g. from Calvin's Christocentric to a more theocentric emphasis) see Alister E. McGrath, *Iustitia Dei: A History of the Christian Doctrine of Justification*, 2 vols. (Cambridge University Press, 1986), II, pp. 40–41.

8 For documentation of this assertion, see Barbara K. Lewalski's summary of "The Protestant Paradigm of Salvation," in *Protestant Poetics and the Seventeenth-Century Religious Lyric* (Princeton University Press, 1979), pp. 13–27.

9 Quoted from *Creeds of Christendom*, ed. Philip Schaff, 3 vols. (1897; Grand Rapids, MI: Baker Book House, 1977), III, p. 497. Predestination is defined here as "the everlasting purpose of God, whereby (before the foundations of the world were laid) he hath constantly decreed by his counsel secret to us, to deliver from curse and damnation, those whom he hath chosen in Christ out of mankind, and to bring them by Christ to everlasting salvation."

10 See, e.g., Theodore de Beza, *A briefe and piththie [sic] summe of the Christian faith*, trans. R[obert] F[yll] (London, [1565]), Cii^v; Dewey Wallace, *Puritans and Predestination: Grace in English Protestant Theology, 1525–1695* (Chapel Hill: University of North Carolina Press, 1982), chs.

1 and 2. Wallace rightly employs the idea of *predestination to holiness* as an identifying feature of Reformed (as opposed to Lutheran) theology. He points out its importance especially to Martyr and Bucer, both of whom were resident and influential in Edwardian England. See, e.g. p. 7.

11 See H. C. Porter, *Reformation and Reaction in Tudor Cambridge* (Cambridge University Press, 1958), p. 339. Porter cites *Institutes,* III.xxiv.5; II, p. 970: "Christ . . . is the mirror wherein we must, and without self-deception may, contemplate our own election. For . . . it is into his body the Father has destined those to be engrafted whom he has willed from eternity to be his own." Porter (p. 340) notes a similar emphasis in Bullinger ("'the end of predestination is Christ'") and in the Second Helvetic Confession.

12 McGrath, *Iustitia Dei,* II, p. 37. The extent of this emphasis is remarkable; see II, p. 38: "faith may be said to play its part in justification by insisting that it does *not* justify, attributing all to Christ. In other words, the possibility that the slogan 'justification *sola fide*' will be understood as 'justification *propter fidem*' is excluded from the outset: justification can only be *propter Christum.*" Cf. Calvin, *Institutes,* III.iii.17; I, pp. 783–84, and the Geneva Bible (1587) notes to Eph. 1.

13 Thomas Becon, *A New Postil* (London, 1566), I, CC7ᵛ.

14 This imputed righteousness corresponds to Luther's conception of "alien righteousness"; as developed in both Lutheran and Reformed traditions, this became "forensic" righteousness. See McGrath, *Iustitia Dei,* II, pp. 24–25, 30–31, 37, 44–45, 49–50.

15 McGrath, *Iustitia Dei,* II, p. 50. Among Spenserians, a similarly absolute view is the norm. Among many possible instances, see Anthea Hume, *Edmund Spenser: Protestant Poet* (Cambridge University Press, 1984), p. 73: "In the Protestant conception of human nature the only 'true' holiness is that of Christ, imputed to the sinful human being *sola gratia, sola fide.*" As we shall see in detail, there is another sort of holiness, different, imperfect, but nonetheless "true."

16 McGrath, *Iustitia Dei,* II, p. 50.

17 Calvin, *Institutes,* III.xvi.1; I, p. 798. Cf. the Tudor homilies, *Certaine Sermons or Homilies,* ed. Ronald B. Bond (University of Toronto Press, 1987), pp. 91–102, and Article 12 of the Thirty-Nine Articles, in *Creeds of Christendom,* III, p. 494. McGrath, *Iustitia Dei,* II, pp. 37–38, credits Calvin with formulating what became the definitive Protestant distinction between justification and sanctification. For Calvin, "the two consequences of the believer's incorporation into Christ are *iustificatio* and *sanctificatio,* which are distinct and inseparable. Thus where Bucer speaks of *iustificatio pii* or 'secondary justification', Calvin speaks of *sanctificatio*; where Bucer links the first and second justifications on the basis of the

regenerating activity of the Holy Spirit, Calvin relates them on the basis of the believer's *insitio in Christum* . . . justification is now conceived *Christologically*, thus permitting the essentially moral conception of justification associated with Zwingli and Bucer to be discarded." Cf. Ronald S. Wallace, *Calvin's Doctrine of the Christian Life* (Edinburgh and London: Oliver and Boyd, 1959), esp. pp. v–vii, 12–19.

18 Calvin, *Institutes,* II.iii.6; I, p. 298; cf. II.iii.11; I, pp. 305–6.

19 Ibid., II.v.11; I, p. 330; II.iii.9; I, p. 302; II.iii.11; I, p. 306.

20 See, ch. 6, pp. 148-49, above. Efforts to secure a place for human effort that seem even more self-contradictory than Calvin's appear in the works of Luther. See *Two Kinds of Righteousness* (1519), "*Luther's Works,*" eds. Jaroslav Pelikan and Helmut T. Lehmann, 55 vols. (St. Louis: Concordia, 1955–86), XXXI, pp. 297–306. See, e.g., p. 299: "alien righteousness [is] instilled in us without our works by grace alone . . . [it] is not instilled all at once, but it begins, makes progress . . . The second kind of righteousness is our proper righteousness, not because we alone work it, but because we work with that first and alien righteousness."

21 "*nos praeveniente, ut velimus, et cooperante dum volumus, ad pietatis opera facienda,*" *Creeds of Christendom,* III, pp. 493–94.

22 Virgil K. Whitaker, *The Religious Basis of Spenser's Thought* (Stanford University Press, 1950), p. 37. Richard A. McCabe, *The Pillars of Eternity: Time and Providence in "The Faerie Queene"* (Dublin: Irish Academic Press, 1989), p. 171, agrees, in the main, with Whitaker.

23 In *Calvin and English Calvinism to 1649* (Oxford University Press, 1979), R. T. Kendall elaborates the view that a tradition of "experimental predestinarian" theology developed from the urgency to locate such signs, and so to find reliable evidence of one's faith. William J. Bouwsma, *John Calvin: A Sixteenth-Century Portrait* (New York: Oxford University Press, 1988), pp. 185–86, suggests that Calvin's own pervasive anxiety occasioned his readiness to view "[p]rogress and growth" in faith and sanctification as "the essence of the Christian life."

24 The originator of this view in Spenser scholarship is A. S. P. Woodhouse, "Nature and Grace in *The Faerie Queene,*" *ELH* 16 (1949), 194–228. Reprinted in A.C. Hamilton, ed., *Essential Articles for the Study of Edmund Spenser* (Hamden, CT: Archon Books, 1972), pp. 58–83. For an account of earlier revisions of these arguments, see my "Nature and Grace," in *The Spenser Encyclopedia* (Toronto University Press, 1990).

25 Alan Sinfield, *Literature in Protestant England, 1560–1660* (Totowa, NJ: Barnes and Noble, 1983), pp. 13–14. A sustained effort to identify Hooker's deviations from Calvinist norms appears in Peter Lake, *Anglicans and Puritans? Presbyterianism and English Conformist Thought from Whitgift to Hooker* (London: Unwin Hyman, 1988), ch. 4. On the basis

even of the extensive evidence Lake assembles, the opposite inference – that Hooker's doctrinal positions are often very close to the Calvinists' – remains plausible.

26 Except where otherwise noted, I quote Hooker's works throughout from the most accessible modern edition, Richard Hooker, *Of the Laws of Ecclesiastical Polity*, intro. Christopher Morris, 2 vols. (London: Dent, 1907), 1.8.11; I, pp. 184–85.

27 Hooker, *Laws*, Appendix i ("Dublin Fragments"); II, p. 491. My reading of Hooker's doctrines of grace and free will corresponds to that of Egil Grislis and John E. Booty: "Hooker was not concerned to expand the freedom of the will in Book I, but rather to limit it . . ." *The Folger Library Edition of the Works of Richard Hooker*, ed. W. Speed Hill, 4 vols. (Cambridge, MA: Harvard University Press, 1977–82), IV, pp. xxxix–xl.

28 Hooker, *Laws*, II, p. 501. See also Hooker's *Learned Discourse of Justification*, "*Laws*," I, pp. 60–61. Making a similar point, the Geneva note to Eph. 1:11 (God "worketh all things after the counsel of his own will") remarks that "all things are attributed to the grace of God without exception, and yet for all that, we are not stocks, for he giveth us grace both to will and to do those things that are good. Philippi. 2.13." Likewise James Pilkington, *The Works of James Pilkington,* ed. James Scholefild (Cambridge University Press, 1842), p. 445.

29 William Perkins, *A Treatise Tending to a Declaration whether a man be in the estate of Damnation, or in the estate of grace, "The Workes of That Famous and Worthie Minister of Christ in the University of Cambridge,"* 3 vols. (Cambridge University Press, 1609), I, Ii4ʳ. Such enthusiasm about works, voiced by so famous a "puritan," warns against viewing an emphasis on good works as a reliable indicator of conservative theology.

30 *Certaine Sermons or Homilies Appointed to be Read in Churches in the Time of Queen Elizabeth I* (1547–1571), facsimile edn, intro. Mary Ellen Rickey and Thomas B. Stroup (Gainesville, FL: Scholar's Facsimilies and Reprints, 1968), p. 209. Except where otherwise noted, I quote the *Homilies* from this edition. Cf. Erasmus' *Paraphrase on Romans, "The seconde tome or volume of the paraphrase of Erasmus upon the newe testament"* (London, 1549), II, ✠4ᵛ.

31 In his *Treatise of Election and Free-Will,* John Bradford, an influential predestinarian (and distinguished martyr of Spenser's college, Pembroke Hall) readily adopts voluntarist terms. Proposing to answer the question of "what free-will the regenerate children of God have," Bradford explains that "as a man born of flesh and blood hath the spirit thereof, whereby as he can stir up himself to do more and more the deeds of the flesh, so the other can, by the Spirit of God in him, stir up in himself the gifts and graces of God." See *The Writings of John Bradford,* ed. Aubrey Townsend,

2 vols. (Cambridge University Press, 1848–53), I, pp. 216–18.

32 By, e.g., Paul J. Alpers, *The Poetry of "The Faerie Queene"* (Princeton University Press, 1967), ch. 10.

33 John Calvin, *Commentaries on the Epistles of Paul to the Galatians and Ephesians*, trans. the Reverend William Pringle (1948; Grand Rapids, MI: Eerdmans, 1957), pp. 334–40.

34 I quote the commonplace from Bradford's "The Old Man and the New," *Writings*, I, p. 298. McGrath, *Iustitia Dei*, II, p. 22, points out that: "For Luther, what is being stated is that the believer is *extrinsically righteous* and *intrinsically sinful*; for Karlstadt, what is being stated is precisely what Augustine intended when he stated that the justified sinner is *partly* righteous and *partly* sinful."

35 McGrath, *Iustitia Dei*, II, pp. 34–37, quotations from 37; *Institutes*, III.iii.1; I, p. 593.

36 Hooker, *Learned Discourse of Justification*, "*Laws*," I, pp. 16–17, 22.

37 Ibid., pp. 39–40. Hooker's fluid terminology here displays another complicating feature of sixteenth-century theological texts. "Righteous" and "holiness" are at times synonymous for him; at others, not. Even so systematic a theologian as Calvin can be impressively inconsistent in his terminology. As R. S. Wallace points out in *Calvin's Doctrine of the Christian Life*, pp. 24–25, Calvin employs "many other terms such as repentance, mortification, new life, conversion, regeneration, to denote exactly the same as he means by the word sanctification." See, e.g., Calvin, *Institutes*, III.iii.9; I, p. 601.

38 Hooker, *Learned Discourse of Justification*, "*Laws*," I, pp. 37–38. Cf. to Hooker's formulation here, the similar one of William Whitaker, whose Calvinist credentials stand beyond question: "'that first grace, whereby he hath reconciled us to himself in Christ and wherein our salvation is contained, that alone we place in God which being felt by us faith, hope and charity and other virtues do follow it, which are ours and resident in us.'" Quoted by Peter Lake, *Moderate Puritans and the Elizabethan Church* (Cambridge University Press, 1982), p. 98.

39 Hooker, *Laws*, I, pp. 37–38.

40 Ibid., V.lvi.10; II, p. 232.

41 Henry J. McSorley, C.S.P., *Luther: Right or Wrong? An Ecumenical-Theological Study of Luther's Major Work, "The Bondage of the Will"* (New York: Newman Press, 1969), pp. 140–73. In these pages, McSorley labors to dispel the persistent notion that St. Thomas' theology was Pelagian. Hooker's "Dublin Fragments" provide a partially formulated yet elaborate refutation of various disagreements and misunderstandings for which the authors of *A Christian Letter* found occasion in Hooker's *Laws of Ecclesiastical Polity*. See *Laws*, Appendix 1.

42 Perkins, *Works*, H3ᵛ. Cf. *Reformed Catholic* (1590), "*Works*," I, Hhh2ʳ⁻ᵛ, where Perkins argues that Christ is "both our sanctification, and our righteousness [therefore] he is not only unto us inherent righteousness but also righteousness imputed." Unlike this imputed righteousness, "our inherent righteousness is imperfect and stained with manifold defects."

43 Perkins, *Reformed Catholic*, "*Works*," I, Ddd4ʳ.

44 Ibid., Ccc5ʳ. Cf. Beza, *Summe*, F7ʳ. The two operations of grace described in these passages closely resemble the distinction between "operating" and "cooperating" grace, promulgated in Augustine's *On Grace and Free Will*. See McSorley, *Luther*, p. 101.

45 On the problem of natural reason's dispositional alliance with an ethic of works, see B. A. Gerrish, *Grace and Reason: A Study in the Theology of Luther* (Oxford: Clarendon Press, 1962), esp. p. 86: Luther returns again and again to the "extraordinary difficulty of shaking off the 'legalistic assumption'" – i.e., natural reason's automatic conviction that salvation derives from works performed in obedience to law. Cf. p. 110, "the essence of reason's false religion of works is 'pride,' 'arrogance,' 'egotism.' " And see pp. 133–34: even though St. Thomas presents "a doctrine of salvation which is legalistic without being Pelagian, or even semi-Pelagian" (because all merits earned through works impelled by habitual grace are gifts of grace), Luther considers the Thomistic view erroneous, "for it places salvation at the end of a long process of human endeavour."

46 Perkins, *Works*, I, Ccc5.

48 McSorley, *Luther*, p. 70, points out that the notion that humankind can perform virtues like prudence, temperance, and the rest simply on the strength of natural powers is also an Augustinian idea. Perkins follows Augustine and others in judging these virtues as good in the estimate of human judgment only, not in the Lord's infinitely more exacting view.

47 Perkins, *Works*, I, Hhh2ʳ.

48 Alexander Nowell, *A Catechism*, ed. G. E. Corrie (Cambridge University Press, 1853), p. 181. Cf. Richard Greenham, *The Works of the Reverend and Faithful Servant of Jesus Christ* (London, 1612), K4ᵛ, and Beza, *Summe*, Giiᵛ.

49 *The Canons and Decrees of the Council of Trent*, Chapter XI and Canon XVIII, 39, "*Creeds of Christendom*," II, pp. 102, 114.

50 Despite this area of consensus, differences occurred. Lutheranism inclined to stress the difference between the Old Law and the New, for example. By means especially of its federal theology, however, Reformed Orthodoxy stressed continuity between the Old and the New. See McGrath, *Iustitia Dei*, II, pp. 40–44.

51 Bradford, "Treatise of Election and Free-Will," *Writings*, I, p. 216. Cf. Erasmus, *Paraphrase*, II, ✠✠2ᵛ. Cf. *inter alia*, the second Tudor homily,

"A sermon of the misery of All Mankind and of his Condemnation to Death Everlasting by his own Sin"; Luther, *A Treatise, Touching the Libertie of a Christian*, trans. James Bell (London, 1579), C5ᵛ; Calvin, *Institutes*, II.vii.6; and Andrewes, *Catechistical Doctrine*, "*Works*," VI, p. 72.

52 Matthew 5:21-48; Erasmus, *Paraphrase*, I, ✠✠4ᵛ; Calvin, *Institutes*, II.viii.6–7; I, p. 372; Hooker, *Discourse of Justification*, "*Laws*," I, p. 23. See also Bradford's "Sermon on Repentance," *Writings*, I, p. 54.

53 This tradition more or less consciously underlies many commentators' assessments of Red Cross Knight's spiritual condition at various stages in *The Faerie Queene*. It is overtly employed by Carol V. Kaske, "The Dragon's Spark and Sting and the Structure of Red Cross' Dragon-Fight: *The Faerie Queene*, I.xi–xii," *SP* 66 (1969), 617–28; rpt. A. C. Hamilton, ed., *Essential Articles*, pp. 430–38.

54 Calvin, *Institutes*, III.iii.11; I, pp. 603–4. Cf. Bradford, who in his "Sermon on Repentence," *Writings*, I, 48, challenges all who might trust their own merits to tell him "when they do any thing so in the love of God and their neighbour but that they had need to cry, *Dimitte nobis debita nostra.*" See, too, the homilies' "Sermon on Repentance," *Certaine Sermons*, p. 258.

55 "Discourse of Justification," in *Laws*, I, pp. 23–24.

56 Perkins, *Works*, I, Ccc5ᵛ. On the immense variety of ways one can become blemished by sins forbidden in the Law, see, e.g., Bradford's brief exposition of the Decalogue, in "Sermon on Repentance," *Writings*, I, p. 54; Calvin's lengthier treatment in *Institutes*, II.viii.13–50; and, most elaborately, Andrewes' commentary in *Catechistical Doctrine*, "*Works*," VI, pp. 76–286.

57 The idea is explicit in Virgil K. Whitaker, "The Theological Structure of *The Faerie Queene*," *That Soveraine Light: Essays in Honor of Edmund Spenser, 1552–1952*, eds. William R. Mueller and Don Cameron Allen (Baltimore: Johns Hopkins University Press, 1952), p. 77; rpt. Hamilton, ed., *Essential Articles*, p. 106. Whitaker is paraphrasing *Laws*, I.vii.7; I, p. 173. The confusion arises partly because Whitaker does not notice that Hooker is concerned here not with all sin, but with sins that reach the final stage of development, outward action.

58 Bradford, "Sermon on Repentance," *Works*, I, p. 47.

59 Calvin, *Institutes*, III.iv.16; I, p. 641. In full accord with these views, Hooker also adduces Psalm 19:12 and declares that "the least sin which we commit in deed, word, or thought, is death, without repentance. Yet how many things do escape us in every of these, which we do not know, how many, which we do not observe to be sins!" *Discourse of Justification*, "*Laws*," I, p. 34. In *Laws*, I.xii.2; I, p. 211, Hooker extols the law of God over natural law because "[h]ereby we know even secret concupiscence to

be sin, and are made fearful to offend though it be but in a wandering cogitation." Cf. Perkins, *A Dialogue of the State of a Christian Man, gathered . . . out of the . . . writings of Master Tindall and Master Bradford,* "*Works*," Ll2ʳ; and *The Estate of a Christian Man in this Life,* "*Works*," Ii5ᵛ.

60 Bradford, *Works,* I, p. 54.

61 Calvin, *Institutes,* III.iv.18; I, p. 643.

62 Ibid., pp. 643–44.

63 Greenham, *Works,* L3ʳ.

64 R. S. Wallace, *Calvin's Doctrine of the Christian Life* (London: Oliver and Boyd, 1959), pp. 54–55.

65 Paul Ricoeur, *The Symbolism of Evil,* trans. Emerson Buchanan (Boston: Beacon Press, 1967), pp. 47–157. We will also notice the different conditions of objective possession of grace and subjective recognition of (or failure to recognize) that state.

66 i.e. that salvation has been purchased by Christ alone. This or a similar proposition constitutes "the foundation," the very core idea of faith presented in Hooker's *Discourse on the Certainty and Perpetuity of Faith in the Elect,* in "*Laws*," I, p. 42. See also, e.g. Becon, *New Postil,* I, CC7ᵛ. Calvin maintains that "we shall possess a right definition of faith if we call it a firm and certain knowledge of God's benevolence toward us, founded upon the truth of the freely given promise in Christ" (*Institutes,* III.ii.7; I, p. 551).

67 Hooker, *Laws,* I, p. 209.

68 Gerrish, *Grace and Reason,* pp. 26–27. See also John Morgan, *Godly Learning: Puritan Attitudes towards Reason, Learning, and Education, 1560–1640* (Cambridge University Press, 1986), esp. ch. 3, "The Limits and Proper Uses of Human Reason."

69 See Beza, *Summe,* Biiiʳ; cf. Biʳ; also Perkins, *Reformed Catholic,* in " *Works*," Ggg5ʳ: "faith contains a knowledge of things to be believed, and knowledge is of the nature of faith . . . God's commandment is that we should grow in knowledge."

70 Hooker, *Laws,* I, p. 209.

71 What follows here contradicts dominant theses of R. T. Kendall's *Calvin and English Calvinism,* which argues (1) that only Calvin maintained that assurance could be based on the weakest variety of faith; and (2) that Beza's and the English "experimental predestinarians"' reluctance to grant assurance to weak faith led them to imply that repentance precedes faith in the *ordo salutis* and to rank works very high in that order.

72 Becon, *New Postil,* I, HH5ᵛ. Cf. Nowell, *Catechism,* p. 144, and Cranmer's "Sermon of Faith," *Certaine Sermons,* p. 22, where the archbishop explains that "a quick or lively faith . . . is not only the common belief of

the articles of our faith, but it is also a true trust and confidence of the mercy of God through our Lord Jesus Christ."

73 Perkins, *Reformed Catholic,* "*Works,*" Ddd5^r.

74 A long-established commonplace among Spenserians maintains that the sixteenth Elizabethan article of faith condemns the "Calvinistic" doctrine of perseverance by declaring that men "may depart from grace given and fall into sin." See Virgil K. Whitaker, "Theological Structure," p. 81; rpt. *Essential Articles,* p. 109. On the basis of Calvin's *Institutes,* III.ii.7, Whitaker also asserts, in *Religious Basis,* pp. 45–46, that Red Cross Knight's fall to Orgoglio contradicts the doctrine of perseverance. But Calvin himself subjects his summary definition to qualifications which easily account for lapses like those of Red Cross Knight. See Calvin, *Institutes,* III.ii.17–19.

75 Although Whitgift and Andrewes were wary, as was Barrett himself, of spiritual overconfidence, which they associated with the word "*securitas,*" Calvinist authorities like William Whitaker employed that word unapologetically as a positive term that describes an important attribute of faith. See H. C. Porter, *Reformation and Reaction,* ch. 13, pp. 317–22, 350–53.

76 Hooker, *Laws* I, pp. 49–50. Hooker's reassuring position was no novelty in Elizabethan theology. As Bradford put it, "faith that is not certain of salvation from God, and that for ever, but doubteth of it, is either a weak faith, or else but a show of faith." "One sparkle of true faith" contains a "certain persuasion of [God's] goodness and love" toward the believer ("Defense of Election," and "Sermon on Repentance," *Writings,* I, pp. 325 and 65). Cf. the words the Calvinist heads at Cambridge obliged William Barrett to read as part of his recantation in May 1595, recorded in Porter, *Reformation and Reaction,* pp. 317–18.

77 Calvin, *Institutes,* III.ii.21; I, p. 567. Bradford, "Sermon on Repentance," *Writings,* I, p. 65. Cf. Hooker, who argues in his sermon on the *Certainty and Perpetuity of Faith in the Elect,* "that our faith may have and hath her privy operations secret to us, in whom, yet known to him by whom they are" (*Laws,* I, p. 4).

78 Hooker, *Certainty of Faith,* "*Laws,*" I, p. 7. See also Greenham's sermon on Christian warfare, in his *Works,* esp. Dd5^r–Ee3^r. As we shall see, this point becomes helpful when readers consider the often puzzling inconsistencies in the effectiveness of human faculties and articles of military equipment in *The Faerie Queene.*

79 Perkins, *A Grain of Mustard Seed,* "*Works,*" Kkk6^r. See also Perkins, *Reformed Catholic,* in "*Works,*" I, Ggg4^v, and *Institutes,* III.ii.5, where Calvin contrasts his idea of implicit faith with the Roman Catholic version of that idea, the latter described (at III.ii.2) as being "prepared to embrace

as true whatever the church has prescribed, or . . . to turn over to it the task of inquiring and knowing." Peter Lake, *Moderate Puritans*, p. 158, discusses Laurence Chaderton's conception of weak faith, as presented in a Paul's Cross sermon of 1580. Like Perkins, Chaderton taught that the weakness can reside either in knowledge or in "apprehension," i.e. the application of saving doctrine to the self.

80 Perkins, *Mustard Seed*, "*Works*," I, Kkk6ᵛ; cf. Perkins, *Reformed Catholic*, "*Works*," I, Ggg4ʳ.

81 Calvin, *Institutes*, III.ii.2, 5; I, pp. 548, 545.

82 Christopher Hill, *Society and Puritanism in Pre-Revolutionary England* (London: Secker and Warburg, 1964), p. 55. Cf. Horton Davies, *Worship and Theology in England from Cranmer to Hooker, 1534–1603* (Princeton University Press, 1970), p. 32.

83 See esp. the first homily, "A Fruitful Exhortacion to the Readyng and Knowledge of Holye Scripture" and the "Homily of Good Woorkes, Part iii," ed. Bond, pp. 61–69, 109–13. The vital importance of discovering what God authentically wills men to do is implied throughout the sequence of homilies on salvation, faith, and good works.

84 Perkins, *Golden Chain*, "*Works*," I, H2ʳ; *Mustard Seed*, "*Works*," I, Kkk6ᵛ; cf. Calvin, *Institutes*, III.ii.19 and 20.

85 Calvin, *Institutes*, III.ii.20; I, 566.

86 Debora Kuller Shuger, *Habits of Thought in the English Renaissance: Religion, Politics, and the Dominant Culture* (Berkeley: University of California Press, 1990), pp. 7–8, notes some of the contradictions in English Calvinist discussions of assurance. At 77–87, she discusses differences of emphasis, and much overlap, in ideas of faith developed by Calvin, Hooker, Andrewes, and Perkins.

87 Perkins, *State of a Christian Man*, "*Works*," I, Ll3ʳ; cf. Hooker, *Certainty of Faith*, "*Laws*," I, pp. 6–7.

88 Cf. the cross-references in the Geneva Bible: Gal. 3:27; Col. 2:12, 3:9; Eph. 4:24; Heb. 12:1.

89 Bradford, "The Old Man and the New," *Writings*, I, pp. 299–300. In his *Pattern of Catechistical Doctrine*, "*Works*," VI, p. 62, Lancelot Andrewes traces this alternating pattern through a surprising variety of passages in both the Testaments.

90 For the metaphor, see Eph. 4:24, which receives cross-references (in the Geneva Bible) to Rom. 6:3; Col. 3:8[–10]; Heb. 12:[1–]2; I Pet. 2:1 and 4:2.

91 Henry Smith, *Sermons* (London, 1593), Y2ʳ⁻ᵛ, Y3ᵛ, Y6ʳ.

92 Ibid., Z3ᵛ–Z4ʳ.

93 Ibid., Y7ʳ. Cf. Calvin's discussion of Eph. 4–7, in *Commentaries on Galatians and Ephesians*, p. 338, where he points out that the conceit of

the "whole armor of God" concerns not the "freely bestowed righteousness" of justification, but "a blameless life." Paul uses the conceit of arming to enjoin us "to be adorned . . . with a devout and holy life." The impulse to read scriptural metaphors of armor as symbols of justification – which Calvin discourages here – requires only that the interpreter concentrate less on the idea of strenuous military endeavor than on the cosmetic functions of armor. At one point, for instance, Hugh Latimer (*The Works of Hugh Latimer*, ed. G. E. Corrie, 2 vols. [Cambridge University Press, 1844–45], I, p. 26), stresses that the armor can represent justification because it "is an apparel to cloth a man, and maketh him seemly and comely, setteth forth his body, and maketh him strong and bold in battle." Cf. Rather more in harmony with Calvin, Erasmus (*Paraphrase*, II, CCii^r), treats the armor passage as "a final conclusion" to the Epistle's sustained treatment of holy living. See also Greenham, "On Christian Warfare," *Works*, esp. Dd5^r–Ee3^v.

94 The latter of these metaphors inspired a genre of practical guides to godliness, quite apart from its widespread influence in belles-lettres. Famous contributions to the genre are Augustine's *Enchiridion*, Erasmus' *Enchiridion*, John Downame's *Christian Warfare*, and Richard Greenham's sermon on "The Christian Warfare."

2 MULTIPLYING PERSPECTIVES

1 A recent instance of the shorthand to which all readers will occasionally resort appears in Humphrey Tonkin's useful introductory book, *"The Faerie Queene,"* Unwin Critical Library (London: Unwin, 1989), p. 85. Cf. Patrick Cullen's resistance to "simplistic expectations of that genre," in *Infernal Triad: The Flesh, the World, and the Devil in Spenser and Milton* (Princeton University Press, 1974), pp. 3–67, quotation from p. 24. Earlier, well-argued opposition to allegory-as-simple-equation appears in, e.g., Rosemond Tuve, *Allegorical Imagery: Some Medieval Books and Their Posterity* (Princeton University Press, 1966), and Thomas P. Roche, Jr., *The Kindly Flame: A Study of the Third and Fourth Books of Spenser's "Faerie Queene"* (Princeton University Press, 1964).

2 See, among other recent instances, Douglas Brooks-Davies, *Spenser's "Faerie Queene": a Critical Commentary on Books I and II* (Manchester University Press, 1977), pp. 3, 13; Kenneth Gross, *Spenserian Poetics: Idolatry, Iconoclasm, and Magic* (Ithaca, NY: Cornell University Press, 1985), p. 18; Michael Leslie, *Spenser's 'Fierce Warres and Faithfull Loves': Martial and Chivalric Symbolism in "The Faerie Queene"* (New York: Barnes and Noble, 1983), p. 102. Among earlier scholars, see, e.g., Virgil K. Whitaker, *The Religious Basis of Spenser's Thought*, Stanford Publications in Language

and Literature 7 (Stanford University Press, 1950), p. 217.

3 In the 1679 *Works*, the Letter to Raleigh followed not only *The Faerie Queene* itself but also a number of the lesser works. The Letter's placement here, and in the editions that appeared during or shortly after the author's lifetime, conforms to Spenser's typical practice in locating allegorical names – well after the figure in question has played an (often) elaborate role in the narrative, and so come to signify meanings that allegorical labels, by summarizing, can only reduce.

4 I quote from the 1590 Ponsonbie edition.

5 In both 1590 and 1596 editions, "Of Holinesse" is italicized; in 1590, "of the Red Crosse" is too.

6 For a diametrically opposed construction of the poet's intentions, see e.g., John D. Guillory, *Poetic Authority: Spenser, Milton, and Literary History* (New York: Columbia University Press, 1983), p. 27: "Spenser desires to ground his text in the origin of the sacred pre-text" for he wishes to write a "redaction" of the book of Revelation. But the poet cannot control his material and *The Faerie Queene's* "romance origin must be seen as a powerfully sustained challenge to that aspiration – indeed, as the inevitable displacement of sacred origin."

7 I use the term "alien associations" as Wolfgang Iser (borrowing the phrase from Pater) defines it: interpretive possibilities unrealized by the meaning ("configurative meaning") currently dominant in the reader's perceptions; though dominant, this meaning is felt semi-consciously to be excluding interpretive possibilities that are quietly soliciting attention. See *The Act of Reading: A Theory of Aesthetic Response* (Baltimore and London: Johns Hopkins University Press, 1978), p. 126.

8 Alastair Fowler, *Kinds of Literature: An Introduction to the Theory of Genres and Modes* (Cambridge, MA: Harvard University Press, 1982), p. 72.

9 "But" replaced "And" in the 1596 edition; "and" did not reappear until the eighteenth-century editors reinstated it.

10 Mother Pauline Parker, *The Allegory of "The Faerie Queene"* (Oxford: Clarendon Press, 1960), pp. 74–75. In *Spenser's Anatomy of Heroism: a Commentary on "The Faerie Queene"* (Cambridge University Press, 1970), p. 91, Maurice Evans offers the same observation.

11 The Geneva gloss, among others, takes the text's "Michael" to mean "Christ and his members."

12 Michael Leslie, *Spenser's "Fierce Warres,"* p. 101; Douglas Brooks-Davies, *Spenser's "Faerie Queene,"* pp. 13–14.

13 E.g. Henry Bullinger, *A Hundred Sermons upon the Apocalypse of Jesus Christ* [trans. J. Daus] (London, 1561), Qq1^r.

14 I shall often need to employ this word, for lack of a better, in its common sense ("having to do with things human, not religious") rather than in the

more specific sense usual in Renaissance scholarship.

15 See ch. 1, pp. 34, 36–37, and Alister E. McGrath, *Iustitia Dei: A History of the Christian Doctrine of Justification*, 2 vols. (Cambridge University Press, 1986), II, pp. 36–39.

16 See also my "Armor of God," in *The Spenser Encyclopedia*, ed. A. C. Hamilton, et al. (University of Toronto Press, 1990).

17 See, e.g., Calvin, *Commentaries on the Epistles of Paul to the Galatians and Ephesians*, trans. the Reverend William Pringle (1948; Grand Rapids, MI: Eerdmans, 1957), p. 208, "The true conviction which believers have of the word of God, [and] of their own salvation . . . does not spring from the judgment of the flesh, or from human and philosophical arguments, but from the sealing of the Spirit, who imparts to their consciences such certainty as to remove all doubt. The foundation of faith would be frail and unsteady, if it rested in human wisdom; and therefore, as preaching is the instrument of faith, so the Holy Spirit makes preaching efficacious." A fascinating treatment of Calvin's theology in relation to the question of anxiety appears in William J. Bouwsma, *John Calvin: A Sixteenth-Century Portrait* (New York: Oxford University Press, 1988).

18 That occurs, as we shall see, when certain later phases of *The Faerie Queene* (e.g. I.iv–v), construed in ways Reformed theological ideas suggest, reveal decisively that the protagonist's inclination to pursue "glory" is a symptom of his sinfulness.

19 John Calvin, *Institutes of the Christian Religion*, trans. Ford Lewis Battles, ed. John T. McNeill, 2 vols. (Philadelphia: Westminster Press, 1960), 3.18.7; I, p. 828. Calvin here paraphrases Gal. 6:17, and adds related quotations from II Cor. 4:10 and Phil. 3:10–11.

20 Seminal studies of the literary and artistic tradition to which Spenser's rich syncretism contributes include Jean Seznec, *The Survival of the Pagan Gods: The Mythological Tradition and Its Place in Renaissance Humanism and Art* (1953; Princeton University Press, 1972); Douglas Bush, *Mythology and the Renaissance Tradition in English Poetry*, rev. edn (1932; New York: Norton, 1967); and Edgar Wind, *Pagan Mysteries in the Renaissance*, rev. edn (1958; Harmondsworth: Penguin, 1967).

21 See Thomas P. Roche, Jr., "Spenser's Muse," *Unfolded Tales: Essays on Renaissance Romance*, eds. George M. Logan and Gordon Teskey (Ithaca and London: Cornell University Press, 1989), pp. 162–88.

22 As noted earlier (p. 209, n. 21), I employ the notion of generic modulation as Fowler formulates it in *Kinds of Literature*, chs. 4 and 7.

23 The allusion is noted in *The Works of Edmund Spenser: A Variorum Edition*, eds. Edwin Greenlaw, et al., 11 vols. (Baltimore: Johns Hopkins University Press, 1932–49), I, p. 178, which also cites Lucretius' *De rerum natura* 1.251. I quote the excellent English translation of *The Georgics* by

L. P. Wilkinson (Harmondsworth: Penguin, 1982), p. 87.

24 Wilkinson, "Introduction," *The Georgics*, p. 28.

25 The plan of Zeus that governs the action in Homer's *Iliad* cannot, for many modern readers, be easily reconciled with notions of universal moral design. Yet Renaissance interpreters could with surprising readiness discover a kindly providence guiding apparently fortuitous turns of Homeric narrative. See, e.g., George Chapman's comment on Nausikaa's errant throw of the ball in *Odyssey* 6.160–68, in *Chapman's Homer*, ed. Allardyce Nicoll, Bollingen Series XLI, 2 vols., 2nd edn (Princeton University Press, 1967), II, p. 109. And however cruel and however mysteriously ironic in its operations, the controlling *fatum* in Virgil's epic can in general be seen to support the rule of law, subduing the proud and defending the weak, as Anchises' interpretation shows (*Aeneid* 6.756–853).

26 See Lodowick Bryskett, *A Discourse of Civill Life*, ed. Thomas E. Wright (Northridge, CA: San Fernando Valley State College, 1970), p. 6. The purpose of moral philosophy is to teach "moral virtues . . . to the end to frame a gentleman fit for civil conversation, and to set him in the direct way that leadeth him to his civil felicity." The "practicke felicitie" this final phrase describes may "be achieved here on earth by man's endeavour, assisted with God's grace and favour." This achievement is wrought chiefly "by the temper of reason . . . guiding us by the mean of virtue to happy life" (pp. 6, 19, 32). As we shall see in chapter 7, awareness of the boundary between "practicke" and more exalted felicities can have significant consequences for interpreters of *The Faerie Queene*, Book II.

27 Cullen, *Infernal Triad*, pp. 26–27, notes the belatedness of a firm moral interpretation for Spenser's wood.

28 On the classical genesis and medieval development of the tree catalogue, see Ernst Robert Curtius, *European Literature and the Latin Middle Ages*, trans. Willard Trask (1948; New York: Harper and Row, 1963), ch. 10, esp. pp. 194–95. Spenser's persistent listing of the human uses and conventional associations of trees gives his catalogue georgic affinities.

29 Alastair Fowler, "The Beginnings of English Georgic," *Renaissance Genres: Essays on Theory, History, and Interpretation*, ed. Barbara Kiefer Lewalski (Cambridge, MA: Harvard University Press, 1986), pp. 105–25, esp. 110–18.

30 Moreover, intelligent delight in the natural world was prescribed, as a legitimate variety of private devotion, by ethically severe Reformed confessions. See Barbara K. Lewalski, *Donne's "Anniversaries" and the Poetry of Praise: the Creation of a Symbolic Mode* (Princeton University Press, 1973), p. 93.

31 See Fowler, "English Georgic," pp. 107–8, for the observation that Elizabethan England's (at least theoretical) commitment "to an austere course

of industrious labor" was frequently "embodied in georgic poetry rather than pastoral, the genre of contemplation or ease."

32 An especially informative treatment of the Wood of Error's antecedents in epic and romance appears in William Nelson, *The Poetry of Edmund Spenser: A Study* (New York: Columbia University Press, 1963), pp. 158–64. See also A. Bartlett Giamatti, *The Earthly Paradise and the Renaissance Epic* (Princeton University Press, 1966).

33 Richard Hooker, *Of the Laws of Ecclesiastical Polity*, intro. Christopher Morris, 2 vols. (London: Dent, 1907), II, p. 319.

34 See, for example, Michel Foucault, *Discipline and Punish: The Birth of the Prison*, trans. Alan Sheridan (Harmondsworth: Penguin, 1979), Part III, "Discipline," esp. pp. 189–92, on the individualizing functions of discipline.

35 Calvin, *Institutes* 2.4.7; I, p. 315.

36 Calvin, *Commentary on Ephesians*, p. 334.

37 The usual reference is to iconographic ancestors who are notable for being specious, like Wind's example of Froda. Hamilton, *FQ* I.i.14.9n, lists the references.

38 See above, ch. 1, p. 32, and *Laws*, I, pp. 184–85, for Hooker's point that grace must be immediately active if human capacities of any sort are to fulfill their "natural" roles.

39 E.g., Maureen Quilligan, *Milton's Spenser: The Politics of Reading* (Ithaca and London: Cornell University Press, 1983), pp. 80–84. For another fascinating and quite different treatment of the Error episode, see Gordon Teskey, "From Allegory to Dialectic: Imagining Error in Spenser and Milton," *PMLA* 101 (1986), 9–23.

40 More strikingly still, the armor abets the dragon's assault on Red Cross in I.xi.27.9. Later on, the otherwise reliable shield admits the dragon's sting I.xi.38.5–6. For further discussion of these moments, see ch. 6, pp. 163–64.

41 See, among many similar instances, Gerald Morgan, "Holiness as the First of Spenser's Aristotelian Moral Virtues," *MLR* 81 (1986), 829. Cf. Hamilton, *FQ* I.i.19.2–4n.

42 Patrick Collinson, *The Religion of Protestants: The Church in English Society 1559–1625* (Oxford: Clarendon Press, 1982), ch. 5, "Popular and Unpopular Religion," esp. p. 202. Cf. above, Introduction, pp. 12–13.

43 Cullen, *Infernal Triad*, p. 31; John N. King, *Spenser and the Reformation Tradition* (Princeton University Press, 1990), pp. 187, 197. Red Cross demonstrates here his recurrent incapacity to grasp the issues at hand; for a positive version of such incomprehension, see ch. 7, pp. 196–97, which examine Britomart's conquest of Busyrane, *FQ* III.xi–xii.

44 See Paul Alpers, *The Poetry of "The Faerie Queene"* (Princeton University

Press, 1967), pp. 336–39, for the point that Spenser's descriptions of Red Cross' combats often reveal an implicit identity between the combatants. An instructive context for evaluating Red Cross Knight's anger could have been provided, for many readers, by Torquato Tasso's recurrent contrasts between worthy and frantic anger, illustrated, respectively, by Rinaldo and Armida in *Jerusalem Delivered,* trans. Edward Fairfax (1600; New York, Capricorn, n.d.), XVI.34, 66. Cf. the wizard's sermon on "noble wrath" and "godly anger" at XVII.63.

45 Bullinger, *Apocalypse,* Aa8^r.

46 Ibid., Kk8^{r-v}.

47 In a passage to which we shall return below, Perkins makes the point especially clear: "a prisoner fitly resembleth a natural man, but yet such a prisoner must he be, as is not only sick and weak, but even stark dead." *A Reformed Catholic,* in *"The Works of the Famous and Worthie Minister of Christ in the University of Cambridge,"* 3 vols. (Cambridge, 1609), I, Ccc5^v.

48 Readings that severely exclude the cooperative work of human will can find theological grounding among the formulations of Luther himself, not among those characteristic of Lutheran or Reformed orthodoxy; see McGrath, *Iustitia Dei,* II, pp. 28–32, and Martin Luther, *Two Kinds of Righteousness* (1519), *Luther's Works,* ed. Jaroslav Pelikan and Helmut T. Lehmann, 55 vols. (St. Louis: Concordia, 1955–86), XXXI, pp. 297–306.

49 Attention to Reformed theology, therefore, yields a somewhat more complex reading of the episode of wood and Error than can easily be captured in the moral precepts or simpler dogmas to which interpreters often resort – that Red Cross "should always use his reason and be on his guard," that he "fails to acquire that wariness which Spenser sees as essential to life in a misleading world," or even, simply, "that man is incapable of achieving his own salvation." These summary assessments are quoted, in sequence, from Virgil Whitaker, *Religious Basis,* p. 26; Hume, *Protestant Poet,* p. 77; and Nelson, *Poetry of Edmund Spenser,* p. 174.

50 Book I's insistence that authentic victories in spiritual warfare participate in the evils they combat reappears in later books of *The Faerie Queene.* See, e.g., Arthur's battle with Cymochles and Pyrochles, II.viii.42; ch. 7, pp. 189–90, above.

51 Quilligan, *Milton's Spenser,* p. 80.

52 Stephen Greenblatt, *Renaissance Self-Fashioning* (University of Chicago Press, 1980), p. 2.

53 On "discipline" as a goal especially important to the "puritan" party in England, see Peter Lake's exposition of the dispute on this issue between Whitgift and Cartwright, *Anglicans and Puritans? Presbyterianism and English Conformist Thought from Whitgift to Hooker* (London: Unwin Hyman, 1988), esp. pp. 28–34.

54 William Tyndale, *Doctrinal Treatises and Introductions to Different Portions of the Holy Scriptures*, ed. the Reverend Henry Walter (Cambridge University Press, 1848), pp. 65–66. Cf. I Cor. 15:10, "By the grace of God, I am that I am," a text quoted in canon 5 of the proceedings of the Council of Orange (529 AD), as Gordon Rupp points out in *Luther and Erasmus: Free Will and Salvation*, ed. and trans. Gordon Rupp and Philip S. Watson, Library of Christian Classics 17 (London: SCM Press, 1969), p. 11.

55 Hooker, *Laws*, V, Appendix 1 (Dublin Fragments); II, p. 502.

56 "Sermon for Witsunday," *Certaine Sermons or Homilies Appointed to be Read in Churches in the Time of Queen Elizabeth I (1547–1571)*, facsimile edn, intro. Mary Ellen Rickey and Thomas B. Stroup (Gainesville, FL: Scholar's Facsimiles and Reprints, 1968), p. 210.

3 CONSTRUCTING EVIL

1 Richard Hooker, *Learned Discourse of Justification*, in *"Of the Laws of Ecclesiastical Polity,"* intro. Christopher Morris, 2 vols. (London: Dent, 1907), I, pp. 22, 39. Cf. Calvin, *Institutes of the Christian Religion*, trans. Ford Lewis Battles, ed. John T. McNeill, 2 vols. (Philadelphia: Westminster Press, 1960), III.ii.5.

2 This self-isolating individualism might seem especially threatening to readers aware of the doctrinal view that humankind is always one of its own greatest enemies. See R. S. Wallace, *Calvin's Doctrine of the Christian Life* (Edinburgh and London: Oliver and Boyd, 1959), p. 228: "men must enforce and constrain themselves to do violence against a mortal enemy when they want to progress in goodness. And who are our enemies? . . . all our own thoughts, all our own affections, all our desires are all deadly enemies that labour to bring us to destruction."

3 See, e.g., Isabel G. MacCaffrey, *Spenser's Allegory: The Anatomy of Imagination* (Princeton University Press, 1976), p. 159; and Anthea Hume, *Edmund Spenser: Protestant Poet* (Cambridge University Press, 1984), p. 81.

4 On the symbolic implications of monastic figures, including hermits, in the literature of Protestant England, see Darryl J. Gless, *"Measure for Measure," the Law, and the Convent* (Princeton University Press, 1979), ch. 1.

5 See John N. King, *Spenser's Poetry and the Reformation Tradition* (Princeton University Press, 1990), p. 24, and ch. 1 generally, which demonstrates the persistence of ecclesiastical satire in Spenser's generic repertoire.

6 Cf. Celia at x.3.8–9, who does good works during the day and prays at night. Hamilton (*FQ* I.x.3.8–9n) notes a comparable contrast between Celia and Corceca.

7 Rosemond Tuve, *Allegorical Imagery: Some Medieval Books and Their Posterity* (Princeton University Press, 1966), p. 106.

8 E.g., Hamilton, *FQ* I.i.50.2–3n, where "halfe enraged" is glossed "almost frantic," and "despight" becomes "indignation."

9 In *A Treatise of Anger*, published with *"The Works of the Reverend and Faithful Servant of Jesus Christ"* (London, 1612), S6ᵛ–T2ʳ, Richard Greenham provides a Protestant version of the conventional distinction between good and evil anger. Good anger overlooks injuries to self but deals harshly with offenses against God's law. However "moral" it might be in motivation, Red Cross' vexation with Una could not stand up to so demanding a test of authenticity: "Long after lay he musing at her mood, / Much griev'd to thinke that gentle Dame so light, / For whose defence he was to shed his blood" (55.1–3). A more combative version of "godly anger," directed against the foes of Christ, appears in Tasso's *Jerusalem Delivered*, trans. Edward Fairfax (1600; New York, Capricorn, n.d.), XVII.63.

10 Erasmus, *The seconde tome or volume of the paraphrase of Erasmus upon the newe testament* (London, 1549), I, E8ᵛ. Cf. Calvin, *A Harmonie upon the Three Evangelists*, trans. E[usebius] P[aget] (London, 1584), L6ᵛ. See also Alexander Nowell, *A Catechism*, ed. G. E. Corrie (Cambridge University Press, 1853), p. 133; Augustine, *Confessions* 2.13; and Aquinas, *Summa theologica*, Part I of the Second Part, Q. 46, Art. 2ff.

11 At I.ii.12, jealousy is again stressed: "The true *Saint George* was wandred far away, / Still flying from his thoughts and gealous feare."

12 Philip Sidney, *An Apology for Poetry*, ed. Geoffrey Shepherd (London: Nelson, 1965), p. 119. Sidney cites *Phaedrus* 250D, *De finibus bonorum et malorum* II.xvi.52, and *De officiis* I.v.14 as his authorities.

13 The quotation is from Chaucer's Parson. Hooker recalls the commonplace in his "Learned Sermon of the Nature of Pride," *The Works of That Learned and Judicious Divine Mr. Richard Hooker*, ed. John Keble, rev. R. W. Church and F. Paget, 7th edn, 3 vols. (Oxford: Clarendon Press, 1888), III, p. 605.

14 For a related point, see Hamilton, *FQ* I.ii.15.1n: "'Pricked with wrath' (8.4), as Sansfoy is 'Spurring . . . with rage' (2), he meets himself."

15 For an account of early allegorizations, see Robert Lamberton, *Homer the Theologian: Neo-Platonist Allegorical Reading and the Growth of the Epic Tradition* (Berkeley: University of California Press, 1986), pp. 130–32. In "The Neoplatonists and the Spiritualization of Homer," *Homer's Ancient Readers: The Hermeneutics of Greek Epic's Earliest Exegetes*, eds. Robert Lamberton and John J. Keaney (Princeton University Press, 1992), p. 129, Lamberton remarks that "[t]he Cyclops . . . was simply the narrative expression of the life of the senses, the life embedded in matter." In

The Choice of Achilles: the Ideology of Figure in the Epic (Stanford University Press, 1992), pp. 334–36, Susanne Lindgren Wofford points out that giants could also serve positive symbolic uses in Spenser's England.

16 Several commentators have noticed instances of this. See, for example, Mark Rose, *Spenser's Art: A Companion to Book One of "The Faerie Queene"* (Cambridge, MA: Harvard University Press, 1974), pp. 31–32; Donald Cheney's comment on Red Cross Knight's battle with Sansjoy, in *Spenser's Image of Nature: Wild Man and Shepherd in "The Faerie Queene"* (New Haven: Yale University Press, 1966), p. 50; and Wofford, *Choice of Achilles*, pp. 284–85.

17 Nowell, *Catechism*, p. 181.

18 See Calvin, *Commentary on Ephesians*, p. 340: "The head is protected by the best *helmet*, when, elevated by hope, we look up towards heaven to that salvation which is promised. It is only therefore by becoming the object of *hope* that *salvation* is a *helmet*."

19 On unconscious faith, see ch. 1, pp. 42–43.

20 Cf. Patrick Cullen, *Infernal Triad: The Flesh, the World, and the Devil in Spenser and Milton* (Princeton University Press, 1974), p. 38.

21 Hamilton, *FQ* I.ii.24.1n; James Nohrnberg, *The Analogy of "The Faerie Queene"* (Princeton University Press, 1976), p. 173. See also D. Douglas Waters, *Duessa as Theological Satire* (Columbia, MO: University of Missouri Press, 1970).

22 Rosemond Tuve, *Allegorical Imagery*, p. 363.

23 This association has been proposed by J. W. Bennett, *The Evolution of "The Faerie Queene"* (University of Chicago Press, 1942), p. 109, and adopted by John Erskine Hankins, *Source and Meaning in Spenser's Allegory: A Study of "The Faerie Queene"* (Oxford: Clarendon Press, 1971), pp. 106–8; John M. Steadman, "Una and the Clergy: The Ass Symbol in the *Faerie Queene, JWCI* 21 (1958), 134–37; and Hamilton, *FQ* I.iii.3.4n; 4.7n.

24 Henry Bullinger, *A Hundred Sermons upon the Apocalypse of Jesus Christ,* [trans. J. Daus] (London, 1561), Aa6ᵛ. Bullinger adds (Aa7ʳ) that "all the light that she hath, she hath it of Christ, the light of her righteousness increaseth and decreaseth . . . she gathereth always some spots of the nature of flesh, which she can not leave but by death."

25 The Geneva Bible's introduction to the book of Numbers summarizes this common reading: "Forasmuch as God hath appointed that his Church in this world shall be under the cross, both because they should learn not to put their trust in worldly things, and also feel his comfort, when all other help faileth: he did not straightway bring his people, after their departure out of Egypt, into the land which he promised them: but led them to and fro for the space of forty years, and kept them in continual

exercises before they enjoyed it, to try their faith, and to teach them to forget the world and to depend on him."

26 Cf. Kathryn Walls, "Abessa and the Lion: *The Faerie Queene*, I.3.1–12," *SSt* 5 (1984), 1–30, argues that Abessa and her context recall Genesis 21's treatment of the expulsion of Hagar, allegorized in Galatians 4. According to Walls, Abessa at first represents "the Jewish faith before the advent of Christianity"; she later represents Roman Catholicism.

27 Hamilton, *FQ* I.iii.10.6n.

28 McGrath, *Iustitia Dei*, II, p. 42: partly (but not exclusively) as a result of Reformed emphasis on the idea of covenant, "both the Old and New Testaments may be regarded as the same in substance, in that both contain the promise of grace linked with the demand of obedience: their difference lies primarily in the manner in which the covenant is administered. The dialectic between law and gospel, so characteristic of contemporary Lutheranism, is thus conspicuously absent."

29 Lancelot Andrewes, *Pattern of Catechistical Doctrine*, in *"The Works of Lancelot Andrewes,"* ed. J. P. W., 6 vols. (1854; New York: AMS Press, 1967), VI, p. 71: "Mt. Sinai was such a hill as no man might ascend unto it; but Sion the hill of grace, must be ascended."

30 Readings comparable to this one, which is common among twentieth-century biblical interpreters, were disseminated officially to Spenser's contemporaries. See Richard Taverner, ed., *The Epistles and Gospels with a Brief Postil . . . from Advent until Low Sunday with Certain Fruitful Sermons* (London, 1540), O1^r, where the waterpots of John 2 are taken to "signify . . . that none is received unto the feast of this great marriage, that is to say to the communion of saints, if first he be not purged . . . by the water contained in the pots of stone, that is by the mercy of our savior and redeemer Jesus which is the true . . . rock, from whence the water did spring out in figure, in the desert." Immediately afterward, this useful water is nonetheless compared unfavorably to the wine to which it is transformed, and comes retrospectively to represent a watered-down "small charity" and doctrines corrupted by "mingling . . . with the water of our own worldly wits." The miracle represents the transformation of merely human "understanding of holy scripture . . . into wine of spiritual doctrine, embraced with charity."

31 Erasmus, *Paraphrase*, II, E2^r.

32 The lion's biblical functions as symbol of divine power and as God's scourge authorize this response. As Augustine points out in *On Christian Doctrine* III.xxv, the lion in Revelation 5:5 represents Christ; in I Peter 5:8, he represents the devil. See II Kings 17:25, where the Lord sends lions to strike fear into the hearts of the Samaritan woman's ancestors. The Geneva (1587) note asserts that these lions "show [God's] mighty power."

33 Hamilton, *FQ* iii.11.5–9n.
34 Because, together with her lion, Una embodies the fearful attractiveness of both the Savior and his word, they participate in the pattern of enigmatic images and events that receive summary expression in Fidelia's beautiful and frightening cup of gold (I.x.13).
35 Reformers often drew an analogy between magic and monastic ritual. See Theodore de Beza, *A briefe and piththie [sic] summe of the Christian faith*, trans. R[obert] F[yll] (London, [1565]), Jii^r, Li^r, who views Roman Catholic celebrants as "charmers [performing] their charms," because they believe that their rituals' efficacy derives not from the secret operation of the Spirit but from "the pronunciation of words." Cf. Perkins, *Reformed Catholic*, "*The Works of the Famous and Worthie Minister of Christ in the University of Cambridge*," 3 vols. (Cambridge, 1609) I, Hhh^5v; Hugh Latimer, *The Works of Hugh Latimer*, ed. G. E. Corrie, 2 vols. (Cambridge University Press, 1844–45), II, p. 230. See also King, *Reformation Tradition*, pp. 47–52.
36 See the healing of the blind at, e.g. John 9:6–7 and Mark 8:22, together with their glosses in the Geneva Bible (1587).
37 Quoted in *The Works of Edmund Spenser: A Variorum Edition*, eds. Edwin Greenlaw, et al., 11 vols. (Baltimore: Johns Hopkins University Press, 1932–49), I, p. 208.
38 Calvin, *Institutes* 2.3.1; I, p. 290. Cf. *Commentary on Ephesians*, p. 292.
39 Hooker, *Laws*, I.viii.11; I, pp. 184–85. As usual in language that employs characteristic locutions of scripture, the heart is considered the locus of cognition, emotion, will, and hence all forms of depravity: "evil thoughts, murders, adulteries, fornications, thefts, false testimonies, slanders" (Matt. 15:19n, Geneva 1587; cf. Gen. 6.5, 8.21; Mark 7.21).
40 Tyndale elaborates the conceit with characteristically energetic sarcasm: "If thou bring a bowl of blood and set it before God to flatter him, to stroke him, and to curry and claw him, as he were an horse, and imaginest that he hath pleasure and delectation therein, what better makest thou of God than a butcher's dog?" Quoted from *Expositions and Notes on Sundry Portions of the Holy Scripture*, ed. the Reverend Henry Walter (Cambridge University Press, 1849), pp. 214–15.
41 Perkins, *Reformed Catholic*, "*Works*," I, Hhh5^r.
42 Michel de Montaigne, *The Complete Works of Montaigne*, trans. Donald M. Frame (1958; Stanford University Press, 1965), p. 393.
43 Mother Mary Robert Falls makes the latter argument in "Spenser's Kirkrapine and the Elizabethans," *SP* 50 (1953), 547–75. Her view has been endorsed by Frank Kermode, *Shakespeare, Spenser, Donne: Renaissance Essays* (New York: Viking, 1971), p. 46; Nohrnberg, *Analogy*, p. 218 and n. 239; and Hamilton, *FQ*, iii.18.4n.

44 See my "Law, Natural and Divine," in *The Spenser Encyclopedia* (Toronto University Press, 1990).
45 Lust's rape of Amoret in *FQ* IV.vii.4–9 provides an instructive contrast to Sansloy's attempted rape of Una. Sexual passion is primary in Lust; angry self-assertion in Sansloy.
46 In his perfectly consistent obedience to Una (e.g., at 9.6–9), the lion can represent both natural law as image of the divine mind, and divinity's awesome power to effect its less regular ends – vengeance not least among them. The lion can therefore symbolize, more particularly, the executive power exercised by princes and their functionaries or, still more specifically as Upton pointed out, the English king as defender of the faith (*Variorum*, I, p. 208).

4 ACHIEVING SIN

1 Isabel G. MacCaffrey, *Spenser's Allegory: The Anatomy of Imagination* (Princeton University Press, 1976), p. 159, who considers Red Cross "guiltless" until canto vii. Cf. Hamilton, *FQ* iv.15.6n; Rosemond Tuve, *Allegorical Imagery: Some Mediaeval Books and Their Posterity* (Princeton University Press, 1966), p. 123; Anthea Hume, *Edmund Spenser: Protestant Poet* (Cambridge University Press, 1984), p. 81; Kathleen Williams, *Spenser's World of Glass: A Reading of "The Faerie Queene"* (Berkeley and Los Angeles: University of California Press, 1966), p. 16; and Sean Kane, *Spenser's Moral Allegory* (University of Toronto Press, 1989), p. 38.
2 Hamilton, *FQ* iv.37.7n, reminds us that "good" is Red Cross' "epic epithet . . . which he deserves in this company."
3 See, e.g., Richard McCoy, *The Rites of Knighthood: The Literature and Politics of Elizabethan Chivalry* (Berkeley: University of California Press, 1989); Stephen Mullaney, *The Place of the Stage: License, Play, and Power in Renaissance England* (University of Chicago Press, 1988).
4 Henry Bullinger, *A Hundred Sermons upon the Apocalypse of Jesus Christ* [trans. J. Daus] (London, 1561), P8ʳ.
5 Erasmus, *The seconde tome or volume of the paraphrase of Erasmus upon the newe testament* (London, 1549), ✠✠ʳ; see also William Perkins, *The Works of the Famous and Worthie Minister of Christ in the University of Cambridge*, 3 vols. (Cambridge, 1609), I, H3ᵛ.
6 As opposed to "pride," which is its "head," in one prominent medieval distinction, as in Aquinas, *Summa theologica*, Part I of the Second Part, Q. 84, Art. 2.
7 Chaucer's *Pardoner's Tale* provides a well-known literary application of the medieval method of dividing sin into numerous "twigs" that branch off from the familiar seven boughs.

8 Hamilton, *FQ* I.iv.43.5–6n, points out that "jollity" can mean specifically sexual pleasures.

9 Ibid., *FQ* I.v.1.1–4n.

10 Darryl J. Gless, *"Measure for Measure," the Law, and the Convent* (Princeton University Press, 1979), ch 4.

11 For an interpretation of this episode which is more severe in its judgments of Red Cross because less drawn to the text's invitations to find positive ethical aims in the knight's behavior, see Patrick Cullen, *Infernal Triad: The Flesh, the World, and the Devil in Spenser and Milton* (Princeton University Press, 1974), pp. 47–50.

12 On the symbolism of light and the sun in *The Faerie Queene*, see C. S. Lewis, *The Allegory of Love: A Study in Medieval Tradition* (1936; New York: Oxford University Press, 1958), pp. 312–15, and Alastair Fowler, *Spenser and the Numbers of Time* (New York: Barnes and Noble, 1964), pp. 63–79.

13 Cf. Paul Alpers, *The Poetry of "The Faerie Queene"* (Princeton University Press, 1967), p. 340; Cullen, *Infernal Triad*, p. 49; Donald Cheney, *Spenser's Image of Nature: Wild Man and Shepherd in "The Faerie Queene"* (New Haven and London: Yale University Press, 1966), p. 50.

14 Drawing on iconographic traditions, Hamilton, *FQ* v.8.2n, finds somewhat different implications in the image's ambivalence.

15 On Elizabethan magnates' egotistical and political investments in such pageantry, see McCoy, *Rites of Knighthood*.

16 Such allusions began to appear during the battle, I.v.10, 15. See the notes in Thomas P. Roche, Jr., *The Faerie Queene* (New Haven and London: Yale University Press, 1981), I.v.10. At I.v.30.2–5, Spenser appears to offer a copious elaboration of *Aeneid* 6.257–58.

17 A. C. Hamilton, *The Structure of Allegory in "The Faerie Queene"* (Oxford: Clarendon Press, 1961), p. 70.

18 Quoted from *The Aeneid of Virgil*, trans. Allen Mandelbaum (Berkeley: University of California Press, 1971), 6.180–82.

19 On grounds much favored by contemporary patriarchal authority: that "the husband is the wife's head, even as Christ is the head of the Church," Eph. 5:23.

20 James Nohrnberg, *The Analogy of "The Faerie Queene"* (Princeton University Press, 1976), pp. 172–73; Hamilton, *Structure of Allegory*, p. 71.

21 For conspicuous *loci classici* in epic, see the death of Palinurus (*Aeneid* 5.840–71) and the voyage of Carlo and Ubaldo to Armida's isle (Tasso, *Jerusalem Delivered* XV.6–9).

22 See Fowler, *Numbers of Time*, p. 69.

23 Calvin, *Institutes of the Christian Religion*, trans. Ford Lewis Battles, ed.

John T. McNeill, 2 vols. (Philadelphia: Westminster Press, 1960), 2.3.3; I, p. 292.

24 The dominant generic modulation here is pastoral idyl; see *The Princeton Encyclopedia of Poetry and Poetics*, ed. Alex Preminger (Princeton University Press, 1974, pp. 362–64, s.v. "idyl."

25 This doubleness seems to be true of both fauns and satyrs in Spenser's presentation, though classical myth distinguished between the two sorts of creatures.

26 Theologians often defined the essence of natural law as a charitable love of others, founded on perceived mutual likeness of sensations, emotions, and desires. Quoting Matthew's treatment (22:37–40) of the "Great Commandments," for instance, Hooker remarks that "all other specialties [of natural law] are dependent" on love of God and the corresponding love of fellow men: *Of the Laws of Ecclesiastical Polity*, intro. Christopher Morris, 2 vols. (London: Dent, 1907), I, p. 181.

27 *Caritas* is, by widely adopted Augustinian definition, love of another founded on love of self, both elements being grounded in love of God. See esp. Augustine's *On Christian Doctrine* I.6.

28 Nohrnberg argues, in *Analogy*, p. 221, that "even in the worship of the ass, [the fauns and satyrs] may achieve some faint approximation of the worship of the one god, the word for ass in Greek being *onos* (vocative *one*)."

29 On Virgil's depiction of *pietas* in the context of late Republican politics, see Donald Earl, *The Moral and Political Tradition of Rome* (Ithaca: Cornell University Press, 1967), pp. 68–69.

30 As, e.g. Alpers contends in *Poetry of "The Faerie Queene"*, p. 335.

31 The quoted phrase is Sidney's, from *An Apology for Poetry*, ed. Geoffrey Shepherd (London: Nelson, 1965), p. 96.

32 Hamilton, *FQ* I.vi.26.1n.

33 In *Spenser's Poetry and the Reformation Tradition* (Princeton University Press, 1990), pp. 206–7, John N. King follows Donald Cheney (*Spenser's Image of Nature*, pp. 64–65) in considering Satyrane to be permanently excluded from "the Christian dispensation." Adopting more purely "humanist" perspectives, Maurice Evans, *Spenser's Anatomy of Heroism: a Commentary on "The Faerie Queene"* (Cambridge University Press, 1970), p. 102, views Satyrane as a " symbol of [the] instinctive stirring of the moral will."

34 See Nelson, *Poetry of Spenser*, p. 162.

35 King, *Spenser's Poetry and the Reformation Tradition*, p. 207. King's point differs from mine in that the Satyrane he perceives must depend on "natural virtue" because the divine will has not included him among the elect.

5 RECONSTRUCTING HEROISM

1 This parallel has been noted by Hamilton, *FQ* I.vi.39.8n and vii.2.7n, who refers the reader to John W. Shroeder, "Spenser's Erotic Drama: The Orgoglio Episode," *ELH* 29 (1962), 140–59.

2 E.g., Vern Torczon, "Spenser's Orgoglio and Despaire," *TSLL* 3 (1961–62), 124–25. Cf. Rosemond Tuve, *Allegorical Imagery: Some Medieval Books and Their Posterity* (Princeton University Press, 1966), pp. 123–24; James Nohrnberg, *The Analogy of "The Faerie Queene"* (Princeton University Press, 1976), p. 263.

3 Hamilton, *FQ* I.vii.2.8n.

4 Henry Bullinger, *A Hundred Sermons upon the Apocalypse of Jesus Christ*, [trans. J. Daus] (London, 1561), P8^r. At II.vii.66.9, as we shall see, Guyon's collapse can manifest a loss of the implicitly present power of grace (ch. 7, p. 188, above).

5 Another use of the *locus amoenus*, less threatening but no less illusory, describes the setting of Colin Clout's vision on Mt. Acidale, VII.x; ch. 7, p. 203, above.

6 Richard Greenham, *The Works of the Reverend and Faithful Servant of Jesus Christ* (London, 1612), L2^r.

7 See, for example, Hamilton, *FQ* I.vii.5.4n, and S. K. Heninger, Jr., "The Orgoglio Episode in *The Faerie Queene*," *ELH* 26 (1959), 174, who read Spenser's nymph as an abbreviated replication of Ovid's. Cf. *Metamorphoses* 4.300-20, where the nymph who haunts the "ever-living Spring" is "unpractiz'd in the chace . . . Of all the Water-Nymphs, this Nymph alone / To nimble-footed Dian was unknowne . . . in her owne Fountaine bathes her faire / And shapefull lims now kembs her golden haire . . ." Quoted from George Sandys, *Ovid's Metamorphosis Englished, Mythologized, and Represented in Figures*, eds. Karl H. Hulley and Stanley T. Vandersall (Lincoln: University of Nebraska Press, 1970), p. 180. Golding's nymph seems even more self-indulgent than Sandys'. See Arthur Golding, *Shakespeare's Ovid, Being Arthur Golding's Translation of the Metamorphoses*, ed. W. H. D. Rouse (London: Centaur, 1961), p. 89, lines 370–83.

8 The metaphor of the race appears also in Eccl. 9:11 and in Psalm 19:5, which is echoed at the beginning of I.v; it receives elaborate treatment at I Cor. 9:24–27. In both Ecclesiastes and in I Corinthians, it is used in conjunction with the metaphor of spiritual battle. At the opening of Heb. 12, the Geneva Bible provides cross-references to seminal Pauline discussions of holiness figured in human imitations of the dying and rising Christ: Rom. 6:4; Eph. 4:23; Col. 3:8. It adds also I Pet. 2:1.

9 See Josephine Waters Bennett, *The Evolution of "The Faerie Queene"* (University of Chicago Press, 1942), ch. 9, and John Erskine Hankins, *Source and Meaning in Spenser's Allegory: A Study of "The Faerie Queene"* (Ox-

ford: Clarendon Press, 1971), pp. 99–119. Hankins restates here the widely accepted argument he promulgated in 1954: that "[t]he Revelation of St. John and related passages in other parts of the Bible provide Spenser's basic pattern and much of his imagery" for Book I (p. 119), and that the elements Spenser selected were those which contain (as Protestants read them) anti-papal satire and lead directly to the eschaton.

10 Patricia A. Parker, *Inescapable Romance: Studies in the Poetics of a Mode* (Princeton University Press, 1979), pp. 75, 77.

11 Preserving this distinction is recommended by Bernard McGinn, "Early Apocalypticism: the Ongoing Debate," *The Apocalypse in English Renaissance Thought and Literature: Patterns, Antecedents, and Repercussions*, eds. C. A. Patrides and Joseph Wittreich (Ithaca, NY: Cornell University Press, 1984), pp. 9–10.

12 Ibid., pp. 7, 10.

13 John Bale, *The Image of Both Churches*, "*Select Works of John Bale*," Parker Society, ed. the Reverend Henry Christmas (Cambridge University Press, 1849), p. 252. This notion was widely disseminated, in part because it helped to bolster the Protestant argument that Revelation's canonical authority should not be doubted. Invoking the authority of Tremellius, for example, the Geneva editors' 1587 preface to the book argues for the authenticity of John's Apocalypse on the grounds that "there appeareth in all parts of it a great majesty of the spirit of prophecy, and the very steps and sentences of, yea and the words of the old prophets."

14 Bullinger's extensive commentary, he tells us in *Hundred Sermons*, B3^v–B4^r, derives from eclectic sources. He has adopted interpretations not only from Augustine and other patristic authorities and Reformed colleagues, but also from Erasmus and Valla, from Aquinas, and from the *Glossa ordinaria*.

15 This will be evident to readers who recall the concluding chapter of Revelation in some detail. Even after its vision of the river and tree of life – a vision that extends only through the first five verses of chapter 22 – the remaining seventeen verses contain a variety of things. These conclude with a brief prayer not celebrating conclusion but yearning for it: "Even so come, Lord Jesus . . . Amen."

16 Extending John Erskine Hankins' views (note 9, above), David Norbrook, in *Poetry and Politics in the English Renaissance* (London: Routledge and Kegan Paul, 1984), pp. 12, 15, 119, 122, argues that *The Faerie Queene*'s structure is "apocalyptic, prophetic" because modelled on Revelation. He equates "the apocalyptic view of history" with "[t]he conviction that the life of society as a whole as well as of each individual was soon to come to an end." Cf. Frank Kermode, *Shakespeare, Spenser, Donne: Renaissance Essays* (New York: Viking, 1971), p. 40. In *The Apocalyptic Tradition in*

Reformation Britain, 1530–1645 (Oxford University Press, 1979), pp. 6, 8, 24, and elsewhere, Katharine Firth limits her exposition exclusively to interpretations that seek to correlate historical events with episodes in Revelation.

17 *Hundred Sermons*, E8^{r-v}; A6^r.

18 As is nearly unavoidable, readers of Revelation create coherent narratives out of discontinuous material. In *Source and Meaning*, p. 108, Hankins provides an especially helpful instance of this. For an instructive contrast, see Erasmus, *Paraphrase*, I, CCc5^r, where Leo Juda asserts that, as all the learned know, there is no more "observed order" in Revelation than there is in "other writings of the prophets," all of whose books are "compact together of many and diverse visions."

19 As my quotations in this and other chapters reveal, these doctrines dominate the commentaries of Bale, Bullinger, Fulke, and Juda, as well as those of the Geneva editors.

20 On the conjugal depiction of the Lord's relationship with the human soul, see the second commandment, where graven images, whose appeal (like Duessa's) is to the carnal eye, are forbidden on the ground that "I the Lord thy God [am] a jealous God" (Exod. 20:5). See also Alexander Nowell's standard gloss, *A Catechism*, ed. G. E. Corrie (Cambridge University Press, 1853), p. 124.

21 Hugh Latimer, *The Works of Hugh Latimer*, ed. G. E. Corrie, 2 vols. (Cambridge University Press, 1844–45), I, p. 28.

22 Torczon, "Spenser's Orgoglio and Despaire."

23 A. C. Hamilton, *The Structure of Allegory in "The Faerie Queene"* (Oxford: Clarendon Press, 1961), p. 75.

24 See, e.g., John Bradford, *The Old Man and the New*, *"The Writings of John Bradford"*, ed. Aubrey Townsend, 2 vols. (Cambridge University Press, 1848–53), I, p. 298: in the unrelenting struggle between the Old and the New Man within the elect and justified soul, the Old Man sometimes so completely prevails that "even the children of God themselves, think that they be nothing else but 'old,' and that the Spirit and seed of God is lost and gone away."

25 See ch. 4, p. 106, above. Red Cross' current aid reflects the far preferable operation of grace, which Bradford describes (*Writings*, I, p. 298): "God . . . always . . . holdeth his hand under his children in their falls, that they lie not still . . . continually in their sin as do the wicked, but at length do return again by reason of God's seed, which is in them hid as a sparkle of fire in the ashes." Cited also by Elizabeth Heale, *"The Faerie Queene": A Reader's Guide* (Cambridge University Press, 1987), p. 40.

26 See Hamilton, *FQ* I.vii.9.8n;12.8n.

27 The Spirit was, as we have seen, especially prominent in the soteriology

of Bucer and of Martyr (Introduction, p. 14, above)

28 The progressive stages of supinity have been noted by Spenser's commentators; see Hamilton, *FQ* I.vii.6.2n. Reformation interpreters of Ephesians 6 discussed a similar series of postures. Latimer, *Works*, I, p. 26, is representative: "'That ye may stand,' saith he. Ye must stand in this battle. . . We may not sit, that is, nor rest in sin, or lie along in sluggishness of sin; but continually fight against our enemy, and under our great Captain and Sovereign Lord Jesus Christ."

29 This useful discussion of points of agreement and disagreement between Catholic and Protestant doctrine is provided by William Perkins, *A Reformed Catholic*, in "*The Works of That Famous and Worthie Minister of Christ in the University of Cambridge*," 3 vols. (Cambridge, 1609), I, Ccc5ᵛ.

30 See also, *FQ* II.viii.11–29; ch. 7, 188–89, above.

31 Cf., e.g., Ovid, *Metamorphoses* 9.68–74.

32 Bullinger employs this conventional numerology throughout his *Hundred Sermons*. See, for instance, Aviʳ, where he explains that "the seventh number, which is most used in this book . . . is the number of fullness."

33 Quoting the list of sins which Paul uses to excoriate human nature in Romans 3:10–18, Calvin's treatment in *Institutes of the Christian Religion*, trans. Ford Lewis Battles, ed. John T. McNeill, 2 vols. (Philadelphia: Westminster Press, 1960), II.iii.2; I, p. 291, also employs the hydra image: "If these are the hereditary endowments of the human race, it is futile to seek anything good in our nature. Indeed, I grant that not all these wicked traits appear in every man; yet one cannot deny that this hydra lurks in the breast of each."

34 William Fulke, *Praelections upon the Sacred and Holy Revelation of St. John*, trans. George Gyffard (London, 1573), L1ᵛ. Cf. Juda, in Erasmus' *Paraphrase*, II, CCc5ᵛ.

35 Scripture offers ample precedent for viewing subsidiary lights as secondary sources of the true "light." Revelation, for instance, often represents Christ as the ultimate source of all illumination and, consequently, employs stars to symbolize the patriarchs, prophets, and apostles "which have their light" from Him "and pour out the same into the church." See Bullinger, *Hundred Sermons*, Aa7ʳ.

36 This citation refers to the Latin text in the Loeb Library *Aeneid*, trans. H. Rushton Fairclough, 2 vols. (New York: G. P. Putnam's Sons, 1916).

37 Geoffrey of Monmouth, *History of the Kings of Britain*, trans. Sebastian Evans (New York: Dutton, 1958), IX.4; p. 188.

38 The view of the dragon as "defensive" and "enervated" is Michael Leslie's, *Spenser's "Fierce Warres and Faithfull Loves": Martial and Chivalric Symbolism in "The Faerie Queene"* (New York: Barnes and Noble, 1983), p. 53.

39 Cf. a related, similarly salient passage: I Cor. 15:55–57, "O death, where is thy sting! . . . The sting of death is sin: and the strength of sin is the Law. But thanks be unto God which hath given us victory through our Lord Jesus Christ."

40 Thomas Becon, *A New Postil* (London, 1566), I, EE5ᵛ.

41 Ibid. In *Hundred Sermons*, V8ᵛ, Bullinger says that Christ called James and John "thunderers, that is to wit excellently sharp in preaching and to be feared."

42 Becon, *New Postil*, I, EE7ʳ–EE8ʳ. Cf. A. C. Hamilton, *Structure of Allegory*, p. 81n, who quotes Calvin's description of contrasting "repentances," of the Law and of the Gospel.

43 Carrying with it, as has been said, intimations of the Last Judgment (cf. Rev. 8:5). See Heninger, "The Orgoglio Episode."

44 Kathleen Williams is unusual, I think, in noticing the importance of this mood; see *Spenser's World of Glass: a Reading of "The Faerie Queene,"* (Berkeley and Los Angeles: University of California Press, 1966), p. 22. But see also Maurice Evans, *Spenser's Anatomy of Heroism: a Commentary on "The Faerie Queene"* (Cambridge University Press, 1970), p. 104.

45 The point has sometimes been noted, but it has not as yet been pointed out that winds are also ambivalent symbols; they can represent "Pharisaical doctrine," and hypocrisy springing from it. See Bullinger, *Hundred Sermons*, Q3ᵛ.

46 Williams, *Spenser's World of Glass*, p. 22; Hamilton, *FQ* vii.32.5–9n.

47 As opposed, say, to Guyon's, II.viii.17.7n; 38.3; see ch. 7, p. 189, above.

48 For the associations between rock and the Messiah, see esp. Num. 20:8–11; Ps. 40.2; Matt. 7:24–27; I Pet. 2:4–8; cf. Rom 9:32. Another Spenserian version of adamantine armor, which supports less consistently optimistic implications, appears at *FQ* V.i.10; ch. 7, p. 200, above.

49 Natalis Comes, *Natalis Comitis mythologiae* (Frankfurt, 1581), Q5ʳ.

50 *A Treatise, Touching the Libertie of a Christian*, trans. James Bell (London, 1579), C5ᵛ.

51 Many have noted the typological pattern of Arthur's actions in I.viii. See esp. Hamilton, *Structure of Allegory*, pp. 77–78; and *Books I and II of "The Faerie Queene"*, eds. Robert Kellogg and Oliver Steele (Indianapolis: Bobbs-Merrill, 1965), pp. 33–35.

52 Paul Alpers, *The Poetry of "The Faerie Queene"* (Princeton University Press, 1967), pp. 337–39. This observation supports Alpers' broader argument that Spenser's treatment of the problem of human heroism is guided by the endeavor "to make us aware of a puzzle, and not to render a structured judgment about it" (p. 336, and ch. 10, *passim*).

53 See ch. 7, p. 190, above, for analysis of the battle in *FQ* II.viii, in which Arthur pointedly does share the vice his opponent embodies.

54 Wariness is an attribute that Red Cross achieves only when he is in the very act of falling to Orgoglio, after "heavenly grace . . . him did blesse" (I.vii.12.3–8).

55 Bradford, *The Old Man and the New*, "*Writings,*" I, pp. 297 ff; quoted by Philip Edgcumbe Hughes, *Theology of the English Reformers* (Grand Rapids, MI: Eerdmans, 1965), p. 85.

56 Bradford, *Writings*, I, pp. 54–55; Calvin, *Institutes*, III.ii.6; I, p. 549; III.xxiv.12; II, p. 978. Cf. H. C. Porter, *Reformation and Reaction in Tudor Cambridge* (Cambridge University Press, 1958), p. 339, and see Dante, *Purgatorio* 9.94–96.

57 For a comparable reading see John N. King, *Spenser's Poetry and the Reformation Tradition* (Princeton University Press, 1990), pp. 97–99.

58 Cf. William Tyndale, *Doctrinal Treatises and Introductions to Different Portions of the Holy Scriptures*, ed. the Reverend Henry Walter (Cambridge University Press, 1848), p. 303, who remarks that the Pope had stolen the Bible's literal sense, and "locked it up with false and counterfeit keys of his traditions."

59 Williams, *Spenser's World of Glass*, p. 23, argues that Red Cross now grasps this doctrinal point.

60 Among many instances, see, ibid., pp. 22–23, which forcefully argues that the rationality Arthur promotes is equivalent to faith. A somewhat more critical interpretation of Arthur's heroism appears in Evans, *Spenser's Anatomy of Heroism*, p. 29.

6 DISCOVERING HOLINESS

1 On Despair's adroitness in echoing scriptural passages taken out of context, see Ann E. Imbrie, "'Playing Legerdemaine with the Scripture': Parodic Sermons in *The Faerie Queene,*" *ELR* 17 (1987), 142–55. See also Patrick Cullen, *Infernal Triad: The Flesh, the World, and the Devil in Spenser and Milton* (Princeton University Press, 1974), pp. 59–63; John N. King, *Spenser's Poetry and the Reformation Tradition* (Princeton University Press, 1990), pp. 213–16; and Harold Skulsky, "Spenser's Despair Episode and the Theology of Doubt," *MP* 78 (1981), 227–42.

2 Richard Greenham, *The Works of the Reverend and Faithful Servant of Jesus Christ* (London, 1612), sigs. K5ᵛ–K6ʳ.

3 Ibid.

4 Imbrie, "'Playing Legerdemain,'" p. 148.

5 Scholars usually maintain that the specific allusion is to Luke 2:35; see, for instance, Imbrie, "'Playing Legerdemain,'" p. 148.

6 Richard Hooker, *Of the Laws of Ecclesiastical Polity*, intro. Christopher Morris (London: Dent, 1907), 1.12.2; I, p. 211.

7 For analyses of ways by which the poetry confuses or effects a merger of Red Cross' and Despair's identities, see Hamilton, *FQ* I.x.417n, 42n, and Paul J. Alpers, *The Poetry of "The Faerie Queene"* (Princeton University Press, 1967), p. 355.

8 Useful reminders that the debate constituted "a prominent medieval-Renaissance genre drawing upon both dialogic and rhetorical traditions, in which more or less evenly-matched speakers argue opposed positions and an audience is expected to judge which has the better case" appear in Barbara K. Lewalski's *"Paradise Lost" and the Rhetoric of Literary Forms* (Princeton University Press, 1985), pp. 16, 22, 156–60.

9 In "'All the Good is God's': Predestination in Spenser's *Faerie Queene*, Book I," *Christianity and Literature* 32 No. 3 (Spring, 1983), 11–18, Daniel W. Doerksen points out that the force of Una's statement derives from its echoes of the predestinarian doctrine as presented in Article XVII of the Thirty-Nine Articles and affiliated biblical texts (e.g. Rom. 8).

10 Calvin, *Institutes of the Christian Religion*, trans. Ford Lewis Battles, ed. John T. McNeill, 2 vols. (Philadelphia: Westminster Press, 1960) III.xxiv.10; II, p. 976.

11 Calvin, *Institutes* III.xxiv.8; II, p. 974.

12 See Introduction, p. 24, above.

13 As Judith H. Anderson, for instance, has put it in *The Growth of a Personal Voice: "Piers Plowman" and "The Faerie Queene"* (New Haven: Yale University Press, 1976), p. 42, *The Faerie Queene* I.x is "an exposition of truth, much like a sermon." Cf. Isabel G. MacCaffrey, *Spenser's Allegory: The Anatomy of Imagination* (Princeton University Press, 1976), pp. 43, 188–90, 222, 406; and King, *Reformation Tradition*, pp. 58–65.

14 These views appear, respectively, in Mother Pauline Parker, *The Allegory of "The Faerie Queene"* (Oxford: Clarendon Press, 1960), p. 98; Virgil K. Whitaker, *The Religious Basis of Spenser's Thought*, Stanford University Publications in Language and Literature 7 (Stanford University Press, 1950), pp. 45–46, and Gerald Morgan, "Holiness as the First of Spenser's Aristotelian Moral Virtues," *MLR* 81 (1986), 830; Jerome Oentgen, O.S.B., "Spenser's Treatment of Monasticism in Book I of *The Faerie Queene*," *ABR* 22 (1971), 120; Carol Kaske, "Spenser's Pluralistic Universe: The View From the Mount of Contemplation (F.Q. I.x)," *Contemporary Thought on Edmund Spenser*, eds. Richard C. Frushell and Bernard J. Vondersmith (Carbondale and Edwardsville: Southern Illinois University Press, 1975), 121–49; and Alpers, *Poetry of "The Faerie Queene,"* ch. 10, esp. pp. 348–49.

15 The echoes are recorded by (among others) Hamilton, *FQ,* I.x.1.6–9n, and Naseeb Shaheen, *Biblical References in "The Faerie Queene"* (Memphis State University Press, 1976), p. 84.

16 Alpers, *Poetry of "The Faerie Queene,"* p. 335. Cf. Anthea Hume, *Edmund Spenser: Protestant Poet* (Cambridge University Press, 1984), p. 68. For other antivoluntarist readings of I.x.1, see Kathleen Williams, *Spenser's World of Glass: A Reading of "The Faerie Queene"* (Berkeley and Los Angeles: University of California Press, 1966), pp. 20, 27, and Whitaker, *Religious Basis*, p. 44. Cf. also Kaske, "Spenser's Pluralistic Universe," p. 124, which assigns a total "Calvinist" antivoluntarism to the lines that echo Philippians 2:13. According to Kaske's interpretation, I.x.i.6–9 "ascribes all to God," and II.i.33.2–4 ("His be the praise . . . More than goodwill to me attribute nought") "credits the power to God and the will to man."

17 The Geneva translators make the point somewhat less lucidly: "make an end of your own salvation."

18 See John Bradford's "Sermon on Repentance," *The Writings of John Bradford*, ed. Aubrey Townsend, 2 vols. (Cambridge University Press, 1848–53), I, p. 75. See also I, p. 218. For Bradford as for Calvin, an essential point of Philippians 2:12–13 is that the regenerate do indeed possess a will which cooperates with the impulsions of grace experienced by believers who have received God's call. That good will cannot, however, be considered the sinner's own autonomous possession. Cf. ch. 1, above, pp. 30–31, and Calvin's related treatments of Philippians 2:12–13, in conjunction with seminal verses from Ephesians, at *Institutes* II.iii.6; I, pp. 296–98; II.iii.7; I, p. 299; II.v.11; I, p. 330. See also the Elizabethan Archbishop (of York) Toby Matthew's comparable view, quoted in Nicholas Tyacke, *Anti-Calvinists: The Rise of English Arminianism, c. 1590–1640* (Oxford: Clarendon Press, 1987), pp. 18–19; Aquinas' similar reading, *Commentary on Saint Paul's First Letter to the Thessalonians and the Letter to the Philippians*, trans. F. R. Larcher and Michael Duffy (Albany, NY: Magi Books, 1969), pp. 87–88; and Augustine's *On Nature and Grace*, *"Basic Works of St. Augustine,"* ed. Whitney J. Oates, 2 vols. (New York: Random House, 1948), I, p. 544.

19 See chapters ix–xvi of *The Canons and Decrees of the Council of Trent*, *"Creeds of Christendom,"* ed. Philip Schaff, 3 vols. (1897; Grand Rapids, MI: Baker Book House, 1977), II, pp. 98–110. An epitome of the relevant implications of these sections appears in ch. xvi: "whereas Jesus Christ himself continually infuses his virtue into the said justified . . . and this virtue always precedes and accompanies and follows their good works . . . we must believe that nothing further is wanting to the justified, to prevent their being accounted to have, by those very works which have been done in God . . . merited eternal life" (pp. 108–9). Cf. ch. 1, above, p. 37.

20 Whitaker, *Religious Basis*, p. 46. Cf. D. Douglas Waters, *Duessa as Theological Satire* (Columbia, MO: University of Missouri Press, 1970), p. 107.

21 Alpers, *Poetry of "The Faerie Queene,"* pp. 348–49.

22 That the features and inhabitants of the House of Holiness should be viewed as metaphors has been easily assumed by C. S. Lewis, *Allegory of Love: A Study in Medieval Tradition* (1936; New York: Oxford University Press, 1958), pp. 321–23, and just as easily dismissed by Whitaker, *Religious Basis*, pp. 46–47, *inter alia*.

23 Greenham, *Works*, T2$^{r–v}$.

24 Greenham elsewhere counts the outward works of worship among the "sweet and sure signs of election," calling it "a sowing of the Spirit, by the use of the means, as of the word, prayer, etc."(*Works*, M1^v).

25 Thomas Becon, *A New Postil* (London, 1566), I, pp. 80ff; quoted in Philip Edgcumbe Hughes, *Theology of the English Reformers* (Grand Rapids, MI: Eerdmans, 1965), p. 80.

26 Greenham, *Works*, M1^v. Cf., among many other possibilities, the Geneva (1587) comment on Rom. 7:18. Also Bradford, *Writings*, I, p. 297, as cited in Hughes, *Theology of the English Reformers*, p. 86.

27 Cf., for example, Frank Whigham, *Ambition and Privilege: The Social Tropes of Elizabethan Courtesy Theory* (Berkeley and Los Angeles: University of California Press, 1984).

28 William Tyndale, *Expositions and Notes on Sundry Portions of the Holy Scripture*, ed. the Reverend Henry Walter (Cambridge University Press, 1849), p. 202; *Certaine Sermons or Homilies Appointed to be Read in Churches in the Time of Queen Elizabeth I* (1547–1571), facsimile edn, intro. Mary Ellen Rickey and Thomas B. Stroup (Gainesville, FL: Scholar's Facsimiles and Reprints, 1968), C2^v, C3^r. On II Peter 1:10, which reads "brethren, give rather diligence to make your calling and election sure," the Geneva gloss comments: "Albeit it be sure in itself forasmuch as God can not change, yet we must confirm it in ourselves, by the fruits of the Spirit, knowing that the purpose of God electeth, calleth, sanctifieth, and justifieth us." Cf. the Elizabethan Article 17, and Thomas Rogers, *The Catholic Doctrine of the Church of England, an Exposition of the Thirty-Nine Articles*, ed. the Reverend J. J. S. Perowne (1607; Cambridge University Press, 1854), p. 123.

29 As we shall see, this point illuminates later episodes in *The Faerie Queene*, as when Guyon "feedes" himself with "comfort" "Of his owne vertues," II.vii.2 (ch. 7, p. 187, above).

30 Commenting on Revelation 10:1, Henry Bullinger, *A Hundred Sermons upon the Apocalypse of Jesu Christ*, [trans. J. Daus] (London, 1561), V7^v, says that "The bright face of Christ bringeth joy and unspeakable gladness to the beholders, and pacifieth the minds. And the same is seen of us spiritually and by faith." An appropriate symbol for faith is the "mirror" of "the glory of the Lord," which believers may eventually "behold . . .

with open face" and so be "changed into the same image, from glory to glory, as by the spirit of the Lord" (II Cor. 3:18). Like Fidelia and the unveiled Una, the gospel shines like "Christall" (I.x.13.7), "yet," as the Geneva comment (1587) on this scriptural passage puts it, "doth it not dazzle their eyes, which look in it, as the law doth."

31 Many Protestant theologians promoted this idea of faith. Among the most influential proponents in England of intellect's importance to faith was Peter Martyr. See, e.g., John P. Donnelly, *Calvinism and Scholasticism in Vermigli's Doctrine of Man and Grace* (Leiden: Brill, 1976), p. 85. See also ch. 1, above, pp. 41, 43–44, above.

32 Cf. Darryl J. Gless, "Nature and Grace," *The Spenser Encyclopedia* (University of Toronto Press, 1990).

33 It is instructive here to consider the often-cited "analogy" or "proportion" of faith established as a "strategic criterion" to guarantee accurate interpretation of scripture. This is defined by William Whitaker, for example, in *A Disputation on Holy Scripture against the Papists*, trans. and ed. The Reverend William Fitzgerald (Cambridge University Press, 1849), pp. 484–86, who maintains that the "sum" of faith which should guide interpretation includes the articles in the Creed, the contents of the Lord's Prayer, the Decalogue, and "the whole Catechism." Given the volume of inexplicit meaning that interpreters have always discovered in these texts, such guides to interpretation clearly require guides themselves.

34 Taverner, *Postil*, T4^r; Perkins' remark is from *The Workes of That Famous and Worthie Minister of Christ in the University of Cambridge*, 3 vols. (Cambridge University Press, 1609), I, Ll3^r.

35 This phenomenon recurs conspicuously at *FQ* III.i.12–18; see ch. 7, p. 192, above.

36 God's gratuitous love for humankind enables its answering love for God, expressed both directly toward Him and indirectly, through love for fellow mortals. See, e.g., Bullinger, *The Decades of Henry Bullinger*, trans. H.I., ed. Rev. Thomas Harding, 4 vols., Parker Society 7–10 (Cambridge University Press, 1849) I.x; I, pp. 180–92. Bullinger's prime authority is Augustine's seminal treatment of *caritas* in *On Christian Doctrine*.

37 See Alexander Nowell, *A Catechism*, ed. G. E. Corrie (Cambridge University Press, 1853), p. 180. The interrelations between Mercy and Charissa, as well as the alternative directions of the virtues they embody and their mutual dependence on grace, are well expressed by Tyndale (*Doctrinal Treatises*, I, p. 109): the believer who has God's spirit understands "that that unspeakable love and mercy which God hath to us . . . and that love wherewith we love God, and that love which we have to our neighbor, and that mercy and compassion which we show on him . . . are altogether the gift of God through Christ's purchasing."

38 Both Erasmus and Calvin could be convinced of this, despite their anti-
    monastic attitudes; see Gless, *"Measure for Measure," the Law, and the
    Convent* (Princeton University Press, 1979), pp. 87–88.
39 Of this mutual reinforcement of action and contemplation, "Tully, Cato,
    Pompeius, Lucullus, and such like singular men among the Ethnics" were
    instances. So too was Christ, who periodically undertook contemplative
    withdrawal to mountains and wilderness: Peter Martyr, *The Common Places
    of Peter Martyr* (London, 1583), Piii^{r-v}. Cf. Donnelly, *Calvinism and
    Scholasticism*, p. 88. King, *Reformation Tradition*, p. 218, argues that "*The
    Faerie Queene* places action and contemplation on an equal footing."
40 Greenham, *Works*, Y4^v. Richard Rogers, *Seven Treatises, Containing Such
    Direction as is Gathered Out of the Holie Scriptures, Leading and Guiding
    to True Happiness . . . the Practice of Christianity* (London, 1603), Y4^r,
    presents comparable views on the uses and timing of contemplation.
41 For contrasting interpretations, see, for instance, MacCaffrey, *Spenser's
    Allegory*, p. 222; Joseph B. Collins, *Christian Mysticism in the Elizabethan
    Age: With Its Background in Mystical Methodology* (Baltimore: Johns Hop-
    kins University Press, 1940), p. 193; and King, *Reformation Tradition*, p.
    217, all of whom see Spenser's mysticism more as a replication than a
    revaluation of medieval precedents.
42 St. Bonaventura, *The Mind's Road to God*, trans. George Boas, The Li-
    brary of Liberal Arts (Indianapolis: Bobbs-Merrill, 1953), pp. 44–45,
    quoting Dionysius' *Mystic Theology*. Cf. *Paradiso* 33.46–145: "And I, who
    was drawing near to the end of all desires, ended perforce the ardour of
    my craving . . . From that moment my vision was greater than our speech,
    which fails at such a sight." Quoted from *Dante's Paradiso*, trans. John D.
    Sinclair (New York: Oxford University Press, 1961).
43 "A Meditation of the Life Everlasting" and "Of the Blessed State and
    Felicity of the Life to Come" climax in scriptural paraphrases and quota-
    tions, often from the later chapters of St. John's Apocalypse. In Bradford,
    Writings, I, pp. 268, 275.
44 Richard Rogers, *Seven Treatises*, Y4^r. On the Protestant inclination to
    assimilate meditation to the aims and typical structure of Protestant ser-
    mons, see Barbara K. Lewalski, *Donne's "Anniversaries" and the Poetry of
    Praise: The Creation of a Symbolic Mode* (Princeton University Press, 1973),
    pp. 84–87. Cf. Lewalski's treatment of meditation in *Protestant Poetics
    and the Seventeenth-Century Religious Lyric* (Princeton University Press,
    1979), ch. 5.
45 E.g. Lawrence Stone's description of hostile human relations, which he
    believes to have been characteristic of early modern society, in *The Fam-
    ily, Sex and Marriage in England, 1500–1800* (New York: Harper and
    Row, 1977). See also Keith Thomas, *Religion and the Decline of Magic*

(New York: Scribner, 1971), and Michael MacDonald, *Mystical Bedlam: Madness, Anxiety, and Healing in Seventeenth-Century England* (Cambridge University Press, 1981).

46 Cf., e.g. *FQ* III.i.12.7–8 and IV.viii.30–31.

47 Cf. Stephen Greenblatt's "Fiction and Friction," in *Reconstructing Individualism: Autonomy, Individuality, and the Self in Western Thought*, eds. Thomas C. Heller, Morton Sosna, and David E. Wellbery (Stanford University Press, 1986), pp. 30–52. The strange and fascinating narrative of sexual identity explored "here suggests that individual identity in the early modern period served less as a final goal than as a way station on the road to a firm and decisive identification with normative structures'" (p. 35).

48 For the allusion, see Nohrnberg, *Analogy*, p. 155.

49 Carol V. Kaske, "The Dragon's Spark and Sting and the Structure of Red Cross' Dragon-Fight: *The Faerie Queene*, I.xi-xii," *SP* 66 (1969), 609–38; rpt. A. C. Hamilton, ed., *Essential Articles for the Study of Edmund Spenser* (Hamden, CT: Archon Books, 1972), pp. 425–46.

50 See the anthology of scriptural quotations assembled in Hamilton, *FQ* x.29–30nn.

51 Hume, *Protestant Poet*, p. 105.

52 See, e.g., Kaske, "Dragon's Spark," p. 637; rpt. Hamilton, *Essential Articles*, p. 445.

53 Hughes, *Theology*, p. 195, quoting John Jewel. See also the discussion of competing sacramental doctrines that appears in D. Douglas Waters, *Duessa as Theological Satire*, pp. 113–19. Some additionally useful materials on the sacraments appear in H. F. Woodhouse, *The Doctrine of the Church in Anglican Theology, 1547–1603* (London: SPCK, 1954), pp. 37–40.

54 Bullinger, *Decades* 5.7; IV, p. 326. Cf. *Decades* 5.7; IV, p. 316. Elizabeth Heale, *"The Faerie Queene": A Reader's Guide* (Cambridge University Press, 1987), p. 44, quotes Calvin's statement on the usefulness, when one has sinned, of remembering the import of one's baptism.

55 Hughes, *Theology*, p. 197; quoting Jewel and Sandys.

56 See Nowell, *Catechism*, p. 205; Beza, *Summe*, D7ʳ–J8ᵛ; Hooker, *Laws*, V.lvii; II, pp. 235–37. Cf. Horton Davies, *Worship and Theology in England: From Cranmer to Hooker, 1534–1603* (Princeton University Press, 1970), pp. 76–123, esp. 80–85.

57 The Elizabethan *Book of Common Prayer, 1559*, ed. John E. Booty (Charlottesville: University Press of Virginia, 1976), p. 273.

58 William Tyndale, *Doctrinal Treatises*, p. 466. See also Bullinger, *Decades* 5.7; IV, p. 339.

59 See the *Book of Common Prayer 1559*, p. 269: "Baptism should not be ministered but upon Sundays and other holy days when the most number

of people may come together . . . because in the baptism of infants every man present may be put in remembrance of his own profession made to God in his baptism."

60 Nowell, *Catechism*, p. 209: to use our baptism rightly, we must "with assured confidence hold it determined in our hearts, that we are cleansed by the blood of Christ." We must also "with all our power and endeavour, travail in mortifying our flesh . . . and must by godly life declare to all men that we have in baptism as it were put on Christ . . . Furthermore, the supper of the Lord doth admonish us of brotherly love and charity, and of the unity we have with all the members of Christ." Cf. *The Book of Common Prayer, 1559*, pp. 274–75.

61 Calvin, *Institutes* III.ii.21; I, p. 567. Cf. Heale, *"The Faerie Queene,"* p. 44, which notes Calvin's point that faith will prevent sin from inflicting a death-blow upon the faithful.

62 Tuve, *Allegorical Imagery*, pp. 110–12; Hume, *Protestant Poet*, pp. 104–5.

63 Nowell, *Catechism*, p. 152.

64 As argued, e.g., by Harold L. Weatherby, "The True St. George," *ELR* 17 (1987), 121, "the Redcrosse Knight . . . is not only sanctified but deified, transformed, as Frank Kermode aptly remarks, from '*miles Christi*' into 'Christ himself (whose bride Una is the Church).'"

65 Bradford, *Writings*, I, p. 99; quoted in Hughes, p. 210. Cf. Cranmer, *Works*, I, p. 43; quoted in Hughes, p. 210. See also Becon, *New Postil*, I, Y1[r], which prescribes anyone who doubts that Christ will save them to "resort . . . unto the Lord's Supper. For Jesus Christ . . . hath instituted the sacrament . . . that . . . thou shouldest not doubt . . . that . . . his blood [was] shed for thy sins."

66 This idea would be especially evident to readers who adopted something like Calvin's focus on incorporation as the solution to the theological problem of adjusting intrinsic to extrinsic causes and consequences of salvation. See above (ch. 1, p. 29); see also R. S. Wallace, *Calvin's Doctrine of the Christian Life* (Edinburgh and London: Oliver and Boyd, 1959), pp. 18–19: sacraments were instituted "to make [the spiritual union of Christ and the church] continually effective in the life of the Church, and to impress upon us continually that this union is the source of our justification and sanctification."

67 This part of the event has been acutely noted. See Hamilton, *FQ* I.xi.53.5–9n, and King, *Reformation Tradition*, pp. 199, 224.

7 "SPENSER" AND DOGMATIC MUTABILITY

1 The primary allusions are noted in Douglas Brooks-Davies, *Spenser's "Faerie Queene": A Critical Commentary on Books I and II* (Manchester

University Press, 1977), pp. 110–11. See also the always useful citations in Hamilton, *FQ.*

2 See, e.g., Patricia Parker, *Inescapable Romance: Studies in the Poetics of a Mode* (Princeton University Press, 1979), pp. 74, 77; and Jonathan Goldberg, *"Endelesse Worke: Spenser and the Structures of Discourse* (Baltimore and London: Johns Hopkins University Press, 1981), p. 2n.

3 See, e.g., John Erskine Hankins, *Source and Meaning in Spenser's Allegory: A Study of "The Faerie Queene"* (Oxford: Clarendon Press, 1971), pp. 111–13, and Harold L. Weatherby, "The True St. George," *ELR* 17 (1987), 124–29.

4 Though he attends to other elements of the canto, the drift of John N. King's interpretation, in *Spenser's Poetry and the Reformation Tradition* (Princeton University Press, 1990), p. 226, can induce a more homogenizing perception: "Generic boundaries disappear at the conclusion of Book I . . . within the all-embracing category of divine comedy. This ultimate simplification fittingly brings to a close a book that moves from generic multiplicity to the primal unity of truth embodied in Una."

5 Henry Bullinger, *A Hundred Sermons upon the Apocalypse of Jesu Christ*, [trans. J. Daus] (London, 1561), Pp3ʳ.

6 R. S. Wallace, *Calvin's Doctrine of the Christian Life* (Edinburgh and London: Oliver and Boyd, 1959), pp. 78–79. See also Greenham's similar reflections, noted above, ch. 6, p. 151.

7 This restriction is applied by Anthea Hume in *Edmund Spenser: Protestant Poet* (Cambridge University Press, 1984), see esp. pp. 108–9. Thanks in part to C. S. Lewis' treatment of "vision cantos," many Spenserians have been inclined to accept their status as given, concrete features of the poem. Teaching *The Faerie Queene* to new groups of students often freshly demonstrates, however, that readers can locate moments of primary significance in a surprising range of alternative locations.

8 Ibid., pp. 68–70.

9 The quotation is from ibid., p. 68; a more recent restatement of it occurs in Richard A. McCabe, *The Pillars of Eternity: Time and Providence in "The Faerie Queene"* (Dublin: Irish Academic Press, 1989), p. 90.

10 Hume, *Protestant Poet*, p. 70.

11 Ibid., p. 111.

12 Because they represent a subclass of works of holiness, Guyon's acts will be inwardly virtuous to a degree that the pagan or "natural" man's performance of them could not be. The best humankind can do by natural means alone is to perform the "outward actions of civil virtues.". See also ch. 4, p. 110–12.

13 See Lodowick Bryskett's *A Discourse of Civill Life*, ed. Thomas E. Wright (Northridge, CA: San Fernando State College, 1970).

14 See Hamilton, *FQ* II.55.6nn.

15 Even the clearest-eyed interpreters have been obliged to project onto this moment some unspecified persisting influence of Acrasia's "charm of 'lust and lewde desyres.'" See Kathleen Williams, *Spenser's World of Glass: A Reading of "The Faerie Queene"* (Berkeley and Los Angeles: University of California Press, 1966), p. 41.

16 Mortdant's name (death giving) may in this context represent (by synecdoche, effect for cause) human nature, which always seeks, and ultimately achieves, death unless grace intervenes.

17 Cf. A. C. Hamilton, "A Theological Reading of *The Faerie Queene*, Book II," *ELH* 25 (1958), 155–62, who considers original sin to be the "whole subject" of Book II, and finds it manifested in the fiction of the bloody-handed babe. Guyon reveals the powers and limits of temperance. Cf. also Hamilton's "'Like Race to Runne': The Parallel Structure of *The Faerie Queene*, Books I and II," *PMLA* 72 (1958), 327–34.

18 This reading requires, of course, that we at least momentarily join Guyon in responding to Pyrochles as a brother knight in trouble, not simply to his name, which asks that he be thought of merely as a personified moral concept. Such slippage seems an almost unavoidable reaction, induced by the poem's persistent alteration of locally dominant generic signals, from moral philosophy to romance and back.

19 See Peter Lake, *Anglicans and Puritans? Presbyterianism and English Conformist Thought from Whitgift to Hooker* (London: Unwin Hyman, 1988), pp. 34–42, for a detailed exposition of the conformist and the puritan views on membership in the church.

20 Hume, *Protestant Poet*, p. 112.

21 I read "comfort" here, II.vii.2.4, in its strong Elizabethan sense, as strengthening, support, etc. *OED* 1.

22 Frank Kermode, *Shakespeare, Spenser, Donne: Renaissance Essays* (New York: Viking, 1971), pp. 70–71; John Erskin Hankins, *Source and Meaning in Spenser's Allegory: a Study of "The Faerie Queene"* (Oxford: Clarendon Press, 1971), pp. 132–33; Patrick Cullen, *Infernal Triad: The Flesh, the World, and the Devil in Spenser and Milton* (Princeton University Press, 1974), ch. 2; and Hamilton, *FQ* II.vii.8–63nn.

23 Hume, *Protestant Poet*, p. 117.

24 Hamilton, *FQ*, II.viii.44n.

25 For a fascinating study of this episode's relation to venerable ideas of corporate identity, see David Lee Miller, *The Poem's Two Bodies: The Poetics of the 1590 "Faerie Queene"* (Princeton University Press, 1988), ch. 4.

26 For a sobering and powerful description of this aim, see Stephen Greenblatt, *Renaissance Self-Fashioning* (University of Chicago Press, 1980), p. 179, and ch. 4 *passim*. Greenblatt's explorations in "cultural

poetics" find in Guyon's destruction of the Bower a "reiteration" of "the European response to the native cultures of the New World, the English colonial struggle in Ireland, and the Reformation attack on images."

27 A darker reading of Arthur's desire is offered by Sheila T. Cavanagh, "'Beauties Chace': Arthur and Women in *The Faerie Queene*," *The Passing of Arthur: New Essays in Arthurian Tradition*, eds. Christopher Baswell and William Sharpe (New York and London: Garland, 1988), p. 215.

28 Quoted by Hamilton, *FQ* III.iii.1n.

29 See Miller, *The Poem's Two Bodies*, pp. 199–209, which discusses Harry Berger's and Jerry Leath Mills' important work on the chronicles of Book II. Drawing especially on Mills ("Prudence, History, and the Prince in *The Faerie Queene*, Book II," *HLQ* 41 [1978], 83–101), Miller remarks that "[t]he function of prudential judgment in reducing this succession of accidents to essential form is precisely to reassimilate agents and events, through a dialectical canceling-and-preserving, to the sacred body they have torn and scattered" (pp. 202–3).

30 Or of "prudence," comprehensively defined; see Miller, *The Poem's Two Bodies*, pp. 200–1.

31 The most persuasive version of this kind of interpretation remains that of Thomas P. Roche, Jr., *The Kindly Flame: A Study of the Third and Fourth Books of Spenser's "Faerie Queene"* (Princeton University Press, 1964).

32 Cf. the comparable if rather different symbolic use of magic in Jonson's "To Penshurst," as interpreted by Raymond Williams, *The Country and the City* (New York: Oxford University Press, 1973), pp. 32–33.

33 As always, interpretive difficulties which seem self-evident to one reader's construction of the text remain invisible to others. For one among many untroubled readings of this episode, see Elizabeth Heale's *"The Faerie Queene": A Reader's Guide* (Cambridge University Press, 1987), pp. 113–14.

34 Richard Hooker, *Of the Laws of Ecclesiastical Polity*, intro. Christopher Morris, 2 vols. (New York: Dent, 1907), 1.3.1; I, pp. 154–55.

35 See Darryl J. Gless, "Law, Natural and Divine," *The Spenser Encyclopedia*, ed. A.C. Hamilton, *inter alia* (University of Toronto Press, 1990).

36 See especially the description of Mercilla's throne, V.ix.28–29, and commentaries that stress the scriptural origins of the imagery, as does Hume, *Protestant Poet*, pp. 136–37.

37 Cf. Jonathan Goldberg's treatment of *The Faerie Queene*, Book V, in *James I and the Politics of Literature: Jonson, Shakespeare, Donne, and Their Contemporaries* (Baltimore and London: Johns Hopkins University Press, 1983), pp. 1–17. For the opposite emphasis, see Heale, *"The Faerie Queene,"* pp. 139–41. In Heale's construction, "Mercilla's trial of Duessa is both godly and wise. Evidence is heard on both sides, counsel is taken,

and a judgement arrived at that respects both equity and the law."
38 Hume, *Protestant Poet*, pp. 133–37.
39 Goldberg, *James I*, p. 8.
40 See Stephen Greenblatt, "Murdering Peasants: Status, Genre, and the Representation of Rebellion," *Representing the English Renaissance*, ed. Stephen Greenblatt (Berkeley: University of California Press, 1988), pp. 19–23.
41 Cf. Humphrey Tonkin, *"The Faerie Queene"* (London: Unwin Hyman, 1989), pp. 186–87: Spenser's graces "are models of gracious conduct, of the social graces that Guazzo, Castiglione and the rest prescribed, but they are also Neoplatonic parallels to the heavenly grace of the Christians . . . It is, of course, an irresistible grace: it cannot be conjured up and it comes when and where we least expect it." Cf. Tonkin's more elaborate treatment of the subject in *Spenser's Courteous Pastoral: Book Six of "The Faerie Queene"* (Oxford: Clarendon Press, 1972), pp. 231–37, 256–64. A reading of Book VI that focuses on contradictions rather than harmonious syncretism appears in Gary Waller, *English Poetry of the Sixteenth Century* (London: Longman, 1986), pp. 194–205.
42 Edgar Wind, *Pagan Mysteries in the Renaissance*, rev. edn (Harmondsworth: Penguin, 1967), chs. 7–8; Gerald Snare, "Spenser's Fourth Grace," *JWCI* 34 (1971), 350–55. As Waller notes, however, the fact that the shepherd's own beloved supplants the Queen in Book VI's climactic vision "seems to call into question the value and power of the court" (*English Poetry*, p. 204). Cf. Annabel Patterson, *Pastoral and Ideology: Virgil to Valéry* (Berkeley: University of California Press, 1987), pp. 132–33.
43 Shakespeare, *Midsummer Night's Dream* V.i.14–15, 19–21.

LIST OF WORKS CITED

PRIMARY WORKS

Andrewes, Lancelot, *A Pattern of Catechistical Doctrine, "The Works of Lancelot Andrewes,"* ed. J. P. W., 6 vols., 1854, New York: AMS Press, 1967.

Aquinas, Thomas, *Commentary on Saint Paul's First Letter to the Thessalonians and the Letter to the Philippians,* trans. F. R. Larcher and Michael Duffy, Albany, NY: Magi Books, 1969.

The Summa Theologica of Saint Thomas Aquinas, trans. Fathers of the English Dominican Province, rev. Daniel J. Sullivan, 2 vols., Chicago: Encyclopedia Britannica, 1952.

Augustine, St. *Basic Works of St. Augustine,* ed. Whitney J. Oates, 2 vols., New York: Random House, 1948.

On Christian Doctrine, trans. D. W. Robertson, Jr., The Library of Liberal Arts, Indianapolis: Bobbs-Merrill, 1958.

Bale, John, *Select Works of John Bale,* Parker Society, ed. the Reverend Henry Christmas, Cambridge University Press, 1849.

Becon, Thomas, *A New Postil Containing Most Godly Sermons upon the Sunday Gospels,* London, 1566.

Beza, Theodore de, *A briefe and pithie summe of the Christian faith,* trans. R[obert] F[yll], London, 1565.

Bonaventura, St., *The Mind's Road to God,* trans. George Boas, The Library of Liberal Arts, Indianapolis: Bobbs-Merrill, 1953.

Bradford, John, *The Writings of John Bradford,* ed. Aubrey Townsend, 2 vols., Cambridge University Press, 1848–53.

Bryskett, Lodowick, *A Discourse of Civill Life,* ed. Thomas E. Wright, Northridge, CA: San Fernando State College, 1970.

Bullinger, Henry, *A Hundred Sermons upon the Apocalypse of Jesus Christ* [trans. J. Daus], London, 1561.

The Decades of Henry Bullinger, trans. H.I., ed. Rev. Thomas Harding, 4 vols., Parker Society 7–10, 1587; Cambridge University Press, 1849.

Calvin, John, *A Harmonie upon the Three Evangelists,* trans. E[usebius] P[aget], London, 1584.

Commentaries on the Epistles of Paul to the Galatians and Ephesians, trans. the Reverend William Pringle, 1948; Grand Rapids, MI: Eerdmans, 1957.

Institutes of the Christian Religion, trans. Ford Lewis Battles, ed. John T. McNeill, Philadelphia: Westminster Press, 1960.

Church of England, *The Book of Common Prayer, 1559,* ed. John E. Booty, Charlottesville: University Press of Virginia, 1976.

Certaine Sermons or Homilies Appointed to be Read in Churches in the Time of Queen Elizabeth I (1547–1571), facsimilie edn, intro. Mary Ellen Rickey and Thomas B. Stroup, Gainesville, FL: Scholar's Facsimiles and Reprints, 1968.

Certaine Sermons or Homilies, ed. Ronald B. Bond, University of Toronto Press, 1987.

Comes, Natalis, *Natalis Comitis Mythologiae*, Frankfurt, 1581.

Creeds of Christendom, ed. Philip Schaff, 3 vols., 1897; Grand Rapids, MI: Baker Book House, 1977.

Dante, *The Divine Comedy of Dante Alighieri*, trans. John D. Sinclair, 3 vols., New York: Oxford University Press, 1961.

Erasmus, Desiderius, *On Copia of Words and Ideas [De Utraque Verborum ac Rerum Copia]*, trans. D. B. King and H. D. Rix, Milwaukee, WI: University of Wisconsin Press, 1963.

The First [and Second] Tome or Volume of the Paraphrase of Erasmus upon the Newe Testamente, London, 1548–49.

Fulke, William, *Praelections upon the Sacred and Holy Revelation of St. John*, trans. George Gyffard, London, 1573.

The Geneva Bible, a Facsimile of the 1560 Edition, intro. Lloyd E. Berry, Madison, WI: University of Wisconsin Press, 1969.

The Geneva Bible, Geneva, 1587.

Golding, Arthur, trans., *Shakespeare's Ovid, Being Arthur Golding's Translation of the Metamorphoses*, ed. W. H. D. Rouse, London: Centaur, 1961.

Greenham, Richard, *The Works of the Reverend and Faithful Servant of Jesus Christ*, London, 1612.

Homer, *Odyssey, "Chapman's Homer,"* ed. Allardyce Nicoll, Bollingen Series XLI, 2 vols., 2nd edn, Princeton University Press, 1967.

Hooker, Richard, *The Folger Library Edition of the Works of Richard Hooker*, ed. W. Speed Hill, 4 vols., Cambridge, MA: Harvard University Press, 1977–82.

Of the Laws of Ecclesiastical Polity, intro. Christopher Morris, 2 vols., London: Dent, 1907.

The Works of That Learned and Judicious Divine Mr. Richard Hooker, ed. John Keble, rev. R. W. Church and F. Paget, 7th edn, 3 vols., Oxford: Clarendon Press, 1888.

The Jerusalem Bible, London: Darton, Longman, and Todd, 1966.

Latimer, Hugh, *The Works of Hugh Latimer*, ed. G. E. Corrie, 2 vols., Cambridge University Press, 1844–45.

Luther, Martin, *Luther and Erasmus: Free Will and Salvation*, ed. and trans. Gordon Rupp and Philip S. Watson, Library of Christian Classics XVII, London: SCM Press, 1969.

A Treatise, Touching the Libertie of a Christian, trans. James Bell, London, 1579.

Two Kinds of Righteousness, "Luther's Works," ed. Jaroslav Pelikan and Helmut T. Lehmann, 55 vols., St. Louis: Concordia, 1955–86.

Martyr, Peter, *The Common Places of Peter Martyr*, London, 1583.

Montaigne, Michel de, *The Complete Essays of Montaigne*, trans. Donald M. Frame, 1958; Stanford University Press, 1965.

Nowell, Alexander, *A Catechism*, ed. G. E. Corrie, Cambridge University Press, 1853.

Perkins, William, *The Works of the Famous and Worthie Minister of Christ in the University of Cambridge*, 3 vols., Cambridge University Press, 1609

Pilkington, James, *The Works of James Pilkington*, ed. James Scholefild, Cambridge University Press, 1842.

Rogers, Richard, *Seven Treatises, Containing Such Direction as Is Gathered Out of the Holy Scriptures, Leading . . . to True happiness . . . The Practice of Christianity*, London, 1603.

Rogers, Thomas, *The Catholic Doctrine of the Church of England, an Exposition of the Thirty-Nine Articles*, ed. the Reverend J. J. S. Perowne, 1607; Cambridge University Press, 1854.

Sandys, George, trans., *Ovid's Metamorphosis Englished, Mythologized, and Represented in Figures*, eds. Karl H. Hulley and Stanley T. Vandersall, Lincoln, NE: University of Nebraska Press, 1970.

Sidney, Philip, *An Apology for Poetry*, ed. Geoffrey Shepherd, London: Nelson, 1965.

Spenser, Edmund, *Books I and II of "The Faerie Queene,"* eds. Robert Kellogg and Oliver Steele, Indianapolis, IN: Bobbs-Merrill, 1965.

The Faerie Queene, ed. A. C. Hamilton, London: Longman, 1977.

The Faerie Queene, ed. Thomas P. Roche, Jr., New Haven and London: Yale University Press, 1981.

The Works of Edmund Spenser: A Variorum Edition, eds. Edwin Greenlaw, et al., 11 vols., Baltimore: Johns Hopkins University Press, 1932–49.

The Yale Edition of the Shorter Poems of Edmund Spenser, eds. William A. Oram, Einar Bjorvand, Ronald Bond, Thomas H. Cain, Alexander Dunlop, and Richard Shell, New Haven and London: Yale University Press, 1989.

Tasso, Torquato, *Jerusalem Delivered*, trans. Edward Fairfax, intro. John Charles Nelson, New York: Capricorn, 1963.

Taverner, Richard, ed., *The Epistles and Gospels with a Brief Postil . . . from Advent until Low Sunday with Certain Fruitful Sermons*, London, 1540.

Tyndale, William, *Doctrinal Treatises and Introductions to Different Portions of the Holy Scriptures*, ed. the Reverend Henry Walter, Cambridge University Press, 1848.

Expositions and Notes on Sundry Portions of the Holy Scripture, ed. the Reverend Henry Walter, Cambridge University Press, 1849.

Virgil, *Aeneid*, trans. H. Rushton Fairclough, Loeb Library, 2 vols., New York:

G. P. Putnam's Sons, 1916.

The Aeneid of Virgil, trans. Allen Mandelbaum, Berkeley: University of California Press, 1971.

The Georgics, trans. L. P. Wilkinson, Harmondsworth: Penguin, 1982.

Whitaker, William, *A Disputation on Holy Scripture against the Papists*, trans. and ed. The Reverend William Fitzgerald, Cambridge University Press, 1849.

SECONDARY WORKS

Alpers, Paul J., *The Poetry of "The Faerie Queene,"* Princeton University Press, 1967.

Anderson, Judith H., *The Growth of a Personal Voice: "Piers Plowman" and "The Faerie Queene"*, New Haven: Yale University Press, 1976.

Armstrong, Paul B., *Conflicting Readings: Variety and Validity in Interpretation*, Chapel Hill: University of North Carolina Press, 1990.

Bennett, J. W., *The Evolution of "The Faerie Queene,"* University of Chicago Press, 1942.

Berger, Jr., Harry, "'Kidnapped Romance': Discourse in *The Faerie Queene*," *Unfolded Tales: Essays on Renaissance Romance*, eds. George M. Logan and Gordon Teskey, Ithaca, NY: Cornell University Press, 1989, pp. 208–56.

Revisionary Play: Studies in the Spenserian Dynamics, Berkeley: University of California Press, 1988.

Bleich, David, "Intersubjective Reading," *New Literary History* 17 (1986), 407–8.

Bouwsma, William J., *John Calvin: A Sixteenth-Century Portrait*, New York: Oxford University Press, 1988.

Brooks-Davies, Douglas, *Spenser's "Faerie Queene": A Critical Commentary on Books I and II*, Manchester University Press, 1977.

Bush, Douglas, *Mythology and the Renaissance Tradition in English Poetry*, rev. edn 1932; New York: Norton, 1967.

Cavanagh, Sheila T., "'Beauties Chace'": Arthur and Women in *The Faerie Queene*," *The Passing of Arthur: New Essays in Arthurian Tradition*, eds. Christopher Baswell and William Sharpe, New York and London: Garland, 1988, pp. 207–18.

Cheney, Donald, *Spenser's Image of Nature: Wild Man and Shepherd in "The Faerie Queene,"* New Haven: Yale University Press, 1966.

Colie, Rosalie L., *The Resources of Kind: Genre-Theory in the Renaissance*, ed. Barbara K. Lewalski, Berkeley: University of California Press, 1973.

Collins, Joseph B., *Christian Mysticism in the Elizabethan Age: With Its Background in Mystical Methodology*, Baltimore: Johns Hopkins University Press, 1940.

Collinson, Patrick, "The Elizabethan Church and the New Religion," *The Reign of Elizabeth I*, ed. Christopher Haigh, Athens, GA: University of Georgia Press, 1985.

"England and International Calvinism, 1558–1640," *International Calvinism, 1541–1715,* ed. Menna Prestwich, Oxford: Clarendon Press, 1985, pp. 197–224.

The Religion of Protestants: The Church in English Society, 1559–1625, Oxford: Clarendon Press, 1982.

Conrad, Peter, *The Everyman History of English Literature,* London: Dent, 1985.

Cullen, Patrick, *Infernal Triad: The Flesh, the World, and the Devil in Spenser and Milton,* Princeton University Press, 1974.

Spenser, Marvell, and Renaissance Pastoral, Cambridge, MA: Harvard University Press, 1970.

Culler, Jonathan, *On Deconstruction: Theory and Criticism after Structuralism,* Ithaca, NY: Cornell Unversity Press, 1982.

Curtius, Ernst Robert, *European Literature and the Latin Middle Ages,* trans. Willard Trask, 1948, New York: Harper and Row, 1963.

Davies, Horton, *Worship and Theology in England: From Cranmer to Hooker, 1534–1603,* Princeton University Press, 1970.

Dent, C. M., *Protestant Reformers in Elizabethan Oxford,* Oxford University Press, 1983.

Dickens, A. G., *The English Reformation,* rev. edn, London: Collins, 1967.

Doerksen, Daniel W., "'All the Good is God's': Predestination in Spenser's *Faerie Queene,* Book I," *Christianity and Literature* 32, no. 3 (Spring, 1983), 11–18.

Donnelly, S. J., John Patrick, *Calvinism and Scholasticism in Vermigli's Doctrine of Man and Grace,* Leiden: Brill, 1976.

Duffy, Eamon, *The Stripping of the Altars: Traditional Religion in England, c. 1400–c.1580,* New Haven and London: Yale University Press, 1992.

Eagleton, Terry, *Literary Theory: An Introduction,* Minneapolis: University of Minnesota Press, 1983.

Earl, Donald, *The Moral and Political Tradition of Rome,* Ithaca, NY: Cornell University Press, 1967.

The Encyclopedia of Religion and Ethics, ed. James Hastings, 13 vols., New York: C. Scribner's Sons, 1908–27.

Evans, Maurice, *Spenser's Anatomy of Heroism: a Commentary on "The Faerie Queene,"* Cambridge University Press, 1970.

Falls, Mother Mary Robert, "Spenser's Kirkrapine and the Elizabethans," *SP* 50 (1953), 547–75.

Firth, Katharine, *The Apocalyptic Tradition in Reformation Britain, 1530–1645,* Oxford University Press, 1979.

Fish, Stanley, *Is There a Text in This Class? The Authority of Interpretive Communities,* Cambridge, MA: Harvard University Press, 1980.

Foucault, Michel, *Discipline and Punish: The Birth of the Prison,* trans. Alan Sheridan, Harmondsworth: Penguin, 1979.

Fowler, Alastair, "The Beginnings of English Georgic," *Renaissance Genres: Essays on Theory, History, and Interpretation*, ed. Barbara Kiefer Lewalski, Cambridge, MA: Harvard University Press, 1986, pp. 105–25.

  Kinds of Literature: An Introduction to the Theory of Genres and Modes, Cambridge, MA: Harvard University Press, 1982.

  Spenser and the Numbers of Time, New York: Barnes and Noble, 1964.

Gerrish, B. A., *Grace and Reason: A Study in the Theology of Luther*, Oxford: Clarendon Press, 1962.

Giamatti, A. Bartlett, *The Earthly Paradise and the Renaissance Epic*, Princeton University Press, 1966.

Gless, Darryl J., *"Measure for Measure," the Law, and the Convent*, Princeton University Press, 1979.

Geoffrey of Monmouth, *History of the Kings of Britain*, trans. Sebastian Evans, New York: Dutton, 1958.

Goffman, Erving, *Frame Analysis: An Essay on the Organization of Experience*, Cambridge, MA: Harvard University Press, 1974.

Goldberg, Jonathan, *"Endlesse Worke:" Spenser and the Structures of Discourse*, Baltimore and London: Johns Hopkins University Press, 1981.

  James I and the Politics of Literature: Jonson, Shakespeare, Donne, and Their Contemporaries, Baltimore and London: Johns Hopkins University Press, 1983.

Gombrich, E. H., *Art and Illusion: A Study in the Psychology of Pictorial Representation*, 2nd edn, Princeton University Press, 1961.

  The Sense of Order: A Study in the Psychology of Decorative Art, Ithaca, NY: Cornell University Press, 1979.

Goodman, Nelson and Catherine Z. Elgin, "Interpretation and Identity: Can the Work Survive the World?" *Critical Inquiry* 12 (1986), 564–75.

Grafton, Anthony and Lisa Jardine, *From Humanism to the Humanities: Education in Fifteenth- and Sixteenth-Century Europe*, London: Duckworth, 1986.

Greenblatt, Stephen, "Fiction and Friction," *Reconstructing Individualism: Autonomy, Individuality, and the Self in Western Thought*, eds. Thomas C. Heller, Morton Sosna, and David E. Wellbery, Stanford University Press, 1986.

  "Murdering Peasants: Status, Genre, and the Representation of Rebellion," *Representing the English Renaissance*, ed. Stephen Greenblatt, Berkeley: University of California Press, 1988.

  Renaissance Self-Fashioning: From More to Shakespeare, University of Chicago Press, 1980.

Gross, Kenneth, *Spenserian Poetics: Idolatry, Iconoclasm, and Magic*, Ithaca, NY: Cornell University Press, 1985.

Guillory, John D., *Poetic Authority: Spenser, Milton, and Literary History*, New York: Columbia University Press, 1983.

Guy, John, *Tudor England*, Oxford and New York: Oxford University Press, 1988.

Haigh, Christopher, "The Church of England, the Catholics and the People," *The Reign of Elizabeth I*, ed. Christopher Haigh, Athens, GA: University of Georgia Press, 1985.

"The Recent Historiography of the English Reformation," *The English Reformation Revised*, ed. Christopher Haigh, Cambridge University Press, 1987.

Hamilton, A. C., ed., *Essential Articles for the Study of Edmund Spenser*, Hamden, CT: Archon Books, 1972.

"'Like Race to Runne': The Parallel Structure of *The Faerie Queene*, Books I and II," *PMLA* 72 (1958), 327–34.

The Structure of Allegory in "The Faerie Queene," Oxford: Clarendon Press, 1961.

"A Theological Reading of *The Faerie Queene*, Book II," *ELH* 25 (1958), 155–62.

Hankins, John Erskine, *Source and Meaning in Spenser's Allegory: A Study of "The Faerie Queene,"* Oxford: Clarendon Press, 1971.

Heale, Elizabeth, *"The Faerie Queene": A Reader's Guide*, Cambridge University Press, 1987.

Heninger, Jr., S. K., "The Orgoglio Episode in *The Faerie Queene*," *ELH* 26 (1959), 171–87.

Hill, Christopher, *Society and Puritanism in Pre-Revolutionary England*, London: Secker and Warburg, 1964.

Hill, W. Speed, "The Evolution of Hooker's *Laws of Ecclesiastical Polity*," *Studies in Richard Hooker*, ed. W. Speed Hill, Cambridge, MA: Harvard University Press, 1982.

Hirsch, Jr., E. D., *Validity in Interpretation*, New Haven and London: Yale University Press, 1967.

Hughes, Philip Edgcumbe, *Theology of the English Reformers*, Grand Rapids, MI: Eerdmans, 1965.

Hume, Anthea, *Edmund Spenser: Protestant Poet*, Cambridge University Press, 1984.

Hutton, Ronald, "The Local Impact of the Tudor Reformations," *The English Reformation Revised*, ed. Christopher Haigh, Cambridge University Press, 1987.

Imbrie, Ann E., "'Playing Legerdemaine with the Scripture': Parodic Sermons in *The Faerie Queene*," *ELR* 17 (1987), 142–55.

Iser, Wolfgang, *The Act of Reading: A Theory of Aesthetic Response*, Baltimore and London: Johns Hopkins University Press, 1978

Jameson, Fredric, *The Political Unconscious: Narrative as a Socially Symbolic Act*, Ithaca, NY: Cornell University Press, 1981.

Johnson, Lynn Staley, *"The Shepheardes Calender": An Introduction*, University Park and London: Pennsylvania State University Press, 1990.

Johnson-Laird, P. N., *Mental Models: Towards a Cognitive Science of Language, Inference, and Consciousness*, Cambridge, MA: Harvard University Press, 1983.

Jones, Norman L., *Faith by Statute: Parliament and the Settlement of Religion 1559*, London: Royal Historical Society, 1982.

Kahn, Victoria, *Rhetoric, Prudence, and Skepticism in the Renaissance*, Ithaca, NY: Cornell University Press, 1985.

Kane, Sean, *Spenser's Moral Allegory*, University of Toronto Press, 1989.

Kaske, Carol V., "The Dragon's Spark and Sting and the Structure of Red Cross's Dragon-Fight: *The Faerie Queene*, I.xi–xii," *SP* 66 (1969), 609–38.

"Spenser's Pluralistic Universe: The View from the Mount of Contemplation (*F.Q.* I.x)," *Contemporary Thought on Edmund Spenser*, eds. Richard C. Frushell and Bernard J. Vondersmith, Carbondale and Edwardsville: Southern Illinois University Press, 1975.

Kendall, R. T., *Calvin and English Calvinism to 1649*, Oxford University Press, 1979.

Kermode, Frank, *Shakespeare, Spenser, Donne: Renaissance Essays*, New York: Viking, 1971.

King, John N., *Spenser's Poetry and the Reformation Tradition*, Princeton University Press, 1990.

Lake, Peter, *Anglicans and Puritans? Presbyterianism and English Conformist Thought from Whitgift to Hooker*, London: Unwin Hyman, 1988.

Moderate Puritans and the Elizabethan Church, Cambridge University Press, 1982.

Lamberton, Robert, *Homer the Theologian: Neo-Platonist Allegorical Reading and the Growth of the Epic Tradition*, Berkeley: University of California Press, 1986.

"The Neoplatonists and the Spiritualization of Homer," *Homer's Ancient Readers: The Hermeneutics of Greek Epic's Earliest Exegetes*, eds. Robert Lamberton and John J. Keaney, Princeton University Press, 1992, pp. 115–33.

Leslie, Michael, *Spenser's "Fierce Warres and Faithfull Loves": Martial and Chivalric Symbolism in "The Faerie Queene,"* New York: Barnes and Noble, 1983.

Lewalski, Barbara K., *Donne's "Anniversaries" and the Poetry of Praise*, Princeton University Press, 1973.

Protestant Poetics and the Seventeenth-Century Religious Lyric, Princeton University Press, 1979.

"Paradise Lost" and the Rhetoric of Literary Forms, Princeton University Press, 1985.

Lewis, C. S., *Allegory of Love: A Study in Medieval Tradition*, 1936; New York: Oxford University Press, 1958.

Lieb, Michael, *Poetics of the Holy: A Reading of "Paradise Lost,"* Chapel Hill:

University of North Carolina Press, 1981.

MacCaffrey, Isabel G., *Spenser's Allegory: The Anatomy of Imagination*, Princeton University Press, 1976.

Macdonald, Michael, *Mystical Bedlam: Madness, Anxiety, and Healing in Seventeenth-Century England*, Cambridge University Press, 1981.

McCabe, Richard A., *The Pillars of Eternity: Time and Providence in "The Faerie Queene,"* Dublin: Irish Academic Press, 1989.

McCoy, Richard, *The Rites of Knighthood: The Literature and Politics of Elizabethan Chivalry*, Berkeley: University of California Press, 1989.

McGinn, Bernard, "Early Apocalypticism: the Ongoing Debate," *The Apocalypse in English Renaissance Thought and Literature: Patterns, Antecedents, and Repercussions*, eds. C. A. Patrides and Joseph Wittreich, Ithaca, NY: Cornell University Press, 1984.

McGrath, Alister, *Iustitia Dei: A History of the Christian Doctrine of Justification*, 2 vols., Cambridge University Press, 1986.

McLane, Paul E., *Spenser's "Shepheardes Calender": A Study in Elizabethan Allegory*, Notre Dame, IN: Notre Dame University Press, 1961.

McNeill, John T., *The History and Character of Calvinism*, 1954; Oxford University Press, 1967.

McSorley, C.S.P., Henry J., *Luther: Right or Wrong? An Ecumenical-Theological Study of Luther's Major Work, "The Bondage of the Will,"* New York: Newman Press, 1969.

Merleau-Ponty, Maurice, *The Primacy of Perception: and Other Essays on Phenomenological Psychology, the Philosophy of Art, History, and Politics*, ed. James M. Edie, Evanston, IL: Northwestern University Press, 1964.

Miller, David Lee, *The Poem's Two Bodies: The Poetics of the 1590 "Faerie Queene,"* Princeton University Press, 1988.

Mills, Jerry Leath, "Prudence, History, and the Prince in *The Faerie Queene*, Book II," *HLQ* 41 (1978), 83–101.

Montrose, Louis Adrian, "The Elizabethan Subject and the Spenserian Text," *Literary Theory / Renaissance Texts*, eds. Patricia Parker and David Quint, Baltimore and London: Johns Hopkins University Press, 1986, 303–40.

Morgan, Gerald, "Holiness as the First of Spenser's Aristotelian Moral Virtues," *MLR* 81 (1986), 817–37.

Morgan, John, *Godly Learning: Puritan Attitudes towards Reason, Learning, and Education, 1560–1640*, Cambridge University Press, 1986.

Mullaney, Stephen, *The Place of the Stage: License, Play, and Power in Renaissance England*, University of Chicago Press, 1988.

Neisser, Ulreich, *Cognition and Reality: Principles and Implications of Cognitive Psychology*, New York: Freeman, 1976.

Nelson, William, *The Poetry of Edmund Spenser: A Study*, New York: Columbia

University Press, 1963.

The New Catholic Encyclopedia, ed. Most Rev. William J. MacDonald, 14 vols., Washington, DC: The Catholic University of America, 1967.

Nohrnberg, James, *The Analogy of "The Faerie Queene,"* Princeton University Press, 1976.

Norbrook, David, *Poetry and Politics in the English Renaissance,* London: Routledge and Kegan Paul, 1984.

Oberman, Heiko Augustinus, *Masters of the Reformation: The Emergence of a New Intellectual Climate in Europe,* trans. Dennis Martin, Cambridge University Press, 1981.

Oentgen, O.S.B., Jerome, "Spenser's Treatment of Monasticism in Book I of *The Faerie Queene,"* *ABR* 22 (1971), 109–20.

Palliser, D. M., "Popular Reactions to the Reformation During the Years of Uncertainty," *The English Reformation Revised,* ed. Christopher Haigh, Cambridge University Press, 1987.

Parker, Mother Pauline, *The Allegory of "The Faerie Queene,"* Oxford: Clarendon Press, 1960.

Parker, Patricia A., *Inescapable Romance: Studies in the Poetics of a Mode,* Princeton University Press, 1979.

Patterson, Annabel, *Pastoral and Ideology: Virgil to Valéry,* Berkeley: University of California Press, 1987.

Porter, H. C., *Reformation and Reaction in Tudor Cambridge,* Cambridge University Press, 1958.

The Princeton Encyclopedia of Poetry and Poetics, ed. Alex Preminger, Princeton University Press, 1974.

Quilligan, Maureen, *Language of Allegory: Defining the Genre,* Ithaca, NY: Cornell University Press, 1979.

  Milton's Spenser: The Politics of Reading, Ithaca, NY and London: Cornell University Press, 1983.

Ricoeur, Paul, *The Symbolism of Evil,* trans. Emerson Buchanan, Boston: Beacon Press, 1967.

Roche, Jr., Thomas P., *The Kindly Flame: A Study of the Third and Fourth Books of Spenser's "Faerie Queene,"* Princeton University Press, 1964.

  "Spenser's Muse," *Unfolded Tales: Essays on Renaissance Romance,* eds. George M. Logan and Gordon Teskey, Ithaca, NY, and London: Cornell University Press, 1989.

Rose, Mark, *Spenser's Art: A Companion to Book One of "The Faerie Queene,"* Cambridge, MA: Harvard University Press, 1974.

Scarisbrick, J. J., *The Reformation and the English People,* Oxford: Blackwell, 1984.

Seznec, Jean, *The Survival of the Pagan Gods: The Mythological Tradition and Its Place in Renaissance Humanism and Art,* 1953; Princeton University Press, 1972.

Shaheen, Naseeb, *Biblical References in "The Faerie Queene,"* Memphis, TN: Memphis State University Press, 1976.

Shroeder, John W., "Spenser's Erotic Drama: The Orgoglio Episode," *ELH* 29 (1962). 140–59.

Shuger, Deborah Kuller, *Habits of Thought in the English Renaissance: Religion, Politics, and the Dominant Culture,* Berkeley and Los Angeles: University of California Press, 1990.

Sinfield, Alan, *Literature in Protestant England,* Totowa, NJ: Barnes and Noble, 1983.

Skulsky, Harold, "Spenser's Despair Episode and the Theology of Doubt," *MP* 78 (1981), 227–42.

Snare, Gerald, "Spenser's Fourth Grace," *JWCI* 34 (1971), 350–55.

The Spenser Encyclopedia, eds. A. C. Hamilton, Donald Cheney, W. F. Blissett, and David Richardson, University of Toronto Press, 1990.

Spufford, Margaret, *Contrasting Communities: English Villagers in the Sixteenth and Seventeenth Centuries,* Cambridge University Press, 1974.

Steadman, John M., "Una and the Clergy: The Ass Symbol in the *Faerie Queene,*" *JWCI* 21 (1958), 134–37.

Stone, Lawrence, *The Family, Sex and Marriage in England 1500–1800,* New York: Harper and Row, 1977.

Strier, Richard, *Love Known: Theology and Experience in George Herbert's Poetry,* University of Chicago Press, 1983.

Teskey, Gordon, "From Allegory to Dialectic: Imagining Error in Spenser and Milton," *PMLA* 101 (1986), 9–23.

Thomas, Keith, *Religion and the Decline of Magic,* New York: Scribner's, 1971.

Tompkins, Jane P., "The Reader in History: The Changing Shape of Literary Response," *Reader-Response Criticism: From Formalism to Post-Structuralism,* ed. Jane P. Tompkins, Baltimore: Johns Hopkins University Press, 1980.

Tonkin, Humphrey, *Spenser's Courteous Pastoral: Book Six of "The Faerie Queene,"* Oxford: Clarendon Press, 1972.

"The Faerie Queene," Unwin Critical Library, London: Unwin, 1989.

Torczon, Vern, "Spenser's Orgoglio and Despaire," *TSLL* 3 (1961–62). 124–25.

Tuve, Rosemond, *Allegorical Imagery: Some Medieval Books and Their Posterity,* Princeton University Press, 1966.

Tyacke, Nicholas, *Anti-Calvinists: The Rise of English Arminianism, c. 1590–1640,* Oxford: Clarendon Press, 1987.

Walker, Cheryl, "Feminist Literary Criticism and the Author," *Critical Inquiry* 16 (1990), 551–71.

Wall, John N., *Transformations of the Word: Spenser, Herbert, Vaughan,* Athens and London: University of Georgia Press, 1989.

Wallace, Dewey, *Puritans and Predestination: Grace in English Protestant Theology,*

Chapel Hill: University of North Carolina Press, 1982.

Wallace, R. S., *Calvin's Doctrine of the Christian Life*, London: Oliver and Boyd, 1959.

Waller, Gary, *English Poetry of the Sixteenth Century*, London: Longman, 1986.

Walls, Kathryn, "Abessa and the Lion: *The Faerie Queene*, I.3.1–12," *SSt*, 5 (1984). 1–30.

Waters, D. Douglas, *Duessa as Theological Satire*, Columbus, MO: University of Missouri Press, 1970.

Weatherby, Harold L., "The True St. George," *ELR* 17 (1987), 119–41

Whigham, Frank, *Ambition and Privilege: The Social Tropes of Elizabethan Courtesy Theory*, Berkeley: University of California Press, 1984.

Whitaker, Virgil K., *The Religious Basis of Spenser's Thought*, Stanford University Press, 1950.

"The Theological Structure of *The Faerie Queene*," *That Soveraine Light: Essays in Honor of Edmund Spenser, 1552–1952*, eds. William R. Mueller and Don Cameron Allen, Baltimore: Johns Hopkins University Press, 1952.

White, Hayden, "Historical Pluralism," *Critical Inquiry* 12 (1986), 480–94.

Williams, Kathleen, *Spenser's World of Glass: A Reading of "The Faerie Queene,"* Berkeley and Los Angeles: University of California Press, 1966.

Williams, Raymond, *The Country and the City*, New York: Oxford University Press, 1973.

Wind, Edgar, *Pagan Mysteries in the Renaissance*, rev. edn 1958; Harmondsworth: Penguin, 1967.

Wofford, Susanne Lindgren, *The Choice of Achilles: the Ideology of Figure in the Epic*, Stanford University Press, 1992.

Woodhouse, A. S. P., "Nature and Grace in *The Faerie Queene*," *ELH* 16 (1949), 194–228.

Woodhouse, H. F., *The Doctrine of the Church in Anglican Theology, 1547–1603*, London: SPCK, 1954.

Wrightson, Keith, *English Society 1580–1680*, New Brunswick, NJ: Rutgers University Press, 1982.

INDEX